# Incorporating Rights

# Incorporating Rights

## *Strategies to Advance Corporate Accountability*

ERIKA GEORGE

OXFORD
UNIVERSITY PRESS

**OXFORD**
UNIVERSITY PRESS

Oxford University Press is a department of the University of Oxford. It furthers the University's objective of excellence in research, scholarship, and education by publishing worldwide. Oxford is a registered trade mark of Oxford University Press in the UK and certain other countries.

Published in the United States of America by Oxford University Press
198 Madison Avenue, New York, NY 10016, United States of America.



---

Library of Congress Cataloging-in-Publication Data

Names: George, Erika, author.
Title: Incorporating rights : strategies to advance corporate accountability / Erika George.
Description: New York, NY : Oxford University Press, [2021] |
Includes bibliographical references and index.
Identifiers: LCCN 2020041618 | ISBN 9780199941483 (hardback) | ISBN 9780190666736 (epub) |
ISBN 9780199366378 (updf) | ISBN 9780199366385 (digital-online)
Subjects: LCSH: Social responsibility of business—Law and legislation. |
International law and human rights. | Corporate governance—Law and legislation.
Classification: LCC K1329.5 .G46 2021 | DDC 346/.065—dc23
LC record available at https://lccn.loc.gov/2020041618

---

DOI: 10.1093/oso/9780199941483.001.0001

1 3 5 7 9 8 6 4 2

Printed by Integrated Books International, United States of America

**Note to Readers**

This publication is designed to provide accurate and authoritative information in regard to the subject matter covered. It is based upon sources believed to be accurate and reliable and is intended to be current as of the time it was written. It is sold with the understanding that the publisher is not engaged in rendering legal, accounting, or other professional services. If legal advice or other expert assistance is required, the services of a competent professional person should be sought. Also, to confirm that the information has not been affected or changed by recent developments, traditional legal research techniques should be used, including checking primary sources where appropriate.

*(Based on the Declaration of Principles jointly adopted by a Committee of the American Bar Association and a Committee of Publishers and Associations.)*

*For*
*Betty Ann George*

# Contents

# Detailed Contents

## PART II CHANGE: HUMAN RIGHTS, CORPORATE RESPONSIBILITY CODES, AND COMPLIANCE WITH COMMITMENTS

# Acknowledgments

This book is the product of nearly a decade of participant observer research conducted among human rights activists, investors, lawyers, sustainability professionals, and policymakers, as well as hundreds of conversations with colleagues from around the world.

Many of these ideas were initially inspired by my work with Human Rights Watch as the organization started to investigate corporate complicity in human rights violations led by the groundbreaking work of Arvind Ganesan, Bronwen Mamby, and others. I owe a debt to the dedicated researchers and advocates who introduced me to human rights research and advocacy early in my career.

For their thoughtful comments on portions of this book and earlier ideas, I thank: Lea VanderVeld, Bobbi Olson, Erika Stevens, Nadia Bernaz, Tara Van Ho, Marcia Nance Weldon, Jena Martin, and Karen Bravo; my American Bar Foundation (ABF) colleagues: Elizabeth Mertz, Terence Halliday, Laura Beth Nielsen, Jothie Raja, Bryant Garth, and Ajay K. Mehrotra; and, my Lutie A. Lytle Black Women Law Faculty Workshop sisters in law: Hope Lewis, Marcella David, Veronica Root, Victoria Shannon Sahani, Laura Beny, Kristin Johnson, and Lolita Buckner Ennis. I especially appreciate my current and former University of Utah colleagues for their support: Antony Anghie, Hiram Chodosh, Daniel Medwed, Leslie Francis, Carissa Byrne Hessick, Manuel Utset, Joy Pierce, Daniel Greenwood, Harris Sondack, Chibli Mallat, and Scott Balderson.

I thank my students at the University of Utah, Loyola University Chicago, and the University of Cape Town, who have taken different incarnations of my seminar courses on corporate citizenship, business and human rights, international business transactions, and international trade.

I have also tested these ideas in presentations at different institutions over the years. For their attention and thoughtful responses to earlier versions of this work, I thank the faculty and students at University of Texas at Austin School of Law, Northwestern University School of Law, Boston College Law School, Brigham Young University School of Law, HEC Paris, University College London Centre of Ethics and Law, Georgetown University Law Center's O'Neill Institute, Washington and Lee University School of Law, University of Connecticut's Dodd Research Center, West Virginia University College of Law, University of St. Thomas School of Law, Vanderbilt University School of Law, University of Washington School of Law, University of California Davis School of Law, NYU School of Law's Institute for International Law and Justice, the Mellon

Sawyer Seminar on Corporations and International Law at Duke University's John Hope Franklin Humanities Institute, Harvard Law School's Center on the Legal Profession, members of the Global Business and Human Rights Scholars Association and my colleagues at the ABF.

The valuable insights offered by Bennett Freeman, David Deisley, Desta Raines, Clifton Henry, Robert Durkee, Adam Greene, John Wilson, Jeffrey S. Collins, Rebecca MacKinnon, Andrew Behar, Beth Ginsberg Holzman, Yann Wyss, Jaren Dunning, Daniel Fibiger, Dominic Renfry, Sasha Lezhnev, Wim Leereveld, Patrica Jurewicz, Komala Ramachandra, and Arvind Ganesan truly improved this project. I have benefited immensely from my exchanges with Surya Deva, Christine Bader, Michael Addo, Beth Stephens, Caroline Reese, Benedict Kingsbury, Sally Engle Merry, David Wilkins, Penny Andrews, Heinz Klug, Karen Engle, Daria Roithmayr, Richard McAdams, Jide Okechuku Nzelibe, Lisa Laplante, David Restrepo-Amariles, David Millon, Lynn Stout, Joan McLeod Heminway, Amol Mehra, Sheldon Leader, Larry Catá Backer, Isabella Bunn, Michael Santoro, Megg Roggensack, James Thuo Gathii, Anita Raamasastry, Philip Stern, Rachel Brewster, Gregory Tzeutschler Regaignon, Valerie Haas, Katherine Young, Darren Rosenblum, Anupam Chander, Stephen Lee, Ernesto Hernandez-Lopez, Karin Buhmann, Paloma Muñoz Quick, Justine Nolan, Dorothée Baumann-Pauly, Chris Jochnick, Rachel Chambers, John Sherman, Sara Labowitz, Michael Posner, Muno Ndulo, Lara Blecher, Tyler Gianni, Rebecca Bratspies, Steve Hitov, Nina Luzzatto Gardner, Joanne Bauer, and Anthony Ewing as well as my colleagues in the Teaching Business and Human Rights Forum.

I thank the many research assistants at the University of Utah S.J. Quinney College of Law who have worked with me over the years for their help, especially: Haden J. Goebel, Mariah McAfee, Laurie Abbott, Pablo Hapsel, Elizabeth Thomas, Martha Munezhi, Stina Peterson, Sheena Christman, Ilsy Melendez, Jess Morrision, Jennifer Ku, Robert Spjuie, Adam Miller, Adam Duncan, Nathan Hart Jackson, Matt O'Connor, Erin Reid, Mikayla Irvin, Alexandra Maeschal, John Plimpton, Ashley Walker, Savannah Schoon, Tyler Hubbard, Stratton McCausland, Brian Andrew Flach, Jessica Ramirez, and Skylar Walker. I thank Scott McMurtrey, Talley Timms Ransil, Rebekah Watts, and Hannah Taub for their assistance with cite checking and formatting footnotes. American Bar Foundation Montgomery Summer Fellow Kimberley Quick also helped with research. Many Utah law librarians provided invaluable assistance: Melissa Bernstein, Felicity Murphy, and Kerry Lohmeier. I especially appreciate Ross McPhail and Donna Ziegenfuss for their help. My administrative assistant, Maggi Spight, worked wonders scheduling travel and interviews. I truly enjoyed collaborating with Dessi K. Price and thank her for cover design.

Finally, I am especially grateful to Gina Gottardo and Smita Narula for their unwavering encouragement and enthusiasm for this project. I credit them with enabling me to complete it.

I dedicate this book to my mother, Betty Ann George, a courageous activist, compassionate educator, and my first teacher.

# Introduction

*The social responsibility of business is to increase its profits.*[1]
*Underlying most arguments against the free market is a lack of belief in freedom itself.*[2]

—Milton Friedman

*To be free is not merely to cast off one's chains, but to live in a way that respects and enhances the freedom of others.*[3]

—Nelson Mandela

Chinese journalist Shi Tao did not report on the 2008 Olympic Games in Beijing because he was serving a prison sentence for divulging a "state secret." Using his Yahoo! email account, Shi Tao sent a message about restrictions imposed on local journalists to the U S-based Asia Democracy Foundation. Chinese authorities tracked him down with the assistance of Hong Kong–based Yahoo! Holdings Ltd., a Yahoo! foreign subsidiary that provided China's state security apparatus with details allowing the communications to be traced back to Shi Tao's computer. Privacy rights and free expression advocacy organizations accused the company of complicity in the government's violation of Shi Tao's rights. When challenged by rights activists concerning his corporation's role in the journalist's imprisonment, Jerry Yang, Yahoo!'s US-based co-founder reportedly claimed his company was simply complying with local laws.

Nigerian environmental and human rights activist Ken Saro-Wiwa did not vote in Nigeria's democratic elections that ended years of military rule because he was executed by the ruling military dictatorship in 1995 for engaging in dissent. An ethnic Ogoni, Saro-Wiwa had campaigned for increased autonomy for his community, a minority group residing in the oil-producing region of the country. He had organized protests against the environmental damage created

[1] Milton Friedman, *The Social Responsibility of Business Is to Increase Its Profits*, N.Y. TIMES MAGAZINE, Sept. 13, 1970, at 32.
[2] MILTON FRIEDMAN, CAPITALISM AND FREEDOM 15 (40th Anniversary ed. 2002).
[3] NELSON MANDELA, LONG WALK TO FREEDOM: THE AUTOBIOGRAPHY OF NELSON MANDELA 624 (1995).

*Incorporating Rights.* Erika George, Oxford University Press. © Erika George 2021.
DOI: 10.1093/oso/9780199941483.003.0001

by the drilling operations of Royal Dutch Shell and other oil companies in his community. Saro-Wiwa was "tried" by a special military court under procedures inconsistent with international fair trial standards, convicted along with the other "Ogoni Nine," and hanged. When criticized for its silence with respect to the Saro-Wiwa's trial, a member of Shell's general management reportedly stated the company was not in a position to question or comment on the country's rules, regulations, or procedures.

Colombian trade unionist "Pablo Perez 50" did not live to see the Colombian government reach a peace accord with the FARC guerrilla movement and adopt sweeping land restitution to return those forcibly displaced by violence during the country's conflict to their homes. "Pablo Perez 50" worked on a banana plantation that supplied Chiquita Brands International until the evening he was kidnapped and killed by the armed paramilitary organization that provided the company with security. In a settlement of criminal charges with the US Justice Department, Chiquita was fined for violating US antiterrorism laws for making payments to designated foreign terrorist organizations. Yet, the civil claims of thousands of Colombians who suffered abuses allegedly due to Chiquita's complicit conduct were rejected by a federal court in the United States, leaving victims with fewer forums for accessing a judicial remedy. Company representatives maintained there was no choice but to cooperate with paramilitaries given the complicated context of the country's conflict situation.

These illustrations raise questions concerning the social responsibility of business with respect to human rights. These stories highlight only some of the ways in which rights are denied to people due to failure on the part of business enterprises to identify and address the risks that particular policies and practices may present to human rights. These examples also bring into high relief the challenges transnational corporations (TNCs) operating in countries with poor human rights records confront.[4] When conducting business in countries where there is open conflict or where local norms and practices are inconsistent with international human rights legal standards, TNCs run the risk of aiding and abetting abuses. While local laws and practices in China, Nigeria, or the complicated context Colombia's armed conflict may have permitted, or perhaps even required the unfortunate ends met by Shi Tao, Saro-Wiwa, and "Perez 50," international human rights law would arguably at minimum have required respect for Shi Tao's privacy, respect for Saro-Wiwa's right to a fair and public hearing by an

[4] The terms "transnational corporations" (TNCs), "multinational corporations" (MNCs), and "multinational business enterprises" (MBEs) will be used interchangeably throughout this book. TNCs, MNCs, and MBEs are used to refer to business enterprises with substantial operations and interests outside of the nation in which it is incorporated, organized or maintains a principle place of business where executive decisions that direct the course of the business are made.

independent and impartial tribunal, and respect for the right of "Perez 50" to live and to join a trade union.

The imprisonment of Shi Tao by China and the execution of Saro-Wiwa by Nigeria were widely condemned. Significantly, human rights activists also condemned companies operating in these countries for being complicit in the human rights violations resulting in the imprisonment, torture, and execution of individuals attempting to exercise their rights and advocate change within their respective societies. Ultimately, these corporations were forced to defend lawsuits filed in the United States seeking compensation because the actions or omissions of the corporation were alleged to have contributed to human rights abuses that occurred abroad.[5]

The increase in allegations of human rights abuses leveled against business enterprises coupled with the apparent inability to hold business enterprises accountable for the harmful effects of activities that cross international borders calls into question whether traditional business practices and traditional understandings of international law are sufficient to protect and promote human rights where multinational business enterprises are involved.

## The Social Responsibility of Business

Economist and Nobel Laureate Milton Freidman's assertion that the social responsibility of business is to make profits within the boundaries of the law is often repeated. While it provides a simple and elegant account of the purpose of the corporate form and a clear guiding principle by which to govern corporate conduct, it seems unsatisfying and inadequate when presented with the complexities of operating in different social contexts where human rights are put at risk by the conduct of commercial actors. Friedman forged his formulation in the context of a free society using a free market as the primary frame of reference.

Freedom is not a reality in much of the world. Maintaining that sufficient corporate social responsibility (CSR) simply entails abiding by the law and making profits misses the fact that business enterprises accused of aiding and abetting human rights abuses may not be acting contrary to local law. Sometimes locals are harmed by business conduct that is wholly consistent with local laws. In many instances local laws are either incompatible with respect for human rights or inadequate to ensure that rights are properly protected. In other instances, local laws are exemplary but simply are not enforced. On occasion, laws intended

[5] *See, e.g.*, Wiwa v. Royal Dutch Petroleum Co., 226 F.3d 88 (2d Cir. 2000); Zheng v. Yahoo!, Inc., No. C-08-1068, 2009 WL 4430297 (Dec. 2, 2009); *In re* Chiquita Brands, Int'l Inc., 792 F. Supp. 2nd 1301 (S.D. Fla. 2011).

to provide protection are perceived as contrary to the interests of a particular industry sector and encounter significant opposition. Indeed, Friedman's formulation would seem to invite incidents of abuse in certain contexts because it does not understand the business of business as being concerned with broader social concerns. Further, Friedman's formulation and others like it fail to appreciate complexity or context.

A more expansive view of the responsibility of business is emerging based on the changing role of business in society. The maxim that the social responsibility of businesses is to make profits within the bounds of law has been met with resistance as some segments of society have grown increasingly concerned with the growing power and influence of the business community around the globe and the consequences of change in an interdependent and interconnected global economy.

Indeed, in a departure from the often-repeated wisdom of Friedman that "the social responsibility of business is to increase its profits"[6] and nothing more, certain segments of the business community have indicated through their activities a willingness to do more. Many corporations are voluntarily assuming commitments to protect human rights and to promote economic development. Corporations are voluntarily incorporating human rights into codes of conduct. Corporations are reporting on more than financial matters voluntarily. Corporate sustainability reports address environmental and social performance. What do these developments mean for international law and human rights protection? Could responsible business practices and corporate codes of conduct consistent with the responsibility to respect international human rights serve to create a body of soft law to supplement the human rights regime and strengthen protections?

## The Subject of International Law

International human rights law in general is created by and binding upon nation states. Yet, as a practical matter some multinational corporations control budgets larger than those of the states in which they operate and are able to wield significant power and influence as a result. While states are no longer thought to be the only entities that can be implicated in human rights violations, the independent obligation of multinational enterprise to conform commercial activities with international human rights standards, if any, is far from clear at this stage in the development of international law. As corporations have grown in power and

[6] Friedman, *supra* note 1.

influence so too have concerns about the adverse impact of corporate activities on human rights.

Private commercial actors with international operations largely have not been treated as bound by the public international human rights obligations that countries around the world have assumed as a matter of law through treaty accords or custom. Because business enterprises do not have the requisite international legal personality, no corporation can become party to an international human rights legal instrument and assume the obligations to protect human rights pursuant to it as a nation state may. For example, Facebook is not a party to the International Covenant on Civil and Political Rights that recognizes the right to privacy and enshrines an obligation to protect it. Pfizer is not a party to the International Covenant on Economic, Social and Cultural Rights that recognizes the human right to health and establishes an obligation to ensure the right is protected. Neither Facebook nor Pfizer can assume human rights obligations under international law, yet both businesses have the ability to influence the enjoyment of human rights.

## The Global Human Rights Regulatory Gap

Often human rights abuses occur in regulatory gaps where there may be little law to guide business practices abroad. A host state, a country that receives foreign investment from transnational corporations, may not be willing or able to take measures to ensure that business practices are not inconsistent with protecting human rights for a variety of reasons. The desire to attract foreign investment by having a more relaxed regulatory regime may motivate some governments to resist implementing protections. Host countries wish to remain competitive and do not want to appear unfriendly to investment by imposing regulations a transnational corporation would find burdensome. A home state, the corporation's country of origin, may be unwilling to closely monitor the extraterritorial actions of business operations that occur abroad even if higher standards of conduct are required at home. The desire to keep home corporations competitive in a global market may make some governments reluctant to require transnational corporations to meet the same high standards when operating overseas.[7]

These gaps in global human rights protection and accountability for rights abuses are symptomatic of significant conceptual problems in both corporate

[7] *See, e.g.*, Steven R. Ratner, *Corporations and Human Rights: A Theory of Legal Responsibility*, 111 Yale L.J. 443 (2001); Beth Stephens, *The Amorality of Profit: Transnational Corporations and Human Rights*, 20 Berkeley J. Int'l L. 45 (2002); Emeka Duruigbo, *Corporate Accountability and Liability for International Human Rights Abuses: Recent Changes and Recurring Challenges*, 6 Nw. J. Int'l Hum. Rts. 222 (2008).

law and international law. As conventionally concerned with internal governance of business organizations and the regulation of relations between management and ownership of the entity, corporate law fails to adequately address the external effects of the modern corporation and its relationship to society. As conventionally conceived to regulate relations between nations, public international law fails to adequately govern the conduct of private nonstate actors. Another approach is in order.

## Bridging the Human Rights Regulatory Gap

A number of efforts have attempted to fill the gap created by the absence of international human rights standards that are legally binding on transnational business enterprises. Among other things these efforts have included adjudication, advocacy campaigns, reporting and rankings, certifications, and codes promulgated by corporations, industry associations, and intergovernmental agencies to set standards of conduct. As advanced by people affected by abuses and their advocates, public entities, and in some instances even private enterprise, these efforts have met with varying levels of success.

To date, efforts to generate strong support for a binding international treaty to regulate business and human rights have been unsuccessful. An early set of draft norms developed for the United Nations on the responsibilities of transnational corporations and other business enterprises regarding human rights that envisioned a binding agreement to make corporate actors accountable was abandoned. A more recent proposal before the United Nations for a binding global agreement to ensure corporate accountability for human rights abuses continues to face considerable resistance from powerful countries and corporations. While several lawsuits were brought in the United States against corporations for their conduct abroad, allegedly in violation of international human rights law, under the Alien Tort Statute (ATS) or Alien Tort Claims Act (ATCA), to date, none of these suits has resulted in a judgment for an alien plaintiff. Most ATS cases were settled out of court. Recently, access to judicial remedy for these types of tort cases in US courts has narrowed significantly.

Other international standards and strategies are now emerging alongside existing legal instruments and outline the obligations of businesses to respect human rights and to refrain from violating human rights. For example, the UN Framework and Guiding Principles on Business and Human Rights unanimously endorsed by the UN Human Rights Council in 2011 clarifies the roles and responsibilities of countries and commercial enterprises with respect to human rights and provides concrete and practical recommendations for conduct consistent with respect for human rights. I believe these standards and strategies to actually operationalize respect for human rights in business enterprises to be more promising avenues for progress than the path of promulgating still more international human rights treaties.

## Incorporating Rights: The Corporate Responsibility to Respect Rights

Given the enforcement problems already inherent in public international law and the existing incentives embedded in corporate law, I argue that a new approach to CSR in the international arena may be the best option for improving standards and practices and assuring corporate conduct consistent with the existing international human rights law already applied to states. I argue that more than law will be required to bridge the human rights regulatory gap. Indeed, a broader business ethic, one that embraces human rights, is imperative.

This book shows how voluntary standards, soft law norms, and CSR initiatives can evolve to become sufficiently strong and influence corporate conduct to become better aligned with respect for fundamental human rights and basic human dignity. By tracing how certain initiatives have hardened and become more significant, this study shows that change could happen under certain conditions and is currently occurring in certain industry sectors.

Closing the human rights protection gap through promulgating voluntary codes of conduct and promoting CSR initiatives that incorporate rights may result in more meaningful reform. When reinforced by access to information, responsible business conduct could under certain circumstances contribute to significant improvement in human rights protection. Voluntary efforts on the part of corporations may offer a path toward greater human rights protection. Self-regulation by corporations has been dismissed by critics who would prefer binding regulation to guarantee protection for human rights. Yet, in the absence of a binding international regulatory regime to govern corporate conduct with respect to human rights, an "order without law" is emerging. This evolving transnational order could serve to advance human rights protection and to close the accountability gap.

Certainly, many will continue to see CSR as a second best and unsatisfactory stopgap solution to the global human rights protection gap. Voluntary social responsibility initiatives are viewed with suspicion and skepticism by some human rights campaigners who maintain that CSR is simply cosmetic and corporations engaging in it lack a real commitment to addressing human rights. Rights campaigners advocate binding international law to regulate the conduct of multinationals. Similarly, some in the business community argue that CSR is a dangerous distraction from the central purpose of profit-making or have simply become cynical. They oppose efforts by corporations to formally commit to principles that reach beyond economic profit as the primary purpose of a business enterprise.

This book posits that neither position is correct or fully complete in its understanding of the potential consequences of the growing proliferation of CSR codes. While both positions do present valid concerns about the limitations of CSR, campaign groups suspicious of CSR may overestimate the power of "binding" international law to protect human rights, and business interests skeptical of CSR may underestimate the power of evolving social norms to protect human rights. Neither fully appreciates the avenues for informal market enforcement of social norms that CSR strategies characterized by explicitly incorporating human rights may catalyze.

This book examines the incorporation of human rights into CSR as a growing portion of the commercial sector has voluntarily stepped into the regulatory gap and promulgated CSR codes. This book also examines governance developments in the sphere of "regulation" at the intersection of CSR and human rights. Accordingly, this book explores and explains how social pressure from activists and investors influences corporate conduct with respect to human rights claims. Appreciating that many are skeptical about the potential for change unless and until binding regulations are adopted, this book proposes a different way of understanding the drivers and dynamics of voluntary global standards and the sustainability of the business and human rights movement—as potentially generative of social norms to influence corporate conduct in a manner consistent with many norms of international human rights law. To the extent that CSR initiatives incorporating rights are informed by and are emerging from a process of communication and from cycles of conflict resolution between corporations, states, and civil society stakeholders, all of these actors are shaping expectations about appropriate and inappropriate conduct for the responsible business enterprise. This interplay between stakeholders can serve to give substantive content to the business responsibility to respect rights rooted in the international human rights legal regime. Certain voluntary codes of conduct could become binding on corporations, if not in a strictly legal sense, then in a sense that makes pragmatic sense to corporate leaders.

Even in the absence of binding international law to regulate business conduct with respect to human rights, through the interplay of interest convergence and increasing information access on the part of investors and consumers where corporations will necessarily seek the respect of the consumer community and wish to avoid reputational risk. There is growing evidence that new norms of conduct consistent with respect for human rights are emerging and may evolve to become binding on businesses.

This book proceeds in two parts. Part I, "Context and Challenges: International Law, Corporate Law, and Responsibility for Human Rights Risks," contextualizes the underlying problem of the global governance gap by identifying the limitations of international law for regulating the conduct of nonstate actors and the limitations of corporate legal theory for defining the role of a corporation in globalized economy. Next, Part I provides a historical overview of the evolution of international efforts to address abuses and align commerce with universal principles on human rights principles and offers a critical assessment of recent global policy initiatives on business and human rights. Part I concludes with an examination of some of the conflicts and challenges that have led to the creation of multistakeholder initiatives and industry sector efforts to articulate and advance responsible business conduct with respect to human rights.

Part II, "Change: Human Rights, Corporate Responsibility Codes, and Compliance with Commitments," conceptualizes the present promulgation of voluntary codes of conduct and the promotion of CSR as an opportunity to close parts of the regulatory protection gap with respect to human rights more effectively than other efforts. What appears to be a voluntary self-regulation situation is best understood as an example of co-creation of norms and expectations for corporate behavior. The new norm of business responsibility to respect human rights can be enforced, provided that material information about corporate social impacts is made accessible to concerned stakeholder constituencies. Greater transparency holds promise for giving power to a shared responsibility to avoid adverse human rights impacts as investors and consumers could choose to reward business enterprises that address issues of human rights effectively and avoid complicity in human rights abuses. Voluntary codes in some cases may become obligatory compacts when conduct deemed irresponsible by the community stands to damage an industry's reputation. Industry inaction will no longer be an option where rights abuses are alleged.

The book concludes by explaining that what appears to be voluntary corporate self-regulation is actually a co-creation with a global citizenry of concerned consumers increasingly demanding changes to corporate conduct. In other words, voluntary codes are more appropriately seen as obligatory compacts between new nonstate actors in the international arena: corporations and conscious consumers. There is untapped potential in private ordering.

New normative standards for corporate conduct are emerging from the dignity demands made by members of civil society. Private ordering is playing a significant role in generating standards in the form of codes of conduct, corporate philanthropy, ethical business alliances, and international declarations. With a view toward advancing a more expansive understanding of the subjects and sources of international law, I propose a different way of understanding and interpreting the norm-generating conduct of private actors when corporations and communities come into conflict. CSR initiatives are more properly understood as a form of soft law regulation enforced by a constellation of consumers, activist investors, and affected communities. Conscious/concerned informed communities can influence the progressive development of corporate governance.

To understand the dynamics of how a human rights controversy comes to be translated into policy reform and more responsible business practices, I conducted qualitative empirical field research among stakeholders. This book draws from my interviews with activists, lawyers, policymakers, professionals, and investors. The analysis is also informed by participant observation ethnographic field research among CSR professionals and policymakers. Based on research conducted over eight years on three continents, this book provides insights into how pressure is promoting positive change and a strong form of soft law. My conclusions and observations are based on a variety of primary and secondary source material gathered from 2010 to 2018, including semistructured interviews; ethnographic research conducted as a participant and observer at the UN Annual Forum on Business and Human Rights; and annual meetings and training sessions hosted by industry associations and investors, including Business for Social Responsibility and the Interfaith Center on Corporate Responsibility. I also studied court pleadings, documents generated by those involved in crafting global policy initiatives on business and human rights, reports by those leveling allegations of abuse against corporate actors, responses by corporations to allegations of abuse, and research articles published in law reviews, journals, newspapers, and magazines.

Chapter 1, "International Law, Corporate Law, and Governance Gaps," explains how domestic US corporate law ignores human rights considerations and contributes to governance gaps. It offers an overview of the conceptual foundations of the corporate form that serves to place rights at risk. It argues that voluntary CSR initiatives, leadership on the part of management, and more inclusive configurations of corporate governance can contribute to creating better business practices consistent with respect for human rights. This chapter also explains how international human rights law is inadequate to address human rights abuses where corporate actors are implicated. It offers an overview of the conceptual foundations of international law that render global business enterprises difficult to regulate and hold to account for alleged abuses. It argues that a wide array of actors beyond states must be recognized as possessing the potential to participate in the creation of policies to regulate business practices with respect to human rights.

In view of the shortcomings of corporate law and international law, chapter 2, "Global Policy Initiatives to Regulate Business Responsibility and Human Rights," argues that pragmatic global policy instruments can provide a strong foundation for promoting changes in business practices and for providing greater protection by closing the governance gaps that place human rights and the environment at risk. This chapter traces the trajectory of international policy initiatives advanced to address the governance gap culminating in the endorsement of the UN Framework and Guiding Principles on Business and Human Rights, which seek to translate human rights issues into corporate responsibility imperatives. Based on my analysis of primary UN documents and commentaries; my interviews with different stakeholder constituencies in the policymaking process, including corporate representatives and rights activists; ethnographic research, including participation in and observations of the annual proceedings of the UN Forum on Business and Human Rights; and interviews with members of the UN Working Group on Business and Human Rights, this chapter will show that while the consensus formed around global policy instruments is fragile, certain aspects of the Framework appear to be gaining traction as authoritative among those stakeholders best situated to address or avoid human rights abuses.

Chapter 3, "Human Rights Conflicts and the Creation of Corporate Responsibility Collaborations," provides comparative accounts of the creation of industry sector–specific regulatory instruments and governance institutions arising from allegations of corporate complicity in human rights abuses after conflicts with concerned constituencies and affected communities. The selected case studies demonstrate that there are consequences for conduct inconsistent with social expectations for business. It considers cases originating in emerging market economies and complex operating environments comparing the advocacy strategies of human rights activists and corporate responses. Cases studied include: the controversial role of transnational corporations in the internet communications technology sector in censorship and surveillance practices and the risks presented to the right to freedom of expression and the right to privacy; the labor conditions in factories and on farms; and the relationship of transnational corporations in the extractives sector to human rights and the risks presented to the environment and human security when extractive sector companies contract with security forces that abuse violent force and use deadly force to silence dissent. This chapter explains how conflicts over corporate complicity in alleged abuses served to catalyze the creation of the different industry-specific multistakeholder initiatives, including: the Global Network Initiative, a private multistakeholder project to promote more responsible business practices; the Fair Labor Association, a multistakeholder collaboration to end abusive labor conditions; and the Voluntary Principles on Security, a tripartite multistakeholder initiative to address security and human rights. Chapter 3 will show that crisis and conflict appear to serve as catalysts for change.

Chapter 4, "Information and Accountability: Regulating the Corporate Responsibility to Respect Human Rights through Ranking and Reporting," argues that regulation can occur through rankings and reporting by providing information about risks to rights, allowing concerned investors and consumers to exercise informed choices. This chapter examines the emergence and evolution of selected ranking and reporting frameworks in the expanding realm of business and human rights advocacy. Specifically, it examines how indicators in the form of rankings and reports evaluating the conduct of transnational corporate actors can serve as regulatory tools with potential to bridge a global governance gap that has placed human rights at risk. It explains the conditions that have led to coordination and collaboration among those entities engaged in creating reporting frameworks and rankings while nevertheless relying upon the competitive impulses of the business enterprises being ranked to assert influence. It also identifies why the businesses being ranked have been slow to deploy effective counterstrategies despite efforts to contest emerging reporting requirements. It considers the interaction of selected business and human rights indicators with recent laws regulating supply chain transparency in the United States and with recent global policy initiatives calling for business enterprises to conduct human rights impact assessments. It reviews some of the methodological and moral risks raised with respect in ranking rights. In conclusion, I argue that in the ecology of global governance these new business and human rights indicators will provide rights advocates with greater power and will have the potential to play an important role in solidifying emerging soft law standards and strengthening corporate self-regulation. I argue strategic use of indicators in the business and human rights realm could ultimately prove to make the commitments contained in voluntary codes of conduct to respect human rights obligatory.

Initiatives to promote information about business human rights impacts on the part of civil society activists demonstrate a shifting consciousness and increasing concern that could introduce moral considerations into capital and consumer markets at a scale sufficient to create an incentive for corporate actors to consider the risks particular business practices may present for human rights.

Chapter 5, "Competition, Choice, and Change: Activist Investors and Concerned Consumers as Ethical Enforcement Agents," considers how enforcement of corporate commitments to respect human rights could occur through the provision of actionable information on corporate performance to concerned constituencies of investors and consumers. It considers competitive pressures that could be brought to bear on particular industries by virtue of greater transparency, including the connected nature of communication enjoyed by a significant segment of consumers. A connected and concerned community of consumers and investors could leverage concerns into change. It contemplates ways to generate adverse market consequences for business activities that have adverse human rights consequences. Specifically, it considers the changes generated by shareholder activism on human rights issues and the advances achieved by a "worker driven, consumer powered and market enforced" fair food program. It also considers examples of corporations that have reaped rewards for responsible conduct consistent with the responsibility to respect human rights. I argue that expectations on business with respect to avoiding adverse human rights impacts and complicity in abuses are increasing and that choices will reflect concerns aligned with rewarding responsible business conduct.

Chapter 6, "From Voluntary to Obligatory: Corporate Reporting and Codes of Conduct to Promote Respect for Human Rights," examines what corporations are doing to address human rights risks presented by particular business practices in particular contexts. It offers an overview of the different strategies being used by transnational business enterprises to respond to concerns expressed by investors, consumers, and affected communities. Among the self-regulation strategies used by businesses examined are participation in multistakeholder initiatives designed to address human rights issues, human rights impact assessments, audits and certifications, supply chain contract provisions, and corporate responses to ratings and reports by concerned stakeholder constituencies. It presents the findings of a discourse analysis of codes created by competing corporations in selected industry sectors assessing over time, the extent to which codes incorporate reference to human rights standards. Corporate responses to allegations of complicity in abuse are analyzed. I argue that the discursive frame asserted by corporate responsibility incorporating rights increasingly treats voluntary norms as obligatory to maintaining a "social license" to operate.

My research is intended to fill a gap in the literature by emphasizing the role of concerned and informed communities as potential "enforcers" and "regulators" of corporate behavior. Too often, these efforts are invisible, marginalized, or seen as irrelevant to "hard" legal processes such as courtroom advocacy or binding international accords. It is my hope that this research will encourage further strategic and analytical inquiry into how concerned and informed communities can influence the progressive development of corporate governance and international standards in the absence of agreement on a binding international instrument. It is critical that we expand our understanding of the private actor as both a subject and source of international human rights law because of the norm-generating power of nonstate actors. Under present conditions, the exchange between nonstate actors—corporations, communities, and consumers—may be the most promising possibility for closing the global governance gap into which the unregulated conduct of multinational corporations often falls. The increasing prominence of private nonstate actors internationally presents unique challenges, but it may also provide an opportunity to globalize norms of social and environmental justice.

Milton Friedman imagined a freedom where the market economy would support liberty. Nelson Mandela imagined a freedom that included responsibility. Present challenges require us to imagine ways various stakeholders can share in the responsibility to change the conditions that contribute to adverse human rights and environmental impacts through examining the consequences of our public and personal procurement choices.

# PART I

# CONTEXT AND CHALLENGES

## *International Law, Corporate Law, and Responsibility for Human Rights Risks*

# 1
# International Law, Corporate Law, and Governance Gaps

*The rise of the modern corporation has brought a concentration of economic power, which can compete on equal terms with the modern state.*

—Adolf Berle, *The Modern Corporation* (1932)

## Introduction

Today, large and powerful private corporations operate in and across many nations. These transnational corporations pose a significant conceptual challenge to international law.[1] The operative concepts of the law of nations do not clearly delineate the duties of entities that are not nations. Conventional approaches to international law are inadequate for addressing the challenges that transnational corporations present. Public international law, as conventionally conceived, fails to adequately govern the conduct of private nonstate actors, such as transnational business enterprises. The resulting gap in global human rights protection and accountability when a private business enterprise contributes to or causes rights violations presents a theoretical problem for international law. To fully appreciate the implications of this global human rights governance gap, it is important to understand the conceptual foundations, the structure, and the basic sources of international law.

This chapter explains why international human rights law has been inadequate to address human rights abuses where nonstate corporate actors are implicated. It offers an overview of the conceptual foundations of international law that render global business enterprises difficult to regulate and hard to hold to account for alleged human rights abuses. It also explains how domestic US corporate law ignores human rights considerations, further widening global human rights governance gaps. This chapter also provides an overview of the conceptual

[1] Steven R. Ratner, *Corporations and Human Rights: A Theory of Legal Responsibility*, 111 Yale L.J. 443, 443–545 (2001).

*Incorporating Rights.* Erika George, Oxford University Press. © Erika George 2021.
DOI: 10.1093/oso/9780199941483.003.0002

foundations of the corporate form that serve to place rights at risk. It argues that voluntary corporate social responsibility initiatives, leadership on the part of management, and more inclusive configurations of corporate governance can contribute to creating better business practices consistent with respect for human rights. It concludes that a wide array of actors, beyond states, must be recognized as possessing the potential impact human rights.

## I. International Law

International law has conventionally been understood as limited to laws that govern relations between nations. Made by and for nations to regulate relationships among independent, sovereign nation-states, international law is literally the "law of nations." As influential international jurist Philip C. Jessup has explained in his 1947 article, "The Subjects of a Modern Law of Nations," states are the subjects of international law, other entities or individuals are only its objects.[2]

### A. The Position of the "Legal Person" in International Law: Sovereign Powers and Privileges

Historically, international law has drawn a sharp distinction between the subjects of international law that have rights and responsibilities, and mere objects, presumably without rights or responsibilities. The sovereign state enjoys its status as a "legal person" in international law.[3] As legal persons, sovereign states possess power to own property, to make international agreements, and to join international organizations. Sovereign states also have the power to seek legal remedies.[4]

States are accepted as the sole "subjects" of international law imbued with "international legal personality." Recognized states enjoy full participation in the international legal system and "can affect and be affected by international law and can enforce international law by bringing at least some international claims."[5] In contrast, "objects" of international law neither enjoy the powers of the subjects of international law; nor are they understood to possess legal personality. Objects are nonstate actors, such as natural persons, private corporations, natural resources, and nongovernmental organizations. In international law, power is

[2] Philip C. Jessup, *Subjects of a Modern Law of Nations*, 45 MICH. L. REV. 383, 383 (1947).
[3] Restatement, (Third) of Foreign Relations Law of the United States, 206 (1987).
[4] *Id.*
[5] Jose E. Alvarez, *Are Corporations "Subjects" of International Law?*, 9 SANTA CLARA J. INT'L L. 1, 3 (2011).

understood to reside with sovereign nation-states, the subjects of international law, while all objects must submit to the power or will of these subjects.

## B. Sources of International Law: State Conduct, Conventions, Custom, and Common Principles

States create the substance of international law. Sovereign states make international law in cooperation with other states, through treaties or by establishing patterns of conduct and practices over time. The commonly recognized sources of international law are codified in Article 38(1) of the Statute of the International Court of Justice (ICJ).[6] The statute provides that treaties, custom, and general principles of law are the primary sources of international law. In addition, judicial decisions and the writings of jurists and scholars may offer evidence of the existence of emerging rules or norms regulating the conduct of states.

The ICJ also recognizes the additional "subsidiary" sources of judicial decisions, and scholarly works demonstrate the acceptance that can transform a nonbinding standard into a binding rule of international law. Conventions, custom, and common principles remain the best evidence of the existence of a binding rule of international law.

### 1. Conventions

The terms "treaty," "convention," "covenant," and "accord," are often used interchangeably to describe an international agreement created by states that consent to be legally bound by its contents. The international law of treaties has been codified in the Vienna Convention on the Law of Treaties. Article 2 defines a treaty as "an international agreement concluded between States in written form and governed by international law, whether embodied in a single instrument or in two or more related instruments and whatever its particular designation."[7] Treaties may be bilateral (an agreement between two states, such as an investment treaty), or multilateral (an accord among several states, such as an environmental treaty). Treaties may also create international institutions and regulate a range issues from taxes, trade, and investment, to human rights and the environment. States enter into treaties.

[6] Statute of the Int'l Court of Justice, art. 38, para. 1. Art. 38, June 26, 1945, 59 Stat. 1055 [hereinafter ICJ Statute].

[7] Vienna Convention on the Law of Treaties, May 23, 1969, 1155 U.N.T.S. 331, 8 I.L.M. 679 (1969); *see also* Vienna Convention on the Law of Treaties Between States and International Organizations or Between International Organizations.

### 2. Custom and State Conduct

Custom is a "general practice accepted as law."[8] Customary international law is created after a general and consistent pattern of state conduct emerges over time that states understand to be obligatory.[9] To be considered international law, a rule or principle must be accepted by states as being legally binding. Customary law is created in part by the conduct of states, which constitutes state practice.

The actions or omissions of states are the practices that generate principles of customary international law. Official government acts are state practices. Acts illustrative of state practice include official statements made at international meetings, representations made in diplomatic exchanges and correspondence, as well as legislation and judicial decisions that address international issues.[10]

There is a customary law of international human rights. Customary international law binds even those states that have refused to ratify human rights treaties or that have ratified treaties but taken reservations intended to nullify particular rights protections.[11] For example, any country that "practices, encourages, or condones" as a matter of state policy: "1) genocide, 2) slavery or the slave trade, 3) murder or disappearances, 4) torture or other cruel, inhuman or degrading treatment or punishment, 5) prolonged arbitrary detention, 6) systematic racial discrimination, or 7) a consistent pattern of gross violations of internationally recognized human rights" violates customary international law.[12]

In sum, state conduct determines international law. Whether through developing custom or ratifying conventions, sovereign nations are the only entities currently recognized in international law with the capacity to create binding legal obligations. Yet there are other nonstate entities operating in the international arena and engaged in conduct with economic, political, social, and security consequences.[13]

## C. Others in International Law: Empire, Global Business Enterprise, and Economic Influence

While not imbued with legal personality for the purpose of creating law, business enterprises can exert considerable influence on international relations.

[8] Ian Brownlie, Principles of Public International Law 6 (6th ed. 2003).

[9] John J. Kirton & Michael J. Trebilcock, Hard choices, soft law: Voluntary standards in global trade, environment and social governance 9 (2017).

[10] *See* Brownlie, *supra* note 8, at 6–29.

[11] *Id.* at 47–48.

[12] Lori E. Damrosch et al., Int'l Law Cases and Materials 602–603 (4th ed. 2001) (citing Restatement (Third) §702).

[13] *See* Philip Alston, *The "Not-a-Cat" Syndrome: Can the International Human Rights Regime Accommodate Non-State Actors?*, in Non-State Actors and Human Rights 3, 3–5 (Philip Alston ed., 2005).

Corporations are nonstate actors that enjoy economic and political influence, if not international legal personality. The relationship between countries and corporations has been simultaneously symbiotic and strained.[14] Anxieties over corporate power eclipsing the power of the sovereign state are not new but rather persist.

The "proper mix of functions" for the colonial-era crown-charter companies was contested from the early days of the corporate form. The example of the British East India Company is instructive. At the height of its power, it "ruled over one-fifth of the world's people, generated a revenue greater than the whole of Britain and commanded a private army a quarter of a million strong."[15]

The company's activities in India influenced trade across the British Empire. Historian Nick Robins explains: "A terrible triangle was formed with African slaves being purchased in part with Indian cotton goods, then being sold in the Americas for new-mined gold and silver, which in turn found its way via London to India where it procured more textiles."[16] The money made in Bengal, India, enabled the company to triple the funding devoted to its tea trade in China.[17] As the demand for tea increased, so did the desire to trade with China.[18] The company facilitated the export of opium produced in Bengal to China. The company later financed the Opium Wars that were precipitated by China's efforts to reject the opium trade due to the social disruption opium addition was causing in the country.[19] The company's tea trade would also come to symbolize oppression in America. The Boston Tea Party, the symbolic start to America's Revolutionary War, was a protest over the influence the East India Company exercised.[20]

In his 1776 book, *The Wealth of Nations*, philosopher Adam Smith argued that the role of trader and sovereign were incompatible.[21] During the age of empire, it was for a time presumed that commercial actors were traders first, with

[14] *See generally* ANDREW CLAPHAM, HUMAN RIGHTS OBLIGATIONS OF NON-STATE ACTORS 195–247 (1995); JOSEPH E. STIGLITZ, MAKING GLOBALIZATION WORK 188–210 (2006); Daniel J.H. Greenwood, *The Semi-Sovereign Corporation*, in LEGAL STUDIES RESEARCH PAPER SERIES (Research Paper No. 05-04, 2005). *Cf.* P.T. MUCHLINSKI, MULTINATIONAL ENTERPRISES AND THE LAW 3–56 (1995).

[15] Nick Robins, *Loot: In Search of the East India Company, the World's First Transnational Corporation*, 14 ENV'T & URB. 79 (2002).

[16] *Id.* at 80–81.

[17] NICK ROBINS, THE CORPORATION THAT CHANGED THE WORLD: HOW THE EAST INDIA COMPANY SHAPED THE MODERN MULTINATIONAL 3–4 (2006).

[18] Robins, *supra* note 15, at 81.

[19] *Id.*

[20] *Id.* at 82.

[21] ADAM SMITH, AN INQUIRY INTO THE NATURE AND CAUSES OF THE WEALTH OF NATIONS 343–44 (Edwin Cannan ed., 1977) ("No two characters seem more inconsistent than those of trader and sovereign. If the trading spirit of the English East India Company renders them very bad sovereigns, the spirit of sovereignty seems to have rendered them equally bad traders. While they were traders only, they managed their trade successfully. . . . Since they became sovereigns. . . . they have been obliged to beg the extraordinary assistance of government in order to avoid immediate bankruptcy.").

responsibility for territorial rule a distant second.[22] However, as the revelation of atrocities, excesses, and corrupt conduct of the East India Company became increasingly difficult to deny, agents and employees of the East India Company were no longer mere merchants but rather had become de facto emperors or quasi sovereigns extending Britain's reign over the far reaches of the world.[23] Robins described the East India Company as "a monstrous combination of trader, banker, conqueror and power broker."[24] Ultimately, the British public rejected the company's overreach and called for reforms while people living under colonial rule resisted and revolted against the Company.

Generations after the imperial expansion of the East India Company and its collapse, a different way of globally exercising commercial power to promote good was introduced as an experiment for addressing apartheid in South Africa. The Reverend Leon Sullivan, an African American pastor, used his influence as a member of the Board of General Motors to oppose racial inequality. Apartheid, South Africa's entrenched system of separation and oppression based on race was an organizing principle of life in the country and a fact of doing business there. South African law required strict categorization and separation of the races, and public policies were designed to ensure exclusion and inequality in every sphere of life and death. With cemeteries even segregated by race, the workplace was no exception.

General Motors was the largest employer of Blacks in South Africa. Beginning with employment, Sullivan sought to dismantle discrimination based on notions of racial superiority and inferiority. Ultimately, he arrived at the conclusion that "companies must practice corporate civil disobedience" against racist laws. Sullivan issued an ultimatum that "Mandela must be freed, apartheid must end, and blacks must vote." With anything short of these aims, Sullivan threatened that he would "bring every American company I can out of South Africa."[25]

His was no idle threat. The estimated $2.3 billion invested in South Africa by US companies comprised one-fifth of the country's foreign direct investment, primarily in the important industry sectors of oil, automotive, computer technology, and minerals.[26] Three US firms controlled approximately 44 percent of the country's petroleum market.[27] The US firms GM, Ford, and Chrysler controlled one-third of the country's automotive manufacturing.[28] The three largest

22 Janet McLean, *The Transnational Corporation in History: Lessons for Today?*, 79 Ind. L.J. 363, 368 (2004).

23 H.V. Bowen, The Business of Empire: The East India Company and Imperial Britain, 1756–1833, at 3, 9–10 (2006).

24 Robins, *supra* note 15, at 83.

25 *See* The Rev. Leon Sullivan Website, *The Global Sullivan Principles*, http://muwww-new.marshall.edu/revleonsullivan/indexf.htm.

26 Brian J.F. Clark, *United States Labor Practices in South Africa: Will a Mandatory Fair Employment Code Succeed Where the Sullivan Principles Have Failed?*, 7 Fordham Int'l L.J. 358, 361 (1984).

27 *Id.*

28 *Id.*

US employers in South Africa were mining concerns. US companies dominated the computer market, with five US firms among the country's top seven in sales.[29]

As a private individual, Sullivan introduced a voluntary code of practice for US companies operating in South Africa. It would come to be adopted by many of the world's major multinational corporations.[30] The Sullivan Principles as issued in 1977 called for:

1. Nonsegregation of the races in all eating, comfort, and work facilities.
2. Equal and fair employment practices for all employees.
3. Equal pay for all employees doing equal or comparable work for the same period of time.
4. Initiation of and development of training programs that will prepare, in substantial numbers, Blacks and other nonwhites for supervisory, administrative, clerical, and technical jobs.
5. Increasing the number of Blacks and other nonwhites in management and supervisory positions.
6. Improving the quality of life for Blacks and other nonwhites outside the work environment in such areas as housing, transportation, school, recreation, and health facilities.[31]

In 1984 he added a seventh and final principle:

7. Working to eliminate laws and customs that impede social, economic, and political justice.[32]

Promulgated by a private individual and adopted by many of the world's major multinational corporations, the Sullivan Principles were crafted to offer ways in which business enterprises operating in South Africa, a country with racist laws and a racist system of government that violated the human rights norms, could conduct business more consciously. This required corporations to operate in a manner contrary to prevailing laws and attitudes in a sovereign state.

Initially, twelve major US multinationals with South African operations would adhere to a code of conduct for conducting business in the country concerning the treatment of nonwhite workers.[33] As participants grew in number

[29] Clark, *supra* note 26, at 358, 361.

[30] *Id.*

[31] *See* Rev. Sullivan, Statement of Principles 1–4 (July 6, 1978) (available from the offices of the American Committee on Africa, New York City).

[32] *See* The Rev. Leon Sullivan Website, *supra* note 25.

[33] S. Prakash Sethi & Oliver F. Williams, *Creating and Implementing Global Codes of Conduct: An Assessment of the Sullivan Principles as a Role Model for Developing International Codes of Conduct—Lessons Learned and Unlearned*, 105 Bus. & Soc'y Rev. 169, 169–170 (2000). Among the founding

and the principles became important domestically and internationally, Sullivan was credited with "accelerating the process of socio-political change in South Africa."[34]

Sullivan successfully managed to persuade the corporate community that complicity with a racist regime was bad for business. However, after little change in South Africa, Sullivan joined calls for divestment and more than one hundred companies adhering to the principles left the South African market.[35] By the end of apartheid in 1994, over one hundred fifty US corporations and their South African subsidiaries had spent millions to bring their business practices into compliance with them.[36]

## D. Economic Globalization and Business Enterprises

The classic state-centered view of international law is increasingly difficult to reconcile with the rise of private nonstate actors that have a significant effect on nations and individuals.[37] Traditional approaches to international law are no longer descriptively or conceptually adequate. The process of economic globalization fueled by private enterprise is eroding the hegemonic place of the state in international law as the subject and source of international law.[38] As a result of globalization, the place where power resides in the international system is growing more diffuse. Authority for traditionally public functions is being ceded to or assumed by private enterprise.

Now nearly half of the world's largest economic entities are corporations, not countries.[39] Commercial enterprises may not have international legal personality, but they do have relative clout in the international arena with revenues that eclipse the gross domestic products of some of the sovereign states in which they operate.

Despite the growing influence of corporations on and in sovereign states, international law continues to treat corporations as objects without international

signatories were: Citicorp, Ford Motor Company, General Motors Corporation, IBM Corporation, International Harvester Company, Mobil Corporation, and Union Carbide Corporation. *Id.* at 170.

[34] *Id.* at 171.

[35] *See The Sullivan Principles, supra* note 25.

[36] Sethi & Williams, *supra* note 33.

[37] *See generally,* NON-STATE ACTORS AND HUMAN RIGHTS (Philip Alston ed., 2005) *and* HUMAN RIGHTS OBLIGATIONS OF NON-STATE ACTORS (Andrew Clapham ed., 2006); *see also,* Steven R. Ratner, *Corporations and Human Rights: A Theory of Legal Responsibility,* 111 YALE L.J. 443, 443–545 (2001).

[38] *See generally,* DAVID KINLEY, CIVILISING GLOBALIZATION: HUMAN RIGHTS AND THE GLOBAL ECONOMY (2009).

[39] *69 of the Richest 100 Entities on the Planet Are Corporations, not Governments, Figures Show,* GLOBAL JUSTICE NOW (Oct. 17, 2018), https://www.globaljustice.org.uk/news/2018/oct/17/69-richest-100-entities-planet-are-corporations-not-governments-figures-show.

legal personality.[40] International law does little to acknowledge or address corporate power even though powerful corporations exert influence on global politics and economics. The growing power and influence of corporate actors calls into question the conventional distinction between subjects and objects, and the status of states as the central focus of in international law. Because private commercial enterprises are merely the objects, not subjects, of international law, they have not been understood to bear the same responsibilities as nations.

The question of whether corporations can be liable for violations of the law of nations is complicated by the doctrinal distinction between subjects and objects, and between the public authority of sovereign nations and the private power of transnational corporations: Facebook is not France. Currently, corporations cannot commit to or become parties to binding international human rights instruments as states can. Under international law, a private commercial enterprise does not have the requisite legal personality to make hard law. The independent obligation, if any, of multinational enterprise to conform to international human rights standards is far from clear.[41] There are often regulatory gaps between the standards of the corporation's home country and its host country. For example, human rights and labor protections may be strong in some countries and weak in others. Therefore, corporate action often occurs in a regulatory gap where there is little international law to guide business practices abroad.

## II. Public International Human Rights Law and Private Corporate Actors

The atrocities of World War II inspired the creation of our contemporary system of international human rights law.[42] In the postwar period, the international community established institutions to prevent threats to peace and executed instruments to promote social and economic progress. The universally agreed-upon system of collective peace and security contained a central commitment to the protection of human dignity and the promotion of freedom.[43] By

[40] Philip C. Jessup, *The Subjects of a Modern Law of Nations*, 45 MICH. L. REV. 383, 387 (1947).

[41] Peter Muchlinski, *Corporate Social Responsibility and International Law: The Case of Human Rights and Multinational Enterprises*, in THE NEW CORPORATE ACCOUNTABILITY 440 (2007).

[42] *See, e.g.*, ELIZABETH BORGWARDT, A NEW DEAL FOR THE WORLD: AMERICA'S VISION FOR HUMAN RIGHTS 196 (2005); PHILIP ALSTON & RYAN GOODMAN, INTERNATIONAL HUMAN RIGHTS, THE SUCCESSOR TO INTERNATIONAL HUMAN RIGHTS IN CONTEXT 10 (2012).

[43] U.N. Charter, pmbl., art. 1; Universal Declaration of Human Rights, G.A. Res. 217 (III), at art. 23, para. 3 (Dec. 10 1948) U.N. Doc. A/810 [hereinafter UDHR]; *See, e.g.*, Makau Mutua, *Savages, Victims and Saviors: The Metaphor of Human Rights*, 42 HARV. INT'L L.J. 201–245 (2001) (challenging the notion of universality of human rights as a cover for the continued expansion of Western values and interests by several countries that are now UN members, which were colonial territories at the time of the Charter and Declaration).

establishing the United Nations in 1945, the international community aimed to create conditions under which justice and respect for international law would be sustained.[44]

The General Assembly of the United Nations unanimously adopted the Universal Declaration of Human Rights (UDHR) on December 10, 1948, a day now celebrated as International Human Rights Day.[45] As with most resolutions of the General Assembly, the UDHR was not understood to be legally binding or enforceable at the time.[46] Unlike many other General Assembly resolutions, however, numerous legally binding international instruments subsequently entered into force and have codified many of the substantive rights contained in the UDHR.[47] As a result, principles contained in the UDHR have become "hard law," requiring a nation's compliance even though it was initially a nonbinding statement of "soft law."

The UDHR remains the international community's central proclamation of "a common standard of achievement for all peoples and all nations,"[48] and contains a range of civil, political, socioeconomic, and cultural rights. Certain rights under the UDHR are understood to be "positive," in that they may require some form of government intervention in order to be realized. For example, the right to education may require governments to provide a system of public education accessible to all without discrimination. Other rights in the UDHR are "negative," in that these rights require governments to refrain from interference in order for them to be protected. For example, freedom from torture requires that governments refrain from engaging in torture. Similarly, enjoyment of the right to freedom of expression depends on governments refraining from censorship.

The UDHR is universal in the sense that it speaks to the entitlement and obligations of everyone, everywhere. It extends beyond states and provides that "every individual and every organ of society" should promote respect for, and

[44] U.N. Charter, pmbl.

[45] G.A. Res. 217 (III) A, Universal Declaration of Human Rights (Dec. 10, 1948).

[46] *See* Dennis J. Driscoll, *The Development of Human Rights in International Law*, in THE HUM. RTS. READER, 41, 45 (rev. ed., 1989) (explaining the nonbinding nature of the Universal Declaration of Human Rights as emphasized by states prior to its adoption).

[47] *See, e.g.*, Int'l Covenant on Civil and Political Rights (ICCPR), Dec. 16, 1966, 999 U.N.T.S. 171; Int'l Covenant on Economic, Social and Cultural Rights (ICESCR), Dec. 16, 1966, 993 U.N.T.S. 3; International Convention on the Elimination of All Forms of Racial Discrimination, Dec. 21, 1965, 660 U.N.T.S. 195; Convention on the Elimination of all Forms of Discrimination Against Women, Dec. 18, 1979, 1249 U.N.T.S. 13; Convention on the Rights of the Child, Nov. 20, 1989, 1577 U.N.T.S. 3; Convention Against Torture and Other Cruel, Inhuman or Degrading Treatment or Punishment, Dec. 10, 1984, 1465 U.N.T.S. 85; G.A. Res. 61/106, Convention on the Rights of Persons with Disabilities (Jan. 24, 2007); G.A. Res. 45/158, Int'l Convention on the Rts. of Migrant Workers (Dec. 18, 1990); G.A. Res. 61/177, Int'l Convention for the Protection of All Persons from Enforced Disappearance (Jan. 12, 2007).

[48] See, supra note 43 Universal Declaration of Human Rights, pmbl.

effective recognition of, the rights contained within it through "teaching and education" and other "progressive measures, national and international."[49]

## A. International Human Rights Instruments and Institutions

Human rights are now enumerated and guaranteed in numerous treaties, and via custom, general principles, and other sources of international law.[50] Chief among the many legally binding international instruments that have codified the substantive rights contained in the UDHR are the International Covenant on Civil and Political Rights (ICCPR) and the International Covenant on Economic, Social and Cultural Rights (ICESCR). The International Bill of Human Rights consists of the UDHR, together with the ICCPR and the ICESCR. The 1993 Vienna Declaration on Human Rights clarifies that all of the rights contained in the International Bill of Rights—civil, political, socioeconomic, and cultural—are interdependent, interrelated, and indivisible.[51]

Labor rights protect the human rights of workers. Fundamental labor rights are set forth in the International Labour Organization's (ILO's) Declaration on Fundamental Principles and Rights at Work, and specified in eight core ILO Conventions.[52] Labor rights include the right to work as well as rights at work. International law enshrines four fundamental labor rights: (1) freedom of association and effective recognition of the right to collective bargaining; (2) the elimination of all forms of forced or compulsory labor; the effective abolition of forced or compulsory labor; (3) the effective abolition of child labor; and (4) the elimination of discrimination with respect to employment and occupation.[53]

There are two levels of international institutional arrangements in place to promote the protection of human rights in the UN system. A new UN Human Rights Council replaced the 1946 UN Commission on Human Rights in 2006.[54] An intergovernmental body composed of forty-seven elected UN member

[49] *Id.*

[50] *See* ICJ Statute, *supra* note 6 (listing the accepted sources of international law as being treaties, custom, general principles, and other sources of international law).

[51] Vienna Declaration and Program of Action, U.N. Doc. A/CONF.157/23 (July 12, 1993).

[52] Int'l Lab. Org. (ILO), *Freedom of Association and Protection of the Right to Organise Convention*, No. 87 (1948); ILO, *Right to Organise and Collective Bargaining Convention*, No. 98 (July 4, 1950); ILO, *Forced Labour Convention*, No. 29 (May 1, 1932); ILO, *Abolition of Forced Labour Convention*, No. 105 (June 25, 1957); ILO, *Minimum Age Convention*, No. 138 (June 26, 1973); ILO, *Worst Forms of Child Labour Convention*, No. 182 (June 17, 1999); ILO, *Equal Remuneration Convention*, No. 100 (June 29, 1951); ILO, *Discrimination (Employment and Occupation) Convention*, No. 111 (June 25, 1958).

[53] ILO, *Declaration on Fundamental Principles and Rights at Work*, 86th Sess., Geneva (June 1998); *see also* Hum. Rts. Watch, *On the Margins of Profit*, Vol. 20, No. 3(G), 32–38 (2008).

[54] G.A. Res. 251, U.N. Doc. A/RES/60/251 (Apr. 3, 2006).

states, it reports directly to the full General Assembly.[55] It oversees the Universal Periodic Review process to assess compliance with human rights commitments by all UN member nations[56] and can also propose new international human rights laws.[57] The council's complaint procedure allows individuals and organizations to bring attention to human rights abuses.[58]

There are also different monitoring mechanisms for each of the basic international human rights treaties. For example, the substantive content of the rights contained in the ICCPR are interpreted by the Human Rights Committee, while the substantive content of the rights contained in the ICESCR are interpreted by the Committee on Economic, Social and Cultural Rights. States that are parties to the basic human rights treaties are to submit reports on their efforts to advance the rights recognized in a given treaty.[59] In addition, there are regional institutions that monitor compliance with regional rights instruments.

The Office of the High Commissioner for Human Rights (OHCHR) supports both the charter-based and treaty-based human rights mechanisms in the UN system. The OHCHR also supports a range of special thematic mandates to monitor human rights conditions conducted by independent experts through its Special Procedures Branch, including the UN Working Group on Business and Human Rights, established in 2011.[60] In 2012, the Human Rights Council established a mandate on human rights and the environment to study human rights obligations relating to the enjoyment of a safe, clean, healthy, and sustainable environment.[61]

International human rights law is evolving to expand into emerging areas that may present risks to the enjoyment of rights. State conduct through participating in policymaking processes serve to generate norms and create custom. There is a trend at the international level toward understanding the relationship of business to the enjoyment of human rights. International law regulates states. States must promote, protect, and fulfill human rights guarantees. Human rights treaties are generally silent as to the obligations of others. The UN human rights

[55] The Council meets in Geneva ten weeks a year. The elected member states serving on the Council serve for a three-year period and cannot serve for more than two consecutive terms.

[56] U.N. Office of the High Commissioner for Hum. Rts., *Universal Periodic Review*, http://www.ohchr.org/EN/HRBodies/UPR/Pages/UPRMain.aspx (last visited Jan. 15, 2016).

[57] U.N. Office of the High Commissioner for Hum. Rts., *How We Do It*, http://www.ohchr.org/EN/AboutUs/Pages/HowWeDoIt.aspx (last visited Jan. 15, 2016).

[58] U.N. Office of the High Commissioner for Hum. Rts., *What We Do*, http://www.ohchr.org/EN/AboutUs/Pages/WhatWeDo.aspx (last visited Jan. 15, 2016).

[59] *See, e.g.*, ICCPR, *supra* note 47, at art. 40, ICESCR, *supra* note 47, at art. 40.

[60] Human Rights Council, *Guiding Principles on Business and Human Rights: Implementing the United Nations "Protect, Respect and Remedy" Framework*, HRC Doc. A/HRC/17/31 (Mar. 21, 2011).

[61] U.N. Office of the High Commissioner for Hum. Rts., *Special Rapporteur on human rights and the environment*, https://www.ohchr.org/EN/Issues/Environment/SREnvironment/Pages/SRenvironmentIndex.aspx (last visited Feb. 13, 2020).

mechanisms are taking on contemporary concerns and creating soft law and standards to address business and human rights and environmental rights.

## B. Human Rights Abuses Involving Corporate Actors

No longer are nations thought to be the only entities implicated in human rights violations; corporations are increasingly implicated along with governments. International human rights advocates have conventionally emphasized abuses perpetrated by governments and the relationship between states and individuals—protecting individual rights from state intrusion and abuse. Greater attention now is being directed toward questioning the role of private nonstate actors, principally multinational corporations, in conduct that contravenes generally accepted principles of international human rights law. Allegations that multinational corporations are directly engaging in human rights violations or are aiding and abetting the efforts of repressive governments to abuse human rights are increasing.

The growing power of the modern multinational corporation brings with it an increased potential to advance or undermine respect for the protection of human rights and the environment.[62] Today, human rights activists, investors, and others are asking how to align the conduct of corporations with human rights standards and how to hold corporations accountable when their conduct deviates from respect for human rights.[63]

Under international law, governments assume obligations to protect, promote, fulfill, and respect human rights. It is therefore incumbent upon the state to ensure that all actors within the state's territorial borders, or under the state's jurisdiction and control, comply with laws enacted to protect human rights. However, in light of the shifting power relationships between the state and the corporation, the picture is more complicated.

Several factors add to the complexity, not least the fact that some poorer states are not as economically powerful as the multinational corporations they host.[64] Compliance and enforcement procedures can be expensive and may exceed the resources of poor and developing nations.[65] Moreover, even if a poorer country were able to enact human rights laws and enforce compliance, it might

[62] *See, e.g.*, Jessica Woodroffe, *Regulating Multinational Corporations in a World of Nation States*, in Human Rights Standards and the Responsibility of Transnational Corporations (Michael K. Addo ed., 1999).

[63] *See, e.g.*, Thom Hartmann, Unequal Protection: The Rise of Corporate Dominance and the Theft of Human Rights (2002).

[64] Henry J. Steiner, Philip Alston, & Ryan Goodman, International Human Rights in Context: Law, Politics, Morals 1388 (3d ed. 2008).

[65] *Id.*

be unwilling to do so because it would risk losing foreign investment.[66] Instead of protecting its citizens by enacting and enforcing environmental and human rights protections, the state may elect to promote foreign investment by rejecting regulations that appear to be burdensome to business. Investors are often perceived to favor regulatory environments with lower standards and low production costs.[67]

## C. Corporate Complicity in International Human Rights Violations

Initially, human rights organizations, such as Amnesty International and Human Rights Watch, focused their monitoring efforts on governments. However, more recently, rights groups have expanded their field of vision to include private actors. Activists working on social, economic, and cultural rights now highlight the role of private industry in impeding and advancing human rights. Allegations that multinational corporations are directly engaging in human rights violations or are aiding and abetting violators have increased.

Human rights activists argue that when corporations "fail to ensure that their operations do not depend upon, benefit from, or contribute to human rights abuses committed by others," they are complicit in violating human rights.[68] The lack of corporate accountability and the inability of individuals and communities to obtain effective remedy to redress violations are subjects being examined by human rights advocates. Human rights organizations have investigated the impact of commercial activity on a range of rights and the environment.[69]

Although international human rights instruments do not directly bind business enterprises as parties to treaties, businesses can affect rights. More frequently than direct involvement in abuses, corporations are indirectly implicated in violations because of their relationships with third parties, such as corrupt or repressive government regimes. There have been allegations leveled against corporations, even claiming corporate complicity in violations of jus cogens—actions that are, without exception, always prohibited under international law.

For example, IBM's technology was used to aid the administration of the genocide of millions of European Jews during World War II; the Nazis were one of

[66] *Id.*

[67] *Id.*; *see* Kinley, *supra* note 38, at 145–203.

[68] Lisa Misol & Smita Narula, *On the Margins of Profit Rights at Risk in the Global Economy*, 20 Human Rights Watch and the Center for Human Rights and Global Justice 11 (2008).

[69] *See id*; Human Rights Watch, On the Margins of Profit: Rights at Risk in the Global Economy 20 (2008); Edwin Black, IBM and the Holocaust: The Strategic Alliance Between Nazi Germany and America's Most Powerful Corporation (Crown Publishers, 2001).

IBM's largest customers.[70] Under the Nazi regime, Germany sent millions of Jewish people and other disfavored minorities to concentration camps, where they were either slaughtered or used for slave labor.[71] IBM's punch card technology ultimately was used by the Nazis to track implementation of Hitler's "Final Solution."[72]

At the start of World War II, IBM was supplying Nazi Germany with more than a billion punch cards per year.[73] IBM provided training, sold replacement punch cards, and employed technicians to service and repair machines for the Nazi regime.[74] Dehomag, IBM's German subsidiary, designed a census package to count and classify citizens. Dehomag recruited, trained, and even fed the large number of temporary workers needed to process the census and track Jewish people.[75] The IBM technology enabled the Nazis to "achieve scale, velocity, [and] efficiency."[76] Ironically, IBM technology also helped the Allies prosecute Nazi defendants during the Nuremberg trials by introducing instantaneous translation.[77]

IBM was not alone in giving aid to a genocidal regime. More than six thousand German firms used forced or slave labor.[78] German chemical company I.G. Farben was one of those firms. It also produced the gas that was used in concentration camp gas chambers to exterminate millions.[79] By 1945, Farben had an estimated one hundred thousand people working in forced labor conditions or as slaves.[80]

At the end of World War II, the United States and the Allies prosecuted the major Nazi war criminals in a series of trials in Nuremberg, Germany.[81] One of the Nuremberg trials was specifically for Farben's twenty-four corporate board members.[82] Farben itself was never tried for any crimes, but the members of the corporation's board were charged with helping Hitler reach power, with waging

[70] Michael Dobbs, *IBM Technology Aided Holocaust, Author Alleges*, Washington Post (Feb. 22, 2001), https://www.washingtonpost.com/archive/politics/2001/02/11/ibm-technology-aided-holocaust-author-alleges/6addc414-ecee-4058-bea6-7f4708912d6f/?utm_term=.4a638715abce.

[71] Michael J. Bazyler, *Nuremberg in America: Litigating the Holocaust in United States Courts*, 34 U. Rich. L. Rev. 1, 38 (2000).

[72] *Id.*

[73] *Id.* (quoting Black, *supra* note 69).

[74] Keith William Diener, *The Restricted Nature of the Profit Motive: Perspectives from Law, Business, and Economics*, 30 Notre Dame J.L. Ethics & Pub. Pol'y 225, 226–227 (2016).

[75] Black, *supra* note 69, at 54–56.

[76] Dobbs, *supra* note 70 (citing Black, *supra* note 69).

[77] *Nuremberg Trials*, History, https://www.history.com/topics/world-war-ii/nuremberg-trials (last updated Oct. 1, 2018).

[78] Alberto L. Zuppi, *Slave Labor in Nuremberg's I.G. Farben Case: The Lonely Voice of Paul M. Hebert*, 66 La. L. Rev. 495, 496 (2006).

[79] *Id.* at 508.

[80] *Id.* at 502.

[81] *Id.* at 496.

[82] *U.S. v. Carl Krauch* et al., Vol. 7-8 (1947), known as the "I.G. Farben Case."

aggressive war, and for the commission of crimes against humanity, including the use of slave labor.[83] The Allies seized Farben, liquidated it, and created a new legal entity called Bayer AG.[84] In 2000, pursuant to an agreement between the United States, Germany, and other governments, the firms that used forced labor during the Nazi regime contributed to the establishment of a fund to compensate those who were enslaved or their heirs.[85]

Leading companies, including Lehman Brothers, Union Pacific Railroad, and JP Morgan Chase, have been sued for unjustly profiting from the institution of chattel slavery in the United States.[86] Many multinational corporations representing a range of industries were sued for their active collaboration with the repressive racist regime of apartheid in South Africa prior to the country's transition to democracy.[87]

### 1. Corporate Contributions to Compromising Civil Rights, Political Rights, and Human Security

Most corporate involvement in rights violations will not rise to the level of a jus cogens violation of international law. More common are instances in which the actions of a corporation or a corporation's failure to act causes or is connected to an abuses. The following offers examples of the ways different industry sectors impact different rights.

International human rights law protects the rights to life, physical integrity, and psychological integrity. Article 3 of the Universal Declaration of Human Rights recognizes that everyone has "the right to life, liberty and security of person."[88] While security is perhaps more associated with antiterrorism concerns and border protection, the operative understanding of security here concerns ensuring that human dignity is protected.[89] Human security also finds protection in Article 9 of the ICCPR, in which the rights to liberty and security of person are protected.[90] Article 6 of the ICCPR protects the right to life, while Article 7 prohibits conduct that is counter to the right to security of the person or that could put human life at risk, such as by torture; by cruel, inhuman, or degrading treatment or punishments; or by medical experimentation without free

[83] Zuppi, *supra* note 78, at 496–497.

[84] *In re Nazi Era Cases Against German Defendants Litig.*, 334 F. Supp. 2d 690, 695 (D.N.J. 2004).

[85] Zuppi, *supra* note 78, at 496.

[86] *In re African-American Slave Descendants Litig.*, 375 F. Supp. 2d 721, 736–737 (N.D. Ill. 2005).

[87] *S. African Apartheid Litig. v. Daimler AG*, 617 F. Supp. 2d 228, 241–243 (S.D.N.Y. 2009).

[88] *See, e.g.*, UDHR, *supra* note 43.

[89] *See, e.g.*, Yaniv Roznai, *The Insecurity of Human Security*, 32 Wis. Int'l L.J. 95, 95–96 (2014); Irene Khan, *A Human Rights Agenda for Global Security*, in Human Security for All: A Tribute to Sergio Vieira De Mello 17 (Kevin M. Cahill ed., 2004).

[90] The Human Rights Committee, the body that monitors the ICCPR has given the term "security of person" a meaning independent from the "liberty and security" provision to encompass personal security and bodily integrity beyond situations of detention.

and informed consent.[91] Nations are called upon to protect the right to security of the person against violence or bodily harm without regard to what type of individual or entity, whether a public agent of the state or a private actor inflicts the abuse—whether a government official, an agent of the state, or a private citizen acting in his or her own personal capacity.[92] Human rights organizations have documented numerous instances of corporate conduct that threatens the right to security of the person.

In recent years, several cases have been brought demanding that corporations be held accountable for playing a role in violating universally recognized fundamental human rights. Extractive industry corporations have been sued in US federal courts for allegedly engaging in human rights abuses associated with operations in Burma,[93] Cameroon,[94] Colombia,[95] India,[96] Indonesia,[97] Nigeria,[98] and Peru.[99] The Royal Dutch Petroleum Company defended itself against allegations that it aided and abetted the brutal destruction of peaceful resistance to aggressive oil development in Nigeria.[100] Peru Copper Corporation defended itself against allegations that pollution from its operations caused the plaintiffs severe lung disease.[101] Freeport-McMoran, Inc., defended itself against allegations that it engaged in cultural genocide by destroying the local Amungme tribe's habitat and religious symbols, forcing the tribe to relocate.[102]

### *The Extractives Industry and Risks to Human Security*

ExxonMobil has defended itself against allegations that their hired security abused villagers in Indonesia.[103] Exxon began developing natural gas fields in the Aceh province of Indonesia pursuant to an agreement with the Indonesian

[91] *See, e.g.*, ICCPR, *supra* note 47, at arts. 6, 7.
[92] G.A. Res. 2106 (XX), *International Convention on the Elimination of All Forms of Racial Discrimination*, art. 5 (b), U.N.T.S. vol. 66, 195 (Dec. 21, 1965).
[93] *Doe v. Unocal Corp.*, 395 F.3d 932 (9th Cir. 2002).
[94] *William v. AES Corp.*, 28 F. Supp. 3d 553 (E.D. Va. 2014).
[95] *Mujica v. AirScan Inc.*, 771 F.3d 580 (9th Cir. 2014); *Giraldo v. Drummond Co.*, 808 F. Supp. 2d 247 (D.D.C. 2011), *aff'd*, 493 F. App'x 106 (D.C. Cir. 2012); *Baloco v. Drummond Co., Inc.*, 767 F.3d 1229 (11th Cir. 2014); *Romero v. Drummond Co., Inc.*, 552 F.3d 1303 (11th Cir. 2008).
[96] *Bano v. Union Carbide Corp.*, 361 F.3d 696 (2d Cir. 2004).
[97] *Doe v. Exxon Mobil Corp.*, 473 F.3d 345 (D.C. Cir. 2007); *Beanal v. Freeport-McMoran, Inc.*, 197 F.3d 161 (5th Cir. 1999); *Alomang v. Freeport-McMoran, Inc.*, 718 So. 2d 971 (La. App. 4th Cir. 1998).
[98] *Abdullahi*, et al. *v. Pfizer*, Inc., 562 F.3d 163); *Bowoto v. Chevron Corp.*, 621 F.3d 1116 (9th Cir. 2010).
[99] *Flores v. Southern Peru Copper Corp.*, 414 F.3d 233 (2d Cir. 2003); *Jota v. Texaco Inc.*, 157 F.3d 153 (2d Cir. 1998).
[100] *Kiobel v. Royal Dutch Petro. Co.*, 569 U.S. 108, 113–114, 133 S. Ct. 1659, 1662-63 (2013).
[101] *Flores v. S. Peru Copper Corp.*, 414 F.3d 233, 236–237 (2d Cir. 2003).
[102] *Beanal v. Freeport-McMoran, Inc.*, 197 F.3d 161, 163–164 (5th Cir. 1999).
[103] *Doe v. Exxon Mobil Corp.*, 69 F. Supp. 3d 75, 83 (D.D.C. 2014).

government. The company hired the Indonesian military to provide security at its natural gas-production fields and facilities in Aceh. Soldiers providing Exxon security raided and razed villages in Aceh and were alleged to have been responsible for, among other offenses, the arbitrary arrest, detention, murders, disappearances, bodily and emotional harm, and wrongful deaths of Aceh residents between 2000 and 2001. Survivors sued Exxon, claiming the company provided "material support" to the Indonesian military—through the provision of supplies and equipment and the funding of weapons purchases. Security forces engaged in abuses while protecting the company's economic interests. The suit sought compensation and punitive damages as well as injunctive relief prohibiting the company from engaging in similar conduct in the future.[104]

In addition to personal security, international human rights law also protects civil and political rights. The ICCPR prohibits discrimination and protects freedom of expression among other rights.[105] Human rights monitoring organizations have documented how corporations in a range of different industries have affected certain civil and political rights. The media has reported on instances of abuses involving business enterprises.

Telecommunications companies have been sued for violating the privacy rights of users and supporting systems of surveillance and repression.[106] Yahoo! was sued for its alleged complicity in the arrest and detention of Chinese dissidents after it provided identifying information to the government.[107] Facebook defended itself against allegations that its data privacy protection policies and practices were deficient and not disclosed to shareholders in the wake of revelations that Cambridge Analytica was misappropriating millions of Facebook user's information for use in political campaigns.[108]

[104] *See, e.g.*, Jonathan Stemple, *Indonesia Torture Case vs Exxon Mobil Revived*, REUTERS (Jul7 8, 2011 5:01 PM), http://www.reuters.com/article/us-exxonmobil-indonesia-idUSTRE7676I120110708; *see also*, *John Doe, Village A, Aceh, Indonesia*, et al., *Appellees v. Exxon Mobil Corporation*, et al., *Appellants*, 473 F.3d 345 (D.C. Cir. 2007).

[105] ICCPR, *supra* note 47, at art. 2 & art. 19.

[106] *See e.g.*, Joseph Menn, *Lawsuit Links Cisco with China Crackdown*, FINANCIAL TIMES, May 23, 2011 https://www.ft.com/content/ed449f78-8567-11e0-ae32-00144feabdc0 (reporting on suit alleging Cisco designed products to help the Chinese government identify and persecute members of the spiritual group, Falun Gong).

[107] Second Amended Complaint, *Wang Xiaoning v. Yahoo! Inc.*, No. C07-02151 CW (N.D. Cal. July 30, 2007).

[108] *In re Facebook S'holder Derivative Privacy Litig.*, No. 18-cv-01792-HSG, 2019 U.S. Dist. LEXIS 48334, at *8 (N.D. Cal. Mar. 22, 2019).

The rise of the internet communications industry has coincided with a worldwide rise in violence attributed to online content in the form of hate speech and disinformation.[109] This rise in violence has impacted minorities in particular.[110]

### *The Internet Communications Technology Industry's Role in Censorship, Surveillance, Incitement, and Intimidation*

The forced displacement and alleged genocide of the Rohingya, a Muslim minority community in Myanmar, was allegedly fueled by the rapid spread of anti-Muslim rhetoric and materials inciting violence that were shared via Facebook.[111] Although much of the violence against the Rohingya was directly carried out by the Myanmar military, Facebook also played a "significant" role in the conflict.[112] By creating and spreading hate speech and false content on Facebook, the Myanmar military was able to exploit the social networking platform's wide reach in the country to incite violence against the Rohingya community.[113] The UN Human Rights Council observed that Facebook's platform provided "a useful instrument for those seeking to spread hate" and called the company's response to the problem "slow and ineffective."[114] Other human rights organizations echoed the Council's concerns.[115] Negative media attention also emphasized Facebook's failure to adequately

[109] *See, e.g.*, Zachary Laub, *Hate Speech on Social Media: Global Comparisons*, CFR.ORG (June 7, 2019), https://www.cfr.org/backgrounder/hate-speech-social-media-global-comparisons.

[110] *Id.*; Minority Rights Group International, *Peoples Under Threat 2019: The Role of Social Media in Exacerbating Violence*, MINORITYRIGHTS.ORG (June 3, 2019), https://minorityrights.org/2019/06/03/peoples-under-threat-2019-the-role-of-social-media-in-exacerbating-violence/.

[111] HUMAN RIGHTS COUNCIL, ADVANCE EDITED VERSION OF REPORT OF THE INDEPENDENT INTERNATIONAL FACT-FINDING MISSION ON MYANMAR 5 (2018), *available at* https://www.ohchr.org/Documents/HRBodies/HRCouncil/FFM-Myanmar/A_HRC_39_64.pdf; *see also Global Conflict Tracker: Rohingya Crisis in Myanmar*, CFR.ORG, https://www.cfr.org/interactive/global-conflict-tracker/conflict/rohingya-crisis-myanmar (last visited Oct. 13, 2019).

[112] HUMAN RIGHTS COUNCIL, *id.* at 14; *see also* Paul Mozur, *A Genocide Incited on Facebook, with Posts from Myanmar's Military*, N.Y. TIMES (Oct. 15, 2018), https://www.nytimes.com/2018/10/15/technology/myanmar-facebook-genocide.html.

[113] *Id.*

[114] HUMAN RIGHTS COUNCIL, *supra* note 111, at 14.

[115] *See, e.g.*, *The Rohingya Crisis*, AMNESTY INTERNATIONAL, https://www.amnestyusa.org/rohingya/ (last visited Oct. 14, 2019); *Rohingya Refugee Crisis a "Human Rights Nightmare," UN Chief Tells Security Council*, UN NEWS (Sept. 28, 2017), https://news.un.org/en/story/2017/09/567402-rohingya-refugee-crisis-human-rights-nightmare-un-chief-tells-security-council; *Live Updates: Rohingya Crisis*, HRW.ORG, https://www.hrw.org/blog-feed/rohingya-crisis (last visited Oct. 14, 2019); *Growing Violence: Myanmar*, RESCUE.ORG, https://www.rescue.org/country/myanmar (last visited Oct. 14, 2019).

address its role in the crisis.[116] After several months of reports about anti-Rohingya propaganda on its platform, the company acknowledged that it had been too slow to act in Myanmar.[117] Facebook blacklisted some of Myanmar's ethnic rebel groups in an effort to control the spread of hate speech and disinformation and to curb incitement on its platform.[118] Facebook increased the size of its team of native Myanmar language speakers and undertook an assessment of its human rights impacts.[119]

### 2. Corporate Complicity in Violations of Socioeconomic Rights

The ICESCR protects entitlements that allow humans to flourish.[120] The rights contained in the covenant encompass the necessities to live a dignified life. Among other rights, the ICESCR guarantees the rights to health in Article 12.[121]

When pharmaceutical companies do not adhere to exacting ethical research, drug promotion, or pricing standards, health can be harmed. Pharmaceutical corporation Johnson & Johnson was forced to defend itself against allegations that the company fueled the US opioid addiction crisis by "serving as a top supplier, seller and lobbyist."[122]

[116] *See, e.g.*, Julia Carrie Wong, *"Overreacting to Failure": Facebook's New Myanmar Strategy Baffles Local Activists*, THE GUARDIAN (Feb. 7, 2019), https://www.theguardian.com/technology/2019/feb/07/facebook-myanmar-genocide-violence-hate-speech; Steve Stecklow, *Why Facebook Is Losing the War on Hate Speech in Myanmar*, REUTERS (Aug. 15, 2018, 3:00 PM GMT), https://www.reuters.com/investigates/special-report/myanmar-facebook-hate/; Megha Rajagopalan, *How Facebook Failed the Rohingya in Myanmar*, BUZZFEED NEWS (Aug. 27, 2018, 6:46 PM ET), https://www.buzzfeednews.com/article/meghara/facebook-myanmar-rohingya-genocide.

[117] Mozur, *supra* note 112.

[118] *Four More Myanmar Ethnic Rebel Groups Banned From Facebook over Hate Speech*, SOUTH CHINA MORNING POST (Feb. 8, 2019, 12:13 AM), https://www.scmp.com/news/asia/southeast-asia/article/2185345/four-more-myanmar-ethnic-rebel-groups-banned-facebook-over.

[119] Alex Warofka, *An Independent Assessment of the Human Rights Impact of Facebook in Myanmar*, FACEBOOK (Nov. 5, 2018), https://newsroom.fb.com/news/2018/11/myanmar-hria/; BSR, HUMAN RIGHTS IMPACT ASSESSMENT: FACEBOOK IN MYANMAR 1, 5–7 (2018), *available at* https://fbnewsroomus.files.wordpress.com/2018/11/bsr-facebook-myanmar-hria_final.pdf; *see also* Jenny Domino, *Gambia v. Facebook: What the Discovery Request Reveals About Facebook's Content Moderation*, JUST SECURITY (July 6, 2020), https://www.justsecurity.org/71157/gambia-v-facebook-what-the-discovery-request-reveals-about-facebooks-content-moderation/.

[120] See generally, ICESCR supra note 47.

[121] ICESCR, *supra* note 47, at art. 12.

[122] Bob Herman, *Oklahoma Says Johnson & Johnson Was the "Kingpin" behind the Opioid Crisis Axios* (2019), https://www.axios.com/johnson-johnson-oklahoma-opioid-crisis-kingpin-5f2a252d-a1b3-4fbd-9e95-dddf415e7cab.html (last visited Mar. 25, 2019); *Kentucky sues Johnson & Johnson over opioid epidemic*, NBCNEWS.COM, https://www.nbcnews.com/storyline/americas-heroin-epidemic/kentucky-sues-johnson-johnson-subsidiaries-over-opioid-epidemic-n867121 (last visited Mar 25, 2019).

*The Right to Health and Pfizer's Experimental Drug in Trials on Nigerian Children*

In 1996, Pfizer, Inc., conducted a drug trial in Kano, Nigeria, during an epidemic of meningitis.[123] The test subjects of the experimental antibiotic were two hundred Nigerian children.[124] Half of the children were given Trovan, Pfizer's experimental antibiotic not yet approved in the United States, and the other half were given Rocephin, the "gold standard treatment" for meningitis.[125] Within a month, eleven children were dead,[126] and others suffered deafness, blindness, seizures, brain damage, and, in one case, an inability to walk or talk.[127]

Pfizer was sued for allegedly violating human rights in Africa by testing experimental drugs on children without obtaining informed consent from the human research subjects.[128] Nigerian plaintiffs in *Abdullahi v. Pfizer, Inc.*, alleged Pfizer violated international law by conducting involuntary medical experimentation on humans in connection with its drug trials on children in Nigeria, citing the Nuremberg Code, the Declaration of Helsinki, and the ICCPR.[129]

In 2009, the Nigerian government and Pfizer agreed to settle the lawsuit out of court.[130] In 2014, nearly twenty years after the drug trial, Pfizer finally paid compensation to the victims in full.[131]

## 3. Corporate Complicity in Violating the Cultural Rights of Indigenous Peoples

Although there is no firm definition of Indigenous peoples, international law recognizes that certain rights are enjoyed when individuals belonging to a

[123] *Pfizer Lawsuit (re Nigeria)*, BUSINESS-HUMANRIGHTS.ORG, https://www.business-humanrights.org/en/latest-news/nigerias-kano-state-sues-pfizer-over-alleged-use-of-children-for-drug-test-that-led-to-deaths-and-deformities/ (last visited Dec. 14, 2020).

[124] Nicole Perlroth, *Pfizer's Nigerian Nightmare*, FORBES (Nov. 20, 2008 5:00 PM), https://www.forbes.com/forbes/2008/1208/066.html#6ac659e123a7.

[125] Jacqui Wise, *Pfizer Accused of Testing New Drug Without Ethical Approval*, NCBI.NLM.NIH.ORG (Jan. 27, 2001), https://www.ncbi.nlm.nih.gov/pmc/articles/PMC1119465/.

[126] Jeanne Lenzer, *Secret Report Surfaces Showing That Pfizer Was at Fault in Nigerian Drug Tests*, NCBI.NLM.NIH.GOV (May 27, 2006), https://www.ncbi.nlm.nih.gov/pmc/articles/PMC1471980/.

[127] Joe Stephens, *Where Profits and Lives Hang in Balance*, WASHINGTON POST (Dec. 17, 2000), https://www.washingtonpost.com/archive/politics/2000/12/17/where-profits-and-lives-hang-in-balance/90b0c003-99ed-4fed-bb22-4944c1a98443/; Donald G. McNeil Jr., *Nigerians Receive First Payments For Children Who Died in 1996 Meningitis Drug Trial*, N.Y. TIMES (Aug. 11, 2011), https://www.nytimes.com/2011/08/12/world/africa/12nigeria.html.

[128] *Abdullahi v. Pfizer, Inc.*, 562 F.3d 163 (2d Cir. 2007).

[129] *Id.*

[130] *Id.*

[131] *Id.*

particular social group come together as a community entitled to protection.[132] Indigenous peoples are members of an identifiable community, often with a consistent or historic connection to a specific region. Indigenous communities may remain distinct from the dominant populations of a nation and may maintain a distinctive language or cultural or social practices.

The UN Declaration on the Rights of Indigenous Peoples (UNDRIP)[133] and ILO Convention 169[134] recognize the rights of Indigenous populations around the world to practice cultural traditions and religious expression in their communities as well as to enjoy traditional forms of communal land tenure.[135]

The principle of "free, prior, informed consent" (FPIC) protects the right of Indigenous peoples to be involved in decisions concerning economic development and infrastructure projects that will impact them. Accordingly, Indigenous populations can withhold or give consent to such projects. At a bare minimum, Indigenous communities must be informed and consulted in advance of government approvals of projects that will impact their resources or territories. A number of the provisions of the UNDRIP support the FPIC principle, and community consultation continues to gain acceptance in practice. FPIC adherence is a priority for many Indigenous populations affected by mining and drilling activities.[136] While there are some limited exceptions, as a general rule, consent is required for extractive projects on Indigenous lands pursuant to FPIC.[137] Accordingly, this category of rights can be especially relevant for the activities of extractive sector companies when natural resources are on or impact Indigenous lands.

When companies in the extractive sector fail to address pollution, human rights are harmed in ways that are interrelated and interdependent. For example, the right to a livelihood for those who fish and farm is placed at risk by unmitigated pollution. When the rights to food and water are placed at risk due to environmental destruction or displacement, the right to health and, in extreme

132 *See* United Nations Declaration on the Rights of Indigenous Peoples, G.A. Res. 61/295, Annex, U.N. Doc. A/RES/61/295 (Sept. 13, 2007) [hereinafter UNDRIP]; *see generally* S. James Anaya, *The Human Rights of Indigenous Peoples: United Nations Developments*, 35 U. Haw. L. Rev. 983 (2013).

133 UNDRIP, *supra* note 132.

134 Int'l Lab. Org. (ILO) No. 169, *Indigenous and Tribal Peoples in Independent Countries* (1989).

135 *Id.*; UNDRIP, *supra* note 132. For an explanation of the FPIC concept as relevant to business operations, *see* Amy K. Lehr & Gare Smith, *Implementing a Corporate Free, Prior, and Informed Consent Policy: Benefits and Challenges*, Foley Hoag LLP (May 2010); Amy K. Lehr & Gare Smith, *Business for Social Responsibility, Engaging with Free, Prior and Informed Consent*, Foley Hoag LLP (Sept. 2012).

136 *See* César Rodriguez-Garavito, *Global Governance, Indigenous Peoples, and the Right to Prior Consultation in Social Minefields*, 18 Ind. J. Global Legal Stud. 1 (2010); Cathal Doyle & Jérémie Gilbert, *Indigenous Peoples and Globalization: From "Development Aggression" to "Self-Determined Development,"* 7 Euro. Y.B. Minority Iss. 199 (2008).

137 *See Report of the Special Rapporteur on the Rights of Indigenous Peoples, Extractive Industries and Indigenous Peoples*, UN. Doc. A/HRC/24/41 (July 1, 2013).

instances, the right to life can be placed at risk if business enterprises do not assess the social and environmental impacts of production.

## Mining Industry Impacts on Indigenous Peoples Rights

Rio Tinto is one of the largest global mining companies in the world. In cooperation with Turquoise Hill Resources and the Mongolian government, Rio Tinto operates the Oyu Tolgoi Project, a copper and gold mining project in Mongolia.[138] The nomadic population surrounding the mine alleges they were neither consulted nor informed prior to the mine's establishment. Local herders are particularly hesitant about the water usage the mine operations will draw—the herders will now be competing for water in the Gobi Desert, where water is already scarce. In 2012, a group of Mongolian herder households filed a complaint against Rio Tinto, demanding just compensation for their forced relocation by Oyu Tolgoi's operations. In 2013, a group of herders from Khanbogd, the village closest to the mine, sent a petition to the Rio Tinto shareholders. A study conducted by the World Bank estimated that the Oyu Tolgoi project demanded 67,000 cubic meters of water per day and was expected to grow dramatically, while the water demand for livestock was only 32,000 cubic meters per day.[139] The study warned that if water usage continues unchecked, water sources in surrounding areas could significantly be depleted by 2022.[140]

### 4. Corporate Complicity in Labor Rights Violations

Human rights and labor rights groups have documented alleged abuses of labor rights in the agriculture, apparel, and extractive industry sectors, as well as instances of disregard for those rights. Labor rights in international law include not only the right to work but also rights at work.[141] The ILO's Declaration

[138] *Oyu Tolgio Project*, RIO TINTO MONGOLIA, http://www.riotintomongolia.com/ENG/index_oyu_tolgoi.asp (last visited Nov. 28, 2014); *see also Rio Tinto Accused of Environmental and Human Rights Breaches*, THE GUARDIAN (Apr. 18, 2013) http://www.theguardian.com/business/2013/apr/18/rio-tinto-environmental-human-rights-breaches (last visited Nov. 20, 2020); Joint Press Release, *Mining and Communities, Mongolian Herders Complain Against Rio Tito Over Oyu Tolgoi Mines*, ESCR-NET, http://www.escr-net.org/node/365339 (last visited Nov. 20, 2020).

[139] THE WORLD BANK, MONGOLIA GROUNDWATER ASSESSMENT IN THE SOUTHERN GOBI REGION, APRIL 2010.

[140] *Id.*

[141] Int'l Labor Org. (ILO), *Declaration on Fundamental Principles and Rights at Work*, 86th Sess., Geneva (June 1998); *see also* Lisa Misol & Smita Narula, *supra* note 68, at No. 3(G), 32–38 (2008).

on Fundamental Principles and Rights at Work sets forth rights that are further specified in eight core ILO Conventions.[142] Freedom of association and effective recognition of the right to collective bargaining are guaranteed by ILO Conventions 87 and 98.[143] The elimination of all forms of forced or compulsory labor is required by ILO Conventions 29 and 105.[144] ILO Conventions 138 and 182 mandate the effective abolition of child labor, with attention to the worst forms of child labor.[145] ILO Conventions 100 and 111 call for the elimination of discrimination with respect to employment and occupation.[146]

These labor rights also find expression in other international human rights instruments. For example, freedom of association and the right to collective bargaining are recognized in Article 22 of the ICCPR and in Article 8 of the ICESCR.[147] A call for the elimination of forced labor is also contained in Article 8 of the ICCPR's prohibition of slavery and servitude.[148] Article 10 of the ICESCR mandates a minimum working age for children and prohibits employment of children in hazardous occupations.[149] The elimination of discrimination in pay and compensation as well as the right to just and favorable conditions of employment are stated in Article 7 of the ICESCR.[150]

Food and beverage corporations have been sued for allegedly aiding and abetting human rights abuses linked to repressing labor organizing in Colombia,[151] in Guatemala,[152] and in Turkey.[153] For example, Coca-Cola faced allegations that it violated human rights in Colombia.[154] The company was

[142] ILO, *Freedom of Association and Protection of the Right to Organise Convention*, No. 87 (1948); ILO, *Right to Organise and Collective Bargaining Convention*, No. 98 (July 4, 1950); ILO, *Forced Labour Convention*, No. 29 (May 1, 1932); ILO, *Abolition of Forced Labour Convention*, No. 105 (June 25, 1957); ILO, *Minimum Age Convention*, No. 138 (June 26, 1973); ILO, *Worst Forms of Child Labour Convention*, No. 182 (June 17, 1999); ILO, *Equal Remuneration Convention*, No. 100 (June 29, 1951); ILO, *Discrimination (Employment and Occupation) Convention*, No. 111 (June 25, 1958).

[143] ILO, *Freedom of Association and Protection of the Right to Organise Convention*, No. 87 (1948); ILO, *Right to Organise and Collective Bargaining Convention*, No. 98 (July 4, 1950).

[144] ILO, *Forced Labour Convention*, No. 29 (May 1, 1932); ILO, *Abolition of Forced Labour Convention*, No. 105 (June 25, 1957).

[145] ILO, *Minimum Age Convention*, No. 138 (June 26, 1973); ILO, *Worst Forms of Child Labour Convention*, No. 182 (June 17, 1999).

[146] ILO, *Equal Remuneration Convention*, No. 100 (June 29, 1951); ILO, *Discrimination (Employment and Occupation) Convention*, No. 111 (June 25, 1958).

[147] ICCPR, *supra* note 47, at art. 22; ICESCR, *supra* note 47, at art. 8.

[148] ICCPR, *supra* note 47, at art. 8.

[149] ICESCR, *supra* note 47, at art. 10.

[150] ICESCR, *supra* note 47, at art. 7.

[151] *In re Chiquita Brands Int'l, Inc. Alien Tort Statute & S'holder Derivative Litig.*, 792 F. Supp. 2d 1301 (S.D. Fla. 2011), on reconsideration in part sub nom. *In re: Chiquita Brands Int'l, Inc.*, No. 07-60821-CIV-MARRA, 2012 WL 12539695 (S.D. Fla. Mar. 27, 2012), and *rev'd sub nom. Cardona v. Chiquita Brands Int'l, Inc.*, 760 F.3d 1185 (11th Cir. 2014).

[152] *Palacios v. The Coca-Cola Co.*, 757 F. Supp. 2d 347, 349 (S.D.N.Y. 2010), *aff'd sub nom. Palacios v. Coca-Cola Co.*, 499 F. App'x 54 (2d Cir. 2012).

[153] *Turedi v. Coca Cola Co.*, 460 F. Supp. 2d 507, 509 (S.D.N.Y. 2006) (plaintiffs alleging a violent attack on them by Turkish police during a labor dispute in Istanbul).

[154] *Sinaltrainal v. Coca-Cola Co.*, 256 F. Supp. 2d 1345 (S.D. Fla. 2003).

implicated in the murder of Isidro Segundo Gil, an activist killed after attempting to organize a trade union.[155] Fresh Del Monte Produce was sued for allegedly engaging in human rights violations in Guatemala.[156] The company allegedly organized an armed gang of employees, agents, and government officials who kidnapped, tortured, and coerced the plaintiffs.[157]

## Chocolate and Child Labor

Behind much of the world's cocoa supply is the work of millions of impoverished children on West African cocoa farms.[158] The US Department of Labor reports that two million children are engaged in hazardous work conditions on cocoa farms in Cote d'Ivoire and Ghana alone.[159] In 2015 and 2018, American consumers filed two separate federal class action lawsuits against chocolate companies, including Hershey and Nestle.[160] In *Dana v. Hershey Co.*,[161] consumers claimed that Hershey had violated California law by not adequately disclosing on their packaging that they sourced some of their cocoa at farms using child labor.[162] The Court dismissed the claim, "stating that it was sound policy not to place duties on manufacturers to disclose certain acts about their products, as the courts are not suited to determine which issues are legitimately important to customers."[163] A second case, *Tomasella v. Nestle USA, Inc.*, brought a similar action against Nestle, alleging unjust enrichment by neglecting to disclose on their packaging the use of child and slave labor to source their chocolate.[164] The Court dismissed the class action, finding that the consumers' claims failed to show how the

155 *Id.*, at 1348.

156 *Aldana v. Del Monte Fresh Produce, N.A., Inc.*, 416 F.3d 1242 (11th Cir. 2005).

157 *Aldana v. Fresh Del Monte Produce, Inc.*, No. 01-3399-CIV-MORE, 2007 U.S. Dist. LEXIS 77020, at *4-5 (S.D. Fla. Oct. 16, 2007).

158 *E.g.*, Peter Whoriskey & Rachel Siegel, *Cocoa's Child Laborers*, WASHINGTON POST (June 5, 2019), https://www.washingtonpost.com/graphics/2019/business/hershey-nestle-mars-chocolate-child-labor-west-africa/.

159 *Child Labor in the Production of Cocoa*, U.S. DEPT. OF LABOR, https://www.dol.gov/agencies/ilab/our-work/child-forced-labor-trafficking/child-labor-cocoa (last visited Oct. 15, 2019).

160 *Hershey Lawsuit (Re Child Labour in Cote d'Ivoire)*, BUSINESS-HUMANRIGHTS.ORG, https://www.business-humanrights.org/en/hershey-lawsuit-re-child-labour-in-côte-d'ivoire (last visited Oct. 15, 2019); *see Dana v. Hershey Co.*, 180 F. Supp. 3d 652 (N.D. Cal. 2016); *Tomasella v. Nestle USA, Inc.*, 364 F. Supp. 3d 26 (D. Mass. 2019).

161 *See Hodsdon v. Mars, Inc.*, 162 F. Supp. 3d 1016 (N.D. Cal. 2016) (granting Mars' motion to dismiss); *McCoy v. Nestle USA, Inc.*, 173 F. Supp. 3d 954 (N.D. Cal. 2016) (granting Nestle's motion to dismiss).

162 180 F. Supp. 3d at 654–655.

163 *Hershey Lawsuit.*, *supra* note 160; *see also Dana*, 180 F. Supp. 3d at 664–665, 670–671.

164 364 F. Supp. 3d at 29.

chocolate companies deceived them.[165] Dismissal of these lawsuits has not ended demands for disclosure in the chocolate industry, however. Public pressure and rights advocacy continues. In 2007, the International Cocoa Initiative is a Swiss-based foundation that has operated in Cote d'Ivoire and Ghana since 2007 and is purely dedicated to child protection in cocoa-growing communities.[166] Hershey now has a program to combat child labor through the Child Labor Monitoring and Remediation System[167] and has launched Cocoa For Good, a program aimed, in part, at ending child labor and empowering youth.[168] Nestle has acknowledged child labor in its supply chain,[169] and in 2017 released a report, "Tackling Child Labour," provided a summary of the company's actions and progress in addressing the problem.[170] Nestle has introduced child labor "monitoring and remediation schemes in Cote d'Ivoire and Ghana,[171] and has partnered with the Fair Labor Association for assistance on addressing supply chain challenges.[172]

Labor violations are not limited to farms and plantations. Factories that manufacture consumer goods such as apparel and electronics have also been implicated in abuses. A number of cases have been filed claiming that business enterprises in apparel and other industries have engaged in or benefited from slave labor linked to human trafficking.[173] In Liberia, the Bridgestone Corporation and Firestone Natural Rubber Company defended themselves against allegations that they used slave and child labor.[174] Gap, Inc., defended

[165] *Id.* at 34–36, 37.

[166] *About the International Cocoa Initiative*, COCOAINITIATIVE.ORG, https://cocoainitiative.org/about-ici/about-us/ (last visited Oct. 15, 2019).

[167] *Id.*

[168] *Introducing Cocoa For Good*, THEHERSHEYCOMPANY.COM, https://www.thehersheycompany.com/en_us/sustainability/shared-business/cocoa-for-good.html (last visited Oct. 15, 2019).

[169] *Does Nestle Have Child Labour in Its Cocoa Supply Chain?*, NESTLE.COM, https://www.nestle.com/ask-nestle/human-rights/answers/nestle-child-labour-supply-chains (last visited Oct. 15, 2019).

[170] NESTLE, TACKLING CHILD LABOUR: 2017 REPORT (2017), *available at* https://www.nestle.com/sites/default/files/asset-library/documents/creating-shared-value/responsible-sourcing/nestle-cocoa-plan-child-labour-2017-report.pdf.

[171] *Does Nestle Have Child Labour in its Cocoa Supply Chain?*, *supra* note 169.

[172] *Protecting Children and Workers*, NESTLE.COM, https://www.nestle.com/csv/impact/respecting-human-rights/workers-livelihoods (last visited Oct. 15, 2019).

[173] *See, e.g., EEOC v. Arabian American Oil Co.*, 499 U.S. 244 (1991); *Doe v. Nestle U.S.A., Inc.*, 766 F.3d 1013 (9th Cir. 2014), *cert denied* 136 S. Ct. 798 (2016); *Chowdhury v. Worldtel Bangladesh Holding, Ltd.*, 746 F.3d 42 (2d Cir. 2014), *cert. denied* 135 S. Ct. 401 (2014); *Wirth v. Mars, Inc.*, No. 15-cv-1470, 2016 U.S. Dist. LEXIS 14552 (C.D. Cal. Sept. 10, 2015); *Sud v. Costco Wholesale Corp.*, 229 F. Supp. 3d 1075 (N.D. Cal. 2017); *Barber v. Nestle USA, Inc.*, 154 F. Supp. 3d 954 (C.D. Cal. 2015); *Hodsdon v. Mars, Inc.*, 162 F. Supp. 3d 1016 (N.D. Cal. 2015); *Dana v. The Hershey Co.*, 180 F. Supp. 3d 652 (N.D. Cal. 2016).

[174] *Roe v. Bridgestone Corp.*, 492 F. Supp. 2d 988, 990–991 (S.D. Ind. 2007); *Flomo v. Firestone Nat. Rubber Co., LLC*, 643 F.3d 1013, 1015 (7th Cir. 2011).

itself against allegations that it violated criminal laws with respect to kidnapping, theft, theft of services, theft by extortion, receiving stolen property, and criminal coercion in Saipain.[175] Apple has come under scrutiny for the poor labor conditions documented in the Chinese factories manufacturing its products.

**The Apparel Industry and Unsafe Labor Conditions**

In the apparel industry, the collapse of an eight-story garment factory in Dhaka, Bangladesh, in April 2013, killed 1,127 people.[176] After evacuating the building the previous day due to large cracks in the walls, workers returned after being told by company officials that conditions were safe.[177] A government report was later released citing substandard materials used in the building's construction, showing blatant disregard for the safety of its workers, a human rights abuse that led to more than a thousand deaths.[178] Brands sourcing from the country came together to create standards to improve factory conditions, with some firms agreeing to an accord and others forming an alliance.

### 5. Climate Change Concerns, Environmental Challenges, and Corporate Conduct

The human right to a clean and healthy environment was not expressly enumerated in early human rights instruments, but a growing body of international declarations and soft law standards provide a firm foundation for the recognition of environmental human rights.[179] Beyond a focus on the natural

[175] *Does I v. Gap, Inc.*, No. CV-01-0031, 2001 U.S. Dist. LEXIS 25035, at 5–8 (D. N. Mar. I. Nov. 26, 2001).

[176] Jason Burke, *Bangladesh garment workers suffer poor conditions two years after reform vows*, The Guardian (Apr. 22, 2014, 9:22 AM), http://www.theguardian.com/world/2015/apr/22/garment-workers-in-bangladesh-still-suffering-two-years-after-factory-collapse.

[177] Human Rights Watch, *Bangladesh: Tragedy Shows Urgency of Worker Protections* (Apr. 25, 2013), https://www.hrw.org/news/2013/04/25/bangladesh-tragedy-shows-urgency-worker-protections.

[178] Jim Yardley, *Report on Deadly Factory Collapse in Bangladesh Finds Widespread Blame*, N.Y. Times (May 22, 2013), http://www.nytimes.com/2013/05/23/world/asia/report-on-bangladesh-building-collapse-finds-widespread-blame.html.

[179] Erika George, *Shareholder Activism and Stakeholder Engagement Strategies: Promoting Environmental Justice, Human Rights, and Sustainable Development Goals*, 2019 Wis. L. Rev. 298, 310–312 (2019); *see also Eco Activists Labelled as Terrorists by Government*, Telegraph (Jan. 27, 2010, 7:00 AM), https://www.telegraph.co.uk/news/uknews/law-and-order/7081209/Eco-activists-labelled-as-terrorists-by-Govemment.html; Anastasia Moloney, *Columbia's Top Court Orders Government to Protect Amazon Forest in Landmark Case*, Reuters (Apr. 6, 2018, 9:46 AM), https://www.reuters.com/article/uscolombia-deforestation-amazon/colombias-top-court-orders-govemment-to-protect-amazonforest-in-landmark-case-idUSKCN1HD21Y.

environment,[180] early international environmental legal norms did recognize a relationship between environmental quality and human dignity in terms of rights. The visionary Stockholm Declaration on the Human Environment,[181] the outcome of the 1972 UN Conference on the Human Environment, sets forth several concepts that continue to influence present debates over the existence of environmental human rights and their content. It laid the foundation for an appreciation of the relationship between the preservation and enhancement of the environment and the enjoyment of basic human rights.

Although a soft law instrument, the Stockholm Declaration provides a strong statement about the imperative of environmental protection. According to Principle 1 of the Declaration:

> Man has the fundamental right to freedom, equality and adequate conditions of life, in an environment of a quality that permits a life of dignity and well-being, and he bears a solemn responsibility to protect and improve the environment for present and future generations.[182]

The Stockholm Declaration presents the relationship between the environment and human rights as inseparable, interrelated, and interconnected.

Climate change is both an environmental protection issue and a human rights issue. For example, "climate change refugees" or "environmental migrants"—those "persons or groups of persons who, predominantly for reasons of sudden or progressive change in the environment that adversely affects their lives or living conditions, are obliged to leave their habitual homes, or choose to do so, either temporarily or permanently"[183]—are already on the move. The Environmental Justice Foundation[184] estimates that extreme weather events related to climate change, such as floods, storms, heat waves, and drought, are already displacing 41 people per minute, or 21.5 million people per year.[185]

As the number of people moving across borders increases, so too has opposition to migration and the mistreatment of migrants.[186] Migration has become a

[180] Rebecca Bratspies, *Do We Need a Human Right to a Healthy Environment?*, 13 SANTA CLARA J. L. 31, 38 (2015).

[181] REPORT OF THE U.N. CONFERENCE ON THE HUMAN ENVIRONMENT, U.N. DOC. A/CONF.48/14, at 2-65, and CORR. 1 (1972).

[182] *Id.*

[183] ENVIRONMENTAL MIGRATION PORTAL, http://www.environmentalmigration.iom.int/environmental-migration (last visited Feb. 14, 2020).

[184] The Environmental Justice Foundation is an environmental advocacy campaign group based in the United Kingdom that places primary emphasis on oceans, pesticides, climate, and cotton. *See* ENVIRONMENTAL JUSTICE FOUNDATION, https://ejfoundation.org (last visited Feb. 14, 2020).

[185] *Protecting Climate Refugees*, ENVIRONMENTAL JUSTICE FOUNDATION, https://ejfoundation.org/what-we-do/climate/protecting-climate-refugees (last visited Feb. 14, 2020).

[186] *See, e.g.*, M. Akram Faizer, *America First: Improving a Recalcitrant Immigration and Refugee Policy*, 84 TENN. L. REV. 933, *933 (2017) (arguing that climate change is a likely

political flashpoint as fears and anti-immigrant sentiments mount in receiving countries.[187] This anti-immigrant sentiment serves to create conditions where the human rights of "climate-change refugees" and other conventional refugees could be put at risk as they seek new places to make a home in the world. People are changing their country of residence in response to the changing climate.[188]

The challenge of addressing climate change is connected to respect for human rights because the adverse impacts of the changing climate disproportionately burdens the most vulnerable populations. The indirect effect of climate change on basic human needs is expected to lead to increased pressures on societies, and potentially to conflict or political instability as prices for food, energy, and other basic commodities essential to human existence increase.[189]

In 2014, all seventy-eight UN Human Rights mandate holders released an unprecedented joint statement to highlight the risks climate change would pose to human rights.[190] The joint statement urged states "to make sure that human rights are at the core of climate change governance."[191] Fossil fuels companies are under growing pressure.

## Corporate Role in Human Rights Impacts Climate Change

Some of the same companies sued for alleged involvement in human rights violations, such as Chevron and Exxon, are now the subject of climate change

factor behind several surging immigration crises and will only increase as a factor, while state failure to constructively respond to these crises has fueled backlashes by nativists and social conservatives); Amelia Hill, *Migration: How Many People Are on the Move Around the World?*, THE GUARDIAN (Sept. 10, 2018, 1:15 AM), https://www.theguardian.com/news/2018/sep/10/migration-how-many-people-are-on-the-move-around-the-world.

187 *See, e.g.*, Ronald F. Inglehart & Pippa Norris, *Trump, Brexit, and the Rise of Populism: Economic Have-Nots and Cultural Backlash* 2, 4 (Harv. Kennedy Sch. Faculty Research Working Paper Series, No. RWPl6-026, 2016) (demonstrating the average vote of populist parties across Europe has doubled since the 1960s, while their share of seats has tripled, and arguing recent populist victories support a "cultural backlash" thesis which implies further political divide is likely); *Migrant Crisis: EU at Grave Risk, Warns France PM Valls*, BBC NEWS (Jan. 22, 2016), http://www.bbc.com/news/world-europe-35375303 (warning that European countries were at risk of being "totally destabilised").

188 *See generally* Sarah Opitz Stapleton et al., *Climate Change, Migration and Displacement*, UNITED NATIONS DEV. PROGRAM 7 (Nov. 2017), https://www.odi.org/sites/odi.org.uk/files/ resource-documents/il 874.pdf. *See also* Mostafa Mahmud Naser, *Climate Change, Environmental Degradation, and Migration: A Complex Nexus*, 36 WM. & MARY ENVTL. L. POL'Y REV. 713, 714 (2012) (arguing for the recognition of and protection for migrants forced to move due to the demonstrated substantial role climate change plays in triggering human migrations, notwithstanding the existence of multicausality).

189 United Nations Env't Programme [UNEP], *Climate Change & Human Rights*, at 7-8 (Dec. 2015).

190 *Id.*

191 John H. Knox, *Climate Change and Human Rights Law: Where We Are Now*, BUSINESS & HUMAN RIGHTS RESOURCE CENTRE: CLIMATE DIALOGUES (2015), https://www.business-humanrights.org/en/climate-change-and-human-rights-law-where-we-are-now.

lawsuits in the United States. Several cities and counties in California, seeking damages and other relief for the costs incurred for adapting infrastructure to address sea-level rise, have sued fossil fuel firms.[192] The state attorney generals for New York and Massachusetts, acting in the public interest and to protect the interests of consumers and investors, have opened investigations into fossil fuel companies for failure to make climate risk-related disclosures.[193] Investors have brought securities fraud class action lawsuits against companies contributing to climate change, alleging that failure to disclose climate change risks breached the fiduciary duty the firms owe to those who provide financing.[194] Activists concerned about the impacts of climate change have appealed to investors to divest from fossil fuels and are advocating investment in alternative renewable energy sources instead.[195]

These are just a few examples of the ways in which businesses can impact the enjoyment of human rights. These examples illustrate the point that particular business decisions can have devastating consequences on communities. In many cases victims of violations remain without remedy. In some industry sectors there is a growing appreciation that impacts are important human rights risks that are real and that the business community has a responsibility to do better. These examples also show the potential to create change in corporate conduct by bringing pressure to bear on business to do better and incorporate rights into planning and operating procedures.

## III. Corporate Law

Conventional conceptions of the corporate form, and theories of corporate governance, contribute to the development of business policies and practices that place human rights at risk. Limiting corporate liability to the institution while

[192] *See, e.g.*, *County of San Mateo v. Chevron*, 3:17-CV-04929-MEJ (N.D. Cal. 2017); *People of the State of California v. BP plc*, RG17875889 (Cal. Super Ct. 2017); *see also* Jeremy Hodges, Lauren Leatherby, & Kartikay Mehrotra, *Climate Change Warriors' Latest Weapon of Choice Is Litigation*, BLOOMBERG (May 24, 2018), https://www.bloomberg.com/graphics/2018-climate-change-lawsuits/.

[193] *See, e.g.*, *Exxon Mobil Corp v. Schniderman*, No. 1:17-CV-02301 (S.D.N.Y 2017).

[194] *See, e.g.*, *Ramirez v. Exxon Mobil Corp.*, 3:16-CV-3111 (N.D. Tex. 2016).

[195] *See, e.g.*, Bill McKibben, *The Movement to Divest from Fossil Fuels Gains Momentum*, THE NEW YORKER (Dec. 21, 2017), https://www.newyorker.com/news/daily-comment/the-movement-to-divest-from-fossil-fuels-gains-momentum; Bill McKibben, *Cashing Out from the Climate Casino*, N.Y. TIMES (Dec. 15, 2017), https://www.nytimes.com/2017/12/15/opinion/finance-global-warming.html; Ben Cushing, *As Divestment Movement Grows, Wells Fargo Feels the Heat*, SIERRA CLUB (Aug. 1, 2017), https://www.sierraclub.org/lay-of-the-land/2017/08/divestment-movement-grows-wells-fargo-feels-heat.

shielding the individuals responsible for making decisions from accountability, combined with incentives to minimize costs at the cost of respect for human rights, has left little room for rights considerations to be taken into account. Market practices emphasizing quarterly earnings reports and pressures to meet analyst estimates in the short term create incentives for a "managerial myopia"[196] that is blind to risks to human rights.

The increasing influence and impact of corporate power in the global economy in general, and the impact of business interests on human rights in particular, warrants an examination of how certain theories of the corporate form operate to reduce the importance of recognizing the social and moral responsibility to respect human rights. To that end, I describe the defining features of the corporate form and competing theories of its purpose. I discuss corporate personhood and the rights and responsibilities of corporations. I present debates about the obligations that private corporate actors owe to the public. Finally, I offer an account of alternative structures or variations of the corporate form and doctrines that provide opportunities for businesses to advance human rights. I argue that these recent developments demonstrate a desire on the part of the public for business enterprises to be responsive to the social and environmental issues confronting society.

## A. The Purpose of the Corporate Person and Shareholder Primacy

The corporation is a form of organizing business activity.[197] It enables a business to raise capital from investors. The business retains managerial control over its activities but distributes a portion of its profits to investors. A corporation is a legal entity separate and apart from those who own or manage it.[198]

Writing in 1819, US Supreme Court Chief Justice Marshall explained the features of the corporate form of organizing commercial relations as follows:

> A corporation is an artificial being, invisible, intangible, and existing only in the contemplation of the law. Being the mere creature of law, it possesses only those properties, which the charter of its creation confers upon it, either expressly, or as incidental to its very existence. These are such as are supposed

[196] See, David Millon, *Why is Corporate Management Obsessed with Quarterly Earnings and What Should be Done About It?*, 70 GEO. WASH. L. REV. 890, 897–900 (2002); Natalie Mizik, *The Theory and Practice of Myopic Management*, 47 J. MARKETING RES. 594 (2010); David Millon, *Two Models of Corporate Social Responsibility*, 46 WAKE FOREST L. REV. 523 (2011).

[197] JAMES D. COX & THOMAS LEE HAZEN, CORPORATIONS 2–3 (2d ed. 2003).

[198] *Id.*

> best calculated to affect the object for which it was created. Among the most important are immortality, and, if the expression may be allowed, individuality; properties, by which a perpetual succession of many persons are considered as the same, and may act as a single individual.[199]

In contrast to international law, US law recognizes the corporation as an independent "legal person" with "legal personality."[200] As independent legal persons, corporations enjoy certain rights, privileges, and immunities comparable to those enjoyed by natural human persons.[201] Corporations can contract, sue, own property, and hold ownership interests in other business enterprises.[202]

In *Santa Clara v. Southern Pacific Railway*, the US Supreme Court extended legal personality to the corporate form of business organization. Writing for a unanimous Court in 1886, Chief Justice Waite simply stated:

> The Court does not wish to hear argument on the question whether the provision in the Fourteenth Amendment to the Constitution which forbids a state to deny to any person within its jurisdiction the equal protection of the laws applies to these corporations. We are all of opinion that it does.[203]

*Santa Clara* rests on an unwritten rationale. The court draws no distinction between the individual natural person and the incorporated business institution. Since the *Santa Clara* ruling, corporate personhood has provided a broader scope of immunity for corporations from government interference because individuals have rights that must be respected by government.[204]

Where commercial interests are at issue, US courts have given wide latitude to the rights of the corporate person. The US Supreme Court, however, has made multiple decisions over the years providing more rights to corporations by conceptualizing companies as comprised of individuals that possess rights. For instance, corporations enjoy due process rights[205] and the right to equal

[199] (*Trustees of Dartmouth College v. Woodward*, 17 U.S. (4 Wheat.) 518, 626 (1819).

[200] *See* Cox & Hazen, *supra* note 197.

[201] *See generally* Kent Greenfield, Corporations Are People Too: And They Should Act Like It Too (2018); Carliss Chatman, *The Corporate Personhood Two-Step*, 18 Nev. L. J. 811 (2018).

[202] *See generally* Adam Winkler, We The Corporations: How American Businesses Won Their Civil Rights (2018); Valerie P. Hans, Business on Trial: The Civil Jury and Corporate Responsibility 84 (2000) (presenting data from interviews with jurors in corporate litigation and demonstrating that "absence of corporeal body appears to shape the way civil jurors consider the corporation and its liability").

[203] *Santa Clara County v. Southern Pacific Railroad Co.*, 18 F. 385 (1886).

[204] Warren J. Samuels, *The Idea of the Corporation as a Person: on the Normative Significance of Judicial Language*, in Corporations and Society: Power and Responsibility 113, 123 (Warren J. Samuels & Arthur S. Miller eds., 1987).

[205] *See Oklahoma Press Publishing Co. v. Walling*, 327 US 186, 66 S. Ct. 494 (1946).

protection.[206] The right to expression has also been extended to corporations through legal doctrines protecting commercial speech and even religious expression.[207]

Professor John Flynn has argued that the development of a doctrine of personhood was inevitable and that, in order to implement laissez-faire capitalism, it had to become a constitutionally mandated ideological baseline for government economic policy.[208] According to Flynn, the decision was consistent with the intellectual and ideological commitments of the Court in the context of the industrial revolution and a postbellum Civil War economy characterized by a shift from an agrarian to a capitalist manufacturing economy. Communications and transportation networks were also expanding rapidly. Because potential for economic progress was understood to depend on the business community, powerful political constituencies did not want economic expansion to be slowed down with government regulations and, as a result, were willing to exclude other social concerns.

Metaphorically and rhetorically, corporate personhood provided support for legal reasoning to recognize rights and privileges for corporations, however, recognition of the corporate form as a unitary entity through corporate personhood also created certain efficiencies that allow for greater administrative ease. Put another way, a corporation is a convenience intended to be an efficient instrument for conducting commerce that allows for the aggregation of capital.

Conducting business in the corporate form brings several advantages and efficiencies including, among others: (1) shareholder exemption from personal liability; (2) immortality for the enterprise; (3) centralized management and standardization of processes/procedures; (4) access to capital; and (5) independence for the enterprise as a separate entity with legal capacity.[209] The shareholder in a company cannot be held personally liable for any harm caused to others. Losses are limited to the amount invested in the company. This creates an incentive to take on risk without personal consequences past a certain point.

In his landmark 1932 book, *The Modern Corporation*, Professor Adolph Berle argued that the private corporation was giving way to a "quasi-public" corporation.[210] For Berle, the private corporation is "quasi-public" because it depends on capital from a group of investors described as the "investing public."[211] He

[206] *Santa Clara County v. Southern Pacific Railroad Co.*, 118 U.S. 394 (1886).

[207] *See Virginia State Board of Pharmacy v. Virginia Citizens Consumer Council*, 425 U.S. 748, 96 S. Ct. 1817 (1976); *Citizens United v. FEC*, 558 U.S. 310, 130 S. Ct. 876 (2010); *Burwell v. Hobby Lobby*, 573 U.S. 682, 134 S. Ct. 2751 (2014).

[208] John J. Flynn, *The Jurisprudence of Corporate Personhood: The Misuse of a Legal Concept*, in Corporations and Society: Power and Responsibility 130 (Warren J. Samuels & Arthur S. Miller eds., 1987).

[209] *See* Cox & Hazen, *supra* note 197, at 6.

[210] Adolf A. Berle & Gardiner C. Means, The Modern Corporation and Private Property 357 (1934).

[211] *Id.* at 5.

posited that a private corporation assumes obligations toward the investing public when it uses the open market to sell its securities. It followed for Berle that the modern corporation had "responsibilities towards owners, the workers, the consumers, and the State . . . In creating these new relationships, the quasi-public corporation may fairly be said to work a revolution."[212]

A competing conception of the corporation in society holds that it is not simply an artificial entity created by state incorporation statutory requirements with quasi-public functions but rather is a natural aggregation of private individuals free to assemble for a common purpose. Conceptualizing the corporation as an aggregation of private individuals implies that the state has less business interfering in business activities.

These competing conceptions of the corporate form have consequences. There are normative implications that a particular conception can have on law, policy, and practice; the relationship between theory and practice is an interactive one. For example, a given conception can be used to justify the expansion or limitation of the obligations that a corporation owes a particular interested or affected constituency. Accordingly, the distinctions drawn between whether a corporation is an artificial creation of law or a natural result of private contractual prerogatives present different challenges for protecting human rights where private commercial actors are involved in abuses.

While there are competing theories of corporate purpose, the concept of shareholder primacy commands significant influence in law and policy. Judicial decisions in the United States have recognized the importance of protecting the investing public against abuses by corporate management such as fraud or self-dealing.[213] For example, in a case often cited as the foundation for shareholder primacy, *Dodge v. Ford*, minority shareholders of the Ford Motor company, the Dodge brothers, challenged Henry Ford's failure to distribute surplus profits.[214] Ford defended, unsuccessfully, that the retained earnings were to be used to finance the company's expansion and to benefit consumers by reducing the cost of cars. Ford claimed that he planned "to employ still more men, to reap the benefits of this industrial system to the greatest possible number, to help them build up their lives and their homes."[215]

Finding against Ford and citing no precedent, the Michigan Supreme Court, in dicta, maintained that corporate management's first priority is to the owners of the corporations:

[212] *Id.* at 6.
[213] *See* Cox & Hazen, *supra* note 197, at 328–331.
[214] *Dodge v. Ford*, 204 Mich. 459, 170 N.W. 668, 671 (1919).
[215] *Dodge v. Ford Motor Co.*, 204 Mich. 459, 505, 170 N.W. 668, 683 (1919).

> A business corporation is organized primarily for the profit of the stockholders, and the discretion of the directors is to be exercised in the choice of means to attain that end, and does not extend to the reduction of profits or the non-distribution of profits among stockholders in order to benefit the public, making the profits of the stock holders incidental thereto.[216]

Commentators have expressed concern that this singular focus on short-term profit maximization to promote the interests of owners sets incentives that may prove counterproductive in the long run, placing human rights and the environment at risk. For example, Professor David Millon has argued that shareholder supremacy leads to "management myopia" while Professor Lynn Stout has argued against seeing shareholders as a monolithic group interested only in profit maximization.[217] Both advance the view that shareholders may see a wider range of matters as material.

The concentration of capital and power the corporate form of business organization currently embodies was created by law and remains protected by law. The corporation is recognized as a legal person and enjoys many of the rights of a human person, with few responsibilities beyond profit maximization. Designed to limit liability and increase efficiency, the conventional corporate form of business organization provides little incentive for responsible conduct or avoiding risks to human rights in the absence of a market for ethical business policies and responsible business practices. Where profits are by design the only focal point in a corporation's field of vision, business leaders may lose sight of the adverse social or environmental impacts that particular policies and practices may cause.

## B. Corporate Social Responsibility

Corporate law, as conventionally conceived, does not mandate that business be conducted in a manner that protects, promotes, or respects human rights. Given the strong emphasis in corporate law on protecting and promoting the interests of shareholders—presumed to be profit maximization—protecting the environment and promoting the human rights of others has not traditionally been a top business priority. Corporate and securities laws do provide some protections for shareholders and detail the duties businesses owe to owners,[218] however pro-social

216 *Dodge v. Ford*, at 684.

217 *See* Millon, *supra* note 196. *See also* LYNN STOUT, THE SHAREHOLDER VALUE MYTH: HOW PUTTING SHAREHOLDERS FIRST HARMS INVESTORS, CORPORATIONS AND THE PUBLIC, 95–102 (2012) David Millon, *Radical Shareholder Primacy*, 10 U. ST. THOMAS L.J. 1013 (2013).

218 *See, e.g.*, Securities Exchange Act of 1934 § 14, 15 U.S.C. § 78m (2000); 15 U.S.C. § 78n; Securities Act of 1933 § 5, 15 U.S.C. § 77e; 15 U.S.C. § 78p(a); Sarbanes-Oxley Act of 2002, Pub.

conduct considering interests beyond those of shareholders has been relegated to the realm of the voluntary assumption of responsibilities that are not legal requirements. The extralegal effort to do good, to go more than the minimum the law requires, is frequently referred to as "corporate social responsibility" (CSR).[219]

There are many and varied definitions and conceptualizations of CSR, from "corporate social responsiveness,"[220] or "corporate social performance,"[221] or "sustainability" to "creating shared value."[222] At its most basic, the concept of CSR captures the idea that the business community should be concerned about society even if the law, domestic or international, does not explicitly mandate or require any action. CSR is voluntary in that it is not legally mandated. Instead, "social responsibility begins where the law ends."[223] The idea that the businesses community owes some manner of obligation to the general public is a long-standing one and has continued to evolve since Berle's 1934 observation about the quasi-public nature of the modern corporation.[224]

Professor Archie Carroll's historical survey of the evolution of CSR concepts and definitions reveals a dynamic academic discourse.[225] Early expressions of CSR in the 1950s and 1960s appealed to individual integrity of the ethical businessman. Conceptions of responsible corporate conduct in American academic literature produced by business scholars in the 1950s that invited business leaders to recognize their broader responsibilities to society were closely associated with Cold War politics.[226] These early articulations of the importance of corporate citizenship were intended to align business interests with building military defense

L. No. 107-204, 116 Stat. 745. *See also* COX & HAZEN, *supra* note 197, at 327–380; Anupam Chander, *Minorities, Shareholder and Otherwise*, 113 YALE L.J. 119 (2003) (explaining how corporate law recognizes protection for minority shareholders as a central part of corporate governance).

[219] *See generally*, KENNETH E. GOODPASTER ET AL., CORPORATE RESPONSIBILITY: THE AMERICAN EXPERIENCE (2012); DAVID P. BARON, BUSINESS AND ITS ENVIRONMENT (7th ed. 2013).

[220] Archie B. Caroll & Kareem M. Shabana, *The Business Case for Corporate Social Responsibility: A Review of Concepts Research and Practice*, 12 INT'L J. MGMT. REV. 87 (2010) (explaining distinction between corporate social responsiveness and CSR, where social responsiveness understands business to be taking a reactive posture to societal needs and responding to the social environment rather than assuming responsibility, citing W.C. Frederick, *From CSR1 to CSR2: The Maturing of Business and Society Thought*, Working Paper 279, Graduate School of Business, University of Pittsburgh (1978))

[221] *See, e.g.*, S. Prakash Sethi, *Dimensions of Corporate Social Performance: An Analytic Framework*, 17 CAL. MGMT. REV. 58–64 (1975) (introducing various aspects of "corporate social performance" and drawing distinctions between corporate "social obligation" in response to market forces or legal constraints, "social responsibility" in response to the normative expectations and values of society, and "social responsiveness" instead of responding to social concerns corporations anticipate and prevent potential problems).

[222] Archie B. Carroll, *Corporate Social Responsibility: Evolution of a Definitional Construct*, 38 BUS. & SOC'Y 268 (1999).

[223] Keith Davis, *The Case For and Against Business Assumption of Social Responsibilities*, 16 ACADEMY OF MGMT. J. 312, 313 (1973), *reprinted in* Carroll, *supra* note 222, at 277 .

[224] Carroll, *supra* note 222, at 273–279.

[225] *Id.*

[226] *See* Carroll & Shabana, *supra* note 235, at 86.

capabilities and expanding free-market capitalism in order to promote patriotism, which would protect against the perceived dangers of Soviet communism.[227]

In the 1970s and 1980s, attention shifted away from the individual ethics of the businessman toward examining business as an institution in the context of society more generally. Scholars focused on understanding what benefits business enterprises derived from and delivered to their communities.[228] Business literature emphasized that a responsible business enterprise must balance a "multiplicity of interests" such that, "instead of striving only for larger profits for its stockholders, a responsible enterprise also takes into account employees, suppliers, dealers, local communities and the nation."[229] Scholars in the years to follow called on business enterprises to commit to taking an active role in solving social problems.[230] Current concepts of stakeholder engagement and stakeholder capitalism echo these earlier insights.

In the 1990s, the late Kofi Annan, former UN Secretary General and Nobel Laureate, recognized the need to address the adverse effects of global business and to generate better corporate citizens. He introduced the UN Global Compact, paving the way for progress on business ethics and corporate social responsibility at the international level.

In 2011, Michael E. Porter and Mark R. Kramer published the popular article, "Creating Shared Value."[231] They argued for a reinvention of capitalism where, "the purpose of the corporation must be creating shared value." Only very recently has the businesses community begun to explicitly incorporate human rights considerations into CSR initiatives and reports. Academic business literature on CSR only rarely addresses international human rights; nevertheless, an understanding of the evolution of CSR provides insight into potential avenues for advancing the incorporation of rights into business policies and performance.

To be sure, CSR has skeptics. For example, Nobel Laureate Economist Milton Friedman saw CSR as suspect at best and as a dangerous distraction at worst. He argued, "few trends could so thoroughly undermine the very foundations of our free society as the acceptance by corporate officials of a social responsibility other than to make as much money for their stockholders as possible."[232]

227 *Id.* citing Bert Spector, *Business Responsibilities in a Divided World: The Cold War Roots of the Corporate Responsibility Movement*, 9 ENTERPRISE & SOCIETY 314–336 (2008).

228 For example, in his 1971 book, *Business in Contemporary Society: Framework and Issues*, Harold Johnson observed: "business takes place within a socio-cultural system that outlines through norms and business roles particular ways of responding to particular situations and sets out in some detail the prescribed ways of conducting business affairs." (HAROLD JOHNSON, BUSINESS IN CONTEMPORARY SOCIETY: FRAMERWORK AND ISSUES (1971), *reprinted in* Carroll *supra* note 222, at 273.

229 Carroll, *supra* note 222, at 273 (quoting Harold Johnson Business in Contemporary Society: Framework and Issues 50 (1971))

230 Carroll, *supra* note 222, at 291–292.

231 Michael E. Porter & Mark R. Kramer, *Creating Shared Value*, HARV. BUS. REV. 62–77 (2011).

232 MILTON FRIEDMAN, CAPITALISM AND FREEDOM 133 (1962); Carroll, *supra* note 222, at 277.

Numerous critiques have been leveled against corporate social responsibility. Some of the more salient critiques question whether CSR efforts are compromising the central purpose of the corporate form. Under this view, the primary responsibility of the corporate form remains profit maximization. Some CSR critics maintain that a free market system can be trusted to solve certain social problems, and where that is not the case, it is the role of government, not business enterprises, to address and redress societal ills.

Nevertheless, present trends point toward more importance being placed by consumers and investors on the social and environmental performance of business. Indeed, economic imperatives could come to necessitate responsible conduct, beyond regulatory requirements, to reach certain market segments. The creation of "benefit corporations," a relatively new form of business organization available in certain states, responds to new demands from a segment of the investing public interested in the social and environmental performance of a business.

B Lab, a nonprofit organization dedicated to using the power of business to solve social and environmental problems,[233] has been the driving force behind a movement to change business as usual for the better.[234] Since 2006, B Lab has been working to build a community of Certified B-Corporations (B-Corps) to accelerate the growth of impact investing and to encourage states to adopt benefit-corporation legislation.[235] In an open letter to business leaders, B Lab explains: "Until recently, corporate law has not recognized the legitimacy of any corporate purpose other than maximizing profits. That old conception of the role of business in society is at best limiting, and at worst destructive."[236] Indeed, B Lab aims to bring about a "B Economy," in which "businesses compete to be best for the world, the people living in it, and the natural environment."[237]

B Lab offers model statutory legislation that states can emulate when drafting their own benefit corporation legislation. The B Lab model statute provides that the purpose of a business must be to create a general public benefit, defined as "a material positive impact on society and the environment, taken as a whole." Specifically, beyond financial reporting, the model statute provides that

[233] *Powered by B Lab*, Benefit Corp Information Center, *available at* http://benefitcorp.net/about-B. Lab. B Lab is currently directed by co-founders, Jay Coen Gilbert, Bart Houlahan, and Andrew Kassoy. *See Our Team*, B Lab, *available at* https://www.bcorporation.net/what-are-b-corps/the-non-profit-behind-b-corps/our-team.

[234] *Our History*, B Lab, *available at* https://www.bcorporation.net/what-are-b-corps/the-non-profit-behind-b-corps/our-history.

[235] *Id.*

[236] *Open Letter to Business Leaders*, B Lab (Aug. 1, 2013), *available at* http://www.bcorporation.net/open-letter-to-business-leaders (letter included over six hundred signatories from benefit corporations).

[237] *See The B Economy*, Certified B Corporation, *available at* https://bcorporation.net/b-economy ("People don't believe the existing economic system is working for them. They're angry, and they're right. That's why we're working to build a B Economy that works for everyone, for the long term . . . To build a B Economy, we need a new kind of business that balances purpose and profit.").

businesses must publicly and annually report an assessment of overall impact on all stakeholders against a third-party standard.

Benefit corporation legislation sets forth specific requirements related to accountability, corporate purpose, and transparency.[238] The requirements for benefit corporations are markedly different than for traditional corporate structure in purpose, fiduciary obligations, reporting, and oversight. The fiduciary duties differ because benefit corporations are required to specify that the fiduciaries must consider the impact of their decision on *nonshareholder constituencies*, such as the local and global environment, society, employees of the corporation, subsidiaries and suppliers, customers, and communities as beneficiaries of the general or specifically stated purpose of the corporation.[239] To that end, the directors' fiduciary obligations for a benefit corporation are more expansive than a traditional corporate formation, where duties are first and foremost owed to shareholders—with a focus to maximize financial gain. Directors of benefit corps have more flexibility to pursue public good, since they are protected from liability on claims that they insufficiently produced public benefits or inadequately pursued profits for shareholders.[240] Benefit corporations could advance corporate accountability and better align business practices with protection for human rights in that a management does not need to be as myopic and focused primarily on financial returns, rather leaders in benefit corporations are free to take a broader perspective of corporate purpose.

## IV. Corporate Accountability for Human Rights Violations

While the business community speaks in terms of "corporate social responsibility," the human rights movement is calling for corporate accountability and liability when corporations are complicit in rights violations.[241] The fact that several Alien Tort Statute cases were filed against leading global firms provides evidence that expectations for responsible business conduct goes beyond the narrow legal obligation to maximize shareholder profits. Where the price of

[238] Dana Brakman Reiser, *Benefit Corporations—A Sustainable Form of Organization*, 46 WAKE FOREST L. REV. 591, 602 (2011). *See*, e.g., MD CODE ANN. § 5-6C-07(a)(1)(2011); VT STAT. ANN. § 21.09(a)(1)(c)(2011).

[239] *Id.* at 594. *See, e.g.*, MD CODE ANN. § 5-6C-07(a)(1)(2011); NJ STATE ANN. § 14A:18-6(a) (2011); VT STAT. ANN. § 21.09(a)(1)(c)(2011); VA CODE ANN. § 13.1-877(A)(1)(2011).

[240] Reiser, *supra* note 238, at 600; Joanne Bauer & Elizabeth Umlas, Making Corporations Responsible: The Parallel Tracks of the B Corp Movement and the Business and Human Rights Movement, 122 BUS. & SOC. R. 285, 324–25 (2017).

[241] *See, e.g.*, Anita Ramasastry, *Corporate Social Responsibility Versus Business and Human Rights: Bridging the Gap Between Responsibility and Accountability*, 14 J. HUM. RTS. 237–259 (2015); Florian Wettstein, *From Side Show to Main Act: Can Business and Human Rights Save Corporate Responsibility?* in BUSINESS AND HUMAN RIGHTS: FROM PRINCIPLES TO PRACTICE (Justine Nolan & Dorothée Baumann-Pauly, eds. 2016).

profit is human suffering that discounts human dignity, businesses are increasingly incurring the costs of public condemnation and litigation.

## A. Alien Tort Statute Litigation

Counsel for victims of human rights violations have sued major multinational corporations in United States courts and the courts of other countries seeking redress.[242] The Alien Tort Statute (ATS), a 1789 federal law enacted in the first session of the US Congress, allows foreign nationals to seek relief in federal courts when the law of nations has been violated.[243] The ATS provides, in pertinent part, that "the district courts shall have original jurisdiction of any civil action by an alien for a tort only, committed in violation of the law of nations or a treaty of the United States."[244]

The principle that private individuals could be held liable for violations of international law—the law of nations—made litigation against private corporations possible.[245] In 1997, *Doe v. Unocal Corp.*[246] was the first suit filed in the United States arguing that corporations should be held liable for being complicit in human rights abuses. Villagers were reportedly murdered, tortured, raped, and forced into labor by members of the Burmese military hired to provide Unocal's gas pipeline project with security. Villagers sued the company, alleging it knew of and enabled the military's abuses. After nearly a decade of litigation, Unocal settled the suit in 2005.

In 2013, in *Kiobel v. Royal Dutch Petroleum*, the US Supreme Court justices unanimously declined to extend jurisdiction over claims that involved a foreign plaintiff suing a foreign defendant for acts in a foreign country. Ester Kiobel sued on behalf of her late husband, an environmental activist and ethnic Ogoni who was killed after the company contracted with the Nigerian government for the military to provide security. The military put down the protests by villagers opposed to the company's operations in the region. Kiobel and others complained

[242] *See e.g.*, Tara Van Ho, *United Kingdom Supreme Court—Extraterritorial Jurisdiction—Business and Human Rights—Civil Claims* 114 Am. J. Int'l L. (explaining *Vedanta v. Lungowe* case in the United Kingdom Supreme Court concerning claims for negligence brought by Zambian claimants against an English parent company and its Zambian subsidiary for damages experienced in Zambia). For current corporate accountability litigation news, pleadings, and commentaries from around the world, *see* Business and Human Rights Resource Center Case Profiles, *available at* https://www.business-humanrights.org/en/big-issues/corporate-legal-accountability/case-profiles/ (listing cases filed in the United Kingdom, the Netherlands, and elsewhere raising human rights claims against business enterprises) (last visited Nov. 19, 2020).

[243] Judiciary Act, ch. 20, § 9, 1 Stat. 73, 77 (1789).

[244] 28 U.S.C. § 1350 (2001).

[245] *Filartiga v. Pena-Irala*, 630 F.2d 876, 878 (2d Cir. 1980).

[246] *Doe v. Unocal Corp.*, 963 F. Supp. 880 (C.D. Cal. 1997).

that "military and police forces attacked Ogoni villages, beating, raping, killing and arresting residents and destroying or looting property."[247] Kiobel argued that the atrocities suffered by residents of the oil-rich region were aided and abetted by business enterprises providing support to the Nigerian government's suppression efforts, including: "food, transportation, and compensation, as well as by allowing the Nigerian military to use respondents' property as a staging ground for attacks."[248]

Rather than reaching the merits of the claims, the Court found that an extension of jurisdiction over claims that occurred overseas would run counter to a presumption against extraterritorial application of US laws. The Court also explained: "On these facts, all the relevant conduct took place outside the United States. And even where the claims touch and concern the territory of the United States, they must do so with sufficient force to displace the presumption against extraterritorial application."[249]

Concurring in the judgment on other grounds, Justice Stephen G. Breyer looked to foreign relations legal principles and practices to conclude that the ATS grants jurisdiction where: "(1) the alleged tort occurs on American soil, (2) the defendant is an American national, or (3) the defendant's conduct substantially and adversely affects an important American national interest."[250] He reasoned that the United States had a distinct interest in not becoming a safe harbor for those who would violate international law.[251] The practical effect of this point is to allow some space for prosecuting violations of international law.

Nevertheless, with its 2018 decision in *Jesner v. Arab Bank*, the Supreme Court handed would-be violators of international human rights a victory by categorically excluding all claims against foreign corporations for violations of the "laws of nations"—no matter the scale or magnitude of the abuse. In *Jesner v. Arab Bank*, the Court rejected claims that victims of terrorist attacks brought against a bank alleged to maintain accounts used by known terrorists to finance attacks and to support the families of suicide bombers. The same Court that continues to recognize the rights of corporations concluded that it did not have authority to impose liability on "artificial entities like corporations." Actual persons can be held liable for violating the laws of nations, but artificial persons incorporated overseas now cannot be. Pointing to foreign policy issues as the institutional responsibility of

[247] *Kiobel v. Royal Dutch Petroleum Co.*, 569 U.S. 108, 113, 133 S. Ct. 1659, 1662, 185 L. Ed. 2d 671 (2013).

[248] *Kiobel v. Royal Dutch Petroleum Co.*, 569 U.S. 108, 113, 133 S. Ct. 1659, 1663, 185 L. Ed. 2d 671 (2013).

[249] *Kiobel v. Royal Dutch Petroleum Co.*, 569 U.S. 108, 115, 133 S. Ct. 1659, 1664, 185 L. Ed. 2d 671 (2013).

[250] *Kiobel v. Royal Dutch Petroleum Co.*, 569 U.S. 108, 127, 133 S. Ct. 1659, 1671, 185 L. Ed. 2d 671 (2013) (Breyer, J., concurring).

[251] *Id.*

the political branches of government, the Court explained it would be "inappropriate for courts to extend ATS liability to foreign corporations absent further action from Congress."[252]

Dissenting, Justice Sonia Sotomayer observed: "in categorically barring all suits against foreign corporations under the ATS, the Court ensures that foreign corporations—entities capable of wrongdoing under our domestic law—remain immune from liability for human rights abuses, however egregious they may be."[253] Moreover, "immunizing corporations that violate human rights from liability under the ATS undermines the system of accountability for law-of-nations violations."[254]

These decisions leave little room for victims of rights violations connected to or caused by corporations to seek and secure remedy through the US federal court system. Litigation to vindicate the rights of victims had limitations even before access to US courts were so sharply curtailed by the *Kiobel* and *Jesner* decisions.

## B. The Limits of Litigation

To date, no ATS cases have resulted in court rulings that have found for corporate liability in the United States.[255] Some cases have been settled, but the terms of settlement are rarely disclosed to the public.[256] The plaintiffs in most ATS cases are poor, Indigenous, and socially excluded people who are able to bring claims only because of the assistance of cross-border coalitions of lawyers.[257]

Often corporations subjected to ATS suits were able to persuade US courts to dismiss claims on procedural grounds pursuant to the doctrine of *forum non conviens*. Some companies settled suits out of court for undisclosed amounts without an admission of liability. The record of successful resolution of these claims has been mixed. The wisdom of the strategy of seeking redress in courts has been questioned because suits are expensive and can span several years.

[252] *Jesner v. Arab Bank, PLC*, 138 S. Ct. 1386, 1390, 200 L. Ed. 2d 612 (2018).

[253] *Jesner v. Arab Bank, PLC*, 138 S. Ct. 1386, 1435, 200 L. Ed. 2d 612 (2018) (Sotomayor J. dissenting).

[254] *Id.*

[255] The United States Supreme Court is set to hear *Doe v. Nestle* arguments on December 1, 2020 and is expected to settle the question of whether courts have authority under the ATS to impose liability on domestic corporations. *See Doe v. Nestle, S.A.*, 929 F.3d 623 (9th Cir. 2019) (certiorari granted).

[256] *See, e.g.*, Jad Mouawad, *Shell to Pay $15.5 Million to Settle Nigerian Case*, N.Y. Times (June 8, 2009), https://www.nytimes.com/2009/06/09/business/global/09shell.html; Duncan Campbell, *Energy Giant Agrees Settlement with Burmese Villagers*, The Guardian (Dec. 14, 2004 7:04 PM), https://www.theguardian.com/world/2004/dec/15/burma.duncancampbell.

[257] Ronen Shamir, *Between Self-Regulation and the Alien Tort Claims Act: On the Contested Concept of Corporate Social Responsibility*, 38 L. & Soc'y Rev. 635, 638 (2004).

There are judicial decisions in other jurisdictions addressing the obligations and potential liability of commercial actors with respect to human rights. Courts in the United Kingdom, the Netherlands, and South Africa have also been asked to address the obligations and potential liability of commercial actors with respect to human rights and torts. Citizens of the Ivory Coast exposed to toxic chemical waste linked to a Dutch petroleum trading company and its subsidiary in the United Kingdom brought legal proceedings against the company in the United Kingdom.[258] A successful criminal prosecution of the company conducted in the Netherlands resulted in fines.[259] Claims against AngloGold Ashanti Ltd., a mining company, were brought by mineworkers in the Constitutional Court of South Africa and resulted in a damages award.[260]

These ATS cases, and the actions pending in other jurisdictions, contribute to our understanding of what responsible business conduct is with respect to human rights, and where failure to act consistently with respect for human rights could result in liability. These cases help shape our understanding and help frame public discourse to bring attention to the plight of victims of rights violations. They teach something of how thinking is evolving about what corporations owe to different stakeholders in society. They also could generate international law on the level of care corporations must take when human rights are at risk.

Nevertheless, given the narrowing of access to the courts in some key jurisdictions—states that are home to many global corporations—it is important to identify other avenues for addressing human rights abuses in which businesses are implicated. Litigation alone will not be sufficient to solve the problems victims of rights violations involving corporate actors confront. Access to remedy remains a problem that requires urgent resolution. In the meantime, a premium should be put on prevention. This will mean finding ways to ensure businesses incorporate rights.

## V. Incorporating Rights

This chapter has explained how international human rights law is inadequate for addressing human rights abuses where corporate actors are implicated. It offered

258 *See, e.g.*, Yao Essaie Motto & Ors V. Traigura Ltd & Trafigura Beheer BV, Claim No. HQ06203370 (Nov. 2006).

259 Rachel Chambers & Katherine Tyler, *The UK Context for Business and Human Rights*, in Lara Blecher, Nancy Kaymar Stafford, & Gretchen C. Bellamy, Corporate Responsibility for Human Rights Impacts: New Expectations and Paradigms (ABA, 2014) (citing Statement from the Management Board of Trafigura Beheer BV (Nov. 16, 2012) at 316–317).

260 *See Mankayi v. AngloGold* (CCT 40/10) [2011] ZACC 3; 2011 (5) BCLR 453 (CC); 2011 (3) SA 237 (CC) (Mar. 3, 2011); *see also* IRIN, *Glimer of Justice for Sick Gold Miners in South Africa*, The Guardian (Mar. 29, 2011).

an overview of the conceptual foundations of international law that render global business enterprises difficult to regulate and hold to account for alleged abuses, and it explained how domestic US corporate law ignores human rights considerations and contributes to governance gaps.

This chapter has also shown that some features of the corporate form can function to compromise respect for human rights. From a human rights perspective, an institutional design that creates distance by separating ownership from management and that limits liability can invite irresponsibility.

Limited liability or sharing the costs of bearing risks was at one point in time required for innovation exploration and exploitation. Indeed, the early charter companies of the imperial project of colonizing regions outside of the European continent were joint stock shares designed to spread the risk of exploration. Shareholders exempt from personal liability can spur innovation but can also invite irresponsibility. The development of benefit corporations signals an increased appetite for better alternatives to business as usual—as are the efforts of shareholder advocates interested in environmental, social, and governance issues.

Too often, "management myopia" continues to contribute to a failure to focus on impacts adverse to rights. As interest in human rights grows along with the costs of failure to respect rights, this can change. Unless and until rights abuses adversely impact the business bottom line and come to be a basis for buy/sell decisions by shareholders, management may continue to miss the adverse impacts of corporate conduct, particularly when human rights risks are not incorporated into corporate decision-making processes.

More than a convenient legal instrument to regulate capital formation, the corporation must be understood as a social institution that can adequately address human rights risks in the global economy. The corporation is an institution that facilitates the accumulation of capital by bringing together people in pursuit of a common purpose, more often than not for the purpose of generating a profit.[261] Therefore, the corporation as a social institution is a means of organizing human economic activity and even belief systems.[262]

Business enterprises are important societal actors. The corporation must be understood to be an "organ of society," as the Universal Declaration of Human Rights provides in its preamble. "Every individual and every organ of society" should strive to promote respect for rights and freedoms and to secure the universal and effective recognition of human rights, both nationally and internationally.[263] In my view, the most human rights–respecting conception of the

[261] Warren J. Samuels, *The Idea of the Corporation as a Person: on the Normative Significance of Judicial Language*, in Corporations and Society: Power and Responsibility 113 (Warren J. Samuels & Arthur S. Miller eds., 1987).

[262] *Id.* at 114.

[263] UDHR, *supra* note 43.

corporate form would be citizens in community. A wide array of actors, beyond states, must be recognized as possessing the potential to participate in the creation of policies to regulate business practices with respect to human rights.

In the next chapter, I will trace the trajectory of international policy initiatives that have advanced in an effort to regulate the social impacts of global corporate capitalism and to address the types of governance gap that gives risks to human rights risks.

# 2
# Global Policy Initiatives to Regulate Business Responsibility and Human Rights

## Introduction

Chapter 1 explained the sources and subjects of international law, the range of human rights enumerated in international law, and the limitations of international law to regulate the conduct of corporations with respect to human rights. Chapter 1 also surveyed cases of businesses accused of human rights abuses. It summarized contrasting approaches to corporate social responsibility (CSR) and showed how theories of corporate governance that favor shareholder profits over a broader set of stakeholder interests can serve to sideline concerns about human rights risks from corporate activity.

In view of these shortcomings of corporate law and international law, this chapter argues that pragmatic global policy instruments can provide a strong foundation for promoting changes in business practices and providing greater protection by closing the governance gaps that place human rights and the environment at risk. This chapter traces the trajectory of international policy initiatives advanced to address the governance gap culminating in the endorsement of the UN Framework and Guiding Principles on Business and Human Rights, which seek to translate human rights issues into corporate responsibility imperatives.

This chapter examines the evolution of international policy initiatives to regulate the conduct of transnational corporations and explores the implications of these efforts for defining the scope of the CSR to respect human rights. It offers a chronology of global policy initiatives developed to address the perceived excesses of private commercial power relative to that of some states and the alleged complicity of commercial actors in human rights abuses. Through an examination of the competing positions advanced by different stakeholders and the substantive content of various proposals considered by international institutions, this chapter explores the dynamics of the development of a framework to regulate global business with respect to human rights. Specifically, it offers an analysis of the 2011 UN Guiding Principles on Business and Human Rights unanimously endorsed by the UN Human Rights Council as part of a continuum of efforts to

*Incorporating Rights*. Erika George, Oxford University Press. © Erika George 2021.
DOI: 10.1093/oso/9780199941483.003.0003

address the influence of concentrated economic power and associated adverse social and political impacts.

The UN Guiding Principles (UNGPs, or Guiding Principles) have been celebrated as marking a break from previous policy failures, creating consensus, and providing an authoritative focal point for progress. This chapter will demonstrate that the instrument is actually iterative and carries forward several of the same concerns and concepts of earlier proposals—it builds on past efforts, but incorporates business principles and perspectives. Further, the chapter will show that despite the growing influence of the UNGPs, the consensus formed around the Principles has become increasingly fragile due to the general failure to provide victims of rights violations access to remedy. Nevertheless, the UNGPs appear to be gaining traction as authoritative, significantly among those stakeholders best situated to address or avoid human rights abuses.

I argue that the UNGPs can provide a foundation for creating lasting and meaningful change in corporate policy and practice. Indeed, the Guiding Principles could come to constitute a stronger international "soft law" standard than is presently anticipated by competing stakeholders involved in policy development. The central contribution of the instrument lies in incorporating the rhetoric of human rights into CSR while clarifying the roles of the public and private sectors in protecting rights.

Based on an analysis of primary UN documents and commentaries from different stakeholder constituencies in the policymaking process, augmented by my ethnographic research, including participation in and observations of the annual proceedings of the UN Forum on Business and Human Rights and interviews with members of the UN Working Group on Business and Human Rights, corporate representatives, and stakeholders, I find that there is an emerging conceptual convergence that could elevate societal expectations of business enterprises and escalate pressure for change. The process of clarifying the concept of the "responsibility to respect" as set forth in the UNGPs will require incorporating an appreciation for human rights into corporate strategy.

First, a chronology of the phases of public and private policy initiatives intended to bring a social conscience to bear on transnational business activities is presented. To demonstrate conceptual shifts in policy approaches to regulating corporate power and protecting human rights, special attention is given to earlier UN efforts and to guidelines promulgated by the Organisation for Economic Cooperation and Development (OECD) on multinational enterprises. Next, the creation of the most recent initiative to address business and human rights, the UN Guiding Principles, is presented to show an emerging clarity on the social responsibility of transnational corporations with respect to human rights. Then, the ways in which the Guiding Principles are being put into practice through the efforts of the UN Working Group on Business and Human Rights, the endorsement of international institutions, and the enthusiasm of a segment of the transnational business community are presented to show a growing imperative to incorporate an appreciation for human rights into corporate strategy. Finally, the contest over the current proposals for a binding international instrument to regulate corporate conduct is presented to demonstrate the persistence of the debate among stakeholders over which modes of regulation can best meet the challenges presented by global business activities and provide remedy to victims of human rights violations. A parallel proposal recently introduced before the United Nations with a view toward drafting a binding international accord on corporate accountability demonstrates a persistent demand that corporations be held accountable for involvement in rights violations.

## I. A Chronology of Conceptual Development

Recent policy debates in international forums are generating a new normative framework to regulate corporate conduct with respect to human rights. The UN Guiding Principles presently dominate global policy debates on business and human rights. Prepared under the leadership of Professor John Ruggie, the UN Secretary General's Special Representative for Business and Human Rights (SRSG), over the course of his mandate from 2005 to 2011 and unanimously endorsed by the Human Rights Council in 2011, the Guiding Principles delineate the roles and responsibilities that governments and business enterprises have in ensuring that human rights are protected and respected.[1]

Prior to the SRSG, there were numerous UN initiatives to address concerns over unregulated or underregulated corporate power. Independent of the SRSG's process, there had been a proliferation of corporate codes of conduct promulgated in the private sector across a range of industries. While some of these codes served to fill existing global regulatory gaps and a few explicitly addressed human rights issues, the field was fragmented and needed a focal point. To that end, the SRSG sought to promote the Guiding Principles as the authoritative focal point to prevent the project from becoming "just another set of voluntary standards vying for attention in an increasingly crowded space."[2] The SRSG has stressed that the Guiding Principles are intended to be the "authoritative UN standards around which the articulated expectations of many public and private

[1] *See Business and Human Rights*, United Nations Human Rights Office of the High Commission, http://www.ohchr.org/EN/Issues/Business/Pages/BusinessIndex.aspx.

[2] Sarah A. Altschuller, *Business and Human Rights: a Convergence of Expectations*, CORPORATE SOCIAL RESPONSIBILITY AND THE LAW BLOG (Dec. 9, 2011), http://www.csrandthelaw.com/2011/12/articles/human-rights/business-and-human-rights-a-convergence-of-expectations/.

institutions have already converged."[3] To appreciate this achievement and its potential, a review of its heritage is helpful.

While momentum to better align business policies and practices with respect for human rights has accelerated in recent years, for nearly half a century there have been various efforts to address the effect of business activity on social conditions. There are distinct phases of policy development that inform one another with each new iteration building on the elements of past policy initiatives. The first phase was characterized by newly independent nations asserting authority in the international system to curtail excessive undue influence on the part of foreign investors and commercial interests in domestic affairs. The second phase was characterized by a retreat from calls for a binding international accord to regulate transnational corporations (TNCs) and by a move toward the promotion of voluntary international standards to guide the conduct of commercial actors operating in emerging markets. The third phase marked a return to calls for mandatory measures and monitoring.

## A. The UN Commission on Transnational Corporations and Draft UN Code of Conduct on Transnational Corporations

In 1974, the UN Economic and Social Council established the Commission on Transnational Corporations to "investigate the effects of TNCs and strengthen negotiating capacity of countries in which they operate" in preparation for drafting a Code of Conduct on Transnational Corporations.[4] An Ad Hoc Inter-Governmental Working Group was tasked with providing a draft text of a code.[5] In 1982, the Commission coordinated a series of deliberations open to all nations based on the draft text.[6] Special sessions followed. In 1988, after years of

[3] *Id.*

[4] Economic and Social Council Resolution 1913 LVII (Dec. 5, 1974) (the term "transnational corporations" as used in the Code was "an enterprise, comprising entities in two or more countries, regardless of the legal form and fields of activity of these entities, which operates under a system of decision-making, permitting coherent policies and a common strategy through one or more decision-making centres, in which the entities are so linked, by ownership or otherwise, that one or more of them may be able to exercise a significant influence over the activities of others, and, in particular, to share knowledge, resources and responsibilities with the others"). For a history of the United Nations Centre on Transnational Corporations established to address issues of global governance in 1975 and later abolished in 1992, *see generally*, Khalil Hamdani & Lorraine Ruffing, United Nations Centre on Transnational Corporations: Corporate Conduct and the Public Interest (2015) (offering "insider perspective" of former staff as a "collective memoir" of efforts to resolve conflict between corporations and countries during the 1970s)

[5] *Draft United Nations Code of Conduct on Transnational Corporations*, United Nations (1983), http://docenti.unimc.it/f1.marongiubuonaiuti/teaching/2015/14427/files/testi-normativi-di-riferimento-generale/progetto-di-codice-di-condotta-delle-nazioni-unite.

[6] *United Nations Commission on Transnational Corporations: Information Paper on the Negotiations to Complete the Code of Conduct on Transnational Corporations*, United Nations (Mar. 7, 1983), https://www.jstor.org/stable/20692548?seq=1#metadata_info_tab_contents.

deliberation, the Secretary General of the United Nations and the Chair of the Special Session of the Commission on Transnational Corporations prepared a revised draft code.[7] In 1990, the chair submitted a text to the Economic and Social Council for consideration.

### 1. Substantive Content of the Code

The text of the Code was strong on state sovereignty. As the core binding international human rights instruments—the International Covenant on Civil and Political Rights and the International Covenant on Economic, Social and Cultural Rights—draw distinctions between types of rights, the Code also divided obligations between those that were "general and political" and those that were "economic, financial and social."[8] The general and political provisions covered sovereignty, economic justice and fairness, rights, and corruption. First and foremost, the text mandated respect for national sovereignty and observance of the domestic laws, regulations, and administrative practices of the host state. Adherence to the economic and development objectives, policies, and priorities of the host country was imperative.

The Code set forth obligations for TNCs and appears to have envisioned the creation of conditions to legally bind business and enforcement provisions to ensure adherence. For example, the Code discussed respect for human rights and fundamental freedoms and fairness in obligatory terms as follows:

> Transnational corporations *should/shall* respect human rights and fundamental freedoms in the countries in which they operate. In their social and industrial relations, transnational corporations *should/shall* not discriminate on the basis of race, colour, sex, religion, language, social, national and ethnic origin or political or other opinion. Transnational corporations *should/shall* conform to government policies designed to extend equality of opportunity and treatment.[9]

The Code called on corporations to respect rights and conform their conduct to government policies that promote equitable treatment.

Significantly, the text also envisioned transparency as an enforcement tool. The provisions on "disclosure of information" emphasized that TNCs should

[7] *Id.* at 1.

[8] *International Covenant on Economic, Social and Cultural* Rights (Jan. 3, 1976), https://www.ohchr.org/en/professionalinterest/pages/cescr.aspx.

[9] *Draft United Nations Code of Conduct on Transnational Corporation as of Summer 1986*, United Nations, https://digitallibrary.un.org/record/156251?ln=en#record-files-collapse-header (emphasis added).

disclose information to the public in a manner that is comprehensible. The information disclosed was to be financial as well as nonfinancial.[10]

Further, with respect to enforcement, the text also envisioned the creation of an international institutional mechanism and a "review procedure."

## 2. Commentary on the Code

The Code was a decolonization document emphasizing primarily the rights of nations and the duties of the TNCs. The Code acknowledged a divide and power differential between the industrialized home countries of TNCs and the developing countries often playing host to TNCs. While the Code did speak to the relationship between nations and multinationals, little discussion in the Code was devoted to the responsibilities of nations toward investors. Professor Steven Ratner has observed:

> The period of decolonization and its immediate aftermath . . . changed the relationship between multinational enterprises and host state governments. The host states in the developing world that were lobbying for a new North-South dynamic also sought to redefine the ties between themselves and the TNEs [transnational enterprises] based in the North. Seeing the TNEs or individual foreign investors as agents of the North in the economic and political domination of the South, they wanted to even the scales.[11]

Competing formulations of the Code proposed during this period portend a contest over whether and the extent to which the effort should create binding obligations to influence the balance of power. For example, one early formulation offered that the text was "open to adoption by all states" regardless of the state's political or economic system or level of development. An alternative proposed formulation offered that the text was "universally applicable to all states."[12]

While the Code failed to find lasting support, it is appropriate to treat it as antecedent to today's efforts. The draft raised concerns that are still relevant today, such as the role of transparency, combating corruption, and the importance of environmental and consumer protection. Notably, relative to other concerns, human rights received only a small mention. The reference to human rights

[10] *The Organisation for Economic Co-Operation and Development Privacy Framework* (2013), https://www.oecd.org/sti/ieconomy/oecd_privacy_framework.pdf.

[11] Steven R. Ratner, *Corporations and Human Rights: A Theory of Legal Responsibility*, 111 Yale L.J. 443, 456–57 (2001).

[12] Draft United Nations Code of Conduct on Transnational Corporations [1983 version], Commission on Transnational Corporations, Report on the Special Session (Mar. 7–18 and May 9–21, 1983), Official Records of the Economic and Social Council, 1983, Supp. No. 7 (E/1983/17/Rev. 1), Annex II at, para 2; *see also*, Philip Kunig, Niels Lau, & Werner Meng, International Economic Law 566 (1989).

emphasized antidiscrimination and equality protections. The text did not make express reference to any of the binding international human rights instruments or detail the full range of protected human rights under international law.

## B. The OECD Guidelines for Multinational Enterprises

In 1976, the OECD put forward its own guidelines apart from the UN process. Wealthy countries advanced the OECD effort in order to counter initiatives at the United Nations to regulate business, such as the Code.[13] Because the UN process to develop the Code was driven primarily by the developing countries that host TNCs, the developed countries that are home to the TNCs that the UN Code proposed to regulate sought solutions through other international organizations. The OECD Guidelines for Multinational Enterprises would become the preferred solution of states and a segment of stakeholders frustrated with the public intergovernmental process to develop laws and policies to police the conduct of TNCs.

The OECD Guidelines are a set of voluntary principles and standards for responsible business conduct in a global context. The Guidelines call for corporate conduct to be consistent with both applicable laws and internationally recognized standards.[14] The Guidelines are addressed to businesses that operate from or in OECD countries and those non-OECD countries that adhere to the OECD Declaration on International Investment and Multinational Enterprises. In contrast to the proposed UN Code that would have become a binding legal instrument had it secured support, the Guidelines are a nonbinding code of conduct that OECD member countries and other "adhering" nations have consented to promote as best practice in the business community.

The OECD Guidelines were founded on the premise that international investment contributes to development and international cooperation. Development and international cooperation can in turn improve the investment climate by maximizing how businesses can contribute to progress while minimizing "difficulties which may arise from their operations."[15] Until the endorsement of the UN Guiding Principles in 2011, the OECD Guidelines had been "the only mutually agreed and comprehensive code of responsible business conduct that governments have committed to promoting."[16] The OECD Guidelines are

[13] Patricia Feeney, *Business and Human Rights: The Struggle for Accountability in the UN and the Future Direction of the Advocacy Agenda*, 161–175 Sur International Journal on Human Rights vol. 6, no. 11 (Biannual English ed. 2009).

[14] *OECD Guidelines for Multinational Enterprises*, 3 (2011), http://www.oecd.org/daf/inv/mne/48004323.pdf.

[15] *Id.*

[16] *Id.*

periodically updated. As a living document, it can be adapted to account for emerging issues as human rights and environmental issues become more salient to members of the international community.

### 1. Substantive Contents of the OECD Guidelines

The current Guidelines are presented in two parts. Part I contains recommendations for responsible business conduct. Part II provides the implementation procedures of the Guidelines. Part I outlines general policies, concepts, and principles before offering recommendations on a range of issues, including disclosure, human rights, employment and industrial relations, the environment, bribery and extortion, consumer interests, science and technology, competition, and taxation. The Guidelines are implemented through a system of National Contact Points (NCPs) established by OECD member governments that adhere to the principles detailed in Part II.[17]

In 2011, the OECD Guidelines were updated to include direct reference to human rights.[18] Governments of the forty-two OECD and non-OECD countries adhering to the OECD Declaration on International Investment and Multinational Enterprises updated the Guidelines "to reflect changes in the landscape for international investment" and "to ensure the continued role of the Guidelines as a leading international instrument for the promotion of responsible business conduct."[19] The human rights update was informed by regional consultations in Asia, Africa, Latin America, the Middle East, and North Africa, with stakeholders and partners. References in the OECD Guidelines to human rights reiterate the obligations set forth in the UN Guiding Principles that all nations must protect human rights and that all business enterprises must respect human rights.

The updated Guidelines now provide that—consistent with the framework of international human rights law, the human rights obligations of the countries in which they operate, and domestic laws and regulations—business enterprises should:

1. Respect human rights, which means they should avoid infringing on the human rights of others and should address human rights violations with which they are involved.
2. Within the context of their own activities, avoid causing or contributing to human rights abuse and address it when it occurs.

[17] Nadia Bernaz, Business and Human Rights: History, Law and Policy—Bridging the Accountability Gap 196–203 (2017) (discussing OECD procedures and the role of NCPs).

[18] *OECD Guidelines for Multinational Enterprises*, *supra* note 14.

[19] *Id.* at 3.

3. Seek ways to prevent or mitigate human rights abuses that are directly linked to their business operations, products, or services by a business relationship, even if they do not contribute to those abuses.
4. Have a policy to respect human rights.
5. Carry out human rights due diligence as appropriate to the size, nature, and context of their operations and the severity of the risks of human rights violations.
6. Provide for or help in the remediation of human rights violations when they identify that they have caused or contributed to these violations.[20]

OECD commentary accompanying the new text on human rights explains: "respect for human rights is the global standard of expected conduct for enterprises independently of States' abilities and/or willingness to fulfill their human rights obligations."[21] The OECD commentary notes business should be guided at a minimum by the International Bill of Human Rights and International Labour Organization (ILO) standards. It also advises that certain enterprises may need to consider additional standards, such as other UN human rights instruments and even international humanitarian law, if rights are placed at greater risk.[22]

Introducing the new guidelines, then OECD Secretary General Angel Gurria emphasized: "[T]he business community shares responsibility for restoring growth and trust in markets . . . these guidelines will help the private sector grow their businesses responsibly by promoting human rights and boosting social development around the world."[23] Revisions to the OECD Guidelines also aimed to establish "a new, tougher process for complaints and mediation" for NCPs.[24]

### 2. Commentary on the OECD Guidelines

Conflicts between corporations and communities have been mediated by OECD NCPs. Done effectively, NCPs could be used to resolve complaints against corporations where judicial venues are not available. However, a 2015 analysis by OECD Watch reviewing fifteen years of cases brought before NCPs to assess the access to remedies for victims of corporate misconduct revealed: "there are very few examples of complaints leading to beneficial results that provided some measure of remedy, and most of these encompass only forward-looking corporate policy changes."[25] According to OECD Watch, "the overwhelming majority of complaints have failed to bring an end to corporate misconduct or provide remedy

[20] *Id.*
[21] *Id.* at 32.
[22] *Id.*
[23] *OECD Guidelines for Multinational Enterprises*, *supra* note 14.
[24] *Id.*
[25] *Remedy Remains Rare*, 5 OECD WATCH (2015), https://www.oecdwatch.org/wp-content/uploads/sites/8/2015/06/Remedy-Remains-Rare.pdf.

for past or on-going abuses, leaving complainants in the same or worse position as they were in before they filed their complaint."[26] The organization based its findings on a quantitative and qualitative analysis of two hundred fifty complaints filed by communities, individuals, and nongovernmental organizations (NGOs) and concluded that in most cases, NCPs are not achieving their central objective, which is to "further the effectiveness of the Guidelines."[27] Nevertheless, OECD Watch maintains that many of the obstacles identified could be addressed "systematically through changes to the Procedural Guidance that promote more effective handling of complaints."[28] NCPs could provide a procedural mechanism for victims of rights violations to bring claims were reforms undertaken to the complaints process and victims made aware of this avenue for dispute resolution.

## C. The UN Global Compact

In his 1999 address to the World Economic Forum in Davos, Switzerland, former UN Secretary General Kofi Annan proposed a new UN initiative to address the social ills perceived to accompany globalization: the UN Global Compact. Inviting the world's business leaders to join a new system of "shared values and principles" that would put "a human face on the global market place,"[29] Annan observed:

> Globalization is a fact of life. . . . The spread of markets outpaces the ability of societies and their political systems to adjust to them, let alone guide the course they take. History teaches us that an imbalance between the economic, social and political realms can never be sustained for very long.[30]

The Global Compact seeks to close the human rights protection gap by bridging the divide between global public interests and global private capital through the creation of a partnership between the United Nations (the public system) and multinational enterprise (the private system). The Global Compact encourages responsible corporate citizenship by engaging business in ameliorating the harms associated with globalization to create "a more sustainable and inclusive global economy."[31] The Global Compact enlists the private sector to work with the United Nations, in partnership with international labor and civil

[26] *Id.*
[27] *Id.*
[28] *Id.*
[29] Alexis M. Taylor, *The UN and the Global Compact*, 17 N.Y.L. Sch. J. Hum. Rts. 975 (2001).
[30] Kofi Annan, *A Compact for the New Century*, Address Before the World Economic Forum (Jan. 31, 1999).
[31] *Corporate Citizenship in the World Economy: The Global Compact, Human Rights, Labour, Environment, Anti-Corruption* (2004), *available at* https://www.unglobalcompact.org.

society organizations, to promote human rights, labor standards, and environmental sustainability within global corporate spheres of influence.

### 1. Substantive Content of the Global Compact

As a strategic policy initiative, the UN Global Compact is a membership-based consortium that invites businesses to commit to align their operations and strategies with ten principles in the areas of human rights, labor, the environment, and anticorruption. The Compact's ten principles are drawn from the Universal Declaration of Human Rights, the ILO's Declaration on Fundamental Principles and Rights at Work, the Rio Declaration on Environment and Development, and the UN Convention Against Corruption. The ten principles are:

Human Rights:

PRINCIPLE 1. Businesses should support and respect the protection of international human rights within their sphere of influence; and
PRINCIPLE 2. Make sure they are not complicit in human rights abuses.

Labor:

PRINCIPLE 3. Businesses should uphold the freedom of association and the effective recognition of the right to collective bargaining;
PRINCIPLE 4. The elimination of all forms of forced and compulsory labor;
PRINCIPLE 5. The effective abolition of child labor; and
PRINCIPLE 6. The elimination of discrimination in respect of employment and occupation.

Environment:

PRINCIPLE 7. Businesses should support a precautionary approach to environmental challenges;
PRINCIPLE 8. Undertake initiatives to promote greater environmental responsibility; and
PRINCIPLE 9. Encourage the development and diffusion of environmentally friendly technologies.

Anticorruption:

PRINCIPLE 10. Businesses should work against corruption in all its forms, including extortion and bribery.[32]

[32] Claude Fussler, Aron Cramer, & Sebastian van der Vegt, Raising the Bar, The UN Global Compact: A Primer on the Principles (2004).

Specifically, participating companies in the Compact are asked to embrace, support, and enact, within their sphere of influence, these ten core principles in areas of human rights, labor standards, the environment, and anticorruption.[33] To achieve better human rights outcomes, the Global Compact "seeks to combine the best properties of the UN, such as moral authority and convening power, with the private sector's solution-finding strengths, and the expertise and capacities of a range of key stakeholders."[34]

### 2. Commentary on the Global Compact

The Global Compact is a complement to, rather than substitute for, global business regulations with respect to human rights. Still, although it is voluntary, there is a measure of accountability with Compact membership, and the Global Compact has periodically expelled participants for failure to comply and to demonstrate progress on conduct consistent with the Compact. Moreover, participating companies must submit a communication on progress to the United Nations.

Understanding business as a driver of globalization and appreciating the challenges and opportunities businesses confront in a global economy, the Global Compact serves as a platform for business to collaborate and partner with governments, civil society, labor organizations, and the United Nations. It is hoped that these partnerships will ensure there are more benefits than burdens to society as a result of cooperation and collaboration to confront common challenges. Proponents maintain that it is a successful flagship UN program.[35] Some more critical commentators have called the project a "bluewash"—rather than promoting change, it provides cover for corporations.[36]

## D. The UN Draft Norms on the Responsibilities of Transnational Corporations and Other Business Enterprises with Regard to Human Rights

In 1998, the Sub-Commission on the Promotion and Protection of Human Rights issued a resolution establishing the Working Group on the Working

[33] *Embedding Human Rights into Business Practice*, 15 United Nations Global Compact and the Office of the High Commissioner of Human Rights (2006).

[34] *Id.*

[35] Teressa Szelest, *Aligning Business to the UN Global Compact Has Benefits Beyond the Bottom Line* (2017), https://www.greenbiz.com/article/aligning-business-un-global-compact-has-benefits-beyond-bottom-line-sponsored.

[36] *NGOs Criticize "Blue Washing" by the Global Compact* (July 2007), https://www.globalpolicy.org/global-taxes/32267-ngos-criticize-qblue-washingq-by-the-global-compact.html.

Methods and Activities of Transnational Corporations to examine the role of TNCs with respect to commercial activities in host countries that could harm human rights and to make recommendations for further discussions of the challenges commercial actors presented.[37] Over several years and a series of expanded mandates and extensions from the Sub-Commission, the Working Group started to craft what would eventually become the Draft Norms on the Responsibilities of Transnational Corporations and Other Business Enterprises with Regard to Human Rights. The Working Group also prepared a commentary that was to "serve as a reference for the practical interpretation of the Norms."[38]

A 2001 Sub-Commission resolution extended the mandate for three years, granting the Working Group authority to create a list of human rights instruments relevant to the activities of TNCs. The Sub-Commission also asked the Working Group to explore the feasibility of establishing a monitoring mechanism and means for sanctioning TNCs to obtain compensation for rights violations.[39] In 2002, the Sub-Commission passed still another resolution inviting the Working Group to complete a version of the draft for public comment and submission to the Sub-Commission for consideration. Over the course of its mandate, the Working Group hosted annual public hearings in Geneva from 2000 to 2003. Participants in the Working Group process included representatives of civil society organizations, commercial enterprise, and members of the academic research community.[40]

In a 2003 resolution, the Sub-Commission finally approved the Norms, affirming that the Norms and the commentary accompanying them "reflect[ed] the most current trends in the field of international law, and particularly international human rights law, with regard to the activities of transnational corporations and other business enterprises."[41] The Sub-Commission Resolution also recommended that the Commission consider establishing a new "open-ended" entity to review the Norms and that the existing Working Group continue to receive reports from stakeholders "concerning the possible negative impact

[37] *See* Pini Pavel Miretski & Sascha-Dominik Bachmann, *The UN Norms on the Responsibility of Transnational Corporations and Other Business Enterprises with Regard to Human Rights: A Requiem*, 17 Deakin L. Rev. 5, 7 (2012); *see also* Dinah Shelton, *Protecting Human Rights in a Globalized World*, 25 B.C. Int'l & Comp. L. Rev. 273, 284 (2002).

[38] *Responsibilities of transnational corporations and other business enterprises with regard to human rights*, Sub-Commission Resolution 2003/16, U.N. Doc. E/CN.4/Sub.2/2003/L.11 at 52 (2003).

[39] Sub-Commission on the Promotion and Protection of Human Rights, The Effects of the Working Methods and Activities of Transnational Corporations on the Enjoyment of Human Rights, ESCOR, 53rd Sess., 25th mtg., U.N. Doc. E/CN.4/Sub.2/2001/40 (Nov. 22, 2001).

[40] *See* Miretski & Bachmann, *supra* note 37, at 16; David Weissbrodt, *Business and Human Rights*, 74 U. Cin. L. Rev. 55, 67–68 (2005); David Weissbrodt & Muria Kruger, *Norms on the Responsibilities of Transnational Corporations and Other Business Enterprises with Regard to Human Rights*, 97 Am. J. Int'l L. 901 (2003).

[41] *Responsibilities of transnational corporations and other business enterprises with regard to human rights*, *supra* note 38.

of the activities of transnational corporations and other business enterprises on human rights, and particularly affecting the implementation of the Norms on the Responsibilities of Transnational Corporations and Other Business Enterprises with Regard to Human Rights."[42] In proposing an open-ended working group, the draft norms contemplated the type of monitoring committee that is usually reserved for treaty bodies that accompany binding human rights instruments.

The Sub-Commission submitted the Norms to the Commission on Human Rights, its parent entity, with the recommendation that they be considered for adoption after comment from interested stakeholders.[43] When the Norms reached the UN Commission on Human Rights, the predecessor to today's Human Rights Council, they were met with significant resistance from the private commercial sector and certain states. After receiving strenuous objections to the substance of the Norms as well as the process leading to their creation, the Commission began to retreat from further development of the Norms. The Commission eventually asserted that it had neither asked for nor authorized the Norms, emphasizing that, as a draft, the document did not create any binding obligations and was not a statement of law.[44]

By a consensus "action without a vote," the Commission asked the newly created Office of the High Commissioner for Human Rights to study the scope and status of legal standards relevant to the responsibility of TNCs.[45] The study concluded that the Norms were not and could not be a law or a statement of law.

### 1. Substantive Content of the UN Draft Norms

The preamble to the Norms relied on the Universal Declaration of Human Rights as a point of reference for establishing the obligations that TNCs and other business enterprises have "as organs of society" to promote and secure human rights. The preamble reaffirmed that "States have the primary responsibility to promote, secure the fulfillment of, respect, ensure respect of and protect human rights," but it also recognized that TNCs and other business enterprises were obligated to "respect generally recognized responsibilities and norms contained in United Nations treaties and other international instruments."[46]

The preamble to the Norms listed a wide range of international instruments business enterprises would be bound to respect. It referred to the widely ratified Covenant on Economic, Social and Cultural Rights and the Covenant on

[42] *Id.*

[43] *Id.*

[44] Miretski & Bachmann, *supra* note 37, at 45; Weisbrodt, *supra* note 40, at 64–68; David Kinley & Rachel Chambers, *The UN Human Rights Norms for Corporations: The Private Implications of Public International Law*, 6 HUM. RTS. L. REV. 447, 463 (2006).

[45] Miretski & Bachmann, *supra* note 37, at 17.

[46] *Norms on the Responsibilities of Transnational Corporations and Other Business Enterprises with Regard to Human Rights*, U.N. Doc. E/CN.4/Sub.2/2003/12/Rev.2 (2003) [hereinafter *The Norms*].

Civil and Political Rights that comprise the International Bill of Human Rights. It listed regional human rights charters, such as the European Convention for the Protection of Human Rights and Fundamental Freedoms, the American Convention on Human Rights, and the African Charter on Human and Peoples' Rights. It also included references to more obscure instruments, including the Plan of Implementation of the World Summit on Sustainable Development and the International Code of Marketing of Breast Milk Substitutes adopted by the World Health Assembly.

The Norms did indicate an appreciation of the fact that TNCs and other business enterprises do have the capacity to promote economic development and to create value, but the Norms primarily called attention to the capacity of TNCs to "cause harmful impacts on the human rights and lives of individuals through their core business practices and operations, including employment practices, environmental policies, relationships with suppliers and consumers, interactions with Governments and other activities."[47]

The Norms anticipated evolution in law and were presented as an instrument to "contribute to the making and development of international law" with respect to the responsibilities and obligations of business enterprises.[48] Consistent with anticipating a living body of international law, the Norms also noted that "new international human rights issues and concerns are continually emerging and that transnational corporations and other business enterprises often are involved in these issues and concerns, such that further standard-setting and implementation are required at this time and in the future."[49]

The Norms contained "general obligations" and "general provisions of implementation." The general obligations in the Norms delineated the duties of nations as follows: "States have the primary responsibility to promote, secure the fulfillment [*sic*] of, respect, ensure respect of and protect human rights recognized in international as well as national law, including ensuring that transnational corporations and other business enterprises respect human rights."

The general obligations set forth in the Norms defined the broad duties of business enterprises: "to promote, secure the fulfillment of, respect, ensure respect of and protect human rights recognized in international as well as national law, including the rights and interests of indigenous peoples and other vulnerable groups."[50] Business enterprises were to fulfill these obligations "within their respective spheres of activity and influence."[51]

[47] *Id.*

[48] *Id.*; *see also*, Larry Catá Backer, *Multinational Corporations, Transnational Law: The United Nations Norms on the Responsibilities of Transnational Corporations as a Harbinger of Corporate Social Responsibility in International Law*, 37 COLUM. HUM. RTS. L. REV. 287, 374 (2005).

[49] *Id.*

[50] *The Norms*, *supra* note 46, at para. 1.

[51] *Id.*

The remaining general obligations addressed particular human rights issues, including the right to equal opportunity and nondiscriminatory treatment; the right to security of persons; the rights of workers; respect for national sovereignty and human rights; as well as obligations with regard to consumer and environmental protection.

Language in the Norms required the proactive engagement of business enterprises to "protect" particular human rights and "contribute to their realization" consistent with relevant international instruments. Provisions detailing obligations with respect to particular rights issues used "shall" to describe what business must do and must refrain from doing in order to "promote," "secure," "ensure," and "protect" human rights. For example, with respect to the right to security of persons, the Norms proclaimed that TNCs "shall not engage in nor benefit from war crimes, crimes against humanity, genocide, torture, forced disappearance, forced or compulsory labor" and "shall observe international human rights norms" in security arrangements.[52] With respect to the rights of workers, the Norms declared TNCs "*shall* not use forced or compulsory labor . . . *shall* respect the rights of children . . . *shall* provide a safe and healthy working environment . . . *shall* provide workers with remuneration that ensures an adequate standard of living . . . *shall* ensure freedom of association and effective recognition of the right to collective bargaining by protecting the right to establish and . . . join organizations."[53] At various points throughout the text, the terms "promote," "secure," "ensure," and "protect" are used with reference to obligations assigned to business enterprises in relationship to different human rights.

The Norms also outlined general provisions for implementation. Implementation provisions called upon business enterprises to "adopt, disseminate and implement internal rules of operation" consistent with the Norms.[54] Pursuant to the implementation provisions, states were to "establish and reinforce the necessary legal and administrative framework for ensuring that the Norms and other relevant national and international laws are implemented by transnational corporations and other business enterprises."[55]

Implementation provisions of the Norms also contemplated the need to address the conditions of victims of human rights violations. To that end, implementation of the Norms would also have required TNCs to "provide prompt, effective and adequate reparation" to those harmed by the failure of a business enterprise to comply with the Norms.[56]

[52] *Id.* at paras. 3, 4.
[53] *Id.*
[54] *Id.* at para. 16.
[55] *Id.* at para. 17.
[56] *Id.* at para. 18.

Significantly, implementation of the Norms also envisioned a monitoring mechanism. Business enterprises would have been subjected to periodic monitoring by the United Nations or by future national or international mechanisms. The monitoring process was to be transparent, be independent, and include the observations of stakeholders. Businesses would also be expected to conduct periodic reviews of the impact of their operations on human rights.

## 2. Commentary on the UN Draft Norms and Critical Assessments

The Norms drew objections primarily from powerful private commercial interests and from the countries in which many of them are incorporated. Opponents representing the private sector raised concerns that the Norms created confusion as to who was responsible for what, expanded the scope of corporate responsibility, and attributed accountability to different commercial actors in ways that were not practicable. A primary objection from private sector opponents was that the Norms, by attempting to extend binding responsibility on business enterprises, would wrongfully alter the balance of power protected in international law where sovereign states are the sole subjects and sources of law. Other objections concerned the TNCs' responsibility for relationships, the supply chain of command as control.[57] Still others complained the Norms were simultaneously too legalistic and too vague because the text failed to distinguish between binding and nonbinding human rights obligations, and it conflated voluntary and mandatory corporate compliance obligations, creating a "legal no man's land."[58]

For example, the US Council for International Business criticized the Norms as constituting "a fundamental shift in responsibility for protecting human rights—from governments to private actors, including companies—effectively privatizing the enforcement of human rights laws."[59] The International Chamber of Commerce and the International Organisation of Employers released a joint statement objecting to the Norms as a vilification of business and an enforced privatization of human rights protection.

The response to the Norms by the government of the United States was consistent with some concerns raised by representatives of the private commercial sector. The United States took issue with the entire enterprise: "Not only was this exercise beyond the mandate of the Sub-Commission—but it was undertaking/undertaken wholly without consideration for the views of the States."[60] Further,

[57] Miretski & Bachmann, *supra* note 37, at 30 (citing Carolin F Hillemanns, *UN Norms on the Responsibilities of Transnational Corporations and Other Business Enterprises with Regard to Human Rights*, 4 German L.J. 1065, 1078 (2003)); Kinley & Chambers, *supra* note 44, at 448–449.

[58] Miretski & Bachmann, *supra* note 37, at 28 (citing Deal, *infra* note 59).

[59] Timothy E. Deal, *The Human Rights Responsibilities of International Business*, paper presented at the Frank Hawkins Kennan Institute of Private Enterprise Seminar, "Are Human Rights the Business of Business?," United States Council for International Business, Washington, D.C., Dec. 10, 2003.

[60] *Id.*

the United States maintained the effort was misguided. Rather than creating new norms from nothing, the United States urged the international community to redirect efforts to enforcing the rule of law consistent with existing obligations assumed by national governments instead of extending human rights obligations to transnational businesses. For the United States, "the key to ending abuses allegedly committed by private business entities is to promote, enforce and respect the rule of law. Governments must act aggressively to prevent, punish and provide adequate redress for violations of law."[61]

The US government took issue with the Norms on both procedural and substantive grounds. Procedurally, the United States maintained that the Sub-Commission "had no authority to create a set of 'norms,' the clearly stated purpose of which is to bind or guide the actions of States or non-State actors."[62] The United States argued that "the sub-commission cannot decide for itself what exercises it wishes to undertake, what powers it wishes to create, or what functions it wishes to perform."[63] In the US view, the very creation of the Norms exceeded authority of the Sub-Commission.

Substantively, the United States objected on grounds of international law, warning that "attempts to craft norms of this nature dangerously shift the focus of accountability for human rights violations away from States and toward private actors, thus creating the perception that States have less of a responsibility to end human rights abuses for which they are responsible."[64] State accountability remains the foundation of human rights law. "Any exercise that attempts to shift focus away from States and toward private actors erodes this foundation and provides States responsible for widespread human rights abuses with excuses and justifications for inaction."[65] The Norms would, the government argued, provide "justifications for inaction."[66] According to the United States: "By attempting to establish duties and obligations for business entities, which are non-State actors, this exercise goes well beyond the present state of international law as well as international legal process."[67] For states to assume obligations under international law to impose international obligations on entities that have not accepted them or been active in their creation would run contrary to the process of international lawmaking.

61 *Id.*

62 See Miretski & Bachmann, supra note 37 at 29 (citing United States Mission to International Organizations to Mr. Dzidek Kedzia Chief of Research and Right to Development Branch—Office of the United Nations High Commissioner for Human Rights (Sept. 30, 2004)).

63 *Id.*

64 *Id.*

65 *Id.*

66 *Id.*

67 *Id.*

Having asserted the position that the Norms were of no legal consequence, having "no status—legal or otherwise," the United States detailed additional reasons why the Norms were fundamentally flawed, starting with the basic assumptions that motivated the entire process: that businesses are responsible for rights violations and that regulatory gaps give rise to violations.[68] For the United States, "any attempt to draft a series of norms to bind private business entities accepts as a baseline assumption that these entities are responsible for widespread human rights abuses in countries where they operate."[69] The United States rejected the premise that business entities were responsible for rights abuses. Rather, according to the United States, "where human rights abuses are widespread, they are the result of either action or inaction of States, not generally by private enterprises."[70]

Taking issue with the premise that there was not an applicable normative framework to regulate TNCs, the United States pointed to the OECD Guidelines on Multinational Enterprises as an example of an existing standard that addressed the role of business in the global economy. The United States also praised the UN Global Compact as a place where the United Nations has added value and increased the efficacy of CSR activities worldwide. Overall, the United States took the position that voluntary initiatives, such as the Compact and public-private partnerships with willing private sector participants, should be the priority of the international community as "voluntary, collaborative efforts to leverage public-private partnerships are the best means for both encouraging responsible business practices by the private sector in this area and for the promotion and protection of human rights."[71] During the international policy debates over the Draft Norms, the US government expressed a strong preference for voluntary initiatives.

## II. An Emerging Conceptual Consensus

### A. The UN Guiding Principles Process

In 2005, at the request of the UN Commission on Human Rights, UN Secretary General Kofi Annan appointed Harvard Professor John Ruggie as the Special Representative on the Issue of Human Rights and Transnational Corporations

[68] *Id.*
[69] *Id.*
[70] *Id.*
[71] *Id.*

and Other Business Enterprises[72] and tasked him with clarifying the "roles and responsibilities of states, companies, and other social actors in the business and human rights sphere."[73]

Ruggie's appointment followed the failure of the international community to take action on the Draft Norms after opposition from powerful stakeholders representing the interests of the business community, including the International Organisation of Employers, the International Chamber of Commerce, and the US government. In 2011, the UN Guiding Principles were endorsed by the UN Human Rights Council, the successor to the Commission on Human Rights.[74]

Ruggie was exceedingly careful to distance his work product and distinguish his process from the Draft Norms the Sub-commission of the UN Commission on Human Rights. After consultation with a broad range of stakeholders, he developed the "Protect, Respect and Remedy" Framework. At the request of the Council, Ruggie next developed a set of "Guiding Principles on Business and Human Rights" to "provide concrete and practical recommendations" for working within the Framework.[75] There were three distinct phases to the process that led to the UN Framework and Guiding Principles. Each phase is discussed in the following.

### 1. The Mandate

In 2006, Ruggie submitted his First Interim Report to the Commission on Human Rights as the SRSG. The Interim Report detailed his approach to the mandate and distanced the project from past UN efforts to address the issue of business and human rights. It presented a new strategic direction of "principled pragmatism" as a departure from the "doctrinal excesses" of past efforts and proposed a path forward through "an unflinching commitment to the principle of strengthening the promotion and protection of human rights as it relates to business, coupled with a pragmatic attachment to what works best in creating change where it matters most—in the lives of people."[76] To that end, Ruggie did

[72] JOHN GERARD RUGGIE, JUST BUSINESS: MULTINATIONAL CORPORATIONS AND HUMAN RIGHTS xviii (2013).

[73] *UN "Protect, Respect and Remedy" Framework*, BUSINESS & HUMAN RIGHTS RESOURCE CENTRE, http://www.reports-and-materials.org/Ruggie-protect-respect-remedy-framework.pdf (last visited Mar. 1, 2013) (brief explanation of the Framework by Special Representative Ruggie).

[74] *See id.*

[75] Report of the Special Representative of the Secretary-General on the Issue of Human Rights and Transnational Corporations and Other Business Enterprises: Guiding Principles on Business and Human Rights: Implementing the United Nations "Protect, Respect and Remedy" Framework, A/HRC/17/31 para. 9, Mar. 21, 2011 [hereinafter *Guiding Principles*].

[76] John Ruggie, *Interim Report of the Special Representative of the Secretary-General on the Issue of Human Rights and Transnational Corporations and Other Business Enterprises*, U.N. Doc. E/CN.4/2006/97 para. 81 (2006) [hereinafter *SRSG Interim Report*].

not purport to be engaged in creating law but rather providing a practical solution to a pressing problem.

Commission Resolution 2005/69 tasked Ruggie with the mandate to "identify and clarify standards of corporate responsibility and accountability for transnational corporations and other business enterprises with regard to human rights."[77] In presenting his plan for work pursuant to the mandate, Ruggie proceeded from the premise "that the objective of the mandate is to strengthen the promotion and protection of human rights in relation to transnational corporations and other business enterprises but that governments bear principal responsibility for the vindication of those rights."[78]

The SRSG's methods of stakeholder consultations on the substance of the mandate to build consensus also marked a departure from past efforts. For instance, the process leading up to the creation of the Norms was critiqued for being top-down and not inclusive. In contrast, the SRSG convened consultations with governments, business associations, labor organizations, and civil society activists and academics in the United States and Europe.

In an Interim Report, Ruggie first framed the issues that would inform his analysis. He identified certain institutional features of economic globalization that made addressing business and human rights challenging. For example, he explained that the presence of "a variety of actors for which the territorial State is not the cardinal organizing principle have come to play significant public roles" presented a regulatory challenge particularly in the economic realm.[79]

The Interim Report explained that international economic activity is transitioning from a system that allowed governments to regulate external trade between national economies to a system that increasingly has

[77] UN Commission on Human Rights, *Human Rights Resolution 2005/69: Human Rights and Transnational Corporations and Other Business Enterprises*, Apr. 20, 2005, E/CN.4/RES/2005/69 para. 1(a), *available at* https://www.refworld.org/docid/45377c80c.htm.

In 2005, the UN Commission on Human Rights adopted Resolution E/CN.4/RES/2005/69, requesting "Secretary-General to appoint a special representative on the issue of human rights and transnational corporations and other business enterprises." The resolution mandated that the special representative:

> To identify and clarify standards of corporate responsibility and accountability for transnational corporations and other business enterprises with regard to human rights;
>
> To elaborate on the role of States in effectively regulating and adjudicating the role of transnational corporations and other business enterprises with regard to human rights, including through international cooperation;
>
> To research and clarify the implications for transnational corporations and other business enterprises of concepts such as "complicity" and "sphere of influence";
>
> To develop materials and methodologies for undertaking human rights impact assessments of the activities of transnational corporations and other business enterprises;
>
> To compile a compendium of best practices of States and transnational corporations and other business enterprises.

[78] *SRSG Interim Report*, *supra* note 76, at para. 7.

[79] *Id.* at para. 10.

become internalized within transnational firms through global supply chains.[80] Transnational firms have also increased their ability to operated and expand globally through trade liberalization. The Interim Report attributed abuse to "distinctive institutional features of global firms" that serve to "multiply and amplify challenges" because transnational business practice is built on "network-based operating models involving multiple corporate entities spread across and within multiple countries."[81]

### 2. The Framework

In 2008, the SRSG delivered his next report to the Human Rights Council. Issued at the conclusion of the original three-year mandate, the 2008 report, " 'Protect, Respect and Remedy': A Framework for Business and Human Right," set a path for moving forward. The Framework rests on three pillars: (1) the state has a duty to *protect* individuals from human rights abuses by third parties, (2) corporations have a responsibility to *respect* human rights, and (3) victims of corporate abuses need greater access to *remedy*.[82] The Framework was well received, and the Council extended the mandate of the SRSG for three more years, requesting that he put the Framework into operation by developing practical guidance to support the three pillars.

## B. The UN Guiding Principles on Business and Human Rights

After consulting with a broad range of stakeholders and allowing a period of public comment, the SRSG issued the Guiding Principles on Business and Human Rights to aid the implementation of the "Protect, Respect and Remedy" Framework. Certain provisions of the Guiding Principles pertaining to human rights due diligence and nonjudicial grievance mechanisms were tested in different business sectors and in different countries. Pursuant to the Human Rights Council mandate to "operationalize" the Framework by providing concrete and practical recommendations, the Guiding Principles "aim not only to provide guidance that is practical, but also guidance informed by actual practice."[83]

### 1. Substantive Content of the Guiding Principles

The Guiding Principles are introduced as "the end of the beginning." To that end, the Guiding Principles are intended to establish "a common global

[80] *Id.* at para. 11.
[81] *Id.* at para. 22.
[82] The Kenan Institute for Ethics at Duke University, The UN Guiding Principles on Business and Human Rights: Analysis and Implementation 6 (2012).
[83] *Guiding Principles*, *supra* note 75 at para. 11.

platform for action."[84] Far from foreclosing future developments in laws or policies to address business and human rights challenges, the introduction to the Guiding Principles acknowledges the possibility of "promising longer-term developments" and invites "cumulative progress."[85] Yet the introductory text of the Guiding Principles disavows any effort to contribute to the creation of new international legal obligations.

The Guiding Principles offer both foundational and operational guidance to states and to business enterprises concerning their respective human rights duties.[86] The Guiding Principles also address access to remedy through state-based and nonstate-based grievance mechanisms.[87] Foundational principles set out general duties while operational principles detail how duties are to be discharged. Taken together, the foundational principles and the operational principles articulate the obligations that states and business enterprises have with respect to human rights and explain how they are to fulfill them.[88]

Grounded in the recognition of the existing obligations of governments to respect, protect, and fulfill human rights and fundamental freedoms, and an appreciation that business enterprises are specialized organs of society performing specialized functions, there are different duties for state and for nonstate actors with respect to human rights detailed in the Guiding Principles. The thirty-one principles are to be understood as a "coherent whole" applying to all states and to all business enterprises regardless of size, structure, sector, or location. Each principle is accompanied by a commentary on the intent and implications of the foundational and operational guidance given.

*a. The State Duty to Protect Human Rights*

The state duty to protect, as a matter of foundational principle, requires a country to guard against rights abuses occurring within its territory, including abuses by business enterprises. To fulfill this duty, a state is obligated to investigate, punish, and prevent rights abuses through the enactment of effective laws and policies. States must make explicit the expectation that all business enterprises based in their jurisdiction respect human rights throughout their operations. By providing clear, coherent, and consistent messages to businesses, states can ensure a measure of predictability. The commentary also notes that, while states are not required to regulate the extraterritorial activities of businesses based within their jurisdiction, they are not prohibited from doing so. Moreover, the general duty

[84] *Id.* at para. 13.
[85] *Id.*
[86] *See also* UN "Protect, Respect and Remedy" Framework, http://www.reports-and-materials.org/Ruggie-report-7-Apr-2008.pdf.
[87] *Guiding Principles*, *supra* note 75, at paras. 25–31.
[88] *Id.* at paras. 13–22.

to protect and promote the rule of law is consistent with crafting law, policy, and remedial measures to address abuses by private actors.

Operational principles detail how states can, through general regulatory and policy functions, meet their duty to protect. States should:

1. Enforce laws that are aimed at, or have the effect of, requiring business enterprises to respect human rights, and periodically to assess the adequacy of such laws and address any gaps;
2. Ensure that other laws and policies governing the creation and ongoing operation of business enterprises, such as corporate law, do not constrain but enable business respect for human rights;
3. Provide effective guidance to business enterprises on how to respect human rights throughout their operations;
4. Encourage, and where appropriate require, business enterprises to communicate how they address their human rights impacts.[89]

Among other things, the UNGPs also provide that states should work to ensure policy coherence across governmental departments such that different agencies implement policies that shape business practices in a manner consistent with the state's human rights obligations. The UNGPs also mandate that "States should maintain adequate domestic policy space to meet their human rights obligations when pursuing business-related policy objectives with other States or business enterprises, for instance through investment treaties or contracts."[90]

Commentary on the foundational principles on state duties offers that fulfillment of general regulatory functions could encompass financial reporting requirements, clarifying that human rights violations may be "material" or "significant" to the economic performance of the business enterprise.[91] The commentary also cautions that the terms of international investment agreements may constrain the implementation of human rights legislation. While providing investor protection through treaties or contracts, states should also ensure they retain the regulatory ability to protect rights under the terms of these agreements.

*b. The Corporate Responsibility to Respect Human Rights*

The first foundational principle pertaining to corporate responsibility provides that business enterprises must respect human rights. This means that businesses should "avoid infringing on the human rights of others and should address

[89] *Id.* at 8.
[90] *Id.* at 12 (Principle 9).
[91] *Id.* at 9 (Principle 3, Commentary).

adverse human rights impacts with which they are involved."[92] At a minimum, the relevant human rights with which a business enterprise must concern itself are those contained in the International Bill of Rights and those in the ILO's Declaration on Fundamental Principles and Rights at Work.[93]

While the UNGPs appreciate that the size and structure of a business enterprise varies, such that the means of meeting responsibilities may similarly vary, the responsibility to respect human rights still extends to all business enterprises without regard to size, sector, or structure.[94] The commentary explains that the methods used by a business to meet its responsibilities will be proportionate to its size, as smaller businesses often will have less capacity and less formal management systems than larger businesses. However, the commentary also cautions that the conduct of a small or midsize enterprise could result in severe human rights abuses. Accordingly, "the responsibility to respect human rights applies fully and equally to all business enterprises."[95]

The responsibility to respect, as a matter of foundational principle, requires that business enterprises "[a]void causing or contributing to adverse human rights impacts through their own activities, and address such impacts when they occur."[96] Further, business enterprises should "[s]eek to prevent or mitigate adverse impacts that are directly linked to their operations, products, or services by their business relationships, even if they have not contributed to those impacts."[97] The commentary acknowledges that businesses may be involved with human rights abuses through their own activities or as a result of relationships with others.

The term "activities" in the UNGPs also extends to omissions. The commentary explains that a corporation's "business relationships" extends to its associations with partners whether those partners represent private industry, NGOs, public institutions, or government agencies. Indeed, much of the litigation against corporations concerns claims of complicity or aiding and abetting and involves acts that could be attributed to a corporation's partners or to issues that flow from particular business relationships.

There are three things a business must do to meet the responsibility to respect. In particular, business enterprises must ensure that they have:

1. A policy commitment to meet their responsibility to respect human rights;
2. A human rights due diligence process to identify, prevent, mitigate, and account for how they address their impacts on human rights;

[92] *Id.* at 13 (Principle 11).
[93] *Id.* at 13 (Principle 12).
[94] *Guiding Principles, supra* note 75 at 14 (Principle 14).
[95] *Id.* at 14.
[96] *Id.* at 14 (Principle 13).
[97] *Id.* (Principle 13).

3. Processes to enable the remediation of any adverse human rights impacts they cause or to which they contribute.[98]

Further elaborating on these foundational norms, the operational principles provide guidance for business enterprises on how to fulfill their responsibility to respect.[99] For example, the operational principles offer that the policy commitment to meet the responsibility to respect human rights should take the form of a statement approved at the highest levels of management and be made available publicly. The statement should detail expectations for conduct consistent with the policy on the part of its personnel, its business partners, and other parties connected to its operations.

The commentary counsels that "Just as States should work towards policy coherence, so business enterprises need to strive for coherence between their responsibility to respect human rights and policies and procedures that govern their wider business activities and relationships. This should include, for example, policies and procedures that set financial and other performance incentives for personnel; procurement practices; and lobbying activities where human rights are at stake."[100]

The commentary is clear: "Business enterprises need to *know and show* that they respect human rights."[101] The operational principles also elaborate on what is expected of companies with respect to due diligence and reporting. In general, human rights due diligence requires a process that "assesses actual and potential human rights impacts, integrating and acting upon the findings, tracking responses, and communicating how impacts are addressed."[102] The process should extend to consideration of human rights violations that the business enterprise "may cause or contribute to through its own activities, or which may be directly linked to its operations, products or services by its business relationships."[103] The operational principles also anticipate that the due diligence process should be ongoing, as human rights risks evolve and business operations are subject to change.

The commentary situates human rights due diligence within "broader enterprise risk-management systems"[104] of businesses. The concept of risk extends beyond managing material risks to the business enterprise to also include risks posed to human rights. The commentary advises that due diligence be done early

[98] *Id.* at 15 (Principle 15).
[99] *Id.*
[100] *Id.* at 16 (Principle 16, Commentary).
[101] *Id.* (Principle 15, Commentary).
[102] *Id.* at 16 (Principle 17).
[103] *Id.*
[104] *Id.* (Principle 17, Commentary).

in the development of a new business operation or relationship in order to reduce human rights risks. Significantly, the commentary on due diligence also considers questions of complicity and standards for aiding and abetting crimes. In essence, the commentary presents due diligence as insurance in the best interest of business enterprises, explaining: "Conducting appropriate human rights due diligence should help business enterprises address the risk of legal claims against them by showing that they took every reasonable step to avoid involvement with an alleged human rights abuse."[105]

The first step in due diligence is to conduct a human rights impact assessment. To assess human rights risks, the operational principles advise that business enterprises have a process to identify and evaluate the actual and potential harm that may result from their own activities or business relationships.[106] This process should "[i]nvolve meaningful consultation with potentially affected groups and other relevant stakeholders, as appropriate to the size of the business enterprise and the nature and context of the operation."[107] The commentary recommends that human rights impact assessments be incorporated within other existing processes, such as environmental impact assessments, but using human rights recognized in international law as a point of reference. The information gathered for impact assessments can be used to guide actions to prevent or mitigate human rights abuses. Where a business enterprise is taking action to address abuses, it should track whether the effort is effective by drawing on feedback from affected stakeholders.[108]

The operational principles also pertain to reporting advise business enterprises to be transparent about how they address human rights abuses. In particular, they recommend that where operations present a risk of severe human rights violations, businesses report formally. Communication on rights abuses should be of a "form and frequency that reflect an enterprise's human rights impacts and that are accessible to its intended audiences."[109] The commentary offers: "Independent verification of human rights reporting can strengthen its content and credibility. Sector-specific indicators can provide helpful additional detail."[110]

## 2. Commentary on the Guiding Principles and Critical Assessments

Some business stakeholders have enthusiastically welcomed the Guiding Principles and are working to understand how the Principles will affect them.

[105] *Id.* at 17 (Principle 17, Commentary).
[106] *Id.* (Principle 18).
[107] *Id.*
[108] *Id.* at 19 (Principle 20).
[109] *Id.* at 20 (Principle 21).
[110] *Id.* (Principle 21, Commentary).

However, some human rights campaign groups have expressed disappointment that the Guiding Principles did not go further in creating binding obligations for corporations. These stakeholders maintain that the international community has so far failed to produce a legally binding framework for ensuring accountability and there is a growing literature questioning the potential of the Guiding Principles to promote change.[111] Proponents of the process that generated the Guiding Principles point out that industry's involvement indicates that it is a pragmatic way of addressing the problems that concern campaigners.

Professor Surya Deva has critiqued the process that produced the Guiding Principles as one of "manufacturing consensus by managing objections."[112] He charges that the SRSG "was not very receptive to or tolerant of ideas that ran against his vision of what human rights responsibilities companies should have or how companies should be regulated."[113] According to Deva, the SRSG's adversarial exchanges with NGOs "polarised the debate and had a chilling effect on the possibility of participants holding diverse opinions on contentious issues."[114] He questions the durability of the consensus on the Principles "when deep disagreements remain on critical key issues."[115]

## III. Putting Principles into Practice

The UN Guiding Principles have gained an impressive following. In addition to being incorporated into the latest revisions to the OECD Guidelines for Multinational Enterprises, the Guiding Principles have been incorporated into the guidance materials of the International Finance Corporation's (IFC's) Performance Standards. The IFC Standards guide the institution's lending determinations. Some states that are home to TNCs are developing national action plans to put the principles into practice. The Principles have been embraced by the IPIECA, the global oil and gas industry association for advancing environmental and social performance, and the International Council on Mining

[111] *Joint Civil Society Statement on the draft Guiding Principles on Business and Human Rights*, FIDH-Worldwide Human Rights Movement (Jan. 31, 2011), http://www.fidh.org/Joint-Civil-Society-Statement-on,9066; *see also* Radu Mares, *A Gap in the Corporate Responsibility to Respect Human Rights*, 36 Monash U. L. Rev. 33, 45 (2010); Tara J. Melish & Errol Meidinger, *Protect, Respect, Remedy and Participate: "New Governance" Lessons for the Ruggie Framework* in The UN Guiding Principles on Business and Human Rights: Foundations and Implementation 311 (Radu Mares ed. 2012); *Justine Nolan, Mapping the Movement: The Business and Human Rights Regulatory Framework* in Business and Human Rights: From Principles to Practice (Justine Nolan & Dorothée Baumann-Pauly, eds. 2016).

[112] Surya Deva, *Treating Human Rights Lightly: A Critique of the Consensus Rhetoric and the Language Employed by the Guiding Principles*, in Human Rights Obligations of Business: Beyond the Corporate Responsibility to Respect? 78, 89 (Surya Deva & David Bilchitz eds., 2013).

[113] *Id.* at 89.

[114] *Id.*

[115] *Id.* at 88.

and Metals. These major trade associations for the oil and mining industries—historically industries that have been the subject of criticism from rights campaigners—have pledged to promote the UNGPs.

The influence of the UNGPs appears to be increasing, in large measure because of the efforts of the UN Working Group on Business and Human Rights and norm entrepreneurs working to create indicators and assessment tools. The adoption of a "principled pragmatism" is driving much of the agenda. The "responsibility to respect" is well on the way to becoming entrenched if adopted by influential business enterprises.

I have conducted ethnographic research at the UN Annual Forum on Business and Human Rights since its inception in 2012, and I have interviewed participating stakeholders. My impressions of the potential strength of international instruments to encourage TNCs to protect human rights are sketched in the following.

## A. The Work of the UN Working Group on Business and Human Rights

At the conclusion of the SRSG's mandate, the Human Rights Council established the Working Group on the Issue of Human Rights and Transnational Corporations and Other Business Enterprises.[116] The Council acknowledged that national legislation would "contribute to the promotion, protection and fulfillment of and respect for human rights and assist in channeling the benefits of business towards contributing to the enjoyment of human rights and fundamental freedoms" but expressed concern that "weak national legislation and implementation cannot mitigate the negative impact of globalization on vulnerable economies."[117] Accordingly, the Council concluded that efforts to bridge governance gaps at the national, regional, and international levels should continue building upon the Guiding Principles "without foreclosing any other long-term development, including further enhancement of standards."[118] Finally, the Council emphasized "the importance of multi-stakeholder dialogue and analysis to maintain and build on the results achieved to date and to inform further deliberations" on business and human rights.[119] These aims continue to shape the agenda of the UN Working Group on Business and Human Rights.

[116] UN Human Rights Council (HRC), *Human rights and transnational corporations and other business enterprises*, A/HRC/RES/17/4 para. 6 (July 6, 2011).
[117] *Id.* at Preamble.
[118] *Id.* at para. 4.
[119] *Id.* at para. 5.

The Human Rights Council constituted the Working Group to consist of five independent experts to be appointed by the Council, with balanced geographical representation, for an initial term of three years. The Working Group is to report annually to the UN Human Rights Council and the UN General Assembly. In the same resolution, the Council established the UN Forum on Business and Human Rights. The Forum is hosted by the Working Group to provide a place for public discourse on trends and challenges in the implementation of the UNGPs and to promote dialogue and cooperation.

## B. Promoting Principles: The UN Forum on Business and Human Rights

The annual Forum on Business and Human Rights brings together various stakeholder constituencies to address pressing business and human rights issues. For instance, the UN Working Group hosted a special session for industry at the 2013 Forum in Geneva to discuss the challenges of putting the Guiding Principles into practice. Representatives of the business community discussed the difference the Principles were making in how they were doing business. Among the issues participants deemed important were effective engagement with external stakeholders and efforts to build a case within corporations for the responsibility to respect human rights. The role of government in promoting human rights was also discussed.

With respect to the influence of the Guiding Principles on business practices, an apparel industry representative shared: "It brought us to thinking about things beyond labor rights, which is, of course, core for us, but the Guiding Principles take on more rights and is more holistic. We are moving from a risk-based to a rights-based impact assessment approach, but it is important to change company mindset. We are using it to transform mindsets."[120] For another participant, the Principles were not "a stretch" since the Principles incorporated concepts already covered by other familiar instruments. On the decision to devote time to putting the principles into practice within the business, this participant shared: "The alignment with the OECD was a driver for us. Our lawyers say it would be prudent to treat this as hard law. So maybe there is not the same reputation risk as violating a law, but the legal department decided that is how to treat it for now."[121]

Putting the principles into practice for many large companies has involved assessing impacts, forming committees to address issues, and figuring out how

[120] Human Rights Council, A/HCR/FBHR/2013/CRP.1/Rev.1 (Dec. 2, 2013); Apparel Industry Representative, UN Forum on Business and Human Rights (Dec. 3–4, 2013).

[121] Human Rights Council, A/HCR/FBHR/2013/CRP.1/Rev.1 (Dec. 2, 2013); Apparel Industry Representative 1, UN Forum on Business and Human Rights (Dec. 3–4, 2013).

to integrate the issue of human rights into existing systems. A representative of a food company shared its successes and offered advice: "First, what do human rights mean for you? We did a gap analysis, then we built out an eight-step process. Yes, it is a journey. It takes time, and you need support at the highest level to be successful."[122] A business industry association representative explained: "We're absorbed with figuring out how to get this integrated into our current systems. [Activists] think things have gone, dark but things are going on. We care about consumer protection and security. We are looking at what we can talk about. It is hard to talk publicly. You have to have information, and people don't want to say we're only halfway there."[123] A representative of the oil and mining industries observed: "We are looking at a more integrated approach to these issues. We have an internal working group with a steering committee."[124]

Some business representatives in attendance shared the view that the task of addressing human rights was not easy. An extractive industry representative expressed frustration that the company's operating constraints were misunderstood despite efforts to address issues: "We have a steering committee. It supervised an external gap analysis. The gap analysis told us what we have, what is good, what we need to do to address the gaps and create cohesion. We knew of the security problems. It is a journey. We're not there yet. Externally it is hard to see, [so the activists think,] 'You have so much money. Surely you can do this.' Because we're so big, it is hard for us."[125]

A representative of a technology firm with a respected corporate citizenship program in place well before the Guiding Principles were drafted discussed the power of technology to promote human rights and shared that his company's approach to rights was therefore "business-led and business-driven."[126] Still, he echoed the sentiment of many others on the difficulty of the task ahead: "Our privacy and terms of use are posted but could be clearer. Parts of our due diligence are integrated, but others are only ad hoc. We are making progress, but it is hard work. I have found it takes cooperation, the support of senior management . . . patience and time."[127]

[122] Human Rights Council, A/HCR/FBHR/2013/CRP.1/Rev.1 (Dec. 2, 2013); Food Company Representative, UN Forum on Business and Human Rights (Dec. 3–4, 2013).

[123] Human Rights Council, A/HCR/FBHR/2013/CRP.1/Rev.1 (Dec. 2, 2013); Business Industry Association Representative, UN Forum on Business and Human Rights (Dec. 3–4, 2013).

[124] Human Rights Council, A/HCR/FBHR/2013/CRP.1/Rev.1 (Dec. 2, 2013); Oil and Mining Industry Representative, UN Forum on Business and Human Rights (Dec. 3–4, 2013).

[125] Human Rights Council, A/HCR/FBHR/2013/CRP.1/Rev.1 (Dec. 2, 2013); Extractive Industry Representative, UN Forum on Business and Human Rights (Dec. 3–4, 2013).

[126] Human Rights Council, A/HCR/FBHR/2013/CRP.1/Rev.1 (Dec. 2, 2013); Technology Industry Representative, UN Forum on Business and Human Rights (Dec. 3–4, 2013).

[127] Human Rights Council, A/HCR/FBHR/2013/CRP.1/Rev.1 (Dec. 2, 2013); Technology Industry Representative, UN Forum on Business and Human Rights (Dec. 3–4, 2013).

Business participants were less forthcoming in response to questions concerning the ways in which they were exercising leverage with their business partners and in their business relationships to ensure respect for human rights, but they did discuss engagement with external stakeholders and offered different strategies. Some participants shared how dealing with external requests for information can raise the profile of human rights issues. For example, discussing requests for information received from investors an extractive sector representative shared: "[Q]uestions are helpful because it gives me internal leverage to make reform proposals."[128] Another participant complained about addressing requests for information from investors: "It is an inefficient system, an imposition. It can't be efficient to answer each request, but we have to take the time."[129]

Providing adequate responses to requests for information about human rights performance from investors and consumers remained a challenge for many participants in the discussion. A representative of a multinational consumer products firm explained that requests from investors was his company's primary concern: "[T]he socially responsible investor requests—if I give information to one in response to a request, should I give the same information to all investors? Now we are putting the information being asked for into our sustainability reports."[130] Another extractive sector representative expressed concerns about sharing information without a clear obligation to report, explaining: "I find that legal wants to know whether policies are being fully implemented. If not, they say don't say anything. The most challenging chapter of our [sustainability] report to write was the one on human rights because you have to balance how to talk about it without causing concern across different constituencies within the company."[131]

In addition to addressing how to respond to external requests for information, participants explored the potential of partnerships and multistakeholder initiatives. With respect to engaging external stakeholders as partners, a representative of an oil and gas company explained: "It is hard to find human rights NGOs to help with any sort of risk management experience. It is hard to find human rights NGOs with a business approach to this as opposed to advocacy on their specific topic."[132] Another extractives sector representative

[128] Human Rights Council, A/HCR/FBHR/2013/CRP.1/Rev.1 (Dec. 2, 2013); Extractive Industry Representative 1, UN Forum on Business and Human Rights (Dec. 3–4, 2013).

[129] Human Rights Council, A/HCR/FBHR/2013/CRP.1/Rev.1 (Dec. 2, 2013); Participant, UN Forum on Business and Human Rights (Dec. 3–4, 2013).

[130] Human Rights Council, A/HCR/FBHR/2013/CRP.1/Rev.1 (Dec. 2, 2013); Representative from a Multinational Consumer Products Firm, UN Forum on Business and Human Rights (Dec. 3–4, 2013).

[131] Human Rights Council, A/HCR/FBHR/2013/CRP.1/Rev.1 (Dec. 2, 2013); Extractive Industry Representative 2, UN Forum on Business and Human Rights (Dec. 3–4, 2013).

[132] Human Rights Council, A/HCR/FBHR/2013/CRP.1/Rev.1 (Dec. 2, 2013); Extractive Industry Representative 3, UN Forum on Business and Human Rights (Dec. 3–4, 2013).

complained: "[I]nternational campaign groups, they raise issues we know we had, but they can't help us to solve them."[133] In contrast, a representative of a food and beverage multinational expressed appreciation for external engagement and issues raised by NGOs: "Civil society tells you what is materially important. They can be all over the place at first, but gradually they do zoom in on what matters to them and where, and then you can leverage your operations. They can help you prioritize."[134]

One extractives sector representative shared the lessons of an encounter with an international human rights campaign group:

> We did not seek this out proactively. We were recently the subject of [a human rights NGO] investigation on our resettlement procedures. It was not a nice report for us . . . but they were able to provide us with recommendations instead of just naming and shaming. It was an interesting approach. They were respectful and fact-based—different from other NGOs that just raise allegations based on nothing. It was not secondhand. But we also got our version out. It scares us to death, no doubt of that, but the more we need the social license to operate, we are not ignoring these reports. We are not callous, but we face complexity in these regions, in these remote areas where rights have not been fulfilled by government. We face different difficult situations and gray areas. We need systemic, cross-sector approaches.[135]

Another extractives sector representative shared: "We do a lot that we don't say on human rights, but the community is engaged and we now have an independent civil society panel of review. They give us information on how bad or well we are doing. They write reports. We respond. While we were building a pipeline, [a human rights NGO] trained the community surrounding it to be witnesses and to monitors. We get a formal second look. We value civil society. We are civil society. Engagement helps us understand our impacts."[136]

Finally, considering what the business community should seek from government, a representative of a multinational consumer products corporation offered that government must "enforce and make laws," explaining "it is a problem for business that we are paying an auditing cottage industry. What if that were done by member states? We supplement states by paying consultants to conduct audits

[133] Human Rights Council, A/HCR/FBHR/2013/CRP.1/Rev.1 (Dec. 2, 2013); Extractive Industry Representative 4, UN Forum on Business and Human Rights (Dec. 3–4, 2013).

[134] Human Rights Council, A/HCR/FBHR/2013/CRP.1/Rev.1 (Dec. 2, 2013); Representative of a Multinational Food and Beverage Firm, UN Forum on Business and Human Rights (Dec. 3–4, 2013).

[135] Human Rights Council, A/HCR/FBHR/2013/CRP.1/Rev.1 (Dec. 2, 2013); Extractive Industry Representative 5, UN Forum on Business and Human Rights (Dec. 3–4, 2013).

[136] Human Rights Council, A/HCR/FBHR/2013/CRP.1/Rev.1 (Dec. 2, 2013); Extractive Industry Representative 6, UN Forum on Business and Human Rights (Dec. 3–4, 2013).

of ourselves. Properly, this is an enforcement matter and a government obligation."[137] He also remarked that government could be making better laws on transparency: "I know this will be controversial, but transparency in communicating our rights impacts is important. We have to come to accept it is coming. Government can help level the playing field in that."[138] Another participant clearly skeptical of government intervention warned: "Be careful what you ask for."[139]

At least some businesses at the UN Forum indicated an intention to treat the Guiding Principles as imperatives. Because the Guiding Principles borrow from concepts of CSR and situate the risk management strategies of due diligence and impact assessments in the context of a global human rights instrument, they could become a legal compliance concern.

My empirical assessment of the panel and presentation topics from the last seven years of the Forum meetings, revealed that between 2012 to 2019 topics related to the corporate responsibility to respect and access to remedy have dominated the discussion. Total mentions of these topics showed that corporate responsibility and access to remedy received more attention than the state duty to protect human rights.

## IV. Continuity and Change: Accounting for Accountability

A comparison of the concepts contained in instruments across time reveals an evolution of understanding and expectations with respect to the role of transnational corporations in society. At different points, the debate fluctuates between whether to impose binding international legal obligations on business enterprises or whether to invite business enterprises to come into compliance with principles that do not have the status of binding legal obligations. The Guiding Principles were an attempt to move beyond this binary. Despite fluctuations back and forth in policy debates, a review of the data demonstrates that there has been forward movement. The rhetoric of human rights and corporate responsibility is becoming increasingly integrated in the global policy arena.

[137] Human Rights Council, A/HCR/FBHR/2013/CRP.1/Rev.1 (Dec. 2, 2013); Representative from a Multinational Consumer Products Firm, UN Forum on Business and Human Rights (Dec. 3–4, 2013).

[138] Human Rights Council, A/HCR/FBHR/2013/CRP.1/Rev.1 (Dec. 2, 2013); Representative from a Multinational Consumer Products Firm, UN Forum on Business and Human Rights (Dec. 3–4, 2013).

[139] Human Rights Council, A/HCR/FBHR/2013/CRP.1/Rev.1 (Dec. 2, 2013); Participant 1, UN Forum on Business and Human Rights (Dec. 3–4, 2013).

This development could allow more room for rights to be discussed in corporate boardrooms. It could also allow for important concerns to become lost in translation.

While the dominant policy discourse set by the Guiding Principles process has detractors for directing the debate away from achieving a binding international accord on corporate accountability for human rights violations, my qualitative empirical research reveals that this approach holds promise to promote change, more so perhaps than another binding human rights international instrument. For example, the corporate "responsibility to respect" increasingly is being seen by business enterprises as an imperative, even though it is currently enshrined in a nonbinding international instrument. Further, evidence suggests that the concepts captured in the Guiding Principles are finding a way to inform existing legal concepts that could lead to greater accountability for abuses attributable to business enterprises, as with the required standard of care in negligence, for example.

The Guiding Principles do carry forward concepts from the earlier initiatives opposed by business community stakeholders. For instance, like the UN Draft Norms, the Guiding Principles reaffirmed the primacy of state responsibility for human rights protection. The Guiding Principles do not provide a detailed list of international instruments, as do the Norms, but they still manage to be rooted in human rights by referencing the International Bill of Rights. Indeed, interviews with business community stakeholders reveal that the reference to these standards has lent the Principles legitimacy among the business constituency and created a demand for ways to document progress on the Principles. However, businesses that believe the Principles will forever end talk of a binding treaty among activists are likely to be disappointed. Projections on the part of some business stakeholders that "adversarial activists will become allies" are similarly overoptimistic. The debate over the meaning of the business "responsibility to respect" will continue until remedy is more readily available for victims of rights violations.

Where the Guiding Principles perhaps make the most significant contribution is in providing business with basic tools to take on human rights issues by framing them as risks to business enterprises and reframing routine business processes such as due diligence and impact assessments in ways that incorporate human rights. The Guiding Principles appear to be succeeding where other initiatives have failed because the preparatory processes that resulted in the final text included business and translates human rights into the terms and technologies of risk management that business enterprises understand. Some commentators have suggested that the interests of business were perhaps too influential in the process that created the text. Whether the Guiding Principles are integrating the rhetoric of human rights into the process of CSR or the other way around, the text brings two languages into the conversation.

Certain common concepts advanced to define elements of corporate responsibility across international initiatives have persisted over time. For the purpose of protecting human rights, perhaps most significant among these concepts are transparency and the scope of CSR. Themes have traveled across time in the debate to develop international instruments to address private commercial power. These recurring concepts, referenced frequently by stakeholders, include respect, credibility, legitimacy, risk, measures and metrics, disclosures, reporting, and relationships and trust.

By placing these emerging policy developments in a broader context of earlier debates, we see a shift not just in the content of international policies but also in a process of changing conceptions of responsibility and what actors assume them when operating globally. We see an expanded range of relevant constituencies and an expanded understanding of the way transnational regulation could work to end abuses. There is also greater policy reinforcement across soft law instruments created through UN institutions.

Where the Guiding Principles set forth a minimum standard, participants in the Global Compact have committed to strive for more than the minimum. For example, while the Guiding Principles speak of undertaking efforts to avoid violations, the Compact speaks of undertaking efforts to advance the realization of human rights.[140] Perhaps for this reason, the Global Compact publications continue to refer to companies possessing "spheres of influence,"[141] a term rejected by the Guiding Principles in favor of the term "leverage." However, because the Compact predated the Guiding Principles, Compact materials are being updated to better reflect the Guiding Principles.[142] The processes and priorities of each are different but complementary: the Guiding Principles and the Compact are part of a wider process within the United Nations to secure business engagement with human rights.[143]

While it is early to assess the likelihood of its success, the Guiding Principles provide a salient starting point from which to advance human rights and to put the issue of business practices that impair the enjoyment of human rights on the

[140] *The UN Guiding Principles on Business and Human Rights: Relationship to UN Global Compact Commitments* (July 2011), http://www.unglobalcompact.org/docs/issues_doc/human_rights/Resources/GPs_GC%20note.pdf (describing the Guiding Principles as providing "further conceptual and operational clarity" for Principle 1 and Principle 2 of the Global Compact), http://www.unglobalcompact.org/docs/issues_doc/human_rights/Resources/GPs_GC%20note.pdf.

[141] UN Global Compact brochure, *available at* http://www.unglobalcompact.org/docs/news_events/8.1/GC_brochure_FINAL.pdf.

[142] E-mail from Michael Addo, member of the UN Working Group on Business and Human Rights, Special Procedures of the UN Human Rights Council to Erika George, Professor of Law, University of Utah, S.J. Quinney College of Law (June 6, 2013) (on file with author).

[143] *See generally Guiding principles on business and human rights*, United Nations Global Compact (July 2011) (explaining that the UN Guiding Principles "reinforce the Global Compact and provide an authoritative framework for participants in implementing this commitment" to "respect human rights.").

agenda of the business community in ways that have to date eluded conventional human rights advocacy strategies calling for binding global regulations.

It was the work of civil society movements that placed business and human rights on the global policy agenda. Nongovernmental human rights groups and faith-based organizations in cooperation with affected communities have worked to raise awareness of the impact of business on human rights. Despite the disappointment of many, it remains the case that their efforts resulted in the adoption of a soft law standard to provide an authoritative framework for stakeholder convergence on the responsibility of business with respect to human rights as distinct from those of sovereign states.

A review of the UN documents reveals an evolving understanding of corporate obligations and roles in global society. The metaphors used to describe the problem are sometimes recurring. The terms that turn up in the debates change, but concerns have remained fairly consistent, as has the resistance to binding standards to regulate corporate conduct. Each iteration of policy had its constituency of opponents and its constituency of proponents.

What distinguishes the present from the past? Why predict success? There are new technologies of law that make compliance with a soft law standard more likely, such as indicators and increasing access to information about abuses implicating private industry. There are opportunities to regulate outside of legal standards and extend a business ethic that reaches further than efforts to enforce human rights law can, provided business enterprises incorporate rights. Increasingly, it will be risky for business enterprises to fail to do so. One development that may make this iteration of efforts different is the convening work of the UN Working Group on Business and Human Rights. Another development is the renewed pressure to promulgate a binding international instrument to regulate global business.

## A. Treaty Talks

In 2014, the Human Rights Council accepted a resolution drafted by Ecuador and South Africa that sought to establish a binding international instrument. The resolution, titled "Elaboration of an Internationally Legally Binding Instrument on Transnational Corporations and Other Business Enterprises with Respect to Human Rights" (the Treaty Resolution), put forward by Bolivia, Cuba, Ecuador, South Africa, and Venezuela for consideration by the Human Rights Council establishes an "an open-ended intergovernmental working group on a legally binding instrument on transnational corporations."[144]

[144] UN Human Rights Council (HRC), *Elaboration of an international legally binding instrument on transnational corporations and other business enterprises with respect to human rights*, A/HRC/

The Council divided on the question of working toward the creation of an internationally binding instrument but not along conventional lines of the "Global North" and the "Global South." The measure was adopted on June 26, 2014, by a majority vote, with twenty votes in support (Algeria, Benin, Burkina Faso, China, the Republic of the Congo, Côte d'Ivoire, Cuba, Ethiopia, India, Indonesia, Kazakhstan, Kenya, Morocco, Namibia, Pakistan, Philippines, Russia, South Africa, Venezuela, and Vietnam), fourteen opposed (Austria, Czech Republic, Estonia, France, Germany, Ireland, Italy, Japan, Montenegro, South Korea, Romania, the former Yugoslavia, the United Kingdom, and the United States), and thirteen abstentions (Argentina, Botswana, Brazil, Chile, Costa Rica, Gabon, Kuwait, Maldives, Mexico, Peru, Saudi Arabia, Sierra Leone, and the United Arab Emirates).

The Elaboration acknowledged the progressive developments in addressing human rights abuse due to transnational corporations to date. Indeed, it reaffirms the SRSG's "Protect, Respect and Remedy" Framework to the extent that it adopts the allocation of responsibilities offered in the "protect" and "respect" pillars set by the UN Framework in its preamble:

> *Stressing* that the obligations and primary responsibility to promote and protect human rights and fundamental freedoms lie with the State, and that States must protect against human rights abuse within their territory and/or jurisdiction by third parties, including transnational corporations, *Emphasizing* that transnational corporations and other business enterprises have a responsibility to respect human rights.[145]

The Treaty Resolution was not unproblematic on its own terms. For example, it addressed only "business enterprises that have a transnational character in their operational activities, and does not apply to local businesses registered in terms of relevant domestic law." This limitation could be a step back from the Guiding Principles, which take into account the risk of harm any commercial enterprise, no matter the size or location, can inflict on human rights.

Professor John Ruggie has cautioned that "the key challenges for the treaty sponsors are a weak political mandate, the proposed treaty's unworkable scope and scale and the sponsors' as well as many supporters' own record with regard to the UN Guiding Principles on Business and Human Rights."[146]

26/L.22/REV.1 para. 6 (June 25, 2014); *see generally* BUILDING A TREATY ON BUSINESS AND HUMAN RIGHTS: CONTEXT AND CONTOURS (Surya Deva & David Bilchitz eds., 2017) (discussing the legal and political challenges of the treaty process and offering substantive proposals).

[145] *Id.* at Preamble.

[146] John Ruggie, *Quo Vadis? Unsolicited Advice to Business and Human Rights Treaty Sponsors*, INST. FOR HUMAN RIGHTS AND BUSINESS (Sept. 9, 2014), https://www.ihrb.org/other/treaty-on-business-human-rights/quo-vadis-unsolicited-advice-to-business-and-human-rights-treaty-sponsors. *See also*

## B. The Zero Draft

On July 16, 2018, pursuant to Human Rights Council Resolution 29/9, the Intergovernmental Working Group released the "Zero Draft" of a "Legally Binding Instrument to Regulate, In International Human Rights Law, The Activities of Transnational Corporations and Other Business Enterprises." The preamble provides: "[E]very person has a right to equal and effective access to justice and remedies in the case of risk of harm or decisive enjoyment of their human rights."[147] Access to remedy was the primary impetus for crafting a legally binding instrument. Rights activists have argued that the nonbinding UN Guiding Principles were simply not sufficient to ensure victims of violations involving business enterprises were made whole, despite acknowledging access to remedy as one of three foundational pillars. Not surprisingly, the Zero Draft places strong emphasis on "effective access to justice and remedy to victims of human rights violations in the context of business activities of transnational character, and to prevent the occurrence of such violations."[148]

The Zero Draft does reflect concepts set forth in previous iterations of policy documents addressing business and human rights challenges. For example, the Zero Draft uses language on the state responsibility to protect mirroring Pillar I of the UNGPs.[149] The Zero Draft also picks up language on the responsibility of businesses to respect human rights.[150] Building upon these two foundational principles the Zero Draft seeks to "strengthen the respect, promotion, protection and fulfilment of human rights in the context of business activities of transnational character."[151] The instrument is intended to "apply to human rights violations in the context of any business activity of a transnational character."[152] It recognizes "all international human rights and those rights recognized under domestic law."[153]

Ten Key Proposals for the Treaty, ESCR-Net and FIDH (Oct. 2016), https://www.escr-net.org/sites/default/files/attachments/tenkeyproposals_final.pdf.; Douglass Cassel & Anita Ramasastry, *Options for a Treaty on Business and Human Rights* (White Paper, May 2015); email from Ariel Meyerstein, to author (July 20, 2015, 12:24 PM MST) (updating on the first session of the Open-Ended Intergovernmental Working Group on a Binding Instrument on Transnational Corporations and Human Rights) (on file with author); Arvind Ganesan, *Towards a Business and Human Rights Treaty* in BUSINESS AND HUMAN RIGHTS: FROM PRINCIPLES TO PRACTICE (Justine Nolan & Dorothée Baumann-Pauly, eds. 2016).

[147] UN Human Rights Council (HRC), *Legally Binding Instrument to Regulate, In International Human Rights Law, The Activities of Transnational Corporations and Other Business Enterprises*, art. 1 (July 16, 2018) [hereinafter *Zero Draft*].

[148] *Id.* at art. 2.

[149] *Id.* at art. 1.

[150] *Id.*

[151] *Id.* at art. 2.

[152] *Id.* at art. 3, para. 1.

[153] *Zero Draft*, *supra* note 147, at art. 3, para. 2.

The Zero Draft's three-part structure contains fifteen articles. Section I contains the preamble and a statement of purpose. Section II is the substantive section that set forth the scope of the instrument[154] and defines terms.[155] Section II addresses procedural concerns and provides the parameters for the exercise of jurisdiction,[156] statutory limitations on actions,[157] and applicable choice of law.[158] Provisions on the rights of victims,[159] prevention,[160] legal liability,[161] mutual legal assistance,[162] and international cooperation[163] are also included in Section II. Section III outlines the institutional arrangements for implementing the instrument and calls for the creation of an oversight committee.[164] State parties are to take all legislative, administrative, and monitoring actions necessary to ensure effective implementation of the proposed obligations contained in the instrument.[165]

Significantly, Section II also contains a dedicated provision on the rights of victims.[166] The Zero Draft discussion differs for the UNGPs in several significant ways.

The provisions that pertain to prevention of rights violations reflect strategies also set forth in the UNGPs, such as conducting due diligence to assess the impact of business activities on human rights.[167] Significantly, the Zero Draft states that state parties are responsible for ensuring that domestic legislation require businesses to conduct human rights due diligence, conduct human rights impact assessments, and consider risks associated with business activities.

Reporting requirements are also addressed. The prevention provisions of the Zero Draft call for reporting "publicly and periodically on non-financial matters, including at a minimum environmental and human rights matters, including policies, risks, outcomes and indicators. The requirement to disclose this information should be subject to an assessment of the severity of the potential impacts on the individuals and communities concerned, not to a consideration of their materiality to the financial interests of the business or its shareholders."[168] Prevention appears to call for bringing the entire length of a supply chain into

154 *Id.* at art. 3.
155 *Id.* at art. 4.
156 *Id.* at art. 5.
157 *Id.* at art. 6.
158 *Id.* at art. 7.
159 *Zero Draft*, *supra* note 147, at art. 8.
160 *Id.* at art. 9.
161 *Id.* at art. 10.
162 *Id.* at art. 11.
163 *Id.* at art. 12.
164 *Zero Draft*, *supra* note 147, at art. 14.
165 *Id.* at art. 15.
166 *Id.* at art. 8.
167 *Compare id.* at art. 9, *with Guiding Principle* 17.
168 *Id.* at art. 9.

compliance with international human rights standards and contributing to the costs of preventing violations.[169]

Unlike the UNGPs, the Zero Draft makes clear that legal liability must extend to corporations. It calls on state parties to "ensure through their domestic law that natural *and* legal persons may be held criminally, civil [*sic*] or administratively liable for violations of human rights undertaken in the context of business activities of transnational character. Such liability shall be subject to effective, proportionate, and dissuasive criminal and non-criminal sanctions, including monetary sanctions."[170] Entities or individuals found liable are to provide reparation/pay damages to victims or to compensate states for the cost of providing redress to victims.[171]

## V. Incorporating Rights

This chapter traced the trajectory of international policy initiatives that have attempted to regulate the role of business enterprise in global affairs. The endorsement of the UN Framework and Guiding Principles on Business and Human Rights, which seek to translate human rights issues into corporate responsibility imperatives, is the latest effort in a long trajectory. Based on my analysis of primary UN documents and commentaries; my interviews with different stakeholder constituencies in the policymaking process, including corporate representatives and rights activists; ethnographic research, including participation in and observations of the annual proceedings of the UN Forum on Business and Human Rights; and interviews with members of the UN Working Group on Business, I believe the UNGPs will prove to make progress where earlier efforts failed. While the consensus formed around the UNGPs has frayed due in large part to continued failures secure remedy for victims of violations, certain important aspects of the Framework appear to be gaining traction as authoritative among those stakeholders best situated to address or avoid human rights abuses: business enterprises.

The push for a binding instrument calls into question whether the UN Guiding Principles are truly the end of the beginning or the beginning of the end of aspirational instruments that are advanced without strong mechanisms for holding corporate actors accountable for abuses. Like the last effort to create binding obligations for business enterprises before it, the Draft Norms, the Treaty Resolution has already drawn objections from powerful private commercial

169 *Zero Draft*, *supra* note 147, at art. 9, para. 2(c).
170 *Id.* at art. 10, para. 1.
171 *Id.* at art. 10, para. 3. A Second Revised Draft was presented by the Intergovernmental Working Group in June 2020.

interests and the countries in which they are incorporated. The momentum of the Guiding Principles is unlikely to be derailed by the pending treaty proposal.

Having observed and participated in each annual UN Forum on Business and Human Rights, I can say that a renewed effort to advance a binding instrument does not come as a complete surprise. While business stakeholders share strategies for developing impact assessments and due diligence programs, the concerns articulated by human rights and labor NGOs have centered on the third pillar of the Framework: access to remedy.

Global policy initiatives provide fertile ground for growth and, if taken seriously, could help the emerging global regulatory ecosystem evolve in a manner that gives meaning to the recognized business responsibility to respect human rights. The next chapter considers how policies and standards continue to emerge from initiatives that bring together different stakeholders from the business community to rights campaigners to determine how best to advance respect for human rights in particular industry sectors.

# 3
# Human Rights Conflicts and the Creation of Corporate Responsibility Collaborations

## Introduction

This chapter provides comparative accounts of the creation of industry sector-specific voluntary regulatory instruments and governance institutions. After allegations of corporate complicity in human rights abuses or conflicts with concerned constituencies and affected communities, in some instances initiatives have been undertaken by a diverse range of stakeholders to address the underlying human rights challenges.

This chapter considers examples of human rights abuses involving corporations that have often originated in emerging market economies and complex operating environments. I compare the advocacy strategies of human rights activists and responses to rights campaigns. Cases studied include: (1) the controversial role of transnational corporations in the internet communications technology (ICT) sector in censorship and surveillance practices and the risks presented to the right to freedom of expression and the right to privacy; (2) the labor conditions and risks to the health and safety of factory workers; and (3) the relationship of transnational corporations in the extractives sector to human rights and the risks presented to the environment and human security when extractive sector companies contract with security forces that have abused the use of force and used deadly force to protect property and to quiet critics.

The chapter also explains how conflicts over corporate complicity in alleged abuses served to catalyze the creation of the different industry-specific multistakeholder initiatives designed to prevent problems including: the Global Network Initiative, a private multistakeholder project to promote more responsible business practices; the Fair Labor Association, a multistakeholder collaboration to end abusive labor conditions; and the Voluntary Principles on Security and Human Rights, a tripartite multistakeholder initiative to address security and human rights. This chapter will show that human rights advocacy has served as a catalyst for change, resulting in the creation of institutional mechanisms to ensure sustained change and continuous improvement. The business community

*Incorporating Rights.* Erika George, Oxford University Press. © Erika George 2021.
DOI: 10.1093/oso/9780199941483.003.0004

and concerned constituencies should use multi-stakeholder initiatives as a means by which to learn, to lead, and to change business as usual.

## I. Conflict: Rights and Risks

Certain industries are by their very nature inextricably intertwined with the realization of certain rights in our modern era of a globalized economy. For example, the right to health relies on access to medicine. Pharmaceutical firms play a significant role in making new medicines after years of research and development. Companies in the ICT industry sector are instrumental in facilitating access to information, amplifying expression, and increasing the exchange of ideas. The fundamental right to freedom of expression relies on the dissemination of information and ideas enhanced by social media and new information technologies. Energy exploration enables economic development in some regions and can contribute to the eradication of poverty when responsibly managed. Millions of people are fed and clothed due to modern methods of mass production in agriculture and apparel. While business enterprises can often enhance the realization of a range of human rights, certain business activities can on occasion pose risks to human rights. In certain industry sectors commercial activities have come into conflict with human rights. Efforts to collaborate to resolve these conflicts and create shared solutions have emerged as a result of stakeholder engagement.

### A. Civil and Political Rights: Freedom of Expression, Public Participation, and the Internet Communications Technology Industry

International human rights law protects the rights of people to exchange ideas and information as freedom of expression. Expression is central to both individual human development and flourishing and democratic institutions and systems of governance. Protecting freedom of expression can serve to promote both civil liberties and open societies. The 1948 Universal Declaration of Human Rights (UDHR) provides: "[e]veryone has the right to freedom of opinion and expression; this right includes freedom to hold opinions without interference and to seek, receive and impart information and ideas through any media regardless of frontiers."[1] Article 19 of the International Covenant on Civil and Political Rights (ICCPR) also protects access to information through recognizing

[1] G.A. Res. 217 (III) A, Universal Declaration of Human Rights (Dec. 10, 1948) [hereinafter UDHR].

the rights to seek and receive information.[2] Freedom of expression encompasses not only the freedom to speak and share information but also the freedom to seek and receive information across all borders through any form of medium—including social media.[3]

Certain restrictions on expression are allowed under international human rights law because the right is also understood to exist in relationship to responsibilities. For example, the Human Rights Committee, the global body that interprets and monitors the ICCPR, has determined that restrictions on the right to expression are permitted to protect the rights or reputation of other individuals or to protect public order or national security. While the right to expression is not unlimited, there are limits on how and when governments may limit expression. For example, any government restrictions on expression must be "necessary" to protect the reputational or security interests under threat and must not be arbitrary.[4] Common restrictions on speech around the world include prohibition on expressions that may incite violence, criminal activity, or public panic.[5]

International human rights law also recognizes the importance of privacy for personal development and human dignity. Article 17 of the ICCPR protects the right to privacy and prohibits invasions of privacy that are unlawful or arbitrary.[6] In 2011, the UN Human Rights Committee issued General Comment 34, explaining that in light of new communications technologies, "States parties should take account of the extent to which developments in information and communication technologies, such as internet and mobile based electronic information dissemination systems, have substantially changed communication

[2] International Covenant on Civil and Political Rights (ICCPR) art. 19, Dec. 16, 1966, 999 U.N.T.S. 171. The International Covenant on Civil and Political Rights (the "ICCPR") protects freedom of expression providing, in pertinent part:

1. Everyone shall have the right to hold opinions without interference.
2. Everyone shall have the right to freedom of expression; this right shall include freedom to seek, receive and impart information and ideas of all kinds, regardless of frontiers, either orally, in writing or in print, in the form of art, or through any other media of his choice.
3. The exercise of the rights provided for in paragraph 2 of this article carries with it special duties and responsibilities. It may therefore be subject to certain restrictions, but these shall only be such as are provided by law and are necessary:
   (a) For respect of the rights or reputations of others;
   (b) For the protection of national security or of public order . . . or of public health or morals.

[3] *Id.*

[4] The Human Rights Committee has rejected arguments from states that public order and national security require restrictions on expression absent a showing of risk to security and has found violations of Article 19, where a state party has failed to specify the precise nature of the threat allegedly posed by an individual's exercise of freedom of expression. *See* Joseph at 534 (citing *Kim v. Republic of Korea* 574/94).

[5] SARAH JOSEPH & MELISSA CASTAN, THE INTERNATIONAL COVENANT ON CIVIL AND POLITICAL RIGHTS: CASES, MATERIALS, AND COMMENTARY 530 (2d ed., 2004).

[6] ICCPR, *supra* note 2.

practices around the world."[7] Accordingly, the Committee maintains: "States parties should take all necessary steps to foster the independence of these new media and to ensure access of individuals thereto."[8]

In 2013, the UN General Assembly adopted Resolution 68/167 on the Right to Privacy in the Digital Age, expressing "deep concern at the negative impact that surveillance and interception of communications may have on human rights."[9] Resolution 68/167 affirms that the right to privacy must be protected and respected in digital communications. Resolution 68/167 calls on states to review their laws and policies related to communications surveillance and personal data collection for consistency with their responsibility to protect the right to privacy.

With respect to the specific aspects of privacy relevant to ICT industry, the Committee in General Comment 16 says of data protection:

> The gathering and holding of personal information on computers, databanks and other devices, whether by public authorities or private individuals or bodies, must be regulated by law. Effective measures have to be taken by States to ensure that information concerning a person's private life does not reach the hands of persons who are not authorized by law to receive, process and use it, and is never used for purposes incompatible with the Covenant. In order to have the most effective protection of his private life, every individual should have the right to ascertain in an intelligible form, whether, and if so, what personal data is stored in automatic data files, and for what purposes. Every individual should also be able to ascertain which public [authorities] or private individuals or bodies control or may control their files. If such files contain incorrect personal data or have been collected or processed contrary to the provisions of the law, every individual should have the right to request rectification or elimination.[10]

There is an affirmative obligation on the state to take measures to protect privacy. States are prohibited from invading privacy and also must protect it. With respect to privacy, the Human Rights Committee has explained the right is protected against interference "whether they emanate from State authorities or from natural or legal persons."[11] States must take legislative and other measures to give effect to the protection of privacy rights.

[7] UN Human Rights Committee, *General comment no. 34, Article 19, Freedoms of opinion and expression*, Sept. 12, 2011, CCPR/C/GC/34, https://www.refworld.org/docid/4ed34b562.html.

[8] *Id.*

[9] G.A. Res 68/167, The Right to Privacy in the Digital Age (Dec. 18, 2013).

[10] UN Human Rights Committee, *CCPR General Comment No. 16: Article 17 (Right to Privacy), The Right to Respect of Privacy, Family, Home and Correspondence, and Protection of Honour and Reputation*, Apr. 8, 1988, https://www.refworld.org/docid/453883f922.html.

[11] *Id.*

### 1. Risks to Rights

We live in the Age of Information, where social media can drive social change. Activists around the world are using social media to promote democracy activists and to voice dissent.[12] The internet played an important role in the uprisings of the Arab Spring in 2011 as activists used various forms of new media to register their opposition, organize protests, and expose state abuses.[13] The spread of such uprisings—dubbed "Revolution 2.0" to highlight the importance of new media both in coordinating protesters and in developing social networks and strategies in advance of the uprisings—demonstrates that new media can play a crucial role in empowering pro-democracy protesters to start and sustain their movements.[14]

While several states that are subject to international human rights law engage in censorship and surveillance, China has been credited with having the most sophisticated system of internet controls. The "Great Firewall" of China, like the Great Wall, was erected to protect the country from outside invaders. China blocks most international Web 2.0 technologies, which support social media.[15] China has the world's largest number of internet users and the world's most sophisticated system of internet censorship.

Journalist Shi Tao was burned after he sent information over China's Great Firewall to a US-based pro-democracy publication using his Yahoo! China email account.[16] Within days, the Beijing State Security Bureau presented a Notice of Evidence Collection to Yahoo! China seeking email content, email account registration information, and account login records for Shi Tao's email address.[17] Beijing-based Yahoo! China employees complied without question with the request on the same day State Security requested the information.[18] After a closed trial lasting less than three hours, Shi Tao was found guilty and sentenced to ten years in prison.[19]

Shi Tao was not the only person to be imprisoned in China for expressing a political opinion at odds with the perspective of government.[20] Chinese court documents obtained and disseminated by human rights organizations cited

[12] Erika George, *Corporate Social Responsibility and Social Media Corporations: Incorporating Human Rights Through Rankings, Self-Regulation and Shareholder Resolutions*, 28 DUKE J. COMP. & INT'L L. 521, 523 (2018).

[13] *Id.*

[14] *Id.*

[15] Uyen P. Le, *Online and Linked In: "Public Morals" in the Human Rights and Trade Networks*, 38 N.C. J. INT'L L. & COM. REG. 107, 112 (2012).

[16] *See id.*; Rebecca Mackinnon, *Shi Tao, Yahoo!, and the Lessons for Corporate Social Responsibility* (Dec. 30, 2007) (Working Paper Version 1).

[17] Mackinnon, *supra* note 16.

[18] *Id.*

[19] *Id.*

[20] *Id.*

Yahoo! Holdings as the source of information in the cases of other individuals.[21] Yahoo! was not the only firm aiding China to engage in censorship and surveillance.[22] For example, Cisco sold technology capable of enhancing the surveillance capacity of China's security forces.[23] Still, it was Shi Tao's case and Yahoo!'s conduct that called into question the nature of industry's collaboration with the Chinese government in repressing dissent and opened debate on the responsible course of conduct.[24] His case perhaps more than any other can be credited with making human rights a corporate social responsibility (CSR) priority in the ICT sector after public outcry.[25]

After Reporters Without Borders, a media rights group, released a report on Yahoo!'s connection to Shi Tao's case, the story received concentrated news coverage in the international media. Headlines highlighted the company's role. The *Daily Telegraph* (UK) reported: *Yahoo! Helps China Track Down and Jail Dissident.*[26] The *Financial Times* reported: *Yahoo! Accused of Helping China Convict Journalists.*[27] The *International Herald Tribune* headline read: *Yahoo! Helped Chinese to Prosecute Journalist.*[28] The *New York Times* reported: *Yahoo! Role Documented in Chinese Trial.*[29] The *Wall Street Journal* said: *Yahoo! Arm's Data Helped China Jail Journalist.*[30]

The story remained in the headlines as the company's response to the allegations fell short of the social expectations expressed concerning responsible business conduct. Media headlines implicating the company read: *Yahoo! Admits Role in China Dissident Case,*[31] *Yahoo! Admits Aiding China in Journalist's Conviction,*[32] and *Yahoo! Says It Gave China Internet Data Later Used to Convict Journalist.*[33] After admitting involvement, the company's efforts to explain

[21] *See generally, id.* (addressing the cases of Wang Xiaoning, Li Zhi, and Jiang Lijun).

[22] *Id.*

[23] *Id.*

[24] *Id.*

[25] *Id.*; Le, *supra* note 15, at 146.

[26] Richard Spencer, *Yahoo! "Helps China Track Down and Jail Dissident,"* TELEGRAPH (Sept. 8, 2005 12:01 AM), https://www.telegraph.co.uk/news/worldnews/asia/china/1497942/Yahoo-helps-China-track-down-and-jail-dissident.html.

[27] Mure Dickie & Richard Waters, *Yahoo Accused of Helping China Convict Journalists*, FINANCIAL TIMES (Sept. 7, 2005), https://www.ft.com/content/97ba5be0-1f62-11da-853a-00000e2511c8.

[28] Joseph Kahn, *Yahoo Helped Chinese to Prosecute Journalist*, INTERNATIONAL HERALD TRIBUNE 2005 WLNR 14137330 (Sept. 8, 2005).

[29] Joseph Kahn, *Yahoo Role Documented in Chinese Trial*, N.Y. TIMES (Sept. 8, 2005), https://www.nytimes.com/2005/09/08/technology/yahoo-role-documented-in-chinese-trial.html.

[30] Wall Street Journal Abstracts, Sept. 8, 2005 (US).

[31] Mure Dickie, *Yahoo Admits Role in China Dissident Case*, FINANCIAL TIMES (Sept. 11, 2005), https://www.ft.com/content/13cbc570-22c9-11da-86cc-00000e2511c8.

[32] Peter S. Goodman, *Yahoo! Admits Aiding China in Journalist's Conviction*, MONTEREY COUNTY HERALD, 2005 WLNR 14301715 (Sept. 11, 2005).

[33] Peter S. Goodman, *Yahoo Says It Gave China Internet Data*, WASHINGTON POST (Sept. 11, 2005), https://www.washingtonpost.com/archive/politics/2005/09/11/yahoo-says-it-gave-china-internet-data/af7a59f6-4b67-4458-bd95-9a6b2c5c2c10/.

also made headlines: *Yahoo! "Following Law" in China Internet Case,*[34] *Yahoo! Founder Explains China E-Mail Move,*[35] *Yahoo! Defends E-Mail Tip-Off,*[36] and *Yahoo! Says It Had to Help China Probe Journalist.*[37] Activist reactions to the company's response also received coverage: *Boycott Threat Shames Yahoo!*[38] and *Yahoo! Faces Flack Over Jailed China Journalist.*[39]

Editorials condemning the company's conduct and implicating it in abuse appeared in multiple US and international media outlets in 2005: *Yahoo! Snoop for Beijing,*[40] *Yahoo Feeds Great Firewall of China,*[41] *Yahoo! Chinese Police and a Jailed Journalist*, and *Year of the Rat: Yahoo! Helps China Catch a Journalist.*[42] The issue remained in international news headlines with reports and editorials implicating Yahoo! in human rights abuses recurring almost annually on the anniversary of Shi Tao's imprisonment for the duration of his detention.

It was only a matter of time before the media optic expanded beyond Yahoo! to include criticism of the conduct of other companies in the ICT industry: *Internet Giants Help Serve Oppression,*[43] *A bargain with China's Censors,*[44] *Web Companies Should Be Castigated for Aiding China Oppression,*[45] *U.S. Firms Shouldn't Trade Their Morals to Work in China,*[46] *U.S. Web Firms Aid in Repression Yahoo!, Google, Microsoft Complicit in China's Stranglehold on Information.*[47]

The rhetoric ratcheting up responsibility on the ICT industry to align conduct with respect for rights began to appear in editorials of media outlets, with headlines such as: *Yahoo! Has Power to End Chinese Net Censorship.*[48] Reporting and editorials can be seen as evidence of expectation elevation on the part of a concerned segment of the public interested in expression and data privacy. Concentrated media coverage created attention and need for the industry to

[34] *Yahoo: "Following Law" in China Internet Case*, VOICE OF AMERICA (Oct. 31, 2009 12:34 AM), https://www.voanews.com/archive/yahoo-following-law-china-internet-case.

[35] *Yahoo Founder Explains China E-Mail Move*, TECHWEBNEWS (Sept. 13, 2005).

[36] *Yahoo! Defends E-Mail Tip-Off*, INDEPENDENT (Sept. 12, 2005).

[37] Allen T. Cheng, *Yahoo! Says It Had to Help China Probe Journalist*, BUFFALO NEWS, 2005 WLNR 14624715 (Sept. 11, 2005).

[38] Michael Logan, Bien Perez, & Jamil Anderlini, *Boycott Threat Shames Yahoo*, SOUTH CHINA MORNING POST (Sept. 13, 2005), http://www.scmp.com/print/article/516008/boycott-threat-shamesyahoo.

[39] Mure Dickie & Richard Waters, *Yahoo Faces Flak over Jailed China Journalist*, FINANCIAL TIMES (Sept. 8, 2005).

[40] *Yahoo! Snoop for Beijing*, ST. PETERSBURG TIMES (Sept. 28, 2005) (US).

[41] *Yahoo Feeds Great Firewall of China*, BANGKOK POST (Sept. 20, 2005) (Thailand)

[42] PITTSBURGH POST-GAZETTE (Sept. 19, 2005) (US).

[43] AKRON BEACON JOURNAL (Sept. 18, 2005) (US).

[44] CHICAGO TRIBUNE (Sept. 17, 2005) (US).

[45] L.A. TIMES (Sept. 15 2005) (US).

[46] SAN JOSE MERCURY NEWS (Oct. 2, 2005) (US).

[47] DENVER ROCKY MOUNTAIN NEWS (Sept. 24, 2005) (US).

[48] Danny O'Brien, *Yahoo Has Power to End Chinese Net Censorship*, IRISH TIMES (Sept. 30, 2005), https://www.irishtimes.com/business/yahoo-has-power-to-end-chinese-net-censorship-1.499366.

respond to growing public concern and calls for more responsible responses on the part of internet communications corporations.

## B. Labor Rights: Slavery and Forced Labor in Agriculture, Apparel, and Consumer Electronics

Labor rights in international law include the right to work as well as rights at work.[49] The International Labour Organization's (ILO) Declaration on Fundamental Principles and Rights at Work sets forth the fundamental labor rights that are further specified in eight core ILO Conventions.[50] Freedom of association and effective recognition of the right to collective bargaining are guaranteed by ILO Conventions 87 and 98.[51] The elimination of all forms of forced or compulsory labor and the effective abolition of forced or compulsory labor is required by ILO Conventions 29 and 105.[52] ILO Conventions 138 and 182 mandate the effective abolition of child labor with attention to the worst forms of child labor.[53] ILO Conventions 100 and 111 call for the elimination of discrimination with respect to employment and occupation.[54] These fundamental labor rights also find expression in other international human rights instruments. For example, the freedom of association and the right to collective bargaining are recognized in Article 22 of the ICCPR and in Article 8 of the International Covenant on Economic, Social and Cultural Rights (ICESCR).[55] A call for the elimination of forced or compulsory labor is also contained in Article 8 of the ICCPR's prohibition of slavery and servitude.[56] Article 10 of the ICESCR mandates a minimum working age for children and prohibits employment of children in hazardous

[49] Int'l Labor Org. (ILO), *Declaration on Fundamental Principles and Rights at Work*, 86th Sess., Geneva (June 1998); *see also* Hum. Rts. Watch, *On the Margins of Profit*, Vol. 20, No. 3(G), 32-38 (2008).

[50] Int'l Labor Org. (ILO), *Freedom of Association and Protection of the Right to Organise Convention*, No. 87 (1948); ILO, *Right to Organise and Collective Bargaining Convention*, No. 98 (July 4, 1950); ILO, *Forced Labour Convention*, No. 29 (May 1, 1932); ILO, *Abolition of Forced Labour Convention*, No. 105 (June 25, 1957); ILO, *Minimum Age Convention*, No. 138 (June 26, 1973); ILO, *Worst Forms of Child Labour Convention*, No. 182 (June 17, 1999); ILO, *Equal Remuneration Convention*, No. 100 (June 29, 1951); ILO, *Discrimination (Employment and Occupation) Convention*, No. 111 (June 25, 1958).

[51] ILO, *Freedom of Association and Protection of the Right to Organise Convention*, No. 87 (1948); ILO, *Right to Organise and Collective Bargaining Convention*, No. 98 (July 4, 1950)

[52] ILO, *Forced Labour Convention*, No. 29 (May 1, 1932); ILO, *Abolition of Forced Labour Convention*, No. 105 (June 25, 1957).

[53] ILO, *Minimum Age Convention*, No. 138 (June 26, 1973); ILO, *Worst Forms of Child Labour Convention*, No. 182 (June 17, 1999).

[54] ILO, *Equal Remuneration Convention*, No. 100 (June 29, 1951); ILO, *Discrimination (Employment and Occupation) Convention*, No. 111 (June 25, 1958).

[55] ICCPR, *supra* note 2, at art. 22; International Covenant on Economic, Social and Cultural Rights (ICESCR) art. 8, Dec. 16, 1966, 993 U.N.T.S. 3.

[56] ICCPR, *supra* note 2, at art. 8.

occupations.[57] The elimination of discrimination in pay and compensation as well as the right to just and favorable conditions of employment are stated in Article 7 of the ICESCR.[58]

### 1. Risks to Rights

Human rights and labor rights organizations have documented how business practices and consumption patterns impact the enjoyment of labor rights.[59] Instances of rights abuses involving corporations producing a range of consumer products from the agriculture and apparel industries to the manufacture of consumer electronics have been reported and in some instances litigated. In 2003, students on university campuses across the United States boycotted Coca-Cola to protest the murder of labor union leaders by paramilitaries in Colombia as the company defended a lawsuit brought by survivors.[60] Chiquita confronted similar allegations stemming from conduct in Colombia. In 2005, former child slaves sued Nestle USA for aiding and abetting the human rights violations "through their active involvement in purchasing cocoa from Ivory Coast."[61] Nike was accused of using sweatshop labor in Indonesia. Several popular brands were sourcing labor from Bangladesh when unsafe conditions lead to a building collapse that killed hundreds.[62] Unsafe conditions and abuses have been documented at factories in China supplying Apple.

57 ICESCR, *supra* note 55, at art. 10.

58 *Id.* at art. 7.

59 *See* Brian Stauffer, Human Rights Watch, When We're Dead and Buried, Our Bones Will Keep Hurting – Worker's Rights Under Threat in US Meat and Poultry Plants (2019), https://www.hrw.org/report/2019/09/04/when-were-dead-and-buried-our-bones-will-keep-hurting/workers-rights-under-threat# ; Mengxin Li, Human Rights Watch, Paying for a Bus Ticket and Expecting to Fly – How Apparel Brand Purchasing Practices Drive Labor Abuses (2019), https://www.hrw.org/report/2019/04/24/paying-bus-ticket-and-expecting-fly/how-apparel-brand-purchasing-practices-drive#; Lynn Kamm, *How Our Greed Keeps Kids Trapped in Foreign Sweatshops*, Wash. Post (Mar. 28, 1993), https://www.washingtonpost.com/archive/opinions/1993/03/28/how-our-greed-keeps-kids-trapped-in-foreign-sweatshops/51fd62c5-7482-4e85-a6b0-f79d876a9fc4/.

60 *See* Steve Matthews, *Coca-Cola Faces Campus Boycotts over Colombia Murder*, Bloomberg (Mar. 2, 2005); Pui-Wing Tam & March Lifsher, *Colombian Killings Land U.S. Company in American Court*, Wall Street Journal (Oct. 6, 2003), https://www.wsj.com/articles/SB10653902002257500; Sibylla Brodzinsky, *Coca-Cola Boycott Launched After Killings at Colombian Plants*, The Guardian (July 23, 2003), https://www.theguardian.com/media/2003/jul/24/marketingandpr.colombia.

61 Tina Bellon, *U.S. Appeals Court Revives Nestle Child Slavery Lawsuit*, Reuters (Oct. 24, 2018 4:38 AM), https://www.reuters.com/article/us-usa-court-nestle/u-s-appeals-court-revives-nestle-child-slavery-lawsuit-idUSKCN1MX2UM.

62 International Labor Organization, The Rana Plaza Accident and its Aftermath (2018), https://www.ilo.org/global/topics/geip/WCMS_614394/lang--en/index.htm; Steven Greenhouse, *Bangladesh Fears an Exodus of Apparel Firms*, N.Y. Times (May 2, 2013), https://www.nytimes.com/2013/05/03/business/factory-owners-in-bangladesh-fear-firms-willexit.html#:~:text=Bangladesh%20Fears%20an%20Exodus%20of%20Apparel%20Firms,-Demonstrators%20outside%20Gap's&text=A%20day%20after%20the%20Walt,corporations%20might%20follow%20Disney's%20lead; Justine Nolan, *Rana Plaza: The Collapse of a Factory in Bangladesh and its Ramifications for the Global Garment Industry* in Business and Human Rights: From Principles to Practice (Justine Nolan & Dorothée Baumann-Pauly, eds. 2016).

## C. Human Security, Socioeconomic, and Cultural Rights: Corruption, Conflict, and the Extractives and Forestry Industries

International human rights law protects the rights to life, physical integrity, and psychological integrity. Article 3 of the UDHR recognizes that everyone has "the right to life, liberty and security of person."[63] ILO Convention 169[64] and the UN Declaration on the Rights of Indigenous Peoples (UNDRIP)[65] recognize rights of indigenous populations around the world to practice cultural traditions and religious expression in community as well as to own traditional forms of communal land tenure.[66] The right to self-determination provides that Indigenous peoples are entitled to "determine priorities and strategies for the development and use of their lands and territories."[67] The principle of "free, prior, informed consent" is consistent with these rights.

### 1. Risks to Rights

The relationship of transnational corporations in the extractives sector to human rights and responses to the risks to human rights when extractive sector companies contract with security forces for protection has been well documented as discussed in chapter 1. Transnational extractive corporations operating in resource-rich regions where conflict and corruption are rife have contributed to insecurity and instability in some instances.

Companies are learning from the litigation generated by conflicts with communities and the reputational risks associated with public scrutiny of policies and practices that put human rights at risk. One lesson, that community opposition to operations can have significant costs, has not been lost on large multinational extractive corporations.[68] Corporations have come to appreciate the risks (reputational and operational) associated with being implicated human rights abuses and environmental damage.[69] It is important to address risks in a more constructive manner consistent with international human rights norms, and many business

[63] *See, e.g.*, UDHR, *supra* note 1.

[64] Int'l Lab. Org. (ILO), *Indigenous and Tribal Peoples in Independent Countries*, No. 169 (1989).

[65] G.A. Res. 61/295, United Nations Declaration on the Rights of Indigenous Peoples (UNDRIP) (Sept. 13, 2007).

[66] *Id.*; ILO No. 169, *supra* note 64.

[67] UNDRIP, *supra* note 65, at art. 32 para. 1.

[68] *See* Rachel Davis & Daniel M. Franks, *Costs of Company-Community Conflict in the Extractive Sector*, Corporate Social Responsibility Initiative Report No. 66. Cambridge, MA: Harvard Kennedy School (2014).

[69] *See e.g.*, Office of the High Commissioner, United Nations Human Rights, *Human Rights Abuses Are Not Just Morally Wrong, They Are Also Bad For Business*, March 23, 2015, https://www.ohchr.org/en/NewsEvents/Pages/DisplayNews.aspx?NewsID=16040&LangID=E ("There can be immense reputational damage to business operations that damage human rights. Share prices and brand identity can be hit by publicity.").

enterprises have agreed to cooperate with critics to create standards to regulate industry practice where state regulatory efforts are inadequate or absent.

## II. Communication and Collaboration: From Stakeholder Engagement to Structured Initiatives

Growing recognition that the global governance gap can place human rights and corporate reputations at risk has given rise to "governance with and without governments"[70] in the CSR and sustainability arena. After confronting human rights challenges associated with operational risks, some companies and civil society organizations have collaborated to create standards and structures to regulate business conduct and to reduce the risk of rights abuses. The result of these collaborations are referred to as multistakeholder initiatives (MSIs). A range of MSIs have emerged to close global regulatory gaps in areas where governments lack either the capacity or commitment to address certain social or environmental problems involving business enterprises. In the business and human rights arena in particular, interested stakeholders have agreed to come together to create policy, identify solutions, implement policies, and improve practices.

### A. What Are MSIs?

An MSI is an agreed institutional arrangement that brings together concerned organizations and individuals to identify and address complicated problems.[71] Because many different factors contribute to many of the human rights and environmental challenges confronting society, many different constituencies must come together to solve complicated problems.[72] Increasing global interdependence necessitates an increase in collaborative efforts to address challenges.[73]

MSIs often are the result of collaborative efforts between disparate actors with different but sometimes overlapping interests.[74] An MSI brings together many different constituencies with sometimes competing and sometimes complementary concerns to solve a particular problem.[75] Different stakeholders come

[70] Sebastien Mena & Guido Palazzo, *Input and Output Legitimacy of Multi-Stakeholder Initiatives*, 22 Bus. Ethics Q. 527, 533 (2012).

[71] Madeline Hung, *Voluntary Measures: Overreliance on MSIs in the U.S. National Action Plan on Responsible Business Conduct*, MSI Integrity (Jan. 12, 2017), http://www.msi-integrity.org/voluntary-measures-overreliance-on-msis-in-the-u-s-national-action-plan-on-responsible-business-conduct/.

[72] *Id.*

[73] *Id.*

[74] *Id.*

[75] *Id.*

together to create an institution to implement policies to address problems that the group creates by reaching a consensus. Impacts differ, as do interests; while stakeholders may share a common concern, different stakeholder constituencies may be affected differently, with some suffering a burden and others gaining a benefit from particular business practices.

While there is no single shared understanding of what defines an MSI, MSI Integrity, a nonprofit research organization that studies the value of voluntary multistakeholder initiatives and designs assessment tools to evaluate MSI performance from a human rights perspective, offers that "at the most basic level, MSIs can be understood as efforts to bring together various stakeholders—such as corporations, civil society organizations, government and affected populations—to collaborate in addressing a specific issues often related to corporate accountability."[76] According to the International Social and Environmental Accreditation Alliance (ISEAL), a global membership association for credible sustainable standards: "stakeholders are individuals or groups with an interest in an initiative's success in achieving its objectives or delivering on its intended results."[77]

## B. MSI Features

A core feature of an MSI is having different constituencies represented in the process of problem-solving and collaborating to address challenges by creating policies and promoting reforms.[78] As the problems associated with business enterprises being connected to or complicit in human rights abuses were brought to public attention stakeholders from civil society organizations and the business community came together to craft solutions through creating standards of conduct. Standards created through stakeholder consultations are serving to close the gaps in governance that give rise to human rights risks. Some MSIs create regulatory standards or "soft law" to address particular issues. MSIs are gaining influence as a new form of regulatory institution.[79] Some MSIs monitor the compliance of particular actors, usually private corporations, with consensus standards of conduct informed by stakeholder input.

Corporations and civil society organizations are communicating about challenges and collaborating to create, implement, and monitor voluntary

[76] *The New Regulators?*, MSI INTEGRITY 6 (June 2017), https://msi-database.org/data/The%20New%20Regulators%20-%20MSI%20Database%20Report.pdf.

[77] Pins Brown, *Principles that make for Effective Governance of Multistakeholder Initiatives* at 2 (citing Patrick Mallet, *ISEAL Emerging Initiatives—Module 1: Overview*, ISEAL ALLIANCE (July 2007)).

[78] *The New Regulators?*, *supra* note 76, at 6.

[79] *Id.* at 2; see, e.g., Dorothée Baumann-Pauly et al, *Setting and Enforcing Industry-Specific Standards for Human Rights: The Role of Multi-stakeholder Initiatives (MSIs) in Regulating Corporate Conduct* in BUSINESS AND HUMAN RIGHTS: FROM PRINCIPLES TO PRACTICE (Justine Nolan & Dorothée Baumann-Pauly, eds. 2016).

standards of conduct to ensure compliance with obligations to respect human rights. Dialogue features prominently in framing understanding of problems and crafting policy and creating possible solutions.

Different stakeholders have different motives for participating in an MSIs. They also have different feeling about the efficacy of MSIs. For example, business enterprises may want to learn about or to quiet criticisms, and in some instances actually want to prevent problems. Civil society organizations may want direct access to the corporate executives who can contribute to solving the problem. Investors may be driven to participate in MSIs to be better situated to evaluate a company's exposure to risk and risk management aptitude. Academics seeking to understand and educate become involved to better understand teach and learn may join as observers.

MSIs are global in reach, but currently, the most influential find origins in home states of global business enterprises, the United States, the United Kingdom, or the European Union. For example, the Ethical Trading Initiative, an alliance of companies, trade unions, and civil society organizations focused on labor rights is based in the United Kingdom. The Fair Labor Association, a labor rights monitoring organization, and the Global Network Initiative, an organization dedicated to developing policies to protect free expression and digital privacy, are both based in the United States.

The geographic reach of an MSI, despite its origin or base of operations, often depends on issues the MSI was developed to address. Stakeholders may be distant and in dispersed locations such as cocoa plantations in the Ivory Coast or banana plantations in Colombia. Sometimes some stakeholders, those likely to suffer adverse human rights impacts may not be direct participants in an MSI. Affected communities with a stake in the issues addressed by an MSI may be diffuse or difficult to reach or represent. Consider for example the millions of users on social media platforms. Affected individuals may live in rural or remote areas, such as villagers in rural regions impacted by extractive activity. In addition, discrimination may operate to exclude certain voices from participating in policy dialogues. Women, youth, and members of disfavored or disadvantaged minority groups may confront barriers to participating in negotiations to develop policy. This exclusion can prove problematic and is inconsistent with human rights principles of fair process and inclusion in decision-making processes.

## C. MSIs as a Corporate Responsibility Resource

As distinct from industry trade association initiatives to avoid human rights risks, collaborative stakeholder engagement in the form of MSIs is seen by some rights advocates as more legitimate than conventional CSR initiatives or industry efforts that fail to integrate the concerns of interested constituencies.[80] A 2017 study by MSI Integrity on the distribution of industry-specific MSIs found the highest concentrations of multistakeholder standard setting efforts in: (1) agriculture, forestry, and fishing; (2) mining and energy; and (3) consumer goods.[81] Only a few MSIs operate in more than one industry. Most MSIs do refer to international law.

To be sure, the self-regulation standards emerging from MSIs could easily be seen as self-serving for certain business stakeholders.[82] However, as the political will of public officials to regulate the social and environmental impacts of business activities appears to be decreasing in strategically significant nations, it is increasingly imperative that concerned constituencies find ways for private ordering to work for the public. Self-governance through MSIs could serve as shared governance to create conditions to improve the human rights performance of particular industry sectors. MSIs provide a much needed service where they serve to create opportunities for collaboration. The following examples are offered to examine the relative efficacy of MSI efforts with respect to business and human rights. It is essential to constructively consider outcomes and impacts of MSI efforts.

## III. Commitments and Compliance: Multistakeholder Initiatives to Promote Responsibility and Protect Rights

Representatives from corporations and civil society organizations have come together, sometimes in fora facilitated by governments, to create standards to regulate corporate conduct and structures to support compliance with standards.

### A. The Fair Labor Association

On January 13, 1999, apparel workers in the Northern Marianas Islands, a US commonwealth, filed what was at the time the largest legal challenge ever brought against sweatshops on American soil.[83] The action named eighteen American apparel companies and retailers, including the Gap.[84] The suit alleged that the

[80] Mariette van Huijstee, Multi-stakeholder Initiatives 19 (2012) (explaining that "MSIs are the only realistic way to motivate sector level change in the face of multiple governance gaps.").

[81] *The New Regulators?*, *supra* note 76, at 4–5.

[82] van Huijstee, *supra* note 80, at 38.

[83] Steven Greenhouse, *Suit Says 18 Companies Conspired to Violate Sweatshop Workers' Civil Rights*, N.Y. Times (Jan. 14, 1999), https://www.nytimes.com/1999/01/14/us/suit-says-18-companies-conspired-to-violate-sweatshop-workers-civil-rights.html?searchResultPosition=1.

[84] *Id.*

companies conspired to force workers into eighty-four-hour work weeks, restricted the liberty and mobility of workers, and confined workers in dilapidated living conditions and substandard unsafe workplace conditions. Activists even documented instances where workers were pressured into aborting their pregnancies.[85] One worker alleged her recruitment contract with a factory supplying the Gap included formal prohibitions on marriage and pregnancy; another worker, upon becoming pregnant, was allegedly returned to China and forced to have an abortion. She was nonetheless refused re-entry into Saipan to return to work.[86] These suits dealt popular apparel brands a significant public relations blow by associating them with slave-like labor conditions and human rights violations.[87] The Gap attempted to mitigate the damage by immediately releasing a statement insisting the company would not tolerate human rights violations at any of the factories supplying Gap products.[88]

Established in 1999, just a few months after the Marianas lawsuits began, the Fair Labor Association (FLA) is a "collaborative effort of socially responsible companies, colleges, and universities, and civil society organizations to protect labor rights globally."[89] According to FLA Board member and former Princeton University Vice President and Secretary Robert Durkee, stakeholder collaboration serves to sustain the FLA's ability to "hold companies accountable for meeting the code of conduct" and to "assess how well the companies were doing in meeting the code of conduct" as companies craft plans for remediation to address labor conditions in factories.[90]

### 1. FLA Mission and Membership

The FLA's mission is to "combine the efforts of business, civil society organizations, and colleges and universities to promote and protect workers' rights and to improve working conditions globally through adherence to international standards."[91] It strives to achieve this aim through a rigorous and public monitoring process, as well as a reputation-based system of accountability. The FLA operates as a nonprofit organization under the laws of the District of Columbia.[92]

[85] *Id.*

[86] Fran Abrams, *Shirts for the Fashionable, at a Price Paid in Human Misery. On US Soil, the Gap Workers Are Forced to Have Abortions*, INDEPENDENT (London) (Sept. 24, 1999), https://www.independent.co.uk/news/shirts-for-the-fashionable-at-a-price-paid-in-human-misery-on-us-soil-the-gap-workers-are-forced-to-1121362.html.

[87] Greenhouse, *supra* note 83.

[88] *Id.*

[89] FAIR LABOR ASS'N, http://www.fairlabor.org/.

[90] Telephone interview with Robert K. Durkee, Vice President and Secretary, Princeton University (April 11, 2019).

[91] *Charter Document*, FAIR LABOR ASS'N, 3 (Feb. 12, 2014) [hereinafter *FLA Charter*].

[92] *Id.* at 8.

The FLA is comprised of companies, colleges, universities, and individuals who are members of civil society organizations. "[N]early 200 colleges and universities in the United States and Canada work with FLA to monitor social compliance and ensure the ethical production of items bearing their marks or logo."[93] Monitoring the manufacturing and production of goods bearing a university's logo and ensuring that such goods are produced in an environment free of abusive labor conditions is the primary function of the FLA.[94] Civil society organizations work with companies to shape programs and monitoring to promote protections for workers.[95] The member companies and suppliers are distributed globally.[96]

Membership in the FLA is conducted by request of the would-be member.[97] A key component of a prospective corporate member's participation with the FLA consists of a monitoring plan, which lays the groundwork through the compliance and monitoring requirements that the applicant would adopt. Monitoring plans provide that a corporate FLA member must allow inspection of their facilities and practices by external independent monitors. Organized labor is notably absent from the FLA membership structure.

### 2. FLA Substantive Policy Commitments and Procedures

A monitoring plan, as laid out in Section III of the FLA charter, helps provide the FLA with the means to ensure that a company, retailer, or seller seeking membership complies with the mission of the association and only manufactures and produces in accordance with ethical labor practices.[98] Some methods of ensuring ethical labor practices involve a company conducting internal monitoring of labor conditions in their facilities, submitting their facilities to monitoring visits by FLA-approved monitors, and submitting a yearly activities and practice report to the FLA.[99] A company's monitoring plan is reviewed by the FLA staff before being passed on to the board of directors with a recommendation whether the applicant is eligible to become a member. If the board reviews and subsequently approves an application, the applicant gains the title of "participating company."[100] Participating companies may be brands, retailers, or suppliers.

Colleges and universities seeking to join the FLA have a slightly different process. They must first participate in the University Advisory Council.[101] Once the

[93] *Benefits of Joining FLA*, FAIR LABOR ASS'N (2012), http://www.fairlabor.org/benefits-joining-fla.

[94] *University of Utah*, FAIR LABOR ASS'N (2012), http://www.fairlabor.org/affiliate/university-utah.

[95] *Civil Society Organizations*, FAIR LABOR ASS'N (2012), http://www.fairlabor.org/affiliates/civil-society-organizations.

[96] *Participating Suppliers*, FAIR LABOR ASS'N (2012), http://www.fairlabor.org/affiliates/participating-suppliers.

[97] *FLA Charter*, *supra* note 91.

[98] *Id.*

[99] *Id.*

[100] *Id.* at 12.

[101] *Id.* at 14.

application is completed, the university will be required to pay annual membership dues to the association. More importantly, if the college or university has a licensing program, "it shall require each of its College or University Licensees to become either a Participating Company or be accepted by the Association in an appropriate College or University Licensee category and to meet the requirements associated with such applicable category."[102] FLA requirements for colleges and universities are not only subject the colleges and universities to its labor requirements, but any of its licensees as well.[103]

External independent monitors inspect facilities for compliance. In order to gain FLA qualification, prospective monitors are required to demonstrate independence from members as well as core competencies for the countries in which they seek accreditation.[104] Those competencies include: sufficient background knowledge, including working knowledge of conduct and monitoring standards; sufficient capability to confidentially and effectively conduct independent external monitoring of FLA members; and the ability to competently and objectively report findings to the FLA.[105]

### 3. FLA Structure and Governance

The governance of the association is divided between a nineteen-member board of directors made up of companies, civil society organizations, and universities and the president/executive director.[106] The board is responsible for amending the FLA charter, workplace codes, and monitoring principles. It appoints the president/executive director and decides whether to suspend accreditation of FLA members.[107] Per the FLA charter, the board is split into eighteen members and one chair. Six of the board members are business representatives selected by a business caucus.[108] Six members are labor/NGO representatives selected by a majority of the then-serving labor/NGO representatives.[109] The remaining six are university representatives selected by a university advisory council.[110] The

[102] *Id.*
[103] *Id.* at 14–15.
[104] *Id.* at 17–18.
[105] *Id.* at 18–19.
[106] *FLA Charter, supra* note 91, at 8, 11. Board members may hold positions as officers, directors, or employees of FLA members, although only one board member may be from any one FLA member. Each board member serves a term of at most three years, although terms are renewable and board members will continue to serve until their successor has been named, even if such service would take them past the three years.
[107] *Id.* at 10.
[108] *Id.* at 8.
[109] *Id.*
[110] *Id.*; as specified in the FLA charter, the UAC is "the advisory council to the Association consisting of colleges, universities, other institutions of higher learning and other entities involved in collegiate licensing. The [UAC] is governed by a set of bylaws adopted by the affirmative vote of a majority of the College or University Affiliates present at the first meeting of the [UAC] and which are

board chair is first nominated by a committee comprised of two members of each caucus.[111]

The president/executive director is elected by the board through a simple majority vote.[112] While the board focuses more on the codification and statutory principles of the FLA, the president/executive director's responsibilities focus more on the implementation of the FLA's regulations, such as reviewing applications for accreditation and renewal of accreditation.[113]

The university liaison is designated by a two-thirds approval of the university board members and serves as the FLA's representative on any university- or college-related issues and actions.[114]

## B. The Voluntary Principles on Security and Human Rights

In May 1998, over a hundred Nigerian activists arrived at a Chevron oil platform to protest the ecological damage caused by the company's dredging.[115] In response, the Nigerian military flew in on helicopters financed by the company and opened fire on the unarmed protestors.[116] Chevron denied responsibility for its role in these human rights abuses,[117] arguing it had to provide equipment to the military upon request per the terms of its joint venture with the government.[118] The company insisted it acted properly by contacting the Nigerian authorities to restore order on the platform. In other words, Chevron claimed it could not be held accountable for what the military did to environmental activists.[119] These arguments were sufficient for a federal jury to clear the company of all liability in 2008.[120]

Similarly problematic relationships between extractive companies and militaries have existed outside the Nigerian delta. In 1968, Mobil—later to be

subject to amendment by the affirmative vote of a majority of College or University Affiliates present at any subsequent meeting of the [UAC]." *Id.*, at 8.

111 *FLA Charter, supra* note 91, at 9.
112 *Id.* at 10.
113 *Id.* at 11.
114 *Id.* at 12.
115 Richard C. Paddock, *Victim Describes Shooting during Chevron Protest*, L.A. TIMES (Oct. 31, 2008), https://www.latimes.com/archives/la-xpm-2008-oct-31-me-chevron31-story.html.
116 *Id*, See also, BRONWEN MANBY, THE PRICE OF OIL, HUMAN RIGHTS WATCH (1999) (detailing rights abuses related to oil industry in Nigeria).
117 *Id.*
118 *Id.*
119 Paddock, *supra* note 115.
120 Bob Egelko, *S.F. Jury Clear Chevron of Protest Shootings*, SFGATE (published Dec. 2, 2008, 4 AM), https://www.sfgate.com/business/article/S-F-jury-clears-Chevron-of-protest-shootings-3183175.php.

acquired by Exxon—began operating in the Arun gas fields of Indonesia.[121] The military's presence there was marked with murder, torture, kidnapping, and rape.[122] The military was allegedly housed in Mobil-owned barracks and used Mobil's machinery to dig mass graves to dispose of victims.[123]

Conflicts such as these between affected communities and corporations in challenging operating environments have served to catalyze change among them the creation of the Voluntary Principles on Security, a tripartite multistakeholder initiative to address security and human rights. The Voluntary Principles on Security were announced in 2000 to address the human rights abuses associated with the use of force to protect the interests and operations of extractive companies. The Voluntary Principles provide an operational approach to conducting assessments of human rights risks associated with security. The Principles aid companies to engage in constructive dialogue with both public and private security forces. The Principles encourage companies to proactively screen and train security forces to ensure that the use of force is lawful and proportionate. The Principles also provide guidance for developing systems to detect and deal with reporting and investigating alleged abuses.

In the decades before the Voluntary Principles provided guidance on security measures, community resistance to rights abuses attracted international attention. For example, in Nigeria the execution of environmental activist Ken Saro-Wiwa by military forces brought Shell under scrutiny. In Colombia, BP was subjected to negative attention after contracting with the Colombian army to provide security for oil pipelines. Occidental was sued for role allegedly aiding and abetting abuses in Colombia.[124] Claims that Chevron was complicit in conduct including forced labor, murder, and rape in Burma were settled out of court.[125]

121 Neela Banerjee, *Lawsuit Says Exxon Aided Rights Abuses*, N.Y. Times (June 21, 2001), https://www.nytimes.com/2001/06/21/business/lawsuit-says-exxon-aided-rights-abuses.html?searchResultPosition=10.

122 *Id.*

123 *Id.*

124 *See, e.g.*, T. Christian Miller, *A Colombian Village Caught in a Cross-Fire*, L.A. Times (Mar. 17, 2002), http://articles.latimes.com/2002/mar/17/news/mn-33266; *Occidental Sued in Human Rights Case*, L.A. Times (Apr. 25, 2003), http://articles.latimes.com/2003/apr/25/business/fi-oxy2; Lawrence Hurley, *U.S. Court Dismisses Colombian Human Rights Claims against Occidental*, Reuters (Dec. 15, 2014, 10:50 AM), http://www.reuters.com/article/usa-courts-rights-idUSL1N0TZ1EE20141215; Jonathan Stempel, *U.S. Court Refuses To Hold Occidental Liable in Colombia Bombings*, Reuters (Nov. 12, 2014, 11:08 AM), http://www.reuters.com/article/us-occidental-colombia-bombing-idUSKCN0IW27020141112; Lawrence Hurley, *U.S. Supreme Court Rejects Human Rights Suit Against Occidental*, Reuters (Dec. 15, 2014, 7:41 AM), http://www.reuters.com/article/us-usa-court-occidental-idUSKBN0TX1QF20151214.

125 *See, e.g.*, *Unocal Settles Burma Human Rights Cases*, Financial Times (Dec. 13, 2004) https://www.ft.com/content/fa24d3a6-4d4d-11d9-b3be-00000e2511c8; *Unocal Pays Out on Burma "Abuses,"* BBC News (Mar. 22, 2005, 2:54 PM), http://news.bbc.co.uk/2/hi/asia-pacific/4371995.stm.

The governments of the United States and United Kingdom, where many companies confronting allegations of abuse have headquarters, hosted a series of discussions with concerned constituencies in the early 1990s. These government-facilitated multistakeholder meetings brought together civil society organizations and corporate officers to discuss problems and develop strategic solutions.

### 1. Voluntary Principles Mission and Membership

Many of the corporations that were the targets of campaigns by rights activists are participants in the Voluntary Principles.[126] The Voluntary Principles are aimed at addressing some of the human rights challenges confronting the extractive industries by providing guidance to companies on safety and security concerns while also encouraging operations consist with a framework that "encourages" respect for human rights.[127] As a multistakeholder initiative, participants of the Voluntary Principles include governments, nongovernmental organizations, and corporations. Participating governments are no longer limited to the United States and European nations with Ghana and Colombia becoming participants. Trade industry associations including the International Council on Mining and Metals (ICMM) and IPIECA, the global oil and gas industry association for environmental and social issues, both continue to serve as observers to the Voluntary Principles. All participants must agree "to proactively implement or assist in the implementation of the [Principles]."[128]

### 2. Voluntary Principles Substantive Policy Commitments and Procedures

The Voluntary Principles are a set of nonbinding standards developed to influence the way extractive companies assess how best to reconcile respect for human rights with security. The Voluntary Principles are best viewed as a risk-assessment instrument, framing the practices for businesses to undertake to avoid conflicts over security with language such as "accurate" and "effective." The Voluntary Principles begin by framing security as an interest shared by communities, corporate interests, and communities. Voluntary Principles are founded on the recognition "that security and respect for human rights can and should be consistent."[129] The Voluntary Principles begin with a series of affirmative

[126] *Id.*, *For Companies*, VOLUNTARY PRINCIPLES OF SECURITY AND HUMAN RIGHTS, http://www.voluntaryprinciples.org/for-companies/.

[127] *See What Are the Voluntary Principles?*, VOLUNTARY PRINCIPLES OF SECURITY AND HUMAN RIGHTS, http://www.voluntaryprinciples.org/what-are-the-voluntary-principles/; *see also,* Scott Jerbi, *Extractives and Multi-Stakeholder Initiatives: The Voluntary Principles on Security and Human Rights; The Extractive Industries Transparency Initiative & The Kimberley Process Certification Scheme* in BUSINESS AND HUMAN RIGHTS: FROM PRINCIPLES TO PRACTICE (Justine Nolan & Dorothée Baumann-Pauly, eds. 2016).

[128] *See Voluntary Principles on Security and Human Rights Participation Criteria*, VOLUNTARY PRINCIPLES ON SECURITY AND HUMAN RIGHTS (2007), http://www.voluntaryprinciples.org/wp-content/uploads/2019/12/TheVoluntaryPrinciples.pdf.

[129] *Id.*

statements and points of consensus. First, the language of the preamble acknowledges that the primary responsibility to protect human rights resides with governments. Next, the preamble asserts that while companies must "act in a manner consistent" with the laws of the host countries, companies must also be "mindful" of "the highest applicable international standards."[130] However, the Voluntary Principles do not directly address potential conflicts between local and international normative systems and standards. The Principles do acknowledge the importance of engaging with civil society organizations and local communities to minimize risk of conflict and to promote community welfare.

In essence, the Voluntary Principles provide a framework for risk assessment and relationship development. The Principles cover three core categories of concern: (1) risk assessment; (2) relations with public security; and (3) relations with private security.

*a. Risk Assessment*

The Voluntary Principles acknowledge a secure operating environment is essential to commercial success. The following six factors for business enterprises to consider in evaluating a potential operating environment are set forth in the Voluntary Principles: (1) identification of security risks; (2) potential for violent conflict; (3) human rights record; (4) rule of law; (5) conflict analysis; and (6) equipment transfer.

The identification of security risks can be challenging in complex contexts where social and political conditions are unstable or constantly changing. For example, BP confronted security challenges in Colombia in connection with its operations in the Casanare region—one of the world's largest oil fields, with reserves reportedly valued at $40 billion.[131] Rival armed insurgent groups, the National Liberation Army and the FARC also operated in Casanare.[132] Armed insurgents in the area often attacked oil pipelines. An oil pipeline linking the remote oil fields near the northern border of the country to the oil ports on the west coast of the country was reportedly attacked thirty-six times in one year.[133] Rather than pay protection money to guerrilla organizations, BP employed private guards and elected to rely on government armed forces for security. The company's Colombian operations then came under scrutiny for corruption, complicity in murder, torture, and intimidation. For its security arrangements, BP pledged to pay $5.4 million to the Colombian army on top of taxes. The firm shared intelligence about and images of local environmental activists protesting its presence in the region allegedly enabling rights abuses. Reporting on BP in 1997, the *Economist* questioned characterizations of BP's conduct in region:

[130] *Id.*
[131] *Colombia: BP at War*, THE ECONOMIST (July 17, 1997)
[132] *Id.*
[133] *Id.*

"A cynical abuser of human rights, or a victim of circumstance—or indeed of misreporting, even malice?"[134]

The Principles explain that proper identification of risk enables firms to better prepare to potentially minimize the risk of being caught in or contributing to violent conflict. The potential for violence may also vary. The Principles caution that risks associated with violence may be sporadic and limited to specific regions, or the risks may be endemic and widespread across an area. For example, some parts of the Democratic Republic of the Congo are not in open conflict, though the country has been embroiled in a long-standing conflict. Similarly, the level of conflict in Colombia varied across the country. The Principles advise firms to examine patterns of violence to predict and prevent risks. The Principles further counsel firms to seek information from host and home governments as well as civil society organizations to aid in an accurate risk assessment.

Firms should assess the reputation and human rights records of the available security service providers in a region. The past human rights performance of national and local law enforcement authorities, private security forces, and paramilitary groups could point to future problems. For example, many complaints were lodged against military state security forces in certain countries, yet firms later went on to employ these same state security forces apparently without asking questions or seeking adherence to standards of conduct. The Principles offer that by paying attention to past abuses and allegations of abuse, a company can avoid repeating a pattern of impunity and promote accountability and perhaps even find alternative ways to address conflict.

Considering the consequences of equipment transfer in environments complicated by conflict or corruption is advised. The Voluntary Principles counsel caution with respect to equipment transfer to avoid complicity in enabling abuses by security forces. For example, a lawsuit against Shell victims alleged that infrastructure and equipment provided to state security forces by the firm were used to perpetrate abuses, forcibly put down peaceful protests, and decimate villages. The Principles suggest that firms put in place procedures to prevent misappropriation and misuse of corporate property.

Finally, a functional legal system with the will and ability to hold those individuals and entities responsible for abuses accountable is also important. There have been instances where local legal authorities have failed to prosecute perpetrators, resulting in impunity, disorder, and damaged community relations. The increased emphasis on operational-level grievance mechanisms is an attempt to compensate for compromised legal systems by providing a private dispute-resolution system.

[134] *Id.*

*b. Relationships with Security Service Providers: Public Sector*

In addition to the basics of risk assessment, the Voluntary Principles offer guidance on relationship management. Corporations are called upon to be the conscious of public actors. The Voluntary Principles emphasize that businesses have an interest in ensuring that actions taken by security forces affiliated with public authorities are "consistent with the protection and promotion of human rights."[135] The Principles draw a distinction between public and private security providers. In sum, the principles recognize different roles and responsibilities between public and private organizations.

To reduce risks of abuse and to promote respect for rights, the Voluntary Principles focus on four issues with respect to working with public security providers:

1. security arrangements;
2. deployment and conduct;
3. consultation and advice;
4. responses to human rights abuses.[136]

In making security arrangements, consultation and communication are of paramount importance. The Voluntary Principles advise companies to consult with host governments and with stakeholders about the impact of security arrangements. Companies are advised to communicate the contents of codes of ethical conduct to security providers. Appreciating the deterrent effect of exposing abuses and the opportunity to generate helpful input from the affected communities, communication is central. Companies are encouraged to engage in advocacy to promote greater governmental transparency such that "security arrangements are accessible to the public."[137]

Appreciating that the primary role of a public security force is to uphold the rule of law, the Voluntary Principles instruct firms to use their influence with host governments to ensure that when security forces are deployed, certain standards are met. By no means should "individuals credibly implicated in human rights abuses" be permitted to provide security services. There must be limits on the use of force and respect for the right to peaceably assemble and to engage in collective bargaining.

With respect to consultation and advice, the Principles advocate participation and cooperation among companies. For example, where firms operating in the same region use security and share common concerns about potential issues

[135] *Voluntary Principles on Security and Human Rights Participation Criteria*, *supra* note 128.
[136] *Id.*
[137] *Id.*

affecting the region or the implications of these issues for human rights, the firms could collectively bring issues to the attention of government. The Principles recommend that companies work with governments to address human rights, safety, and security issues and to advance adherence to international standards of engagement such as the UN Code of Conduct for Law Enforcement Officials and the UN Basic Principles on the Use of Force and Firearms. Companies are also encouraged to provide human rights education and training for security providers.

Significantly, responses to human rights abuses, should allegations of abuse arise, are outlined in the Voluntary Principles. The Principles counsel companies to record and report credible abuse allegations to appropriate host government authorities. Where appropriate, corporations should call for investigations of incidents of abuse and continually monitor the status of investigations. The Voluntary Principles provide that the safety and security of sources of information about violations must be protected.

*c. Relationships with Security Service Providers: Private Sector*

Because of the complications associated with public security forces, many companies opt to employ private security firms to protect property and personnel where state support is insufficient or unavailable. Accordingly, the Voluntary Principles provide guidance on managing relations with private security forces. The Principles call for companies contracting with a private security provider to require the provider to comply with laws to adhere to ethical standards and to aim to implement "emerging best practices" developed by industry, civil society organizations, and public authorities to promote respect for international human rights and humanitarian law.

The Voluntary Principles instruct that companies or independent third parties should monitor the policies and practices of private security providers. Private providers should have disciplinary policies in place to deter abuses. Allegations of abuses or illegal actions should be investigated. Credible allegations of abuses should be reported to the relevant public law enforcement authorities. Companies should advocate for abuses to be addressed and must monitor the status of public investigations into alleged abuses.

The Voluntary Principles reiterate that private providers should—just as public security providers should—"exercise restraint" and limit the use of force consistent with UN standards on appropriate conduct for law enforcement officials. Similarly, private providers must also respect the rights of assembly and association and collective bargaining. In contrast to state security, the Voluntary Principles make clear that private security "should provide only preventative and defensive services and should not engage in activities exclusively the responsibility of state military or law enforcement authorities."[138] To reduce the risk of private security providers exceeding authority, the Voluntary Principles advise companies to incorporate the Voluntary Principles into contracts with providers. Companies are instructed to include terms that allow termination of contracts for security services where there is credible evidence of abuse or illegal conduct.

Companies are advised to do due diligence and review the record of private security providers, particularly with respect to excessive use of force. Companies are also advised to facilitate the exchange of information about abuses committed by private security providers. In addition, the International Code of Conduct for Private Security Service Providers asks its signatory companies to "recognize the importance of respecting the various cultures encounter in their work"[139] and to "affirm that they have a responsibility to respect the human rights of, and fulfill humanitarian responsibilities toward, all those affected by their business activities, including Personnel, Clients, suppliers, shareholders, and the population of the area in which services are provided."

### 3. Voluntary Principles Structure and Governance

The administration of Voluntary Principles is provided by its Secretariat and Compass Consulting International Ltd.[140] Less an organization than a set of collectively agreed-upon principles, Voluntary Principles is focused on the three pillars of its membership: governments, companies, and NGOs.

Ten governments have joined Voluntary Principles, including the United States.[141] Member nations benefit from the opportunity to coordinate in learning and problem-solving with other governments, international extractive companies, and NGOs. Of particular value is coordination of public security services with extractive companies in order to avoid the notorious conflicts that have plagued the industry. The governments also have access to the resources and coordination Voluntary Principles provides.

Chevron, Shell, and ExxonMobil have also joined the Voluntary Principles.[142] Participation in the Voluntary Principles enables companies to align their corporate policies and procedures with international human rights principles. Participation also allows companies to communicate to the public their

[138] *Id.*
[139] *International Code of Conduct for Private Security Service Providers*, International Code of Conduct Association, http://www.icoca.ch/en/the_icoc.
[140] *The Secretariat*, Voluntary Principles (2019), https://www.voluntaryprinciples.org/the-secretariat.
[141] *For Governments*, Voluntary Principles (2019), https://www.voluntaryprinciples.org/for-governments.
[142] *For Companies*, Voluntary Principles (2019), https://www.voluntaryprinciples.org/for-companies.

commitment to these values, to share with one another the best practices for reconciling human rights and security, and to collaborate on difficult issues.

By participating in the Voluntary Principles, NGOs can promote respect for human rights in the historically hostile context of extractive security enforcement.[143] Of all the pillars, NGOs are most representative of the populations affected by the extractive industry. NGOs are thus best placed to foster dialogue and collaboration between the multiple stakeholders and can also verify the successful implementation of the Voluntary Principles.

## C. The Global Network Initiative

The Global Network Initiative (GNI) is a multistakeholder platform created to address how "technology companies [can] best respect the rights of their users—wherever they operate."[144] Following Yahoo!'s provision of information to Chinese authorities in 2005 that led to the arrest of a Chinese journalist, the GNI was established by Yahoo! and others in 2008 to "provide an evolving framework for responsible company decision-making in support of free expression and privacy rights" and to "collectively advocate with governments and international institutions for laws and policies that promote and protect freedom of expression and privacy."[145]

The product of more than two years of deliberation by companies, human rights and press freedom organizations, academics, and investors, the GNI was originally formed in 2008 in response to claims of alleged corporate complicity in human rights abuses, including censorship and surveillance.[146] It was created to determine how technology companies could best respect the rights of their users—wherever they operate.[147]

Architects of the GNI, including tech giants Google, Microsoft, and Yahoo!, constructed the organization along with rights advocates and academics as part of a concerted effort to draw on the perspectives, credibility, and leverage of their stakeholders, with a belief that "the foundation for good law and policy is internationally recognized rights to free expression and privacy."[148]

[143] *For NGOs*, VOLUNTARY PRINCIPLES (2019), https://www.voluntaryprinciples.org/for-ngos.

[144] *About GNI*, GLOBAL NETWORK INITIATIVE (2018), https://globalnetworkinitiative.org/about-gni/. *See generally*, Michael Samway, *The Global Network Initiative: How Can Companies in the Information Communications Technology Industry Respect Human Rights?* in BUSINESS AND HUMAN RIGHTS: FROM PRINCIPLES TO PRACTICE (Justine Nolan & Dorothée Baumann-Pauly, eds. 2016).

[145] *Id.*

[146] *See, e.g.*, Joseph Kahn, *Yahoo Helped Chinese to Prosecute Journalist*, N.Y. TIMES (Sept. 8, 2005), https://www.nytimes.com/2005/09/08/business/worldbusiness/yahoo-helped-chinese-to-prosecute-journalist.html (discussing the imprisonment of Shi Tao, a Chinese journalist imprisoned after Yahoo! provided Tao's computer records).

[147] *See generally*, *About GNI*, GLOBAL NETWORK INITIATIVE, https://globalnetworkinitiative.org/about-gni/ (last visited Sept. 24, 2018).

[148] *Id.*

### 1. GNI Mission and Membership

The stated mission of the GNI is "to protect and advance freedom of expression and privacy in the ICT industry by setting a global standard for responsible company decision making and by being a leading voice for freedom of expression and privacy rights."[149] The GNI aims to accomplish this mission by fostering accountability, providing a framework for responsible decision-making, empowering policy to promote human rights and by enabling learning to shape best practices.[150] More specifically, the recent goals of the GNI have revolved around combating network disruptions, contributing scholarship surrounding intermediary liability, encouraging transparency among governments regarding surveillance, and conducting seminars about the ways jurisdiction affects human rights online.[151]

Membership of the GNI is comprised of academic organizations, civil society organizations, ICT companies, investors, observers, and a panel of academics.[152] GNI membership is open to "companies in the global ICT sector worldwide, and NGOs, investors and academic institutions that commit to the Principles and other core GNI documents."[153] In order to join the GNI, a prospective member must submit a statement of interest with a signature from an authorized representative. The statement of interest must declare a commitment to implementing or advancing the principles of the GNI (described in the next section), promoting accountability with respect to the implementation of the GNI principles, and contributing to shared learning on GNI-related issues among participants.[154]

Member companies are required to adopt certain practices and responsibilities as part of their membership. These include implementing processes and procedures in accordance with GNI implementation guidelines, allowing themselves to be assessed and evaluated by independent assessors, and paying annual dues set by the GNI.[155] Founding corporate members Google, Yahoo! (now Oath), and Microsoft have been joined by BT (British Telecommunications plc), Facebook, Millicom, Nokia, Orange, Telefonica, Telenor Group, Telia Company, and Vodafone.[156]

[149] *Our Mission*, Global Network Initiative, https://globalnetworkinitiative.org/team/our-mission/ (last visited Sept. 25, 2018).
[150] *Id.*
[151] *Network Disruptions*, Global Network Initiative, https://globalnetworkinitiative.org/policy-issues/network-disruptions/ (last visited Sept. 25, 2018)
[152] *Our Members*, Global Network Initiative, https://globalnetworkinitiative.org/#home-menu (last visited Sept. 25, 2018).
[153] *Governance Charter*, Global Network Initiative, https://globalnetworkinitiative.org/governance-charter/ (last visited Sept. 25, 2018). [hereinafter *GNI Charter*]
[154] *Id.*
[155] *Id.*
[156] *Id.*

NGOs, investors, and academic institutions are also required to adopt certain practices as part of their membership. These include paying nominal dues or offering a donation, supporting the GNI principles, and contributing to a shared learning pool among GNI participants.[157]

2. GNI Substantive Policy Commitments and Procedures

The GNI further lays out several core principles (GNI Principles) that members are expected to adopt in order to provide direction and guidance to the ICT industry. Among these principles are the protection of freedom of expression, ensuring privacy as a human right, promoting responsible company decision-making, and enabling multistakeholder collaboration.[158]

In order to encourage participants to act with the GNI's principles in mind, the GNI requires that member groups meet several conditions to maintain their membership status. In addition to adopting the GNI principles, participating companies are expected to implement processes and procedures according to GNI standards, submit to regular evaluation by independent assessors to determine compliance, contribute to shared learning and collective action with participants, pay annual dues set by the GNI, and actively participate in GNI meetings/and or activities.[159]

Members found to have violated GNI participant requirements may have their membership terminated by the GNI board. Specifically, the board may terminate membership for failure to pay dues, failure to attend meetings/activities for more than a twelve-month period, failure to meet reporting requirements, failure to materially participate in voting measures, failure of companies to meet compliance and evaluation requirements, and disclosure of information identified as confidential.[160]

GNI's assessment structure is broken up into "self-reporting from the companies to GNI after one year of membership" and "an independent assessment of each company member held every two years covering both a process review and including the review of specific cases."[161]

Aspiring independent assessors must apply to the executive director for consideration and review by the director and the board.[162] Independent assessor candidates will be evaluated for their independence and competence and are selected by a simple-majority vote of the board.[163]

[157] *Id.*

[158] *The GNI Principles*, Global Network Initiative, https://globalnetworkinitiative.org/policy-issues/ (last visited Sept. 23, 2018).

[159] *GNI Charter*, *supra* note 153, at 7.

[160] *Id.*

[161] *GNI Charter*, *supra* note 153, at 8.

[162] *Id.* at 9.

[163] *Id.*

Once accredited, an independent assessor may serve a two-year term. Assessors may seek renewal of their accreditation at the end of each term.[164] Furthermore, each independent assessor enters into a master services agreement with the GNI, which requires them to meet the GNI's list of independence criteria, competency criteria, confidentiality requirements, and other performance and quality requirements.[165]

### 3. GNI Structure and Governance

The GNI is governed by a board of directors with an independent chair serving as the overseeing entity.[166] The board's purpose is to "further the Principles and to oversee the organization to fulfill the vision of the GNI" as well as to "be responsible for the strategic direction and the fiduciary operations of the GNI."[167] The strategic direction and fiduciary operations of the GNI are monitored and managed by the GNI board of directors.

The board of directors consists of ten members from companies, five from civil society organizations, two from the academic community, two from the investor community, and an independent chair. One additional seat on the board is provided for an academic or investor representative, alternating between the two constituencies every eighteen months. Every board member must also designate an alternate board member from within their organization or constituency.[168]

Board members are nominated and selected by members within their respective constituency group—business and industry associations, civil society organizations, academics, and investors.[169] Each board member may serve up to a three-year term, although terms are automatically renewable for one term. Upon completion of a second term, a board member may receive an affirmative vote from the majority of their constituency to serve a third term.[170] Board members all designate an alternate board member from within their respective constituencies.[171] However, the board may not have more than one representative from a single company, NGO, investor, or academic institution.

The board's independent chair, serves a three-year term that can be renewed only once.[172] The chair is nominated by the board and selected by "(1) the affirmative vote of a majority of each constituency group entitled to vote and (2) the affirmative majority of all constituency group members entitled to vote."[173]

164 *Id.*
165 *Id.*
166 *Id.* at 2.
167 *Id.* at 2.
168 *Board of Directors*, GLOBAL NETWORK INITIATIVE, https://globalnetworkinitiative.org/board/ (last visited Sept. 25, 2018).
169 *GNI Charter*, *supra* note 153, at 3.
170 *Id.*
171 *Id.*
172 *Id.* at 4.
173 *Id.*

The board's voting obligations are divided into two categories, supermajority and simple-majority vote.[174] A supermajority requires a two-thirds majority of the board and at least 50 percent of each constituency.[175] These decisions include adopting or amending core GNI documents, appointing and removing the executive director, and determining the compliance of a GNI participant.[176] A simple majority vote decides the annual operating plan and budget, accrediting independent assessors, and admitting new participants.[177] GNI staff oversee the running of the organization and the enforcement and enactment of the board's policies.[178]

## IV. Change: MSIs as Instruments and Institutions of Global Governance

### A. MSI Debates: Assessing the Efficacy and Impacts of MSIs

According to MSI Integrity, to date "research on MSI functioning has yet to concretely integrate perspectives on MSI functioning from communities and individuals whose rights and well-being MSIs are intended to address."[179] Data on the efficacy of MSIs of rights holders is urgently needed.

Critics of MSIs express concerns that the rise in nongovernmental regulatory experiments are intended to undermine labor organizing efforts and real regulatory reforms.[180] Skeptics suggest that some MSIs, especially those that serve as certifying bodies or issue certifications such as the Kimberley Process, which certifies diamonds, or Forest Stewardship, which certifies that wood is sustainably sourced, will create a false sense among consumers that problems have been addressed. Business participants are perceived to be primarily interested in mitigating reputation risks rather than solving problems.[181] Reducing reputational risks to business and solving problems to reduce risks to human rights are not

[174] *GNI Charter*, *supra* note 153, at 5.
[175] *Id.*
[176] *Id.*
[177] *Id.*
[178] *Id.* at 6.
[179] *Mission and Principles*, MSI Integrity (last visited Nov. 13, 2020), https://www.msi-integrity.org/about/mission-and-principles/#:~:text=Our%20Mission%20and%20Vision%20The%20Institute%20for%20Multi-Stakeholder,initiatives%20%28MSIs%29%20that%20address%20business%20and%20human%20rights; *see also* Bennett Freeman, "Rethinking MSIs: Time to Bury MSIs?—Not so Fast," MSI Integrity (Oct. 1, 2020), https://www.msi-integrity.org/rethinking-msis-time-to-bury-msis-not-so-fast/
[180] Dara O'Rourke, *MSI Regulation: Privatizing or Socializing Global Labor Standards?*, 34 World Dev. 899 (2005)
[181] *Id.*

necessarily mutually exclusive. Indeed, some in the business community are interested in solving problems and do acknowledge the demands for corporate accountability from rights activists, but express concern about "increased pressure on privatizing responsibility for human rights . . . because corporations are not democratically elected representatives of people."[182]

## B. Structural Dynamics of Securing Human Rights through MSIs

The structure of MSIs differ significantly presenting obstacles and creating opportunities of change.

### 1. Obstacles and Opportunities

*a. Efficacy of the FLA: Obstacles and Opportunities*

The overall efficacy of the FLA is difficult to determine. There is no easily accessible evidence that an FLA member has ever lost its accreditation or faced legal repercussions for its labor practices. Unfortunately, it is unclear whether this is indicative of compliance with the FLA's requirements or simply the association's failure to effectively enforce them or to adequately report progress to the public.

The current benefits and efficacy of the FLA's system appear to be mostly tied to the positive reputation that membership creates and the downstream impact of membership. Only once the board approves the participation of a company, retailer, or supplier, the new member and the association may communicate its membership to the public.[183] Furthermore, as discussed earlier, universities and companies seeking membership must ensure that their licensees and those they directly do business with must either become members or must be approved by the association.[184] Therefore, a system is created wherein if a prospective licensee or company wishes to work with a member, they must also become a member.

The aspects of the FLA that have not been disclosed in much detail are changes to its guidelines in certain countries and their acceptance of third-party complaints. The FLA has stated that:

> [In certain countries,] the rights embodied in the standards are not fully recognized or enforced either through law or practice. Despite these difficulties, one of the principal goals of the Association is to promote and encourage positive change in these countries so these standards become fully recognized,

[182] Telephone interview with Daniel Fibiger, Senior Director, Global Sustainability at Gap Inc. (Feb. 24, 2019).

[183] *FLA Charter*, *supra* note 91, at 16.

[184] *Id.* at 13–14.

> respected and enforced. When deemed necessary and appropriate by the Board, the Association shall provide Participating Companies and College or University Licensees with appropriate country guidelines to address such special.[185]

They have further established that complaints "can be initiated by any third party after local remedies have been used to investigate allegations of significant and/or persistent noncompliance with the Workplace Code or Monitoring Principles in the Facilities of Participating Companies and College or University Licensees."[186]

The FLA is an organization with a large member base and the capability of gaining members through downstream requirements and the positive associations that are assumed with membership and access to a reliable market of University consumers. Labor unions are not among the FLA's member base.

*b. Efficacy of the Voluntary Principles on Security: Obstacles and Opportunities*

The Voluntary Principles on Security and Human Rights are another edifice in the "emerging architecture of collaborative arrangements" identified by Professor John Ruggie, the Special Representative of the Secretary General (SRSG) as contributing to progress on human rights and responsible business conduct. The Voluntary Principles are aimed at addressing some of the human rights challenges confronting the extractive industries by providing guidance to companies on safety and security concerns while also encouraging operations consist with a framework that "encourages" respect for human rights.[187]

While commending some participating companies for efforts to develop relevant indicators, Oxfam elected to leave the Voluntary Principles in 2013 over "the lack of meaningful progress in independent assurance."[188] Nongovernmental participants have also express frustration with the lack of progress on aspects of grievance mechanisms.[189] Trade industry associations including the ICMM and the IPIECA continue serve as observers to the initiative.

There are notable positive aspects of the Voluntary Principles which could promote change in the extractives industry. The Principles emphasize a front-end early assessment where many CSR programs do back-end audits, and while

[185] *Id.* at 29.

[186] *Id.*

[187] *See What Are The Voluntary Principles?*, VOLUNTARY PRINCIPLES OF SECURITY AND HUMAN RIGHTS, http://www.voluntaryprinciples.org/what-are-the-voluntary-principles/ (last visited Jan. 21, 2016).

[188] Oxfam America, *Oxfam Leaves Voluntary Principles for Security and Human Rights Multi-Stakeholder Initiative*, BUSINESS AND HUMAN RIGHTS RESOURCE CENTRE (Apr. 17, 2013), http://business-humanrights.org/en/oxfam-leaves-voluntary-principles-for-security-and-human-rights-multi-stakeholder-initiative.

[189] Author's informal interview with NGO staff, 2013.

audits are fine as an ongoing element of monitoring, more done earlier could result in improved human rights performance.

The practice of information sharing about abusive practices or inadequate policies of potential public and private security provides with others in the industry could create the type of leverage needed to change practices. The risk of a contract termination confronting private providers adds the element of accountability and could lessen the likelihood of continued impunity. Paradoxically, while the Voluntary Principles has perhaps "the most stunted governance structure" and is perhaps the least transparent and "opaque on accountability," Bennett Freeman, former US Deputy Assistant Secretary of State for Democracy, Human Rights and Labor who led the stakeholder process resulting in the structure and standards for the government, argues that the Voluntary Principles have been among the most successful of all the MSIs and have made a positive impact on the ground.[190]

While some improvements can be attributed to the Voluntary Principles, some problems remain, which could compromise the ability of stakeholders to ensure that respect for human rights is sustained. The Voluntary Principles provide no guidance on how to reconcile conflicts between local laws and customs and international law where there are inconsistent levels of protection. Imagine a country that does not recognize or adhere to the standard of "free, prior, informed consent" contained in Declaration on the Rights of Indigenous Peoples, which requires that affected communities have a say in development likely to impact their way of life.[191] Suppose a country does not acknowledge the rights of migrant workers as contained in the UN Convention on the Rights of Migrants.[192] In contrast, the United Nations Guiding Principles on Business and Human Rights (UNGPs) provide that international standards should inform the policies and practices of business enterprises even when operating in challenging environments.

Another problem is that the Principles do not provide an explicit temporal element. The recommendation that firms assess the reputation and human rights record of security service providers is a case in point. Ideally, such assessments should occur before a company engages security services.

Nevertheless, the Voluntary Principles still call for a great deal in difficult circumstances. For example, paying attention to the safety and security of sources and the status of investigations can be further complicated by abusive authoritarian governments. There is a role for business in defending the rights of environmental and human rights, and opportunities to do so will depend on context. To make the Voluntary Principles more effective, there should be

[190] Telephone Interview Bennett Freeman, former US Deputy Assistant Secretary of State for Democracy, Human Rights and Labor. January 15, 2019.

[191] *Free, Prior and Informed Consent*, Food and Agriculture Organization of the UN, http://www.fao.org/indigenous-peoples/our-pillars/fpic/en/ (last visited Feb. 12, 2020).

[192] G.A. Res. 45/158, International Convention on the Protection of the Rights of All Migrant Workers and Members of Their Families (Dec. 18, 1990).

a fourth categorical concern, in addition to relationships with private security, relationships with public security, and risk assessment—relationships with communities could be given greater emphasis.

*c. Efficacy of the GNI: Obstacles and Opportunities*

The GNI faces numerous challenges which hinder its ability to be an effective regulating entity. Low participation rates and issues with membership plague the organization.[193] When the GNI was founded, Amnesty International refused to join or even support the initiative because it was "not yet strong enough to allow Amnesty International to endorse them."[194] Despite public outcries and mounting pressures since the inception of the GNI, large tech companies such as Twitter have remain unwilling to join.[195] Furthermore, despite many recent issues with telecom companies, such as warrantless wiretaps, no telecom companies joined the GNI until 2016.[196] While telecom company participation was a great victory for the initiative, it also cost it two founding members from the academic constituency that disagreed with the agreements that had to be made to bring in those companies.[197] Because multistakeholder initiatives are based on the concept of self-monitoring and assessment, they are only as strong as their constituent members. However, in 2020, the GNI had only twelve member companies: BT, Facebook, Google, Microsoft, Millicom, Nokia, Oath, Orange, Telefonica, Telenor, Telia, and Vodafone.[198]

The other key concern with the GNI is the poor accountability to which it holds its members—a perception perhaps due in part to inadequate external transparency.[199] Despite the requirements written in the GNI charter, no companies were assessed for the first three years of the organization's existence.[200] Furthermore, national regulations make it difficult for member companies to be entirely transparent, which cost the GNI another founding member in 2013.[201] While many agree that the GNI is a great start in promoting human rights and

[193] Colin M. Maclay, *Protecting Privacy and Expression Online Can the Global Network Initiative Embrace the Character of the Net?*, ACCESS CONTROLLED: THE SHAPING OF POWER, RIGHTS AND RULE IN CYBERSPACE, OPEN NETWORK INITIATIVE 97–98 (2010).

[194] Bobbie Johnson, *Amnesty Criticizes Global Network Initiative for Online Freedom Of Speech*, THE GUARDIAN (Oct. 30, 2008), https://www.theguardian.com/technology/2008/oct/30/amnesty-global-network-initiative.

[195] Larry Downes, *Why No One Will Join the Global Network Initiative*, FORBES (Mar. 30, 2011), https://www.forbes.com/sites/larrydownes/2011/03/30/why-no-one-will-join-the-global-network-initiative/#14d5a3c7d782.

[196] Sarah Labowitz & Michael Posner, *Why We're Leaving the Global Network Initiative*, N.Y.U. (Feb. 1, 2016), https://bhr.stern.nyu.edu/blogs/why-were-leaving-the-gni.

[197] *Id.*

[198] *Our Members*, GLOBAL JUSTICE INITIATIVE (2018), https://globalnetworkinitiative.org/#home-menu.

[199] Colin M. Maclay, *Protecting Privacy and Expression Online*, ACCESS CONTROLLED 87, 98 (2010).

[200] Downes, *supra* note 195.

[201] *EFF Resigns from Global Network Initiative*, ELECTRONIC FRONTIER FOUNDATION (Oct. 10, 2013), https://www.eff.org/press/releases/eff-resigns-global-network-initiative.

protecting freedom of expression and privacy, they also agree that it is only a start and needs a lot of work to become a successful monitoring and regulating entity.[202] These problems are compounded by the extensive requirements to join the GNI which effectively disqualify start-ups or venture-financed companies that might have been able to lend significant contributions.[203]

The GNI has also struggled to earn and keep the confidence of human rights organizations. One of the world's foremost human rights NGOs, Amnesty International was involved in the initial discussions, but refused to join the GNI after citing disappointment with the weakness of the final organizational structure.[204] Similarly, the Electronic Frontier Foundation (EFF) withdrew from the GNI, citing a lack of confidence that the group's corporate members were able to be transparent about their internal privacy and security systems in the wake of US National Security Agency (NSA) surveillance revelations. An EFF statement on the matter read, "EFF can no longer sign its name on joint statements knowing now that GNI's corporate members have been blocked from sharing crucial information about how the US government has meddled with these company's security practices."[205]

Since its relatively slow start, GNI membership has grown every year since its inception, with major tech companies committing to the GNI. While the addition of major players in the ICT sector may be a net positive, the GNI's goals will continue to be undermined if its most powerful and influential members continue to be implicated in human rights and privacy violations the world over—seemingly in direct opposition to the GNI's stated principles. For example, Google's rumored China-centric search engine (codenamed Dragonfly) has been widely criticized by numerous human rights groups.[206] If the Dragonfly project proceeds as confirmed and Google offers search engine services under the control of the Chinese government, it is difficult to see how Google could reconcile that behavior with its commitments to the GNI principles.

Likewise, Facebook has been implicated in a number of human rights and personal privacy violations in recent years. In Myanmar, where Facebook is seen as the de facto internet,[207] the company was recently accused of censoring activists

[202] Josh Katz, *Initiative Against Internet Suppression Good Start But Lacks Teeth, Some Say*, Finding Dulcinea (Oct. 30, 2008), http://www.findingdulcinea.com/news/international/October-08/Initiative-Against-Internet-Suppression-Good-Start-But-Lacks-Teeth--Some-Say.html.

[203] *Id.*

[204] Bobbie Johnson, *Amnesty Criticizes Global Network Initiative for Online Freedom of Speech*, The Guardian (Oct. 30, 2008), http://www.guardian.co.uk/technology/2008/oct/30/amnesty-global-network-initiative.

[205] *EFF Resigns from Global Network Initiative*, *supra* note 201.

[206] *See* Isobel Asher Hamilton, *14 Powerful Human-Rights Groups Write to Google Demanding It Kill Plans to Launch a China Search Engine*, Business Insider (Aug. 29, 2018, 6:15 AM), https://www.businessinsider.com/human-rights-groups-ask-google-to-kill-china-search-engine-plans-2018-8.

[207] Matthew Ingram, *In Some Countries, Fake News on Facebook Is a Matter of Life and Death*, Colum. J. Rev. (Nov. 21, 2017), https://www.cjr.org/analysis/facebook-rohingya-myanmar-fake-news.php.

and journalists documenting incidences of what the US State Department has called "ethnic cleansing of Myanmar's Rohingya minority."[208] Earlier this summer, a *New York Times* report also revealed that Facebook had formed partnerships with numerous mobile device manufacturers in order to share users' personal information.[209] This was just the latest in a long line of Facebook personal data and privacy scandals, to say nothing of the Cambridge Analytica debacle that directed disinformation to Facebook users in an effort to influence the outcome of electoral politics in some nations.[210]

While it certainly would not be fair to attribute the actions and omissions of social media companies to the GNI, it will struggle to maintain credibility, membership, and funding if there are not more serious consequences for continued conduct in violation of GNI Principles.

Through adherence to its principles, the GNI provides a framework for ICT companies that aim to advance commercial interests and remain accountable to respect rights of users when governments demand personal data.[211] The very existence of the GNI provides concrete evidence that powerful organizations do recognize the value of pursuing ways to promote ethical decision-making in the ICT world.[212] However, stated goals and well-articulated principles will mean little if they do not ultimately contribute to tangible results.

While there is no shortage of criticism for the GNI,[213] it has made some impressive strides in recent years. For example, the GNI grew its membership by nearly a third in 2017. Notably, many of the additions were large ICT-sector companies such as Millicom, Nokia, Orange, and Vodafone, which had been observers in the GNI during the prior year.[214] This shows that the GNI was able to further earn the confidence of more technology firms of considerable size; the newly added ICT companies account for a combined 1.5 billion users.

[208] *Id.*

[209] Gabriel J.X. Dance, *Facebook Gave Device Makers Deep Access to Data on Users and Friends*, N.Y. Times (June 3, 2018), https://www.nytimes.com/interactive/2018/06/03/technology/facebook-device-partners-users-friends-data.html.

[210] Kevin Granville, *Facebook and Cambridge Analytica: What You Need to Know as Fallout Widens*, N.Y. Times (Mar. 19, 2018), https://www.nytimes.com/2018/03/19/technology/facebook-cambridge-analytica-explained.html.

[211] *See* Brian R. Israel, *Make Money Without Doing Evil? Caught Between Authoritarian Regimes in Emerging Markets and a Global Law of Human Rights, U.S. ICTS Face a Twofold Quandary*, 24 Berkeley Tech. L.J. 617, 655 (2009).

[212] *See* Ira Steven Nathenson, *Super-Intermediaries, Code, Human Rights*, 8 Intercultural Hum. Rts. L. Rev. 21, 175 (2013).

[213] Larry Downes, *Why No One Will Join the Global Network Initiative*, forbes (Mar. 30, 2011, 12:20 PM), https://www.forbes.com/sites/larrydownes/2011/03/30/why-no-one-will-join-the-global-network-initiative/?sh=53ef53bfd782; Sarah Labowitz & Michael Posner, *Why We Are Leaving the Global Network Initiative* (Feb. 1, 2016) https://bhr.stern.nyu.edu/blogs/why-were-leaving-the-gni; Anupam Chander, *Googling Freedom*, 99 Cal. L. Rev. 1, 38 (2011).

[214] *See 2017 Annual Report*, Global Network Initiative, https://globalnetworkinitiative.org/gin_tnetnoc/uploads/2018/06/GNIAnnualReport2017.pdf (last visited Sept. 26, 2018).

Given that the GNI has constructed its operations around holding other companies accountable to policy commitments, one way to assess success or failure is by examining how member corporations have complied with the GNI principles. During the 2016 assessment period, Facebook, Google, LinkedIn, Microsoft, and Yahoo! were all found to be in compliance with GNI principles.[215]

The GNI represents a strong collective of companies, academics, investors and human rights organizations aimed at combating human rights abuses in the ICT sector. It has shown an ability to consistently gain high-profile membership and has created a useful framework for companies struggling to reconcile different demands.

### C. Making the Most of MSI Strategies

Some MSI standards do become salient and spread. Some voluntary standards originating from the efforts of civil society organizations have been incorporated into government policy and corporate compliance initiatives.

## V. Incorporating Rights

This chapter explained how conflicts over corporate complicity in alleged rights abuses served to catalyze the creation of the different industry-specific multistakeholder initiatives. It also evaluated the obstacles and opportunities multistakeholder initiative strategy presents as a means of regulating the human rights policies and practices of business enterprises. This chapter provided a foundation for understanding the existing and emerging obligations of business enterprises in key industry sectors with respect to human rights and the institutions evolving to address business operations in challenging contexts.

Although institutional arrangements like the GNI, the FLA, and the Voluntary Principles on Security remain voluntary in that no business is legally obligated to join, they are part of a larger system of efforts to regulate conduct, and they are informed by past conflict and cooperation with affected communities in some measure. There are also relative benefits and drawbacks, evolution is occurring.

[215] *Global Network Initiative Public Report on the 2015/2016 Independent Company Assessments*, Global Network Initiative (July 2016), https://globalnetworkinitiative.org/wp-content/uploads/2018/02/Public-Report-2015-16-Independent-Company-Assessments.pdf (explaining that "only organizations accredited by the multi-stakeholder GNI board are eligible to conduct the independent assessments of member companies. Accredited assessors must meet the independence and competency criteria required by the GNI, and enter into an accreditation agreement with the GNI.").

Bennett Freeman, who on behalf of the US State Department led the development of the Voluntary Principles on Security and Human Rights, served on the board of the FLA, and later co-founded the GNI offered these reflections on the role of these types of institutional arrangements:

> The big challenge in the business in human rights field, including in the MSI field, is how you go beyond setting standards and encouraging or facilitating policy frameworks and due diligence processes and even accountability mechanisms, grievance mechanisms, remedy more generally. Is it sufficient to get to what you're really trying to do, which is to make an impact? We've all been struggling for the last half dozen years with this debate of how do you define and measure impact?[216]

With respect to the efficacy of MSIs, Freeman concedes: "I don't think anybody has fully cracked the code."[217] Yet, he maintains MSIs have contributed to significant and constructive changes in business policies and practices that have served to protect rights and save lives based on his observations and experience working in government and with major multinationals across a variety of industry sectors over the years. As for measuring efficacy of working through MSI structures, he says: "Well, it's hard. It's hard methodologically to hear the dog that doesn't bark."[218]

As SOMO, the Dutch NGO has observed, "strategic alliances between civil society organizations (CSOs), corporations, citizens, research organizations and governments, show great potential in effectively addressing the (many) remaining societal issues of our time. Most of the issues we face today are neither owned nor solved by the individual stakeholders anymore. With growing interdependence comes a growing need to search for collaborative approaches."[219] Arvind Ganesan, founding director of the business and human rights program at Human Rights Watch explains:

> in my experience, there are certain elements that you need to have in place to actually see change from a company where regulation or law or some kind of liability isn't present, and the first is external pressure, which is what civil society does, and to some degree what MSIs do . . . they create an expectation. They create a norm, if not a standard. The second is that you actually have to have internal champions within a company to socialize these expectations of these norms or these standards. Third, you have to have the buy in from senior

[216] Telephone Interview Bennett Freeman, former US Deputy Assistant Secretary of State for Democracy, Human Rights and Labor, January 15, 2019.
[217] *Id.*
[218] *Id.*
[219] VAN HUIJSTEE, *supra* note 80, at 8.

> leadership so it is okay or prioritized to do it. So, from that perspective, if there are internal champions [in a company] then an MSI does help them, because they can say look at the other companies are doing. Look at the pressure we're getting, and things like that.[220]

This chapter provides a foundation for understanding the existing and emerging obligations of business enterprises with respect to human rights grounded in international standards motivated by risks both to business and those at risk of having their rights violated. It presented an overview of the international human rights impacted by business activities and explained the origins of the principal industry-specific instruments and institutions that have been created to protect and promote human rights through collaboration. It offered context for the challenges confronted by MSIs. Finally, it has offered an assessment of the opportunities for and obstacles to cooperation between the advocates of affected communities and corporations implicated in rights violations, using representative MSIs to point to the potential for rethinking regulatory strategies to protect rights. This chapter has not discussed more recent MSIs such as the Bangladesh Accord or long-established entities addressing similar challenges with higher levels of government engagement such as the Extractives Industry Transparency Initiative (EITI) or the Kimberley Process.

In sum, institutional design can influence input and participation, but the promise of the MSI strategy is in peril where the outsized influence of certain partners or the relative power and information asymmetry among stakeholders are not taken into account and adequately addressed in the governance structure of an MSI. These evolving multistakeholder initiatives, sometimes referred to as "self-regulatory" or "private ordering," are often co-created and can provide the means by which to promulgate standards. Implementation can prepare the ground to grow respect for rights, provided that power imbalances between different constituencies are addressed procedurally. While not binding international law, these steps toward standards creation and monitoring by MSIs are promising and have potential to lead to constructive change.

The next chapter presents rankings and indicators, another opportunity to grow respect for rights by incentivizing corporate responsibility.

[220] Telephone interview with Arvind Ganesan, Human Rights Watch, Jan. 19, 2019.

# PART II

# CHANGE

## *Human Rights, Corporate Responsibility Codes, and Compliance with Commitments*

# 4

# Information and Accountability

## Regulating the Corporate Social Responsibility to Respect Human Rights through Ranking and Reporting

### Introduction

This chapter examines the emergence and evolution of selected ranking and reporting frameworks in the expanding realm of business and human rights advocacy. Specifically, it examines how indicators in the form of rankings and reports evaluating the conduct of transnational corporate actors can serve as regulatory tools with potential to bridge a global governance gap that places human rights at risk. It explains the conditions that have led to coordination and collaboration among entities engaged in creating reporting frameworks and rankings that rely on the competitive impulses of the business enterprises being ranked to influence changes in business policies and practices. It also identifies why the businesses being ranked have been slow to deploy effective counterstrategies despite efforts to contest emerging reporting requirements. It considers the interaction of selected business and human rights indicators with recent laws regulating supply chain transparency in the United States and with recent global policy initiatives calling for business enterprises to conduct human rights impact assessments. It reviews some of the methodological and moral risks raised with respect to ranking rights. In conclusion, I argue that in the ecology of global governance, these new business and human rights indicators will provide rights advocates with greater power and have the potential to play an important role in solidifying emerging soft law standards and in strengthening corporate self-regulation. I argue that strategic use of indicators in the business and human rights realm could ultimately prove to make the commitments contained in voluntary codes of conduct to respect human rights obligatory.

*Incorporating Rights.* Erika George, Oxford University Press. © Erika George 2021.
DOI: 10.1093/oso/9780199941483.003.0005

## I. The Primary Elements of Indicators

Quantitative indicators are emerging as regulatory instruments of global governance.[1] Governments and international agencies are using indicators to measure progress and compare performance on a range of issues. Indicators increasingly inform decisions related to resource allocation and budget and policy priorities. For example, the World Bank's *Doing Business Report* provides a benchmark for financing projects. The United States' *Trafficking in Persons Report* ranks countries on different tiers that can determine whether or not or the extent to which the US government will provide aid. There are now even metrics quantifying issues previously understood to be subjective or qualitative, such as "gross national happiness."[2]

### A. Indicator Definitions

In their investigation of the significance of indicators in sociolegal processes, scholars Kevin E. Davis, Benedict Kingsbury, and Sally Engle Merry observe that there is no consensus on the meaning of the term "indicator" but offer the following functional definition:

> An indicator is a named collection of rank-ordered data that purports to represent the past or the projected performance of different units. The data are generated through a process that simplifies raw data about a complex social phenomenon.[3]

The OECD, both an author and an audience for various social indicators, provides another definition:

> In general terms, an indicator is a quantitative or a qualitative measure derived from a series of observed facts that can reveal relative positions (e.g. of a country) in a given area. When evaluated at regular intervals, an indicator can

[1] *See* Kevin E. Davis, Benedict Kingsbury, & Sally Engle Merry, *Introduction: Global Governance Indicators*, in GOVERNANCE BY INDICATORS: GLOBAL POWER THROUGH QUANTIFICATION AND RANKINGS 4 (Kevin E. Davis, Benedict Kingsbury, & Sally Engle Merry eds., 2012) ("The burgeoning production and use of indicators in global governance has the potential to alter the forms, the exercise, and perhaps even the distribution of power in certain spheres of global governance."); Galit A. Sarfaty, *Regulating Through Numbers: A Case Study of Corporate Sustainability Reporting*, 53 VA. J. INT'L L. 575 (2013).

[2] *See* Mathais Siems & David Nelken, *Global Social Indicators and the Concept of Legitimacy*, 13 (4) INT'L J. L. IN CONTEXT 436, 436–449 (2017)

[3] Kevin E. Davis, Benedict Kingsbury, & Sally Engle Merry, *Indicators as a Technology of Global Governance*, 46 L. & SOC'Y REV. 71, 73 (2012).

> point out the direction of change across different units and through time. In the context of policy analysis . . . indicators are useful in identifying trends and drawing attention to particular issues. They can also be helpful in setting policy priorities and in benchmarking or monitoring performance.[4]

In its Rule of Law Indicators Guide, the United Nations explains the function of indicators as follows:

> Indicators are indirect measures of elements that, taken together, can be used repeatedly and over time to assess progress towards specific goals and objectives. The often have the dual role of spurring reform and holding agencies and individuals accountable for their past performance. The use of indicators is becoming increasingly popular in many areas of public policy, science and business as an accountability mechanism for public institutions and private companies and as an early warning sign of disease, famine, economic crisis or other problems with widespread impact . . . Indicators allow the synthesis of complex information to produce easily interpreted measures that are well suited to tracking changes over time and drawing comparisons.[5]

While social realities may be captured in a myriad of ways, Davis and colleagues contrast indicators as distinctive for serving to compile data in a manner that allows for comparisons to be made among particular units of analysis. For instance, an indicator could allow for comparative evaluations to be made of different countries, as does the World Justice Project's Rule of Law Index; or for different companies, as does Oxfam's "Behind the Brands Scorecard." Put simply, "indicators cater to the demand for (and receptivity to) numerical, rank-ordered and comparable data."[6]

Complicating matters, however, indicators are far from simple and may not necessarily satisfy the demand for information or drive truly transformative change. Mathias Siems and David Nelken make this point with respect to the World Bank's ranking, explaining: "indicators are only proxies for good law and can only cover a small proportion of the relevant laws for doing business . . . a country that changes its law according to these indicators quickly rises in the ranking, but this is irrelevant as far as the remainder of their legal system remains unchanged."[7] Significantly for the human rights advocate concerned about the

[4] Siems & Nelken, *supra* note 2 (citing *Handbook on Constructing Composite Indicators: Methodology and User Guide*, Organisation for Economic Co-operation and Development 13 (2013), http://www.oecd.org/sdd/42495745.pdf).

[5] *Id.* at 437 (citing the United Nations Rule of Law Indicators Implementation Guide and Project Tools (UN, 2001), at I).

[6] *Id.*

[7] *Id.* at 441.

conduct of powerful business enterprises, "the indicator represents an assertion of power to produce knowledge and to define or shape the way the world is understood."[8]

Davis and his colleagues have set forth some salient characteristics of indicators. An effective indicator will have a name establishing authority to make measurements. An effective indicator will frequently take the form of a rank ordering that envisions "improvement" and allows for movement in the measurement. An effective indicator has the capacity to take complex information about social phenomena and simplify it to enable ease of comparison across difference. Finally, an effective indicator can be used to inform decisions and make evaluations.[9]

Especially important for the success of indicators to address business and human rights issues is the potential for the index to be presented as authoritative and useful in evaluating the comparative performance of business enterprises in addressing adverse human rights impacts. Indicators can be created to measure progress toward realizing the corporate responsibility to respect human rights. To the extent that an indicator becomes the measure against which conduct is evaluated, in effect it sets a standard for conduct.

Davis and his colleagues identify some specific elements of indicators that make indicators easily accessible for use in decision-making regarding resource allocation or conduct. Consistency, transparency, authority, and impartiality are important elements. A consumer might decide how to allocate his or her disposable income on products and services rated by GoodGuide as the World Bank uses indicators to inform decisions on how to allocate aid. Indicators are attractive for their apparent "objectivity" and the added efficiency of reducing administrative costs of processing disparate information.

Indicators are used to rank things. A clear and common usage is necessary to understand how indicators are being deployed in business and human rights debates.

## B. Indicator Debates

The apparent advantages of indicators notwithstanding, indicators do present problems and disadvantages. In some instances, the creation of indicators can be costly. Multiple conflicting indicators can cause confusion. Missing or incomplete data could compromise the validity of rankings created based on indicators. As Wendy Nelson Espel and Michael Sauder have observed, "collecting the data

[8] *Id.*
[9] *Id.*

that comprises indicators is often more difficult and messy than appears from the outside."[10] Most significant for efforts to craft indicators to assess human rights is the concern that indicators simply oversimplify complex issues.

Davis and his colleagues posit that the growing demand for and reliance on indicators in global governance is related to the scale and intensity of social and economic interactions amenable to governance.[11] Debates over the social responsibility of transnational business enterprises similarly have gained ground as the span and scale of their influence is perceived by many to grow out of proportion to the ability of any one state to regulate commerce. Enterprising advocates interested in bringing business conduct into alignment with respect for human rights have created different rankings based on indicators relevant to adverse human rights impacts to influence business policies and practices and to inform the consumers about various products, goods, and services provided by particular companies.

### C. Dynamics of Indicator Creation

Several of the new indicators used in the rankings and ratings that purport to measure relative corporate human rights performance were created through consultative, collaborative processes often including the very corporations that appear in rights rankings in talks to determine what measures matter.[12] Because business enterprises are involved in the process of building the indicators that ultimately inform rankings, there has been "buy in."[13] A company that does not rank well will nevertheless understand the metrics against which the company's policies and practices were measured and will have had an opportunity to inform the development of indicators.

## II. The UN Guiding Principles on Business and Human Rights: Assessing and Reporting Risks

Assessing and addressing human rights risks through gathering and sharing data is consistent with the operational guidance provided to business enterprises in the UN Guiding Principles on Business and Human

[10] Wendy Nelson Espel & Michael Sauder, *The Dynamism of Indicators*, in GOVERNANCE BY INDICATORS: GLOBAL POWER THROUGH QUANTIFICATION AND RANKINGS 87 (Kevin E. Davis et al., eds. 2012).

[11] Davis, et al., *supra* note 1, at 3.

[12] Telephone Interview with Rebecca MacKinnon, Founder, Ranking Digital Rights–New America (Feb. 15, 2019).

[13] *Id.*

Rights (UNGPs). The UNGPs provide that to respect human rights, business enterprises "should avoid infringing on the human rights of others and should address adverse human rights impacts with which they are involved."[14] Aside from having a policy commitment to respect human rights, the corporate obligation to respect human rights outlined in the UNGPs also mandates that a business enterprise put in place "a human rights due-diligence process to identify, prevent, mitigate and account for how they address their human rights impacts."[15] Companies that take seriously the recommendations contained in the UNGPs by implementing human rights risks assessments, engaging in human rights due diligence, and reporting on the results provide the information used in the indicators created by constituencies concerned about human rights impacts. Companies that disclose salient environmental and social information also tend to perform better in human rights rankings because in most instances the indexes rely in large part on publicly available information provided by the companies.[16]

Many of leading human rights indicators evaluating business enterprises were created to be consistent with the UNGPs. Company rankings that rely on human rights indicators are being deployed to incentivize adherence to central elements of the business obligation to respect human rights. Ultimately, business and human rights indicators and ratings of the human rights performance of commercial actors will serve to strengthen and reinforce the parts of the UNGPs that detail the responsibility to respect human rights.

## A. Human Rights Risk Assessment

When done well, a human rights due diligence process should put a business enterprise in a better position to avoid infringing on the human rights of others by having a better understanding of the way practices may not be consistent with policies and the impacts of particular business practices. Indicators, rankings,

[14] Special Rep. of the Sec'y-Gen., *Guiding Principles on Business and Human Rights: Implementing the United Nations "Protect, Respect and Remedy" Framework*, Guiding Principle 11, U.N. Doc. HR/PUB/11/04 (2011), *available at* https://www.ohchr.org/Documents/Publications/GuidingPrinciplesBusinessHR_EN.pdf [hereinafter UNGP].

[15] *Id.* at Guiding Principle 15(b).

[16] *See* George Serafeim, *Social-Impact Efforts That Create Real Value*, HAR. BUS. REV., https://hbr.org/2020/09/making-sustainability-count (last visited Oct. 10, 2020); John Gerard Ruggie & Emily K. Middleton, *Money, Millennials and Human Rights: Sustaining "Sustainable Investing,"* GLOBAL POLICY (Jan. 3, 2019), https://onlinelibrary.wiley.com/doi/abs/10.1111/1758-5899.12645; Casey O'Connor & Sarah Labowitz, *Putting the "S" in ESG: Measuring Human Rights Performance for Investors*, N.Y.U. CTR. FOR BUS. AND HUMAN RIGHTS (Mar. 2017), https://static1.squarespace.com/static/547df270e4b0ba184dfc490e/t/58cad912e58c6274180b58b6/1489688854754/Metrics-Report-final-1.pdf.

and ratings can provide information to corporations that could help to inform design of better human rights due diligence processes.

According to the UNGPs, a company's human rights due diligence process should evaluate actual as well as potential impacts on human rights.[17] An effective due diligence process also communicates how human rights impacts identified are addressed.[18] The human rights due diligence process corporations should put into practice as envisioned in the UNGPs must recognize that human rights risks will evolve as the operations or operating context of a business enterprise change.[19] To that end, according to the UNGPs, "business enterprises should identify and assess any actual or potential adverse human rights impacts with which they may be involved either through their own activities or as a result of their business relationships" to fully evaluate human rights risks.[20]

Human rights due diligence should seek to identify adverse impacts that a business could "cause or contribute to through its own activities, or which may be directly linked to its operations, products or services."[21] Business enterprises are tasked with conducting due diligence in order to assess and address risks using internationally recognized human rights as a point of reference. The UNGPs envision that effective human rights due diligence and human rights impact assessments would put businesses in a better position to know and to avoid the risk of causing or contributing to human rights abuses. Indeed, a human rights due diligence process provides information to a business about where it can improve performance to avoid having adverse impacts on human rights.

## B. Reporting Risks to Human Rights

Not only should business enterprises know about the human rights impacts of their operations, they should show the public what is known. Guiding Principle 21 explains:

> The responsibility to respect human rights requires that business enterprises have in place policies and processes through which they can both *know and show* that they respect human rights in practice. Showing involves communication, providing a measure of transparency and accountability to individuals or groups who may be impacted and to other relevant stakeholders, including investors.[22]

[17] UNGP, *supra* note 14, at Guiding Principle 17.
[18] *Id.*
[19] *Id.*, at Guiding Principle 17(c).
[20] *Id.*, at Guiding Principle 18.
[21] *Id.*, at Guiding Principle 17(a).
[22] *Id.* 15, at Guiding Principle 21, Commentary, Paragraph 1 (emphasis added).

The UNGPs make explicit reference to indicators in provisions related to information gathering and dissemination. For example, Guiding Principle 20(a) on the efficacy of efforts to address human rights impacts provides that business enterprises should verify whether adverse human rights impacts and use "appropriate qualitative and quantitative indicators" to track implementation of efforts.[23] The UNGPs advise business enterprises to communicate how human rights impacts are being addressed.[24] Reporting on human rights is one of the many forms of communication recognized in the UNGPs as consistent with the responsibility to respect.[25] Commentary to Guiding Principle 21 recommends that corporate reporting "cover topics and indicators concerning how enterprises identify and address adverse impacts on human rights."[26] In particular, the Guiding Principle 21 Commentary offers "[s]ector-specific indicators can provide helpful additional detail."[27]

Reference to indicators is also made in commentary to Guiding Principle 7 explaining how states can facilitate business respect for human rights in areas affected by conflict. The UNGPs provide that in addition to ensuring that laws and regulations are crafted to effectively address increased risks associated with operating in conflict-affected areas, states should "develop early-warning indicators to alert . . . business enterprises to problems."[28] Early-warning indicators developed by governments could conceivably allow businesses enterprises and affected communities to avoid or to mitigate and address risks when operating in complicated contexts.

## C. Indicators and Information: Reporting Initiatives

As expectations on businesses continue to escalate and demands that businesses meet the obligation to respect human rights are becoming more clearly articulated, calls for some means for measuring progress have increased in certain industry sectors. For example, a global online survey of 853 of high-level corporate executives conducted by the Economist Intelligence Unit in 2014 found that respondents identified "public benchmarking on human rights performances (e.g. an index of companies)" as most likely to "enable companies to better fulfill their corporate responsibility to respect human rights."[29] A public index of

[23] *Id.*, at Guiding Principle 20.
[24] *Id.*, at Guiding Principle 21.
[25] *Id.*, at Guiding Principle 21 Commentary, Paragraph 2.
[26] *Id.*, at Guiding Principle 21 Commentary, Paragraph 3.
[27] *Id.*
[28] *Id.*, at Guiding Principle 7, Commentary, Paragraph 3.
[29] The Economist Intelligence Unit, The Road from Principles to Practice: Today's Challenges for Business in Respecting Human Rights (2015).

companies was viewed by respondents as more likely to lead to fulfilling human rights responsibilities than making human rights due diligence a legal requirement for business or strengthening legislative frameworks to ensure level market playing fields at the national level.[30]

Firms may fear risk of leading where other firms do not follow, amoral rivals would remain in the market without a meaningful way for the market to measure the benefits more ethical business cultures provide.[31] Indicators could provide the regulatory instrument needed to ensure that business enterprises incorporate rights by capitalizing on the creation of reputational risks and rewards.

Indicators rely on accurate, relevant information. Measuring the social impacts of business activities is in its relative infancy. In contrast to the regular and regulated financial reports that many corporations are obligated by law to produce, social and environmental reporting remains largely voluntary. Accordingly, there have been efforts to craft reporting frameworks that are consistent with the UNGPs in order to inform the types of salient information about social impacts that businesses enterprises should identify and share. The Global Reporting Initiative, an independent international nongovernmental organization has developed sustainability reporting standards to enable businesses to better "understand and communicate impact on critical sustainability issues such as climate change, human rights, governance and social well-being."[32] Shift, a nonprofit consulting firm founded by former associates of the Special Representative of the UN Secretary General on the issue of human rights and transnational corporations and other business enterprises, developed the first "comprehensive guidance for companies to report human rights issues in line with their responsibility to respect human rights" in 2015.[33]

## III. Business and Human Rights Indicators: Ranking Respect for Rights

New nonbinding international standards that outline the obligations of businesses with respect human rights, such as the UNGPs and other instruments, could hold promise for preventing suffering, provided strategies for enforcing

[30] *Id.*

[31] Ronen Shamir & Dana Weiss, *Semiotics of Indicators: The Case of Corporate Human Rights Responsibility*, in Governance by Indicators: Global Power through Quantification and Rankings 111 (Kevin E. Davis et al., eds., 2012) (these expressions would appear to confirm the observations by Ronen Shamir and Dana Weiss that engagement by business enterprises with human rights issues is increasingly linked to an enterprise risk management approach to strategy).

[32] *About GRI*, https://www.globalreporting.org/Information/about-gri/Pages/default.aspx (last visited Feb. 5, 2020).

[33] UNGP Reporting Framework, https://www.ungpreporting.org (last visited Feb. 17, 2019).

adherence to the principle that business enterprises do have an obligation to respect rights can gain strength among strategic constituencies such as investors and consumers. Indicators have the potential to play an important role solidifying emerging soft law standards and strengthening corporate self-regulation.

There are now reporting frameworks and rankings being developed to evaluate business enterprises based on their practices in general and pertaining to particular salient human rights issues. The features of selected business and human rights rankings based on indicators designed to detect risks to human rights are summarized in the following. These benchmarks address a range of different human rights issues and contribute to creating a broader public interest in the conditions of production and generating demand for greater corporate transparency concerning social and environmental performance intersecting with human rights risks.

## A. The Corporate Human Rights Benchmark Initiative: Preventing Abuses

Launched in 2014 at the UN Annual Forum on Business and Human Rights, the Corporate Human Rights Benchmark (CHRB) provides an "open and public benchmark of corporate human rights performance."[34] The initiative is a collaboration of investors and activists, including Aviva Investors,[35] a global asset manager affiliated with the largest insurer in the United Kingdom; the Institute for Human Rights and Business,[36] a leading UK-based think tank; Calvert Investments,[37] a mutual fund firm focused on responsible investment; the Business and Human Rights Resource Centre,[38] a leading research and advocacy organization; VBDO,[39] the Dutch Association of Investors for Sustainable Development; and EIRIS, a UK-based charitable foundation providing "free and objective information on ethical finance and corporate activity to the public."[40]

After global multistakeholder consultations to inform the technical development of a methodology to measure ways to enhance respect for human rights, the CHRB developed a draft methodology.[41] CHRB launched with an express

[34] *See* CHRB, *Who We Are*, https://www.corporatebenchmark.org/who-we-are (last visited Feb. 6, 2020).

[35] *See* Aviva Investors, https://www.avivainvestors.com/en-us/about/ (last visited Feb. 5, 2020).

[36] *See* Institute for Human Rights and Business, https://www.ihrb.org/about/about-home/ (last visited Feb. 5, 2020).

[37] *See* Calvert Investments, https://www.calvert.com/about-us.php (last visited Feb. 5, 2020).

[38] *See* Business and Human Rights Resource Centre, https://www.business-humanrights.org/en/about-us (last visited Feb. 5, 2020).

[39] *See* VBDO, https://www.vbdo.nl/en/ (last visited Feb. 5, 2020).

[40] *See* EIRIS Foundation, https://www.eirisfoundation.org/about-us/ (last visited Feb. 5, 2020).

[41] Corporate Human Rights Benchmark, *Corporate Human Rights Benchmark Newsletter*, 2 (2015), https://www.business-humanrights.org/sites/default/files/Corporate-Human-Rights-

commitment to "inclusive consultation with diverse actors" and credited the creators of Behind the Brands, the Access to Medicines Index, and the UNGP Reporting Framework for insights on methodology development.[42]

The CHRB is in its infancy and aims to produce a free and public ranking of five hundred major companies from around the world online, based on a transparent public methodology. In its first phase the initiative conducted worldwide consultations to inform the creation of a transparent methodology for measurement. This first phase was to have resulted in a web-based portal and pilot ranking of two hundred fifty companies. The initiative tested a pilot ranking across a diverse range of stakeholders before proceeding to the production of an actual ranking. Ninety-eight different companies were ranked from four different industries, including: (1) agricultural products; (2) apparel; (3) information and communications technology; and (4) extractives. For a full list of the companies ranked, look at "Annex 1—Companies Benchmarked" in the CHRB Key Findings 2017.[43]

While the initiative is a collaboration, it embraces competition in that the proposed benchmark it is working to create relies on the competitive impulse of business. The CHRB maintains that "respect for human rights lies at the heart of [corporate] contribution to the common good, their reputation, and their social license to operate."[44] To that end, the CHRB Standard aims to "build on a competitive approach to drive better human rights performance by companies through developing a transparent, publicly available and credible ranking of corporate human rights policy and performance."[45] According to CHRB:

> There is already considerable evidence that public transparency combined with public rankings of companies' performance is a powerful tool in driving a "race to the top." The initiative can make an important contribution to creating greater corporate accountability, incentivizing business behavior and creating greater leverage for policy-makers, investors, communities and consumers.[46]

The CHRB Standard is to be an "open source" ranking available to the public. It aims to meet the demand for more information about company

Benchmark-newsletter.pdf; *see also CHRB Methodology*, https://www.corporatebenchmark.org/chrb-methodology (last visited Feb. 7, 2020); Corporate Human Rights Benchmark Key Findings 2017, 5 (2017) [hereinafter CHRB Key Findings 2017].

[42] *Id.*

[43] CHRB Key Findings 2017, *supra* note 41, at 46–47.

[44] *See* CHRB, http://business-humanrights.org/en/corporate-human-rights-benchmark (last visited Apr. 27, 2015).

[45] Initiative Information Sheet on file with author.

[46] *Id.*

social performance. The CHRB maintains that there are many benefits to using evidence-based approaches to improve corporate responsibility and accountability through rankings based on human rights indicators. For example, investors "will be better equipped with information to direct investments to companies actually performing against human rights standards and away from those who are not."[47] Members of civil society "will be empowered to make well-informed choices about specific companies and products through greater transparency and better data on performance, and will have better information to encourage and pressure for advances by companies."[48] According to the CHRB, policymakers will benefit by having "an objective means by which to focus on those companies and business sectors that have the greatest human rights impacts and in particular those which are underperforming against significant human rights risks, highlighting where regulation and incentives might be necessary."[49] Included in the users intended to derive benefits from the CHRB Standard are the business enterprises evaluated by the CHRB, as higher rankings could serve to reward companies that are performing well.

The CHRB developed six core measurement themes. Each theme contains a set of indicators. The six core themes measured are: (1) governance and policy commitments; (2) embedding respect and human rights due diligence; (3) remedies and grievance mechanisms; (4) performance: company human rights practices; (5) performance: responses to serious allegations; (6) transparency.[50]

The themes are weighted differently, as follows:

- Governance = 10%
  - Board Level Accountability = 5%
  - Policy Commitments = 5%
- Embedding Respect and Human Rights Due Diligence = 25%
  - Embedding Respect for Human Rights in Culture and Management Systems =1 0%
  - Human Rights Due Diligence = 15%
- Remedies and Grievance Mechanisms = 15%
- Performance: Company Human Rights Practices = 20%
- Performance: Responses to Serious Allegations = 20%
- Transparency = 10%

[47] *Id.*
[48] *Id.*
[49] *Id.*
[50] *See* Corporate Human Rights Benchmark Initiative Pilot Methodology 2017, 40–41 (2017) [hereinafter CHRB IPM 2017].

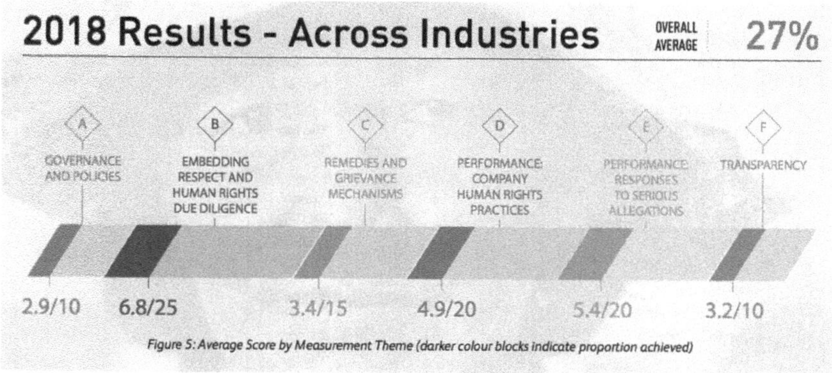


**Figure 4.1** CHRB Average Score by Measurement Theme Across Industries 2018
*Source*: Corporate Human Rights Benchmark, *2018 Key Findings, Apparel, Agricultural Products and Extractives Companies*, at 16 (2018)

Each theme has a series of indicators that are publicly available in the CHRB Initiative Pilot Methodology.[51] The themes consider a corporation's policies, governance, processes, practices, and transparency, as well as how they respond to serious allegations.[52]

In 2016, the CHRB ranked the first set of 100 companies.[53] Due to corporate mergers, CHRB ranked fewer companies in 2017.[54] Of the ninety-eight companies CHRB ranked in 2017, several were incorporated outside of the United States and Europe, including China, India, Brazil, and South Africa. In 2018, CHRB ranked 101 companies. Figure 4.1 is a graphic representation of the scoring distribution of average scores for companies across different industries by themes the CHRB measures. Figure 4.2 shows the "band range" that CHRB has assigned to different companies based on assessed human rights performance.

Some companies have started to report their rankings in sustainability reports and marketing materials.

51 *Id.* at 41. These indicators are found on pages 46 to 132 of the CHRB Initiative Pilot Methodology.
52 *See* CHRB Key Findings 2017, *supra* note 41, at 6.
53 *See* CHRB IPM 2017, *supra* note 50, at 28.
54 *See* CHRB Key Findings 2017, *supra* note 41, at 46–47.

| BAND RANGE | COMPANY | INDUSTRY |
|---|---|---|
| 80–90% | Adidas | AP |
| 70–80% | Rio Tinto | EX |
| | BHP Billion | EX |
| 60–70% | Marks & Spencer Group | AP&AG |
| | Unilever | AG |
| | Vale | EX |
| | ENI | EX |
| | VF | AP |
| 50–60% | The Coca-Cola Company | AG |
| | Kellogg | AG |
| | Royal Dutch Shell | EX |
| | Inditex | AP |
| | Freeport-McMoRan | EX |
| | Anglo American | EX |
| | Gap | AP |
| 40–50% | Hennes & Mauritz | AP |
| | BP | EX |
| | Hanesbrands | AP |
| | Total | EX |
| | Nestle | AG |
| | Repsol | EX |
| | PepsiCo | AG |
| | Diageo | AG |
| | Petrobras | EX |
| | Woolworths | AG |
| 30–40% | Glencore | EX |
| | ConocoPhillips | EX |
| | Next | AP |
| | Ecopetrol | EX |
| | Danone | AG |
| | Heineken NV | AG |
| | Equinor | EX |
| | Tesco | AP&AG |
| | Nike | AP |
| | General Mills | AG |
| | Under Armour | AP |
| 20–30% | Ancher Daniels Midland | AG |
| | Chevron Corporation | EX |
| | Kering | AP |
| | Fast Retailing | AP |
| | Wesfarmers | AG |
| | Coal India | EX |
| | Associated British Foods | AP&AG |
| | Mondelez International | AG |
| | Carrefour | AG |
| | Sasol | EX |
| | Goldcorp | EX |
| | Lukoil | EX |
| | Wal-Mart Stores | AP&AG |
| | Occidental Petroleum | EX |
| | Anheuser-Busch InBev | AG |
| 20–30% (cont.) | Rosneft Oil | EX |
| | McDonald's | AG |
| | Pernod-Ricard | AG |
| | Kroger | AG |
| 10–20% | The Hershey Company | AG |
| | Suncor Energy | EX |
| | Excon Mobil | EX |
| | Ahnold Delhaize | AG |
| | PTT | EX |
| | Grupo Mexico | EX |
| | LVMH | AP |
| | Aeon Company | AP&AG |
| | L Brands | AP |
| | Target | AP&AG |
| | Sysco | AG |
| | Compass Group | AG |
| | Norilsk Nickel | EX |
| | TJX Companies | AP |
| | Anadarko Petroleum | EX |
| | Marathon Petroleum | EX |
| | Yum! Brands | AG |
| | Canadian Natural Resources | EX |
| | Kohl's | AP |
| 0–10% | Tapestry | AP |
| | Philips 66 | EX |
| | PetroChina | EX |
| | BRF | AG |
| | Costco Wholesale | AP&AG |
| | Starbucks | AG |
| | Nordstrom | AP |
| | Falabella | AP&AG |
| | Devon Energy | EX |
| | Oil & Natural Gas Corporation | EX |
| | Gazprom | EX |
| | Ross Stores | AP |
| | Kraft Heinz | AG |
| | China Petroleum & Chemical | EX |
| | China Shenhua Energy | EX |
| | Macy's | AP |
| | Shoprite | AG |
| | Prada | AP |
| | CNOOC | EX |
| | Hermes International | AP |
| | Surgutnerftegas | EX |
| | EOG Resources | EX |
| | Alimentation Couche-Tand | AG |
| | Valero Energy | EX |
| | Monster Beverage | AG |
| | Heilan Home | AP |
| | Kweichow Moutai | AG |

**Figure 4.2** CHRB Band Range Company Rankings Across Industries 2018

*Source*: Corporate Human Rights Benchmark, *2018 Key Findings, Apparel, Agricultural Products and Extractives Companies*, at 17 (2018)

## B. KnowTheChain: Monitoring Modern Slavery

KnowTheChain (KTC) is a resource to raise awareness about modern slavery in corporate supply chains and to promote transparency in compliance with a California law that requires companies to post disclosure statements. In contrast to other rankings, such as the Access to Medicines Index that are not linked to a legal obligation, KTC's benchmark operates to aid enforcement of an existing legal requirement. In 2010, California enacted the first state law requiring manufacturers and retail companies to publicly disclose their policies to eradicate slavery, forced labor, and human trafficking within their supply chains.[55] Effective January 1, 2012, retailers and manufacturers subject to California's law were required to disclose efforts, if any, to ensure that slavery and human trafficking were not present in their supply chains. To be sure, the California law only requires companies to disclose what is being done to detect the presence of trafficking and slavery in sourcing; it does not require companies to do anything beyond disclosure.

Founded in 2013 by Humanity United, a nonprofit foundation, KTC is a partnership of anti-slavery organizations, religious organizations, research centers, and investors, including the Business and Human Rights Resource Centre, Free the Slaves, the Coalition to Abolish Slavery and Trafficking, the Interfaith Center on Corporate Responsibility, Made in a Free World, Verité, and World Vision, among others.[56] KTC was created to educate companies, consumers, investors, and policymakers about the presence of slavery in supply chains. KTC first began by reporting on compliance with the California law. In January 2014, KTC started its own form of citizen civil society enforcement by contacting each company it identified without a statement or with an incomplete statement and providing information about the law. KTC later turned to benchmarking businesses based on the content of disclosures.

[55] CAL. CIV. CODE § 1714.43 (West 2012).

[56] KNOWTHECHAIN, https://knowthechain.org (last visited May 14, 2015); *see also* BUSINESS AND HUMAN RIGHTS RESOURCE CENTRE, https://www.business-humanrights.org/en/about-us (last visited Feb. 5, 2020) ("[W]orking with everyone to advance human rights in business and eradicate abuse."); FREE THE SLAVES, https://www.freetheslaves.net/ (last visited Feb. 7, 2020) ("Liberating slaves and changing the conditions that allow slavery to persist."); COALITION TO ABOLISH SLAVERY & TRAFFICKING, https://www.castla.org/ (last visited Feb. 7, 2020) ("Ending modern slavery through education, advocacy and empowering survivors of human trafficking."); INTERFAITH CENTER ON CORPORATE RESPONSIBILITY, https://www.iccr.org/ (last visited Feb. 7, 2020) ("Through the lens of faith, ICCR builds a more just and sustainable world by integrating social values into corporate and investor actions."); MADE IN A FREE WORLD, https://madeinafreeworld.org/ (last visited Feb. 7, 2020) ("[D]eveloping and implementing high impact solutions to human trafficking by working with the most effective partners to rescue and care for victims worldwide."); VERITÉ, https://www.verite.org/ (last visited Feb. 7, 2020) ("[I]lluminat[ing] labor rights violations in supply chains and remedy them to the benefit of workers and companies alike."); WORLD VISION, https://www.worldvision.org/ (last visited Feb. 7, 2020) ("[H]elping children, families, and their communities overcome poverty and injustice.").

KTC published its first benchmark in 2016, citing the role of benchmarks in helping businesses to identify best practices and to improve procedures.[57] KTC intends for its benchmark to serve as a catalyst to create incentives for business enterprises to identify gaps in different industry sectors.[58]

KTC currently benchmarks companies in three sectors: (1) internet communications technology (ICT), (2) food and beverage, and (3) apparel and footwear.[59] These sectors were selected due to "significant exposure to forced labor in their supply chains."[60] The US Department of Labor identified these sectors as having inputs involving forced labor.[61] The particular companies included in the benchmark were selected based on the size and market capitalization, as well as on the extent to which the companies derived revenues from corporate branded products.[62] Companies in these sectors are sourcing materials and commodities from countries in conflict or where labor regulation is either inadequate or not adequately implemented.[63] For example, companies in the ICT sector source raw materials from the Democratic Republic of the Congo, a country experiencing conflict.

KTC benchmarks for all three sectors include the same seven themes: (1) commitment and governance; (2) traceability and risk assessment; (3) purchasing practices; (4) recruitment; (5) worker voice; (6) monitoring; and (7) remedy.[64] KTC has determined that improvements in these seven areas will aid the abolition of slavery in global supply chains.

Commitment and governance:

- "The company's top-level commitments on forced labor, supply chain standards, management processes, training programs and stakeholder engagement."

[57] Pointing to the success of earlier rankings, including the Access to Medicines Index, the Corporate Human Rights Benchmark, and Ranking Digital Rights, KTC introduced its benchmark explaining: KTC believes that benchmarks can play a powerful role in encouraging companies to uphold labor standards and protect workers' rights. They can harness the competitive nature of markets to drive a "race to the top" by creating brand rewards for leaders and brand risk for laggards. *See* KnowTheChain Benchmarks, https://knowthechain.org/benchmarks (last visited Dec. 30, 2018).

[58] *Id.*

[59] *Id.*

[60] *See id.*

[61] *See* 2018 List of Goods Produced by Child Labor or Forced Labor, U.S. Dep't of Lab. 16, 17, 20 (2018), https://www.dol.gov/sites/dolgov/files/ILAB/ListofGoods.pdf.

[62] *See Overall Company Ranking*, KnowTheChain, https://knowthechain.org/benchmarks/1/ (last visited Jan. 21, 2018).

[63] *See* Profit and Poverty: The Economics of Forced Labour, International Labour Office (ILO), Special Action Programme to Combat Forced Labour (SAP-FL), Fundamental Principles and Rights at Work Branch (FPRW) 12–13 (2014).

[64] *See Company Comparison Tool*, https://knowthechain.org/benchmarks/comparison_tool/6/ (last visited Feb. 7, 2020).

Traceability and risk assessment:

- "The extent to which the company traces its supply chain and conducts forced labor risk assessments, and discloses information about these processes."

Purchasing practices:

- "The company's awareness and action on purchasing practices that can exacerbate forced labor risks, and its process for selecting suppliers, integrating standards into contracts and cascading them down the supply chain."

Recruitment:

- "The company's approach to reducing exploitation by recruitment agencies and eliminating workers' payment of fees for their jobs."

Worker voice:

- "The extent to which the company proactively communicates with workers through the supply chain, enables freedom of association and ensures access to effective and trusted grievance mechanisms."

Monitoring:

- "The company's process for auditing (including whether it includes non-scheduled visits, document review, worker interviews) and disclosure about the audit process and findings."

Remedy:

- "The extent to which the company has corrective action plans for non-compliant factories, as well as processes for remedying workers who are victims of forced labor, and reports on remedies provided." These seven themes are subdivided into additional subcategories.[65] In 2018, KTC used a total of twenty-three different indicators across the seven themes. Indicators are weighted equally.[66] A company can score up to a total of 100 points.[67] KTC does not directly evaluate whether a benchmarked company complies with regulation on forced labor; rather, indicators are intended to

[65] *2018 Benchmark Methodology*, https://knowthechain.org/benchmark-methodology/ (last visited Feb. 7, 2020).
[66] *Id.*
[67] *Id.*

> aid companies to determine and develop best practices for compliance with supply chain transparency laws.[68] To that end, the benchmark is "a measurement of companies' disclosures on their policies and practices to mitigate the risk of forced labor or human trafficking in their supply chains."[69]

KTC's resource research team, led by Sustainalytics, an independent research firm that caters to investors interested in environmental, social, and governance issues, examines company websites for information outlining the procedures used to detect human trafficking in their supply chains.[70] KTC's resource also provides a record of which companies do and do not yet have statements in compliance with the California law.[71] Companies have an opportunity to provide additional information after KTC's assessment, either by updating information on the company website or by providing a response to the Business and Human Rights Resource Centre website.[72] However, companies cannot opt out of being evaluated on the benchmark.[73]

KTC updated its methodology in 2018 in response to lessons it learned after its 2016 benchmarking, incorporating feedback from diverse stakeholders. The focus is mainly on implementing more practical approaches to the issues identified, moving away from a focus on awareness and policy toward action on issues such as worker voice and access to remedy.[74] It also has added retailers to its list of companies benchmarked. KTC ranks each company on a scale of 1 to 100 and includes graphics on its website to demonstrate the companies' relative scores. In addition to company self-reporting, KTC will also include forced labor allegations reported by credible third parties. The benchmark aims to encourage companies to look beyond the first tier of supply chains. KTC urges companies to conduct comprehensive supply chain reviews that would ultimately reach the sourcing of raw materials and commodities.

Industry leaders Kellogg, Unilever, and Nestlé rank consistently near the top of the KTC benchmark—Kellogg scores a 95/100 on the theme of "commitment," the closest to a perfect score available among the various indices. Figure 4.3 shows KTC's 2018 rankings of food and beverage companies. Figure 4.4 shows KTC's 2018 apparel and footwear company rankings. Figure 4.5 shows KTC's 2018 rankings for information communications technology companies.

[68] *See* KnowTheChain Benchmarks, *supra* note 57.
[69] *See* KnowTheChain FAQs, https://knowthechain.org/faqs/ (last visited Jan. 21, 2018).
[70] KnowTheChain, *supra* note 56.
[71] *See generally id.*
[72] *See id.*
[73] *See* KnowTheChain FAQs, *supra* note 69.
[74] *Id.*

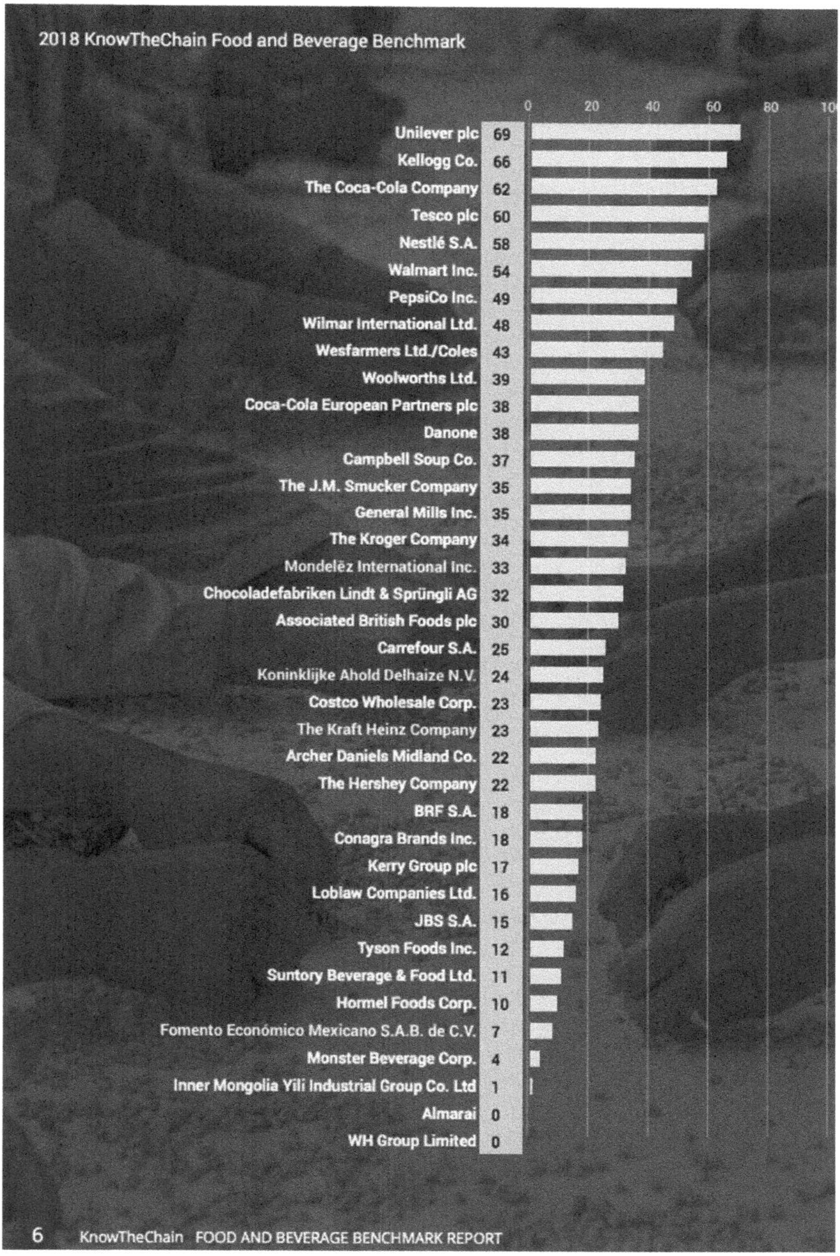


**Figure 4.3** KTC Food and Beverage Benchmark

*Source*: KnowTheChain, *Food and Beverage Benchmark Report*, at 6 (2018)

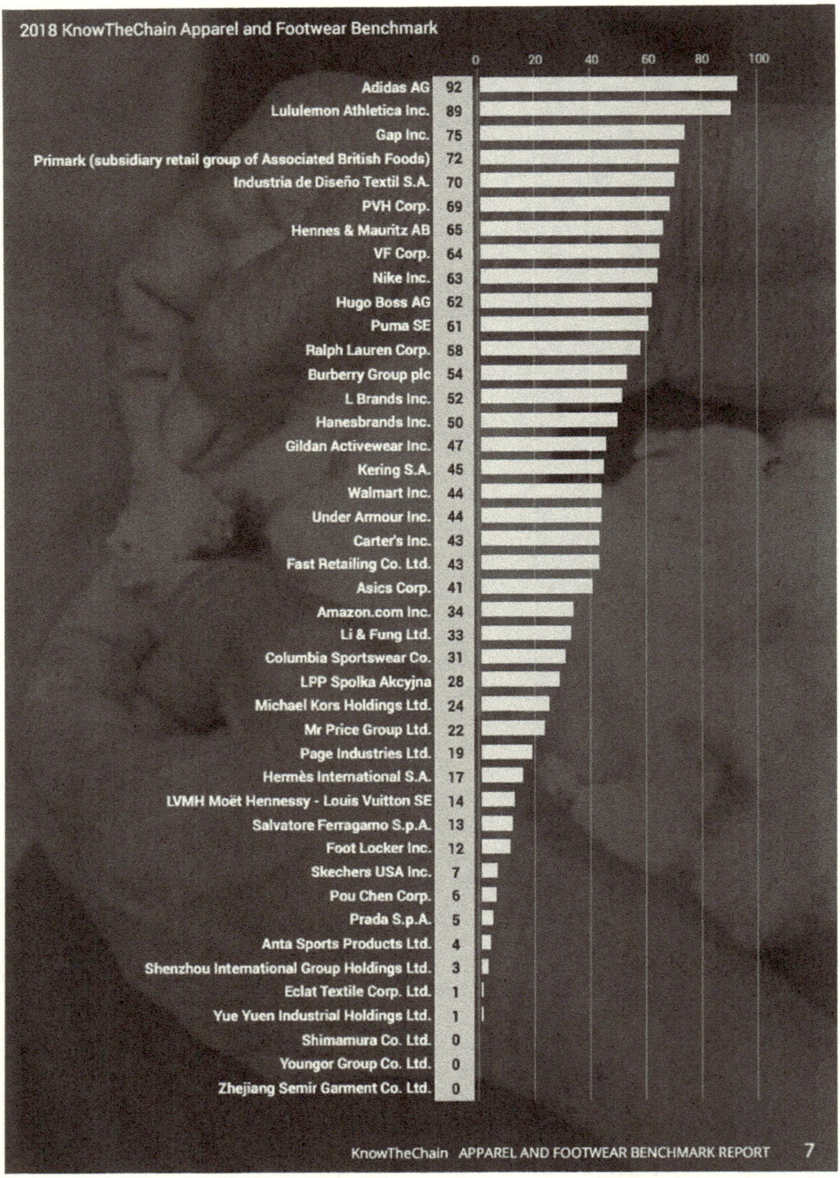


**Figure 4.4** KTC Apparel and Footwear Benchmark

*Source*: KnowTheChain, *Apparel and Footwear Benchmark Report*, at 7 (2018)

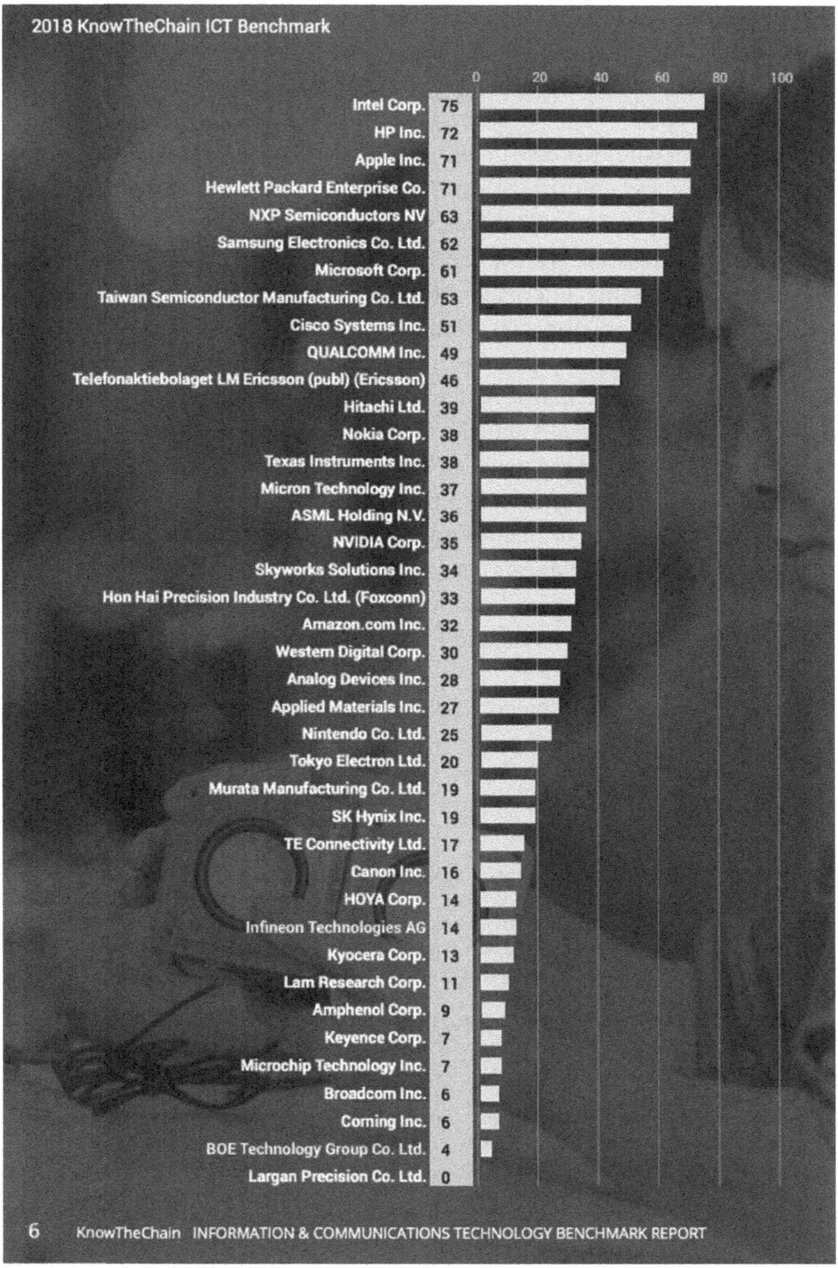


**Figure 4.5** KTC Information & Communications Technology Benchmark
*Source*: KnowTheChain, *Information & Communications Technology Benchmark Report*, at 6 (2018)

Some companies have introduced ethical labor recruitment efforts. For example, Apple created standards to guide hiring.[75] Adidas shared responses to KTC's questions on its website, furthering supply chain transparency.[76]

In 2012, I spoke with an attorney with the California State's Attorney General's Office who expressed concern that the law would be all but impossible to monitor and enforce.[77] However, after KTC's efforts by April 2015, the California Attorney General's Office sent the first enforcement action letters to companies requesting self-reporting of compliance.[78] The example of KTC presents an interesting interplay with legal enforcement as rights activists are using information strategies to influence corporate conduct. KTC began simply by identifying compliant and noncompliant companies. In 2014, KTC's early research revealed that less than half of the companies it identified as having reporting obligations actually made the mandatory disclosures.[79] KTC has stepped in to close a gap between law and practice. Indeed, KTC has characterized itself as "a bridge between the letter and spirit of the law."[80] Unlike other strategies that aim to "name and shame," KTC's strategies aim to "open a meaningful dialogue that assists companies in building ethical and fair supply chains free of forced labor and trafficking."[81] KTC maintains that its benchmark approach "can drive tangible improvements in companies' policy and practice."[82]

These changes speak to the potential success of indicators in shifting corporate policies and practices.

[75] Interview with Desta Raines, External Engagement Manager, Apple Inc. (2018).

[76] William Anderson, *Adidas Group Response to KnowTheChain Apparel & Footwear Benchmark*, ADIDAS GROUP (June 20, 2016), https://www.adidas-group.com/media/filer_public/52/da/52da31a6-93d0-4e01-a4d5-e3d96fefd949/adidas_group_response_to_knowthechain_20june2016.pdf.

[77] Benjamin Greer, Special Deputy Attorney General, California Department of Justice, University of Nebraska (2012).

[78] *See* David F. McDowell & Purvi G. Patel, *California AG Initiates Supply Chain Act Disclosure Review: Enforcement Actions Likely to Follow*, MORRISON & FOERSTER LLP (Apr. 9, 2015). *See generally*, KAMALA D. HARRIS, ATT'Y GEN. CAL. DEPT. OF JUST. THE STATE OF HUMAN TRAFFICKING IN CALIFORNIA (2012).

[79] Know the Chain, *See Which Companies Do and Do Not Have Statements under the California Transparency in Supply Chains Act (2014)*, BUSINESS & HUMAN RIGHTS RESOURCE CENTRE (Jan. 1, 2014), https://www.business-humanrights.org/en/latest-news/know-the-chain-see-which-companies-do-and-do-not-have-statements-under-the-california-transparency-in-supply-chains-act-2014/ (explaining that under the California Transparency in Supply Chains Act (SB-657) only 44 out of 129 companies (34.1%) complied with section (b) of the Act which requires companies to "disclose the efforts they are making to eradicate human trafficking and slavery from their supply chains").

[80] KNOWTHECHAIN: ABOUT US (last updated 2014), https://www.knowthechain.org/about-us/ (last visited May, 12, 2015).

[81] *Id.*

[82] WHY BENCHMARKING?, https://knowthechain.org/benchmarks (last visited Dec. 30, 2018).

## C. Ranking Digital Rights Corporate Accountability Index: Protecting Expression and Access to Information

The Ranking Digital Rights (RDR) Corporate Accountability Index project brings together researchers and advocates to evaluate and rank the world's most influential ICT corporations on policies and practices related to privacy and freedom of expression informed by international human rights law.

Rebecca MacKinnon, a former journalist who covered the Asia region for CNN International, founded RDR in 2013 as a nonprofit research initiative to improve the human rights performance of companies in the industry. MacKinnon explains her theory of change as follows: "[O]ur index offers a roadmap for companies to improve their policies and disclosures affecting users' privacy and freedom of expression. And so, it enables companies to see how they're doing against that roadmap, and to see very specifically how they can improve and how they compare to other companies."[83] Industry competition is used to encourage change.

The RDR Project's ranking aims to:

- Encourage companies to develop, deliver and manage products and services in a manner consistent with international human rights norms;
- Identify what specific legal and political factors prevent or hinder companies from respecting users' and customers' human rights;
- Inform companies, individual users, civil society, academics, investors, governments, and the public about the relationship between the ICT sector and human rights.[84]

After developing metrics through phases of multistakeholder consultations and testing pilot indicators, RDR released its first Corporate Accountability Index in 2015, ranking sixteen leading companies in the ICT sector on public commitments and disclosed policies concerning the privacy and freedom of expression rights of users.[85] RDR used thirty-one indicators across the three categories of governance, privacy, and freedom of expression in the 2015 rankings. No rankings were published in 2016 while RDR reviewed and revised its methodology to include indicators relevant to governance and accountability mechanisms. In 2017, RDR expanded the ranking to twenty-two companies,

[83] Rebecca Mackinnon, LinkedIn, https://www.linkedin.com/in/rmackinnon/ (last visited Feb. 7, 2020).
[84] Interview with Rebecca Mackinnon, Director, Ranking Digital Rights (2019).
[85] *See 2015 Corporate Accountability Index*, Ranking Digital Rights, https://rankingdigitalrights.org/index2015/ (last visited Feb. 7, 2020).

using thirty-five indicators. The companies evaluated in RDR's 2018 Corporate Accountability Index taken together provide products and services used by the majority of the world's population with internet access. RDR plans to continue to increase the number of companies evaluated and will add two telecommunications companies in 2019.

To create the Corporate Accountability Index, a primary team of independent international researchers affiliated with RDR collect data for each company and provide a preliminary assessment of company performance across all indicators. The researchers also assess how companies performed from year to year. Next, a second team of researchers conducts a fact-check assessment provided by primary researchers. Then the RDR team reviews and reconciles these results to resolves any differences that arise in data collection. The RDR team also conducts a "horizontal review" to cross-check the indicators to ensure that data collected has been evaluated consistently for each company in the ranking. RDR provides initial results to companies for comment and feedback. There is an opportunity for companies to correct or contest information. Next, the RDR team conducts another horizontal review in response to feedback collected from companies to again cross-check the indicators for consistency and quality control. Finally, the RDR team calculates company scores.

Companies receive a cumulative score of their performance on specific indicators across all Index categories evaluated, including Governance (G), Freedom of Expression (F), and Privacy (P). Ranking results also show how companies performed in each individual category and on each indicator.[86] Data for measuring these indicators are also derived from company responses to survey questions in addition to publicly available policies with implications for privacy rights and freedom of expression. Company responses to survey questions are assessed and weighted. For instance, an F category question concerning access to information asks whether a company removes, filters, or restricts access to content and how it provides explanations to affected users.[87] RDR assigns a weighted value to assess the quality of a company's answer. A "strong" company would provide a detailed explanation to users, while a "fair" company would provide a general explanation, and a "weak" company might mention that content was restricted without providing a reason.[88] Variable weights are given to different responses.

Category G contains six indicators measuring company disclosure of their commitments to freedom of expression and privacy principles and standards at the corporate governance level.[89] Companies are evaluated for the following.

[86] Ranking Digital Rights, *2017 Corporate Accountability Index Research Indicators*, 7–8 (Sept. 2016), https://rankingdigitalrights.org/wp-content/uploads/2016/09/2017Indexmethodology.pdf.

[87] Ranking Digital Rights, *Phase 1 Pilot Methodology, F8, 13* (Oct. 2, 2014), https://rankingdigitalrights.org/wp-content/uploads/2014/10/RDRmethodology_v3_2Oct2014.pdf.

[88] *Id.*

[89] Ranking Digital Rights, *supra* note 87, at 10–44.

1. Policy commitment
2. Governance and management oversight
3. Internal implementation
4. Impact assessment
5. Stakeholder engagement
6. Remedy

Category F contains eleven indicators measuring company disclosure of their policies and practices that affect users' freedom of expression rights. RDR's F indicators are specific and speak to the issues identified by the UN Human Rights Committee with respect to respecting freedom of expression across multiple forms of media.

1. Access to terms of service
2. Changes to terms of service
3. Process for terms of service enforcement
4. Data about terms of service enforcement
5. Process for responding to third-party requests for content or account restriction
6. Data about government requests for content or account restriction
7. Data about private requests for content or account restriction
8. User notification about content and account restriction
9. Network management (telecommunications companies)
10. Network shutdown (telecommunications companies)
11. Identity policy

Category P contains eighteen indicators measuring company disclosure of their policies and practices that affect users' privacy rights. RDR's P indicators are specific and speak to the issues identified by the UN Human Rights Committee with respect to privacy.

1. Access to privacy policies
2. Changes to privacy policies
3. Collection of user information
4. Sharing of user information
5. Purpose for collecting and sharing user information
6. Retention of user information
7. Users' control over their own user information
8. Users' access to their own user information
9. Collection of user information from third parties (internet companies)
10. Process for responding to third-party requests for user information

11. Data about third-party requests for user information
12. User notification about third-party requests for user information
13. Security oversight
14. Addressing security vulnerabilities
15. Data breaches
16. Encryption of user communication and private content (internet, software, and device companies)
17. Account security (internet, software, and device companies)
18. Inform and educate users about potential risks

RDR's Index is a named and rank-ordered indicator that could be understood as a regulatory instrument in that it is being used to advocate changes in corporate practices that place rights at risk. It its relatively short existence the RDR Index has served to provide a picture of the past and projected performance of leading companies in the ICT industry that have the power and influence to set legal and policy priorities.

The RDR Index can be used to rank and assess the relative position and progress of different companies over time. Google (Alphabet) secured the top spot in RDR's 2018 ranking of twelve internet and mobile ecosystem companies with a score of 63 out of 100.[90] Microsoft earned the number two spot with a score of 61.[91] Facebook came in at number four with a score of 55.[92] Apple's score of 44 landed the company in the bottom half of RDR's ranking.[93] However, Apple earned the largest score improvement of any company in the 2018 index for enhancing its public commitment to privacy protections for users.[94] Microsoft, while still a leader on most individual metrics assessed, suffered a decline in overall scoring for failure to provide clear notice about account restrictions and other adverse actions to users of its Skype service.[95] Google has sustained the top spot since the creation of the RDR Index. Facebook has raised its standing in the rankings by improving from a score of 41 in 2015, to a score of 53 in 2017, to a score of 55 in 2018. Figure 4.6 shows RDR's 2018 rankings of internet and mobile ecosystem companies.

Beyond ranking companies, RDR's Corporate Accountability Index presents an overview of the performance of the industry sector. RDR also identifies issues

[90] *See 2018 Company Ranking*, Ranking Digital Rights, https://rankingdigitalrights.org/index2018/ (last visited Feb. 7, 2020).
[91] *Id.*
[92] *Id.*
[93] *Id.*
[94] *See Year-on-Year Comparison*, Ranking Digital Rights, https://rankingdigitalrights.org/index2018/compare/ (last visited Feb. 7, 2020).
[95] *See* Microsoft Corp., Ranking Digital Rights, https://rankingdigitalrights.org/index2018/companies/microsoft/ (last visited Feb. 7, 2020).

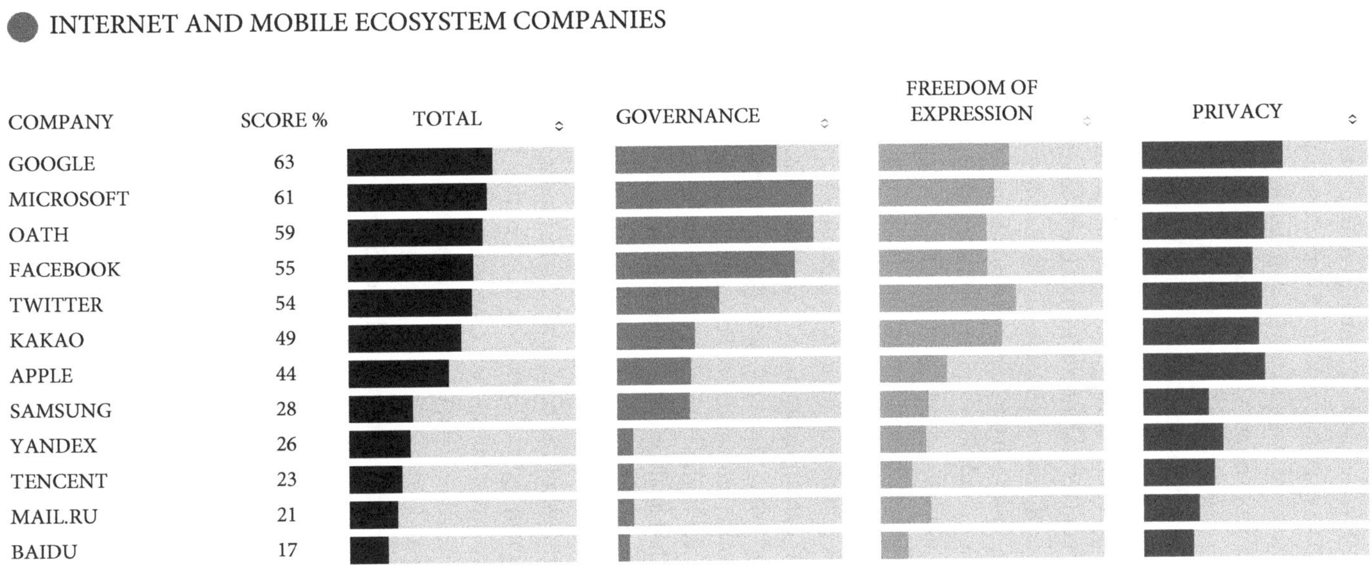


**Figure 4.6** RDR Company Ranking Internet and Mobile Ecosystems.
*Source*: *Ranking Digital Rights Corporate Accountability Index*, at 4 (2018)

that the industry as a whole confronts and provides recommendations for reform. In 2018, RDR concluded that the lack of transparency in the industry on policies and practices affecting freedom of expression and privacy exposed users to a range of undisclosed risks. RDR's 2018 Index Report identified the relative failure of firms to make rights a central priority for risk assessment and corporate management oversight as a key governance challenge. The Index Report found that most firms do not disclose data on the measures taken to protect user data, leaving users vulnerable and noting the costly consequences of data security failures globally. Companies still do not provide the public sufficient to the public about how content and information is mediated and managed. According to RDR, the failure of many companies to disclose more about management of user information—from what information is collected to who has access to the data and under what conditions—places rights at risk of abuse. Information mismanagement or failure to protect personal data on digital platforms may make individuals and institutions more vulnerable to manipulation.

More than half the companies ranked in the 2018 Corporate Accountability Index promptly responded to RDR's findings after the digital rights campaign group Access Now demanded answers.[96] In some instances, company responses did actually report what measures were put in place to improve performance concerning respecting human rights. For example, Microsoft reported that it extended "Data Subject Rights" recognized in Europe to consumers worldwide and now provides tools that allow users to know what data is collected and to correct or delete data.[97] Microsoft also highlighted the company's legal challenge to the process by which the US government issues search warrants and gathers digital evidence as illustrative of the company's commitment to user privacy and respect for other human rights.[98] Facebook reported that since RDR's ranking was released, it had expanded transparency reporting on content restrictions in each country and that it had now put in place an appeals process for content removed from the platform.[99]

In other instances, companies simply reaffirmed a commitment to respect user freedom of expression and privacy. For example, telecommunications company AT&T, criticized by rights advocates for collaboration with intelligence

[96] Peter Micek & Carolyn Tackett, *Access Now Calls on 22 Major Tech Companies to Account for Their Human Rights Practices*, Access Now: Business and Human Rights (Sept. 17, 2018, 9:42 AM), https://www.accessnow.org/access-now-calls-on-22-major-tech-companies-to-account-for-their-human-rights-practices// (open letters calling for responses to ranked companies).

[97] *Microsoft's Response to Access Now's September 12, 2018 Letter*, Microsoft (2018), https://www.business-humanrights.org/sites/default/files/Microsoft%20response_AN_RDR_2018.pdf.

[98] *Id.*

[99] Letter from Alex Warofka, Product Policy Manager, Facebook, to Peter Micek, General Counsel, Access Now (Sept. 26, 2018), https://www.business-humanrights.org/sites/default/files/Facebook%20response_AN_RDR_2018.pdf.

services placing activists at risk, called attention to the fact that the company still received the highest privacy score among companies in its category.[100]

The responsibility to respect, as set forth in the UNGPs, calls for companies to have a policy on human rights and to conduct human rights impact assessments.[101] The indicators in RDR's governance category closely track the UNGPs in particular. Principle 16 operationalizing the corporate responsibility to respect human rights recommends the creation of a policy commitment that clearly sets forth expectations for employees and parties directly connected to the operation, products, or services of a business.[102] A company's policy commitment should be approved by senior company leaders, informed by internal and/or external experts, and included in policies and procedures throughout the entire business enterprise according to Principle 16.[103] Finally, Principle 16 provides that a company's human rights policy commitment should be available to the public and shared with relevant stakeholders including employees and business partners.[104]

In the absence of transparency, corporate social responsibility is compromised and access to remedy reduced. The RDR project is serving to incentivize information sharing and to spur reform. The project has published a guide for investors.[105]

## D. The Access to Medicines Index: Promoting Health

The Access to Medicine Index (AMI) was founded by a Dutch entrepreneur Wim Leerveld and first published in 2008. It is a tool to incentivize action on the part of the pharmaceuticals industry. Intended to "simulate positive change by publicly encouraging pharmaceutical companies to step up their efforts to improve access to medicine worldwide," the index measures seven performance categories and uses a weighted analytical framework to consistently capture and compare company data. Companies are evaluated in each category for commitment, transparency, performance, and innovation.

The index is based on the idea that "problems can be successfully solved by bringing people together to create effective, lasting and transparent solutions." By integrating input from stakeholders from different sectors—public, private,

100 Email from Jeffrey Dygert, Executive Director of Public Policy, AT&T, to Peter Micek, General Counsel, Access Now (Oct. 6, 2018), https://www.business-humanrights.org/sites/default/files/ATT%20response_AN_RDR_2018.pdf.
101 UNGP, *supra* note 14, at 13, Foundational Principle II.
102 *Id.*, at Guiding Principle 16(c).
103 *Id.*, at Guiding Principles 16(a–b) & (e).
104 *Id.*, at Guiding Principle 16(d).
105 Interview with Mackinnon, *supra* note 84.

and nonprofit—the organization has been able to create a robust, balanced AMI. The AMI examines the top twenty research-based pharmaceutical companies, based on the relevance of their product portfolios and market capitalization for their activities in developing countries, using World Bank and UN classifications measuring economic advancement and human development.

Earlier opposition and government efforts to regulate pricing and patents notwithstanding, the index has been well received by the industry. At least two of the companies contained have featured their AMI ranking on their websites. One, GlaxoSmithKline topped the rankings. GSK has established a Developing Countries and Market Access unit as a department supported by a "lower price/higher volume" business model with employee bonuses structured to reward volume growth rather than profit growth.

An Index Research Team, supported by formal committees, teams, and subcommittees, came together to develop the methodology used to measure corporate performance. A cross section of interested stakeholders participated in the process. The methodology report of Access to Medicine explains: "Strategic guidance was provided by the Expert Review Committee (ERC), a panel of independent experts from the WHO, governments, patient organizations, the industry, NGOs, academia, and investors among others. Recommendations on specific topics of the Index were provided by Technical Subcommittees: panels of specialists in different aspects of access to medicine. Other experts from a variety of organizations (academic, industry, non-governmental, multilateral, investors) supported the development of the Methodology."[106] The "methodology report can also be used to prioritize which actions companies should take."[107]

The AMI rests on four strategic pillars, covering seven technical areas, comprised of sixty-nine indicators. Accordingly, "[w]ithin each Technical Area, indicators are linked to four Strategic Pillars . . . The Pillars provide a series of lenses for examining these dimensions of company behavior across the Technical Areas."[108] The four strategic pillars include: (1) commitment; (2) transparency; (3) performance; and (4) innovation.

Commitment evaluates a company's: "positions, strategies, policies and codes of conduct related to access to medicine."[109] AMI maintains that "[c]ommitments are the first step to improving access to medicine: they make clear what the company values, its aims, and how it aims to achieve them."[110]

[106] Access to Medicine Foundation, *Access to Medicine Index 2018*, 56 (2018), https://accesstomedicineindex.org/media/atmi/2017-Methodology-2018-Access-to-Medicine-Index.pdf; *see also id.* at 2 (containing list of contributors included in the teams, committees, and subcommittees).

[107] *Id.* at 3.

[108] *Id.* at 34.

[109] *Id.*

[110] *Id.*

Transparency evaluates the extent to which a company discloses information about any initiatives and activities that influence access to medicine. AMI maintains that "[t]ransparency is key for accountability and promotes the sharing of practices and approaches."[111] Performance assesses the actions a company takes to promote access to medicine. AMI indicators on performance measure "how and where companies put access-related policies and priorities into action, for example, by addressing product gaps through R&D, implementing equitable pricing strategies or licensing products on access-oriented terms."[112] The performance pillar carries the greatest weight. Finally, the innovation pillar includes indicators designed to "capture[] how companies create or employ new and unique means of advancing industry practice. As the pharmaceutical industry penetrates new markets, there are opportunities to develop innovative approaches that respond to local needs, and make access to medicine more sustainable."[113]

The seven technical areas supporting the four pillars include: (1) general access to medicine management; (2) market influence and compliance; (3) research and development; (4) pricing, manufacturing, and distribution; (5) patents and licensing; (6) capacity building; and (7) product donations. General access to medicine management is weighted at 10 percent and contains indicators on access-to-medicine strategy; managing for access-to-medicine outcomes; stakeholder engagement; and innovation. Market influence and compliance is also weighted at 10 percent and contains indicators on ethical marketing and anticorruption; responsible lobbying; compliance; and innovation. AMI methodology places greater weight on research and development at 20 percent, with indicators on product development; planning for access; clinical trial conduct; and innovation. The pricing, manufacturing, and distribution theme is given the greatest weight at 25 percent and includes indicators to measure: filing for marketing approval/registration; equitable pricing strategies; manufacturing and distribution; and innovation. Patents and licensing is weighted at 15 percent and evaluates patenting strategy, licensing, competition, trade policy, and innovation. Capacity building counts for 15 percent of a ranking and includes assessments of R&D capacity building, manufacturing capacity building, supply chain capacity building, pharmacovigilance capacity building, health system strengthening, and innovation in capacity building. Finally, product donations are given the least weight at only (5 percent) and considers indicators relevant to scale and reach, quality and sustainability, and ad hoc donations.[114] Each one

[111] *Id.*
[112] *Id.*
[113] *Id.*
[114] *Id.* at 35–54.

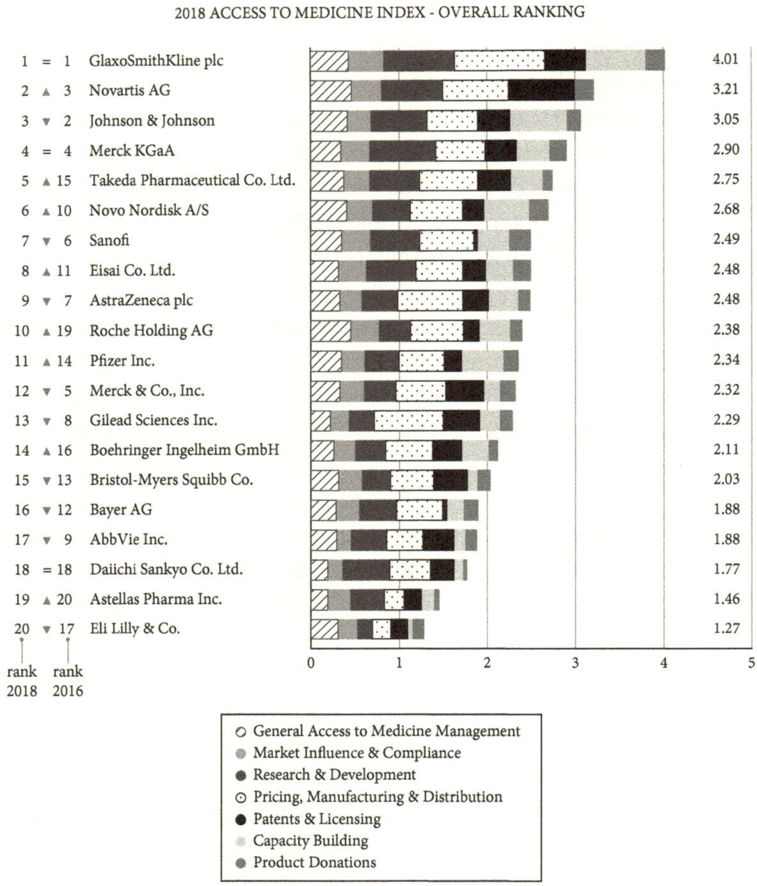


**Figure 4.7** Access to Medicines Index Overall Ranking
*Source:* Access to Medicine Index 2018, at 7 (2018)

of the seven themes has a series of indicators that are publicly available in the Access to Medicine Index's regular Methodology Report.[115] The weight and considerations of each indicator have changed slightly since their inception in 2008.[116] In addition, AMI's yearly reports list and explain the modifications for each indicator from year to year. Figure 4.7 shows AMI's 2018 overall ranking of pharmaceutical companies.

[115] *Id.* at 34–54.
[116] *Id.* at 34–54.

AMI now also issues "report cards" that allow for cross comparison among the companies ranked in the index.[117] The AMI website also now has a section devoted to investors.[118]

Leerveld explains the success of the index as follows:

> I knew the industry very well and I knew that if you compare these big companies with each other on important matters, I was convinced something would happen. If you make a list . . . it is a ranking really, but index has a bit more flavor . . . if you compare these companies that day in day out compete with each other that are thinking constantly of how to beat their competitor. If suddenly a list appears in the Financial Times on an issue where they can compare themselves with their peers . . . they care because their peers care. The World Health Organization cares. When we measure something that is very important it is a bull's eye because the world has for a long time been trying to convince to these companies to do more—we help them. They had no direction what to and suddenly an index tells them how their competitor is doing. Prior to the index they all thought they were doing the best, but after the index comes out they find they are far from leading. They come away with the fact that they are not really leaders . . . Companies are now going to NGOs wanting to be higher on the index asking "help me" "help me" how.[119]

The success of the index turns on capitalizing on the competitive impulse within the industry sector coupled with the longtime horizon of investment returns that counsels a cautious approach among competitors in the sector. As Leerveld explains: "Companies that do things that try to find a product that will be profitable in 12–15 years anticipate relevance in the future sooner than you think. They make it relevant themselves. They anticipate that the list is growing in importance and that is why they make it important."[120] Moreover, investors are especially interested in the index. According to Leerveld: "There are [investment firms] that say if you invest in the companies high on the index you get higher returns. How do they behave towards these markets, what are the implications for future markets how far thinking are they? It's a business risk. Investors care because social issues are more and more on the agenda."[121]

[117] *See Report Cards*, Access to Medicine Index, https://accesstomedicinefoundation.org/access-to-medicine-index/report-cards (last visited Feb. 7, 2020).

[118] *See Investors*, Access to Medicine Index, https://accesstomedicinefoundation.org/about-us/investors (last visited Feb. 7, 2020).

[119] Interview with Wim Leerveld, Founder, Access to Medicines Index (Jan. 8, 2015).

[120] *Id.*

[121] *Id.*

The AMI is an example of an indicator setting standards. The designers devised the standard by which to measure the conduct of pharmaceutical companies on the issue of access.

## E. The Oxfam Scorecards: Behind the Brands and Barcodes

Oxfam's Behind the Brands Scorecard targets the world's ten most prosperous and powerful food and beverage companies, including: Nestlé, Associated British Foods (ABF), Coca-Cola, Danone, General Mills, Kellogg, Mars, Mondelez International (previously Kraft), PepsiCo, and Unilever. Among other things, the Scorecard aims to increase transparency and accountability of the "Big 10" throughout the supply chain. Oxfam evaluates how peer companies compare on policies and ranks companies to create an incentive for a "race to the top" to improve the social and environmental performance of the target companies.[122] "Behind the Brands is part of the Oxfam GROW campaign. The aim of the GROW campaign is to build a better food system: one that sustainably feeds a growing global population and empowers poor people to earn a living income and feed their families."[123]

> The aim of Behind the Brands is to generate a "race to the top" among the Big 10 to improve their policies across seven themes that impact upon food security. It is assumed that these policy improvements will enable companies to reduce negative social and environmental impacts across agricultural supply chains. The Scorecard and its underlying spreadsheet are valuable tools for internal and external stakeholders, including investors, consumers and citizens wishing to identify both examples of best practice and gaps needing improvement. The Scorecard is the core of the Behind the Brands campaign, and promotes transparency and accountability among companies.[124]

Oxfam also aims to use the Scorecard to "[a]mplify the voices of key stakeholders such as farmers, communities, consumers and investors."[125]

The scorecard examines company policies in seven "themes" that Oxfam identifies as critical to sustainable agricultural production that had previously been neglected by the industry. The structure of the scorecard weights each of the

122 Beth Hoffman, Behind the Brands: Food Injustice and the "Big 10" Food and Beverage Companies (2013).
123 *Id.* at 3.
124 *Id.* at 3.
125 Erinch Sahan, The Journey to Sustainable Food: A Three-Year Update on the Behind the Brands Campaign 1 (2016).

seven areas equally. These areas include: (1) corporate transparency; (2) women workers and producers in the supply chain; (3) farm workers in the supply chain; (4) small-scale farmers growing the commodities; (5) rights and access to (and sustainable use of) land; (6) rights and access to and sustainable use of water; and (7) climate consciousness. Scores range from "good" to "very poor."

Within each theme, Oxfam's Scorecard assesses companies on the degree to which agricultural sourcing policies:

1. directly affect the lives of people in communities in developing countries that the company sources from;
2. indirectly affect the lives of people in these communities by enabling or facilitating positive impacts; and
3. are indicative of, or correlate with, the kinds of practices that would have a positive impact.[126]

Oxfam evaluates company awareness, knowledge, commitments, supply chain management, and transparency. Oxfam credits transparency and structures evaluation of disclosures differently to reward reporting of important aspects of agricultural sourcing, including countries of origin and sourcing volumes. The awareness assessment involves considerations such as: "Does the company demonstrate general awareness of key issues relating to that theme and does it conduct projects to understand and address these key issues?"[127] The knowledge measure asks: "Does the company demonstrate it measures, assesses and reports key issues and facts specifically in its supply chains that relate to that theme?"[128] The commitment metric asks: "Does the company commit to addressing the key issues relating to that theme in its supply chains?"[129] Supply chain management considers questions such as: "Does the company require its suppliers to meet relevant standards related to that theme?"[130] Finally, transparency takes an expanded approach to reach disclosures on important corporate level concerns "linked to the practices that are relevant (directly or indirectly) to the lives of those in rural communities in developing countries."[131] Oxfam explains: "[E]ach indicator category includes several indicators and sub-indicators."[132]

[126] *Id.* at 3.
[127] Hoffman, *supra* note 122, at 6.
[128] *Id.* at 6–7.
[129] *Id.* at 7.
[130] *Id.* at 7.
[131] *Id.* at 3–4; Sahan, *supra* note 125 at 6–7.
[132] Hoffman, *supra* note 122, at 10–35; *see also* Oxfam, *The Behind the Brands Scorecard Methodology*, 10–35 (2014), https://www.behindthebrands.org/images/media/Download-files/BtB%20Methodology%20document_final_Sept%202014.pdf.

The Scorecard priorities key commodities used by the Big 10 based on impact to small-scale farmers, farm workers, and local communities, including palm oil, sugar cane, cocoa, coffee, tomatoes, and dairy products, among others.[133]

According to Oxfam, over "700,000 campaign actions were taken by Behind the Brands supporters urging the Big 10 companies to improve their policies."[134] Oxfam reports that after direct action including "targeted online social media to offline mobilizations and email petitions" most company scores improved by at least 10 percent over a three year period.[135] Some investors have also taken action. In 2013, after Oxfam's first ranking was released, thirty-three major investment funds representing nearly $1.4 trillion of assets under management expressed support for Oxfam's initiative and insisted that food industry leaders improve supply chain policies and increase transparency.[136] Significantly, signatories also pledged to cooperate with companies to create policy changes, noting the "broad and urgent need for significant improvement across the sector" demonstrated by Oxfam's data.[137]

Oxfam has found that changes for the better extended beyond the Big 10, explaining the leverage exerted by large players in the market: "The changes have not been limited to the Big 10, as Behind the Brands has seen evidence of major suppliers feeling pressure from the Big 10 to also adjust the way they do business. While there is no systematic analysis of how the suppliers of the Big 10 have changed their practices, there is anecdotal evidence that this is happening."[138]

According to Oxfam, the number of indicators across the themes varies because in some instances the organization was not able to identify clear questions addressing key issues to sufficiently separate high performers from low performers, or in other instances more complexity and nuance was warranted.[139] Each indicator is also weighted equally within each indicator category, as is each subindicator. Oxfam announced updates to the rankings, remarking on improvements that ranked companies have made to their policies over time.

There appears to be slight changes to the methodology regularly. The Scorecard has been released periodically, sometimes within nine months of the

[133] *Id.*

[134] Erinch Sahan, *Using Scorecards to Influence Business: The Behind the Brands Experience*, OXFAM: VIEWS & VOICES (Oct. 11, 2017), https://views-voices.oxfam.org.uk/private-sector/2017/10/using-scorecards-to-influence-business-learning-from-behind-the-brands.

[135] SAHAN, *supra* note 125, at 4.

[136] *See Investors Push Food Industry Giants for Urgent Action on Transparency*, OXFAM INTERNATIONAL (Sept. 16, 2013), https://www.oxfam.org/en/pressroom/pressreleases/2013-09-17/investors-push-food-industry-giants-urgent-action-transparency (last visited May 7, 2015).

[137] *See* BEHIND THE BRANDS—INVESTOR STATEMENT (2013), https://www.oxfam.org/sites/www.oxfam.org/files/oxfam-behind-the-brands-investor-statement-17sept2013.pdf (last visited Feb. 24, 2019).

[138] SAHAN, *supra* note 125, at 7.

[139] *See* Oxfam, *Behind the Brands Methodology Summary* (2013), https://www.behindthebrands.org/images/media/Download-files/BehindTheBrandsMethodologySummary-26Feb13-EN.pdf.

last, three months of the last, or more than a year from the last. The only direction on when the Scorecard is actually released is "regularly."[140] "Oxfam update[s] the Scorecard annually . . . with additional updates being undertaken to reflect noteworthy progress by the Big 10. The annual updates include revisions of the indicators to reflect advancements in best practices within the sector."[141]

The Scorecard seems to be widely accepted by the Big 10 of the food and beverage industry. Some of the companies, including Nestlé and Unilever, publish their rankings and the Oxfam Behind the Brand Scorecard on their company websites.[142] There are also many quotes throughout the Behind the Brand reports from top-ranking officials of the Big 10 companies commending the goals of the Behind the Brand Scorecard and Oxfam. Many of the Big 10 companies are involved in the formulation of the indicators and give feedback to Oxfam regarding indicator development. Additionally, according to Oxfam, the Scorecard has been effective in encouraging companies to change their policies to be more in line with obligations under the UNGPs and other multistakeholder initiatives to improve their rank.

According to Oxfam Scorecard rankings, Nestlé and Unilever perform better than other companies in the sector due in large part to developing policies and making disclosures.[143] In contrast, Kellogg has disclosed fewer public policies addressing impacts of its operations on producers.

The Oxfam Scorecard has attracted the attention of industry. For example, Nestlé issued a public letter responding to the ranking and committing to explore ways to approve its approach to women in its supply chain.[144] Oxfam in turn issued a statement welcoming the company's stated intention to make improvements and commended it for being the first of the three big chocolate companies to make a public commitment.[145] In the same statement, Oxfam announced plans to hold public actions at the headquarters of Mars, Mondelez, and Nestlé to mark International Women's Day and to make a statement about the company performance with respect to gender equality.[146] Oxfam's Behind

140 Hoffman, *supra* note 122, at 9.

141 *Id.* at 6–7.

142 *E.g.*, *Unilever Leads Industry in Oxfam's Behind the Brands Scorecard*, Unilever (Apr. 19, 2016), https://www.unilever.com/news/news-and-features/Feature-article/2016/Unilever-leads-industry-in-Oxfams-Behind-the-Brands-scorecard.html (last visited Feb. 7, 2020); *Nestle Tops Oxfam's Behind the Brands Scorecard Again*, Nestlé (Feb. 26, 2014), https://www.nestle.com/media/news/oxfam-behind-the-brands (last visited Feb. 7, 2020).

143 Hoffman, *supra* note 122, at 3.

144 Letter from Jose Lopez, Executive Vice President, Nestlé S.A., to Frank Michaelson, Policy Advisor, Oxfam Novib (Mar. 7, 2013), https://www.nestle.com/sites/default/files/asset-library/documents/media/news-and-features/2013-march/nestle-letter-to-oxfam-march-7-2013.pdf.

145 *Nestle Responds to Oxfam's Behind the Brands*, Oxfam International: Press releases (Mar. 8, 2013), https://www.oxfam.org/en/press-releases/nestle-responds-oxfams-behind-brands (last visited Feb. 12, 2020).

146 *Id.*

the Brands Scorecard is being widely used as a reliable ranking scheme to which investors and competing businesses in the food and beverage industry are paying attention.

In 2018, Oxfam launched Behind the Barcodes, a Scorecard of the six largest supermarket retailers in the United States ranked for "how they tackle critical issues affecting the people who produce the food they sell."[147] The Scorecard focuses on four main areas: (1) transparency and accountability; (2) workers; (3) farmers; and (4) women.[148] Like Behind the Brands, Behind the Barcodes relies on publicly available information on company policies to produce the Scorecard, which includes: Walmart, Albertsons, Costco Wholesale, Whole Foods Market, and Kroger among other firms.

These Oxfam food sector rankings are examples of rankings using indicators that are setting standards. Oxfam selected and set the seven standards against which to measure the industry sector. The indicator is also used as a tool for engaging industry actors.

## F. Enough! Demand the Supply: Companies Ranked by Progress on Conflict Minerals

More than half of the world's supply of cobalt comes from the Democratic Republic of the Congo (DRC), where artisanal miners, including children, mine by hand unaided by technical or protective equipment, often under conditions that constitute modern slavery. UNICEF estimates that forty thousand children work in mines across southern DRC.[149] Technology firms rely on a steady supply of these rare earth minerals in manufacturing; cobalt is a key component in many consumer electronic devices.[150]

As global demand for cobalt in the technology sector increased, its mining remained largely unregulated and unchecked among technology corporations. Firms often failed to assess the human rights impacts of sourcing decisions and did not conduct adequate due diligence to detect human rights risks.[151] The recognition of a clear business responsibility to identify risks to human rights and to avoid contributing to or causing human rights abuses is a recent development,

[147] *See* OXFAM, BEHIND THE BARCODES (2018), https://www.oxfamamerica.org/explore/research-publications/behind-the-barcodes/ (last visited Feb. 24, 2019).

[148] *Id.*

[149] Jane Wakefield, *Apple, Samsung and Sony Face Child Labour Claims*, BBC (Jan. 19, 2016), http://www.bbc.com/news/technology-35311456.

[150] Amnesty International, *This Is What We Die For: Human Rights Abuses in the Democratic Republic of the Congo Power the Global Trade in Cobalt*, 5–7 (Jan. 2016, AFR 62/3183/2016).

[151] Jessi Hempel, *Apple and Microsoft May Use Cobalt Dug by Kids, Report Says*, WIRED (Jan. 19, 2016, 2:33 PM), http://www.wired.com/2016/01/apple-and-microsoft-may-use-cobalt-dug-by-kids-report-says/.

introduced in international standards and reinforced by domestic regulation in some regions.

The Enough Project, an initiative of the Center for American Progress to end genocide and crimes against humanity, was founded in 2007. In 2010, it started to rank company on progress on eradicating conflict minerals originating in the DRC to end the violent conflict that has plagued the region. The United Nations has established that continued conflict in the DRC has been fueled and financed by the sale of rare earth minerals. Recognizing the region's conflict had long been resistant to conventional approaches to international crisis, the Enough Project turned its advocacy focus on finance in order to target "the political economy of conflict, in particular the violent kleptocratic regimes that we believe are at the heart of the persistence of these conflicts and the massive corruption that enriches the leaders and their international collaborators." To that end, Enough Project advocacy prioritized the use of policy instruments to interrupt corruption emphasizing the need to stop illicit financial flows from war criminals in order to leverage peace agreement processes and human rights protection.[152]

The Enough Project ranking measures the performance of twenty-one leading electronics companies selected based on market share for their ability to "set the tone and direction of wider industry efforts"[153] and for their "potential to be catalytic in the development of new policies and practices regarding responsible sourcing."[154] The ranked companies are also especially attuned to consumer and investor pressure and include Apple, Dell, HP, IBM, Intel, Microsoft, Motorola, Samsung, and Sony, among others.

The Enough Project ranks electronics companies on conduct in five categories selected for impact on curbing the conflict minerals trade: (1) tracing; (2) auditing; (3) certification; (4) legislative support; and (5) stakeholder engagement. The Enough Project collects survey data from the business enterprises it ranks and also refers to but does not incorporate into calculations other rankings including the Greenpeace Guide to Green Electronics and Newsweek's Green Rankings. The rankings are released along with a lengthy narrative discussion providing an overview of industry-wide progress, or lack thereof. It also offers recommendations for individual company action. The Enough Project explains the purpose of its rankings exercise as follows:

[152] *About*, ENOUGH PROJECT, https://enoughproject.org/about (last visited Nov. 16, 2020).

[153] THE ENOUGH PROJECT, GETTING TO CONFLICT-FREE: ASSESSING CORPORATE ACTION ON CONFLICT MINERALS 2 (2010), http://www.enoughproject.org/files/publications/corporateactionI.pdf.

[154] Annie Callaway, *Demand the Supply: Ranking Consumer Electronics and Jewelry Retail Companies on Their Efforts to Develop Conflict-Free Minerals Supply Chains from Congo*, THE ENOUGH PROJECT, at 1–2 (Nov. 2017), https://enoughproject.org/wp-content/uploads/2017/11/DemandTheSupply_EnoughProject_2017Rankings_final.pdf.

> These rankings are an effort to provide consumers with the information they need to purchase responsibly, as well as a means of encouraging companies to continue to move forward in good faith. We are hopeful that as the rankings are updated in subsequent reports, scores will improve along with methodology as the process for tracing, auditing, and conflict-free certification evolves.[155]

Leading companies are given credit, while the laggards are condemned by the Enough Project. However, rankings have not been released regularly.

The Enough Project ranking predated the enactment of regulations requiring companies to make conflict minerals reports to the US Securities and Exchange Commission (SEC). Subsequently, the European Union also introduced conflict minerals reporting requirements. In 2010, the Enough Project released company rankings to increase awareness among companies and to encourage consumer activism to prevent products containing minerals that could be linked to violence from entering the market. That same year, the United States passed Section 1502 of the Dodd-Frank Wall Street Reform and Consumer Protection Act, requiring all publicly traded companies using tin, tantalum, tungsten, and gold in their products to report on their supply chain due diligence. The Enough Project released its second electronics company rankings in 2012, the same year the SEC implemented its Conflict Minerals Rule under Dodd-Frank Section 1502.

Revised Enough Project rankings after the enactment of binding reporting regulations assessed companies based on four core categories of criteria:

1. **Conducting Conflict Minerals Sourcing Due Diligence and Reporting**: Assessing conflict minerals policies, due diligence, smelter and refinery disclosure, third-party audit participation, and supplier and traceability program engagement.
2. **Developing a Conflict-Free Minerals Trade and Sourcing Conflict-Free Minerals from Congo, Particularly Gold**: Sourcing verifiably conflict-free tin, tantalum, tungsten, and gold from Congo and supporting the development of a conflict-free minerals trade in Congo through financial contributions and multistakeholder engagement.
3. **Supporting and Improving Livelihoods for Artisanal Mining Communities in Eastern Congo**: Making financial contributions to projects with the objective of supporting livelihoods and/or improving health, safety, and economic opportunities in artisanal mining communities in eastern Congo.
4. **Conflict-Free Minerals Advocacy**: Actively supporting the maintenance and enforcement of the Dodd-Frank Wall Street Reform and Consumer

155 The Enough Project, *supra* note 153, at 2.

Protection Act's Section 1502, and engaging with financial institutions to enhance their awareness of the risks associated with conflict minerals sourcing.

The Enough Project reports: "The criteria were designed with two main goals in mind: first, to identify the most important areas that need improvement without unfairly moving the goalposts from previous rankings, and promote new opportunities for companies to strengthen their due diligence and reporting practices; and second, to highlight real progress by including certain key criteria from previous Enough rankings where company processes noticeably improved in recent years."[156] Moreover, "[t]wo extra credit opportunities were also offered related to 1) taking steps to ensure the company's minerals did not originate from national parks, and 2) financial contributions to the Conflict-Free Smelter Program (CFSP) Initial Audit Fund."[157] With each iteration of the ranking, the Enough Project observed that many companies improved and some even identified opportunities for creating conflict-free minerals sourcing practices and engaging consumers.[158]

Sasha Lezhnev, previously Deputy Director of Policy for the Enough Project, explained that his "Rank 'Em & Spank 'Em" approach to advocacy can be effective, but in his experience "name and shame" strategies are usually a last resort effort to engage an industry sector or business enterprise. Indeed, the rankings only came after the organization's earlier attempts to pursue an education approach to advocacy with business enterprises implicated in conflict minerals issues did not yield desired results.[159] Nevertheless, he concedes that at least early on "corporations did not know where problems were, they probably suspected problems but could look the other way or not look at them."[160]

That said, rankings and education advocacy alone would not have been sufficient to shift the industry on the conflict minerals issue according to Lezhnev. Legal reporting requirements proved to be essential. Lezhnev attributes approximately 75 percent of successes he has seen to date in the DRC to the conflict minerals legislation. While the Enough Project made inroads using the education approach in some companies before regulatory requirements, Lezhenv attributed these advances to principled and progressive leadership in certain companies. He expressed anxiety about the lack of regulations requiring reporting as follows: "[W]hat if all the good guys retire?" To him, having a law matters because things change. Employees committed to issues leave or interest

156 *Id.* at 10.
157 *Id.* at 11.
158 *Id.* at 8.
159 Interview with Sasha Lezhnev, Deputy Director of Policy, Enough Project, in Washington, D.C. (June 22, 2012).
160 *Id.*

in a particular topic fades over time. Initially, Lezhenv had little faith in the binding regulatory requirements as well but later came to see positive impacts:

> I used to think it was all just on paper but now it is becoming valuable. Because of the law, the International Conference for the Great Lakes Region now has a process for chain of custody [of minerals] that is much improved. Before the law the meetings of the Conference were do-nothings. Now something is being done. The tenor of these meetings has changed. Before these guys were passing time now they actually must provide evidence for buyers—a better chain of custody system has come about how that the threat of a de facto embargo got the attention of people on the ground.[161]

Companies submitted their first conflict minerals reports to the SEC pursuant to regulatory requirements in 2014. In 2015, the international human rights organizations Amnesty International and Global Witness teamed up to review the reports submitted and concluded that 79 percent of the reports failed to meet minimum requirements of the US conflict minerals regulations discussed infra.[162] Subsequent academic studies also found failings. Questions concerning the adequacy and efficacy of the contents of reports remain. The US conflict minerals reporting rule was highly contested from its inception and has been rolled back significantly since the 2016 elections, while the EU regulations will go into effect in 2021. Whether the right mix of regulations and rankings could work to curb the trade in conflict minerals and contribute to ending the conflict in the DRC and associated human rights abuses remains to be seen. Nevertheless, the advocacy was innovative and served to make the conflict minerals problem a priority. Figure 4.8 shows the 2017 Enough Project rankings of companies across different industry sectors for efforts to develop conflict-free supply chains.

## IV. Principles in Practice: Reporting and Ranking Respect for Rights

The previous section surveyed a sampling of rankings and ratings that are related to the impact of business enterprises on the enjoyment of human rights. This section explores trends and themes as these reporting and ranking efforts serve to inform the ecology of global governance and in turn serve to influence corporate governance. How the producers of these indicators coordinate to create then is examined. The lack of significant contestation on the part of the business entities that are the subjects of these indicators is explained. Finally, the ways in which

[161] *Id.*

[162] *See Digging for Transparency: How U.S. Companies Are Only Scratching the Surface of Conflict Minerals Reporting*, Amnesty Int'l & Global Witness 1 (Apr. 2015).

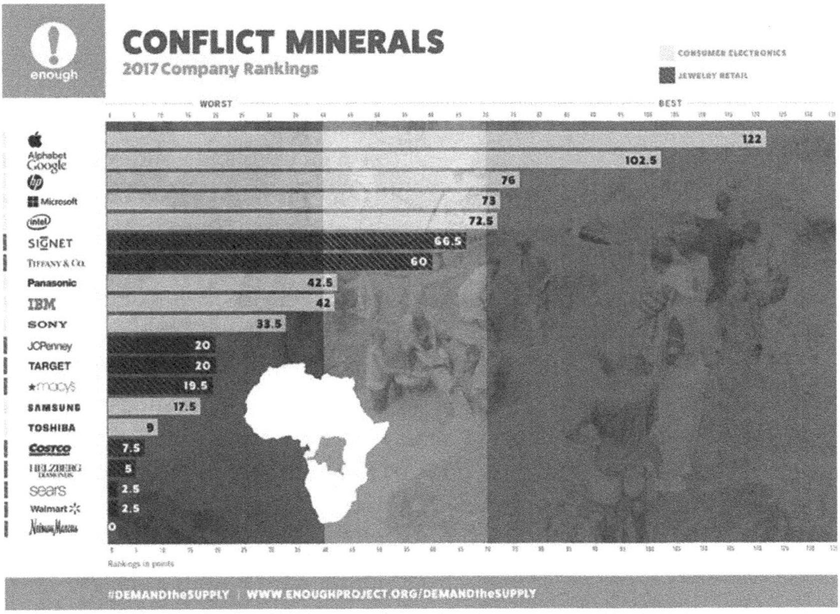


**Figure 4.8** Conflict Minerals 2017 Company Rankings
*Source*: Enough Project, Demand the Supply: Ranking Consumer Electronics and Jewelry Retail Companies on Their Efforts to Develop Conflict-Free Minerals Supply Chains from Congo, at 2 (2017)

information in the form of rankings influence the interrelationship between law, policy, and the production of knowledge about the human rights impacts of particular business practices is outlined in the following.

## A. Indicator Initiatives: Opportunities and Challenges

### 1. Creation and Coordination

Efforts to coordinate are more prevalent than competition in indicator generation for evaluating the impact of business on human rights. Far from seeing competition among producers of indicators in the business and human rights realm, frequently there is collaboration among coalitions of activists to create ratings and rankings. There is often broad public consultation with notice and open comment periods to contribute to the process of creating a rating or ranking. With the exceptions of the rankings and scorecards produced by Oxfam and the Enough Project on specific issue areas within single industries, the emerging indicators are coming from blended stakeholder constituencies composed of investors and activists. KTC is composed of no less than ten different organizations. The RDR Index, the CHRB Standard, and Shift's Human Rights Reporting and Assurance Frameworks Initiative (RAFI) all piloted survey questions and sought public comment.

RAFI, as a new entrant to human rights reporting, states that in December 2013 it signed a memorandum of understanding with the popular and widely used Global Reporting Initiative to "underline their mutual commitment to advancing meaningful corporate human rights reporting."[163] Consistent with this understanding, RAFI will seek to "through an open and multi-stakeholder consultative process, to identify opportunities for the language of the reporting and assurance frameworks to dovetail to the greatest extent possible with the GRI Sustainability Reporting Guidelines."[164]

Conditions favor cooperation for the nonprofit producers of indicators. Ranking producers are under resourced relative to the enterprises they are ranking, so pooling resources rather than competing or duplicating efforts would favor conditions for coordination. NGO activists motivated by specific issues and nonprofits presently dominate the space, not intergovernmental or international agencies like the World Bank as is the case with most indicators examined in the literature that follows the work of Davis, Kingsbury, and Merry.

An important benefit resulting from coordinated efforts of indicator producers is that more consultative inputs go into the creation. More broad inputs in creating indicators may lead to more legitimacy and efficacy. Most of the emerging indicators are the result of processes that are transparent. Many of the activist organizations are accorded a moral authority in the eyes of certain segments of the public. It is this group of conscious consumers and investors that those engaged in creating business and human rights rankings wish to reach.[165] Still for the single issue or single issue ratings systems put forward by a single NGO like Oxfam or the Enough Project there is an aura of authority based on expertise and experience that offers the indicators legitimacy.

The nature of the power imbalances between the ranked and those doing the ranking is not so clear-cut as it might intuitively appear. Activists interviewed were often very knowledgeable about context and impacts of corporate action in, say, the Congo, while a corporation should in theory possess more information about its practices. Activists explain that business do not know because businesses do not ask. Indicators present an opportunity to learn. Several of the indicators rely on survey data and self-reports from companies. Failure to answer a question can cost points in the final rankings so there is incentive for a brand-sensitive and motivated company to gather information about potential human rights impacts.

163 Email from Caroline Rees, President and Co-Founder, Shift Project, to Erika George, Professor of Law, University of Utah S.J. Quinney Coll. of Law (Feb. 24, 2015) (on file with author).

164 *Id.*

165 *See generally* Pat Auger et al., *Do Social Product Features Have Value to Consumers?*, 25 Int'l J. Res. Marketing 183–191 (2008); Karen L. Becker-Olsen, B. Andrew Cudmore, & Ronald Paul Hill, *The Impact of Perceived Corporate Social Responsibility on Consumer Behavior*, 59 J. Bus. Res. 46–53 (2006); C.B. Bhattacharya & Sankar Sen, *Doing Better at Doing Good: When, Why, and How Consumers Respond to Corporate Social Initiatives*, 47 Cal. Mgmt. Rev. 9–24 (2004).

The very few reporting self-assessment standards to advance human rights created by business-only organizations have stalled. For example, the Human Rights Matrix of the Global Business Initiative, a business-led program with fourteen corporate members, including GE, HP, the Gap Inc., and Coca-Cola, among others ceased operation in 2009 after a short span of activity. So it seems the source of an indicator may matter for it to become salient.

### 2. Competition

While the organizations that are the source of these new rights impact reports and rankings are cooperative, evidence suggests that the subjects of the rankings engage in competition. A representative of a food and beverage industry sector company told the author that he aspired to get the company to "best in class" in the rankings.[166] The more effective rankings seem to list companies that are in competition with one another. Where a company is vulnerable to brand damage or reputation injury, such as those appearing on Oxfam's Scorecard, or where the company is in an industry that has confronted a prominent public relations crisis, like the pharmaceuticals sector, it may be more readily responsive to rankings. Through interviews with industry representatives, I learned that some in the business community, especially those charged with the responsibility for implementing corporate social responsibility and sustainability initiatives, actually appreciate the external pressure as it provides them with leverage to justify the need for change internally.[167]

### 3. Information Inputs and Outcomes

Information in the process of indicator construction can play an instructive role. For instance, the interplay between the asking of questions by the producers and those providing answers provide an opportunity for human rights education. For instance, Leerveld of the Access to Medicines Index admitted:

> I see it as very important if we don't ask the companies they will not learn what we want from them. Companies simply don't know what the world wants from them. We invite them here we explain for a day what we want, we explain the questions—otherwise they don't understand our questions we explain why we are asking the questions. I am not interested in an index for measuring. I am interested in progress. I want to make them better. I want to teach them to learn.

[166] Interview with Yann Wyss, Human Rights Specialist, Nestlé, in Geneva, Switzerland (Dec. 3, 2013).

[167] *See* Christine Bader, *Why Corporations Fail to Do the Right Thing*, ATLANTIC: BUSINESS (Apr. 21, 2014), https://www.theatlantic.com/business/archive/2014/04/why-making-corporations-socially-responsible-is-so-darn-hard/360984/ ("If we are to stop harm associated with business, we have to understand why people fighting the good fight inside companies fail, and what they need in order to succeed.").

> We ask questions when we know they don't have that system in place to answer because they have not organized themselves, but they know for next year they need to get better organized.[168]

The most common form of data collection for business and human rights–related rankings is to conduct a survey. For example, the Ranking Digital Rights and the Enough Project instruments rely primarily on surveys. Oxfam's Scorecard draws data from multiple publicly available sources and the availability of information varies.[169] In a sense these indicators are still self-reporting for business enterprises with some added scrutiny. Over time, however, it would not be unreasonable to expect to get more and more information about a corporation as the influence of an indicator becomes stronger.

### 4. Contestation by Corporate Actors

Surprisingly, my research has not revealed a strong and organized corporate counterstrategy to combat human rights rankings beyond the usual commercial advertising that presents a given business enterprise in a positive light. Nor are businesses ignoring the rankings. If anything, according to those who generate them, indicators are becoming important because industry sectors are treating them as important.

Where the stakes are adverse reputational impacts for a corporation or industry, it would not be unreasonable to expect corporations to launch a coordinated attack on the legitimacy of the organizations responsible for the rankings. However, this strategy could be risky and backfire where the organization is well respected and well established. Another strategy could be to create a ranking by business for business. Again, this strategy could backfire as it could be perceived as lacking the legitimacy of an independent assessment and provide NGOs fodder for comparing what a company says it does with respect to rights to what adverse impacts could be attributed to company conduct. Another strategy would be to distract the intended targets of the indicator by identifying a worse issue of industry sector. For example, one representative in the electronics sector reported "buying time" with NGO activists by pointing out how much worse the jewelry industry was and would be a more appropriate starting point for an intervention. Finally, it would be reasonable to expect that contestation on the part of corporations could take the form of silence—refusing to cooperate in surveys and self-reporting, saying nothing. The downside of this strategy, however, would

[168] Interview with Leerveld, *supra* note 119.

[169] Ranking Business and Human Rights: The Potential of Benchmarking the Corporate Respect for Human Rights, Presentation at the UN Business and Human Rights Annual Forum Panel, Geneva, Switzerland (Dec. 1, 2014), https://www.ohchr.org/Documents/Issues/Business/ForumSession3/Programme.pdf.

be giving rights activists the space to create a narrative about a corporation's commitments and conduct in the absence of a corporation's response to requests for information about its human rights performance. A corporation's failure to comment on allegations, explain conduct, or convincingly communicate a policy commitment with respect to rights may lead to further escalation of public actions to embarrass the brand. Moreover, in many of the indicator measurement systems a failure to respond could result in a lower ranking or last place. One representative of a consumer products company informed me that the best-case scenario would be to have an adverse external NGO say something positive about progress. It is generally more credible to be commended by former critics than to engage in self-congratulatory public relations campaigns. Accordingly, it may be strategic for a business enterprise sensitive to brand pressures to comply rather than contest corporate responsibility and human rights indicators.

### 5. Cooperation: Shareholders and Stakeholders

To date there is little evidence of direct and sustained coordination between investors, the authors of human rights rankings, human rights advocates, and victims of human rights violations, but overlapping advocacy networks exist. In some instances, investors have referenced the documentation of human rights reports by advocacy organizations in proxy materials proposing that companies adopt and implement human rights policies and report with greater transparency. Investors have also reached out to rankings for information. RDR founder Rebecca MacKinnon has shared research data with investors she considers shareholders to be stakeholders in the ranking instrument and explains:

> The first set of stakeholders are investors. Investors use the data to make decisions and shape their engagement strategies with companies . . . Domini made a decision to sell its Facebook stock—based partially on our research. But we've had conference calls with Fidelity, Goldman Sachs. We've done several presentations and calls with Rockefeller Investments, BNP Paribas and others . . . We've been hearing from quite a lot of investors. The Investor Alliance for Human Rights recently published a letter, an open letter to companies, urging them to adhere to the standards that the Ranking Digital Rights represents in its indicators.[170]

In sum, there is a powerful opportunity for human rights advocates to work more closely with the authors of human rights rankings given the influence investors and owners have with business enterprises.

[170] MacKinnon interview, *supra* note 84.

### 6. Interaction and Influence: Alignment with Law and Policy

There is a significant degree of interaction between indicators in the business and human rights realm and law and policy. Often indicators make direct reference to international and or domestic laws, regulations, or polices. For instance, the RDR makes express reference the International Covenant on Civil and Political Rights. The RAFI was designed to assess corporate performance against the UNGPs, which provide: "the responsibility of business enterprises to respect human rights refers to internationally recognized human rights—understood, at a minimum, as those expressed in the International Bill of Human Rights and the principles concerning the fundamental rights set out in the International Labour Organization's Declaration on Fundamental Principles and Rights at Work."[171]

Presently, it is at the domestic level the strategic linkages between indicators and law seem the strongest. The Enough Project's rankings of conflict minerals predate reports mandated by federal law. Prior to the passage and implementation of conflict minerals transparency legislation in the US discussed *infra*, the Enough Project's ranking included an assessment of a company's position on the proposed law. The Enough Project considered whether a given company supported or opposed disclosure requirements in reviewing where a company would rank with respect to a commitment to transparency.[172] KTC was essentially informing business enterprises of legal obligations to report pursuant to California's supply chain transparency law discussed infra by publicly reporting on the level of compliance with the state law that different businesses attained.[173]

### 7. Institutional Interactions: Advancing Authoritative Rights Reporting

Some of these emerging human rights ranking systems interact with governmental and intergovernmental institutions charged with monitoring human rights. The successor institution created by the UN Human Rights Council to continue the work of the Special Representative, the UN Working Group on the Issue of Human Rights and Transnational Corporations and Other Business Enterprises,[174] has provided a platform for dialogue and dissemination of developing business and human rights indicators. The UN Working Group is composed of five independent experts, reflecting regional representation. These experts enjoy the discretion to "identify strategic opportunities to further embed the Guiding Principles into global governance frameworks."[175]

[171] UNGP, *supra* note 14, at Guiding Principle 12.

[172] *See* Enough Project, Getting to Conflict-Free: Assessing Corporate Action on Conflict Minerals, Appendix: Methodology (Dec. 2010), https://enoughproject.org/files/corporate_action-1.pdf.

[173] *See* KnowTheChain, *supra* note 80.

[174] *See* A/66/53, chap. III. A, Res. 17/4, para. 6.

[175] *See* A/67/285, Sixty-Seventh Sess., Item 70(c) of the provisional agenda, *Promotion and Protection of Human Rights: Human Rights Situations and Reports of Special Rapporteurs and Representatives* (Aug. 10, 2012).

The UN Working Group first devoted significant time to the discussion of indicators at the third Annual UN Forum on Business and Human Rights in 2014.[176] The Annual Forum is a multistakeholder event led by the Working Group and the Office of the UN High Commissioner for Human Rights (OHCHR). The Forum program consists of high-level plenary sessions and parallel sessions organized by the Working Group and the OHCHR. There are also approved parallel sessions organized by external stakeholders. Under the leadership of the Working Group, the 2014 Forum theme "Advancing Business and Human Rights Globally: Alignment, Adherence and Accountability" focused on key strategic issues and current trends—including indicators.

The Working Group and the OHCHR sponsored a parallel session, "Improving Human Rights Reporting: The Contribution of the Reporting and Assurance Frameworks Initiative."[177] In addition, the AMI, the Ranking Digital Rights Project, the Human Rights Performance Benchmark Project, and Oxfam's Behind the Brands Scorecard were all given time on the formal Forum agenda in a parallel session, "Ranking Business and Human Rights: The Potential of Benchmarking the Corporate Respect for Human Rights."[178] While the authors of these indicators did not explicitly address the nature of their interaction with international human rights institutions, participation in the Forum demonstrates that there is active engagement and dialogue with UN entities.

The UN Working Group is well situated to lend legitimacy to emerging indicators consistent with the charge contained in its mandate to build capacity. The UN Working Group is also well situated to expand support for emerging indicators to other international entities and agencies consistent with the charge contained in its mandate to develop possible areas of cooperation with these entities and with governments. The Working Group is coordinating with various treaty bodies that monitor human rights to assist in the development of general comments and concluding observations and the framing of questions relevant to putting the guiding principles into practice that can be posted to state parties during the review of country reports.[179]

Indicators could provide incentives for businesses to create internal capacity to identify and avoid potential adverse human rights impacts to improve brand

[176] The Working Group reports annually to the Human Rights Council and the General Assembly. For more background information, *see Working Group on the issue of human rights and transnational corporations and other business enterprises*, United Nations Human Rights Office of the High Commissioner, http://www.ohchr.org/EN/Issues/Business/Pages/WGHRandtransnationalcorporationsandotherbusiness.aspx.

[177] Programme from 2014 United Nations Forum on Business and Human Rights, in Geneva, Switzerland (Dec. 1, 2014) (on file with author).

[178] *Id.*

[179] Correspondence from Michael Addo, Expert, UN Working Group on Business and Human Rights, to Erika George, Professor of Law, University of Utah S.J. Quinney Coll. of Law (July 18, 2013) (on file with author).

rankings. To a certain extent, indicators are being used as educational tools by the organizations promulgating them. For instance, a representative of the Enough Project explained that the organization initiated engagement with corporations in the consumer electronics industry to bring awareness to the issue of conflict minerals.[180] The founder of the AMI expects that the preparations a company will need to take to report and respond to rankings assessment inquiries will also require becoming more cognizant of human rights impacts.[181]

In addition to these institutional interactions in the global policy arena, or perhaps further solidifying the interconnections between various institutional actors like the OHCHR and the UN Working Group, there are individuals who carry experience and expertise between institutions as they change affiliations. For example, some of the key staff of Shift, the independent nonprofit center developing the Human Rights Reporting and Assurance Framework Initiative, previously had been members of the UN Special Representative's team central to drafting the UNGPs.[182] Shift lists among its "partner institutions" members of the UN Global Compact Network, the International Labour Organization, the International Organisation of Employers, and Oxfam. It has partnered with institutions that have demonstrated the capacity to influence changes in law and policy.

Finally, information contained in indicators may influence the institution of the market or may serve to support the effective implementation of regulatory efforts to require reporting on nonfinancial performance as a condition of accessing certain capital markets. For instance, under a recent directive adopted by the European Union some companies will be required to disclose nonfinancial information, including human rights impacts by 2017. The creators of the Human Rights Reporting and Assurance Framework Initiative maintain that its standardized framework can catalyze change and make required reporting more meaningful.[183] Reporting could be the first step toward a meaningful rights ranking.

## B. Indicator Initiatives: Criticisms and Concerns

Interestingly, some of the loudest critics of the use of indicators to assess the human rights impacts of business are leading members of the human rights movement. For instance, as Arvind Ganesan of Human Rights Watch puts it, "would we conceive of two or three extra judicial killings as equivalent to ten instances of torture?"[184] What some rights activists are resisting is false

[180] Interview with Lezhnev, *supra* note 159.
[181] Interview with Leerveld, *supra* note 119.
[182] *See Our Story*, Shift Project, http://shiftproject.org/page/our-team (last visited Feb. 7, 2020).
[183] *See First Comprehensive Guidance for Companies on Human Rights Reporting Launches in London*, Shift Project (Feb. 25, 2015), http://shiftproject.org/news/first-comprehensive-guidance-companies-human-rights-reporting-launches-london.
[184] Arvind Ganesan, Director Business and Human Rights, Human Rights Watch, Presentation at BSR Panel (Nov. 5, 2013).

"commensuration and cognition."[185] As explained by Espel and Sauder, the risk presented by commensuration, or put another way, the process of converting qualities into quantities that can share the same metric, is that "commensuration removes information from the particularity of its context and standardizes it."[186] Indeed, a focus on numbers to the exclusion of narrative can numb decision makers to nature of abuse and atrocity.

Beyond commensuration and cognition concerns, there is a risk of methodological mismatch. Malcolm Langford and Sakkiko Fukuda-Parr explain how the qualitative methods dominant in human rights practice are at variance with the "audit"-like tool of indicators.[187] They argue that quantitative indicators could on occasion compensate for shortcomings in qualitative approaches but on other occasions will simply be "ill-fitting proxies."[188]

Other challenges to the use of business and human rights indicators include the concern that indicators, as currently produced by private civil society actors could serve to disempower the legitimate centers of regulatory power that should more properly govern the area, such as the Human Rights Council or national governments.[189]

To be sure, there are authorized and recognized public forums for developing policy, but the proliferation of indicators created by private actors can be a way of empowering members of civil society to exert influence. There does not appear to be a high barrier to entry; it seems anyone can start an index. A low barrier to entry in the creation of indicators could create opportunities for recalibration of the existing power and information asymmetries between rights activists and business enterprises.

The challenge to the use of business and human rights indicators from the business community centers on concerns over the proliferation of competing initiatives. Business representatives present at Forum discussions on developing human rights indicators for business warned against "moving goal-posts" for performance and emphasized the importance of having realistic expectations of what it is possible for businesses to achieve.[190]

## V. Incorporating Rights

This chapter has examined the emergence and evolution of selected ranking and reporting frameworks in the realm of business and human rights advocacy.

[185] Espel & Sauder, *supra* note 10, at 92.

[186] *Id.*

[187] Malcolm Langford & Sakiko Fukuda-Parr, *The Turn to Metrics*, 30 Nordic J. Hum. Rts. 222–238 (2011).

[188] *Id.*

[189] Damiano de Felice, *Measuring Respect for Human Rights by Corporations: Challenges and Opportunities in the Production of Business and Human Rights Indicators*, 37 Hum. Rts. Q. 511–555 (2015).

[190] Panel Discussion, Annual Forum Panel, in Geneva, Switzerland (Dec. 1, 2014).

Specifically, it examined how indicators in the form of rankings and reports evaluating the conduct of transnational corporate actors serve as regulatory tools to bridge a global governance gap that has given rise to human rights risks by providing interested constituencies with actionable information upon which to base decisions. It explained the conditions that have led to coordination and collaboration among entities engaged in creating reporting frameworks and rankings. It described how certain indicators rely upon the competitive impulses of the business enterprises being ranked to assert influence over the businesses. It also identified why the businesses that are being ranked have been slow to deploy effective counterstrategies despite efforts to contest legally binding reporting requirements. It considered the interaction of selected business and human rights indicators with recent laws regulating supply chain transparency in the United States and with recent global policy initiatives calling for business enterprises to conduct human rights impact assessments. Finally, it reviewed some of the methodological and moral risks raised with respect to ranking rights. These risks can be reduced by ensuring narratives are not wholly overtaken by numbers.

The use of rankings informed by indicators is increasing and is increasingly serving as a regulatory instrument to the extent that rankings inform how shareholders and stakeholders will engage with business. Business and human rights rankings are gaining in influence and increasing incentives for businesses to change policies and practices to be better aligned with international human rights standards. The founding director of the business and human rights program at Human Rights Watch, Arvind Ganesan explained how his views on indicators have evolved as follows:

> initially I was more skeptical of them . . . what has been surprising to me is that rankings really matter to the private sector . . . Companies and businesses are inherently quantitative in many ways, and [a ranking] helps them not only benchmark themselves but benchmark themselves against their competitors, which is important to them. There's a value in that.[191]

Businesses are paying attention to rankings and would rather not rank poorly. Aside from avoiding a poor ranking, businesses are using benchmarks to advance accountability. As a sustainability professional working in the apparel and footwear sector explained:

> in some instances [rankings] have helped shine a light on holes in our program that we do have. And then, they can help us get resourced to fill those holes . . . it

[191] Telephone interview with Arvind Ganesan, Director Business and Human Rights, Human Rights Watch, Jan. 19, 2019.

> was helpful to identify some programmatic and some policy improvements that we could make. And it also allowed us to have that conversation with our senior leadership team, the C-suite, because it was in the news and what not.[192]

An inclusive creation process is central to the legitimacy of the rankings that these new business and human rights indicators inform. There are methodological questions to be resolved in human rights rankings, such as what metrics to use and what should be measured, especially as investor interest in evaluating companies based on social and environmental performance increases.

In the expanding ecology of global governance, these new business and human rights indicators will provide rights advocates with greater power to influence change by creating performance incentives. Business and human rights indicators have the potential to play an important role in solidifying emerging soft law standards and strengthening corporate self-regulation. The strategic use of indicators in the business and human rights realm could ultimately prove to make the voluntary commitments contained in corporate codes of conduct to respect human rights obligatory.

[192] Telephone interview sustainability professional working in apparel and footwear, Feb. 24, 2019.

# 5

# Competition, Choice, and Change

## Activist Investors and Concerned Consumers as Ethical Enforcement Agents

### Introduction

This chapter considers market-based strategies for bringing business practices into alignment with the responsibility to respect human rights. I argue that when investors and concerned consumers have access to sufficient information on corporate performance and risks posed to human rights by certain commercial practices, they can change corporate conduct by exercising preferences for companies, products, and services that are not associated with abuse. Transparency is essential for ensuring that human rights are protected. It is not my intention to in any way discount the value and importance of government regulation. Indeed, regulation to promote transparency may well be necessary for encouraging the business community to conduct human rights due diligence and disclose "salient" risks to human rights and the environment that particular business policies and practices may pose. My intention is to describe the ways in which investors and consumers—should they choose to do so—can help to drive change.

The previous chapter examined the role of indicators, ratings, and rankings in creating information incentives to improve corporate human rights performance. Here I examine how shareholder advocacy and certain social and environmental reporting initiatives to share information about the human rights and environmental impacts of business activity demonstrate a shifting consciousness on the part of investors. Reporting could serve to incorporate moral considerations into capital and consumer markets on a scale sufficient to create an incentive for corporate actors to consider the risks that particular business practices may present for human rights and the environment. I argue that the enforcement of corporate commitments to respect human rights could occur through the provision of actionable information on corporate performance to conscious constituencies of investors and consumers. Competitive pressures could be brought to bear on particular industries to improve social and environmental performance.

Specifically, this chapter considers how the growth in socially responsible investment, shareholder advocacy, mandatory reporting regimes, and integrated reporting initiatives could contribute to the promotion of respect for human

*Incorporating Rights.* Erika George, Oxford University Press. © Erika George 2021.
DOI: 10.1093/oso/9780199941483.003.0006

rights in the business community. The connected nature of communications now enjoyed by a significant segment of consumers is also explored as another route to regulate corporate conduct. A connected and concerned community of consumers and investors has increasingly been able to leverage securities law and purchasing power to promote change.

## I. Ethical Investors as Human Rights Enforcement Agents

Socially responsible investing (SRI) integrates traditional financial analysis with analysis of corporate responsibility and sustainability by incorporating the consideration of environmental, social, and governance (ESG) factors in portfolio selection and management. SRI is also referred to as "responsible," "sustainable," "socially conscious," "mission-driven," "green," or "ethical" investing. This section reviews the purpose of ethical investing and explains the processes commonly used by socially responsible investors.

### A. Shareholder Primacy: Protection and Power

Shareholders—owners of the corporations in which they hold shares—occupy an important role in corporate governance and possess the power to influence corporate policy and practices on a range of issues, including, potentially, respect for human rights. Under prominent theories of the firm, protecting the interests of shareholders is a primary corporate responsibility. This is known as *shareholder primacy.*[1]

Shareholders have an important stake in corporate governance because they provide the necessary capital to enable the business to operate. Because investors provide capital, they can claim a share of the profits generated by the business. They have rights to dividends and the distribution of assets upon dissolution of a corporation. The common assumption is that shareholders are interested only in high returns on the investments they make. Some corporate legal scholars have questioned this assumption and are critical of approaches that insist that shareholder primacy must always drive the decisions of management.[2] Shareholder primacy has arguably resulted in short-term thinking and shortsighted conduct.

[1] *See, e.g.*, Adolf A. Berle, *Corporate Powers as Powers in Trust*, 44 HARV. L. REV. 1049 (1931); Michael C. Jensen & William H. Meckling, *Theory of the Firm: Managerial Behavior, Agency Costs and Ownership Structure*, 3(4) J. FIN. ECON. 305 (Oct. 1976); Lynn A. Stout, *Bad and Not-So-Bad Arguments for Shareholder Primacy*, 75 S. CAL. L. REV. 1189 (2002); David Millon, *Radical Shareholder Primacy*, 10 U. ST. THOMAS L.J. 1013 (2013).

[2] Lynn Stout, *The Shareholder Value Myth: How Putting Shareholders First Harms, Investors*, CORP. & THE PUBLIC 24–37 (2012)

Incentives are structured in ways that force the management of a firm into decisions that are "myopic" and look only to quarterly returns.[3] Myopic management compromises the performance of the business enterprise, and managerial strategies that are shortsighted are likely to place people and the planet at risk.

Usually, investors are passive, providing capital to a corporation in return for a portion of the corporation's profits without active engagement in oversight or management of business operations. Active investing, however, may prove to be an important avenue for creating incentives to change corporate social and environmental performance. To the extent that corporations raise capital from lenders and investors, investors and lenders have some power to influence aspects of corporate governance in ways that provide incentives for businesses to respect rights and consider environmental impacts. For example, some lenders have provided better loan terms to businesses that make efforts to conduct human rights impact assessments.[4] Certain investment firms have created sustainable funds informed by ESG principles and now manage client portfolios to give preference to holdings that have ranked relatively high on human rights benchmarks.[5]

Securities regulations empower investors to participate in corporate governance to a certain extent; in the United States, shareholders can introduce proposals for reform and demands for disclosure through proxy voting.[6] Investors who hold shares with voting privileges have the power to change the composition of a corporation's management through board elections. Shareholders are able to exert some influence on corporate social and environmental policies through the proxy process.

### 1. Information as Protection for Shareholders: Disclosure

Publicly traded companies raise capital to support business activities through issuing and selling shares or securities. In the United States, the Securities and

[3] *See* David Millon, *Theories of the Corporation, 1990*, Duke L.J. 201 (1990); Emeka Duruigbo, *Tackling Shareholder Short Termism and Managerial Myopia*, 100 Ky. L.J. (2011–2012).

[4] *See* Rita Mota, *Banks as Human Rights Enforcers? A Comparative Analysis of Soft Law Instruments*, 34 Am. Univ. Int'l L. Rev. 351, 368 (2018).

[5] *See, e.g.*, Larry Fink, *Larry Fink's 2019 Letter To CEOs: Profit & Purpose*, BLACKROCK (2019), https://www.blackrock.com/americas-offshore/2019-larry-fink-ceo-letter (explaining importance of CSR, ESG); Robert G. Eccles & Svetlana Klimenko, *The Investor Revolution: Shareholders Are Getting Serious about Sustainability*, Harv. Bus. Rev. (May–June 2019), https://hbr.org/2019/05/the-investor-revolution; Abby Schultz, *Future Returns: Sustainable Investing is Turning Mainstream*, BARRON'S (Nov. 17, 2020), https://www.barrons.com/articles/future-returns-sustainable-investing-is-turning-mainstream-01605640036; Sean Collins & Kristen Sullivan, *Advancing ESG Investing: A Holistic Approach for Investment Management Firms*, Harv. L. Sch. F. on Corp. Governance (Mar. 11, 2020).

[6] 17 C.F.R. § 240.14a-8(i)(7). Businesses cannot exclude proposals seeking information on social and environmental risks. Exchange Act Release No. 40018 (May 21, 1998) ("[P]roposals relating to such matters but focusing on sufficiently significant social policy issues . . . generally would not be considered to be excludable, because the proposals would transcend the day-to-day business matters and raise policy issues so significant that it would be appropriate for a shareholder vote.").

Exchange Commission (SEC) is the regulatory agency responsible for investor protection and maintaining fair and efficient capital markets. Investors are the primary constituency protected by securities laws and regulations. The SEC protects investors against unreasonable risks, in significant part by requiring corporations to disclose certain "material" information about the securities issued for sale in the market. For example, Section 14(a) of the Securities Exchange Act of 1934 governs public interest disclosures.

The conventional supposition has been that investors are only interested in profits such that a firm need only report financial performance—material information concerns money. However, some scholars have called this conventional wisdom into question. Professor Cynthia Williams argues that it is appropriate for social performance information also to be provided in order to protect the interests of investors and the public,[7] and Professor Lynn Stout maintains that shareholders are diverse and some do care about and consider information deemed to be "nonfinancial" such as potential adverse environmental impacts or child labor as highly relevant when deciding whether to invest in a business enterprise.[8]

### 2. Intervention as Protection for Shareholders: Derivative Litigation

Shareholders can also sue on behalf of the corporation itself to protect the interests of the business enterprise.[9] Derivative litigation allows shareholders to protect a corporation and, by extension, their investment in a corporation. The prerequisites for a shareholder-derivative lawsuit are: (1) the action must be to enforce a right the corporation may properly assert but has failed to do so itself; and (2) the plaintiff must fairly and adequately represent the interests of similarly situated shareholders.[10] These requirements effectively oblige plaintiff shareholders to submit to a preliminary examination of their motivations, which are measured against the leadership's motivations to determine whether the plaintiff is an effective representative of the corporation's interests.[11]

Plaintiff shareholders must demonstrate that damage has been inflicted on a party to whom a duty is owed by management—the corporation itself.[12] This

[7] *See* Cynthia A. Williams, *The Securities and Exchange Commission and Corporate Social Transparency*, 112 HARV. L. REV. 1197, 1208–1209 (1999).

[8] Stout, *supra* note 2.

[9] *Id.*

[10] FED. R. CIV. P. 23.1 (other jurisdictions are substantially similar).

[11] Thomas P. Kane & Amy L. Wadsworth, *The "Entry Requirements" for Shareholder Derivative Litigation*, 25 TORT & INS. L.J. 880 (1990).

[12] David Rosenberg, *Delaware's "Expanding Duty of Loyalty" and Illegal Conduct: A Step towards Corporate Social Responsibility*, 52 SANTA CLARA L. REV. 81, 87, 103 (2012) (arguing combining Delaware's jurisprudence on corporate loyalty with the moral obligations inherent in a corporation should allow shareholders to bring derivative lawsuits claiming disloyalty by directors who approve illegal acts).

can be an issue for committed human rights activists when those most truly damaged by the economic, employment, or ecological consequences of corporate conduct—the victims of violations—have no direct relationship to the corporation itself. For example, it could be difficult to establish standing to bring litigation in the United States as an individual concerned about social media platforms spreading misinformation but as an investor it would be easier. For example, suits involving the integrity of the 2016 US electoral process and user privacy brought against Facebook by shareholders were allowed to proceed because these suits were framed to seek redress for the financial injuries sustained by shareholders when Facebook's stock price fell in July 2018 after revelations connecting the company to speeding the spread of targeted disinformation to voters.[13]

It may well be that when such damages are framed as ineffective risk management by leadership that harms the financial interests of investors, lawsuits will be more likely to survive dismissal and proceed to trial in US federal courts than claims focused on injuries sustained by victims of human rights violations.[14] This means that investor claimants may be able to seek redress for economic harms, while the claims of victims of human rights violations claim remain without access to remedy as readily.

There are other ways that concerned shareholders could leverage their power to promote human rights protections. Not only can shareholders bring derivative suits, they can and should demand disclosure of information relevant to discerning risks presented to human rights by a company's record on ESG issues. Investing in ways that are aligned with providing capital to those business enterprises that operate in ways that respect human rights and protect the environment could promote much needed change.

## B. Socially Responsible Investors and Social Change: The Purpose of Ethical Investment

Historically, SRI strategies have focused on avoiding further contribution to societal injustices through specific investment choices.[15] More recently, the aims and approaches to SRI have extended the individual ethical preference for avoiding association with harmful products and practices to an institutional

[13] *In re Facebook Section 220 Litig.*, 2019 Del. Ch. LEXIS 197, at *3 (Ch. May 30, 2019).

[14] Nir Kossovsky, Opinion, *Food Industry Leaders Face Increased Personal Reputational and Legal Risk*, FOOD DIVE (May 17, 2019), https://www.fooddive.com/news/food-industry-leaders-face-increased-personal-reputational-and-legal-risk/554956/ (written by the CEO of a risk management company, counting six derivative lawsuit filings on these grounds).

[15] KATHERINA GLAC, CENTER FOR ETHICAL BUSINESS CULTURES, THE INFLUENCE OF SHAREHOLDERS ON CORPORATE RESPONSIBILITY (2010).

ambition to improve society. Where before an individual investor may wish to avoid holding shares in alcohol, tobacco, firearms, or fossil fuels, now some institutional investors seek to support businesses that are working to solve global problems. Indeed, some institutional investors are leveraging their holdings to help address certain social challenges.

### 1. Ethical Investing: Origins and Evolution

Initiatives of faith-based organizations formed the foundations of the modern SRI movement.[16] For example, members of the Quaker faith opposed the slave trade and avoided investments in companies that profited from gambling, alcohol, and tobacco.[17] The Methodist Church promoted ethical commercial activity such that business practices should not harm others, and industries likely to have a negative impact on the health of workers should be avoided.[18] These earliest forms of SRI, also known as "ethical investing," used "negative screening"—a method of excluding certain types of securities from the holdings in a portfolio.[19] Negative screens were devised to avoid investment in companies and industries that engaged in activities in conflict with the fundamental tenants of a faith community.[20]

Borrowing from the earlier faith-based ethical approaches, the term "socially responsible investing" came to describe the values-based approach to investment. SRI strategies reflected an increasing awareness of the impact that companies and investors could have on the public good.[21] For example, trade unions

[16] *See, e.g.*, Terrence Guay, Jonathan P. Doh, & Graham Sinclair, *Non-Governmental Organizations, Shareholder Activism, and Socially Responsibility Investments: Ethical, Strategic, and Governance Implications*, 52 J. Bus. Ethics 125–139 (2004).

[17] *See* Julian F. Kölbel, Florian Heeb, Falko Paetzold, & Timo Busch, *Can Sustainable Investing Save the World? Reviewing the Mechanisms of Investor Impact*, 33 Org. & Env't 554, 554 (2020) ("Historically, the Quakers divested to avoid supporting the slave trade."); Benjamin J. Richardson, *Protecting Indigenous Peoples through Socially Responsible Investment*, 6 Indigenous L.J. 205 (2007) (quoting J.R. Soderlund, Quakers and Slavery: A Divided Spirit (1985)).

[18] *See* Simone de Colle & Jeffrey G. York, *Why Wine Is Not Glue? The Unresolved Problem of Negative Screening in Socially Responsible Investing*, 85 J. Bus. Ethics 83, 84 (2008) ("Quakers and Methodists often refused to invest with firms involved in the slave trade . . . The earliest formal investment policies were organized around avoiding 'sinful' companies, those producing alcohol, tobacco, and gambling."); Céline Louche, Daniel Arenas, & Katinka C. van Cranenburgh, *From Preaching to Investing: Attitudes of Religious Organisations Towards Responsible Investment*, 110 J. Bus. Ethics 301, 311 (2012).

[19] *See* Nur Uysal, *Faith-Based Investor Activism for Corporate Environmental Responsibility: Catalysts for Corporate Change?*, in The Handbook of Financial Communication and Investor Relations 245, 248 (Alexander V. Laskin ed., 2018) (citations omitted).

[20] Louche, et al., *supra* note 18, at 311; P.L. Cochran, *The Evolution of Corporate Social Responsibility*, 50(6) Bus. Horizons 449–454 (2007). *See also Encyclical Letter Laudato Si' of The Holy Father Francis on Care for Our Common Home*, Vatican Press, http://i2.cdn.turner.com/cnn/2015/images/06/18/papa-francesco_20150524_enciclica-laudato-si_en.pdf.

[21] Eccles & Klimenko, *supra* note 5, at 3–4; Cochran, *supra* note 20, at 449–454.

recognized that their pension assets could be directed toward investments that increased the overall well-being of society and laborers.[22]

Certain specific issues and industry sectors have attracted the attention of the SRI community. For example, refusal to invest in South Africa in order to cripple the apartheid government demonstrated a willingness on the part of some investors to exert economic influence to advance a particular political outcome.[23] Later, the anti-apartheid movement called for a divestment disinvestment campaign. Anti-apartheid activists lobbied institutions, such as university endowments and public pension funds, to withdraw investments in companies that did not adhere to a set of voluntary antidiscrimination principles.[24] Student protests caused the number of universities participating in the anti-apartheid disinvestment campaign to rise from 53 in 1985 to 155 by August 1988.[25] The disinvestment campaign contributed to a reduction of US direct investment in South Africa from $2.28 billion in 1982 to $1.27 billion in 1988. The adverse impact of the divestment campaign on the South African economy is believed to have played a meaningful role in ending the country's apartheid system of government.[26]

## 2. Ethical Investing: The Process, the Players, and Progress

SRI has now entered into more mainstream investment strategies. SRI strategies emphasize the incorporation of broader social and environmental goals into the investment process. Investors committed to improving social and environmental conditions, or to avoiding complicity in exacerbating societal and environmental ills, have developed a variety of strategies to promote progress.

SRI methodology uses a combination of strategies to align capital with salient social and environmental concerns, including: (1) negative/exclusionary screening; (2) positive/best-in-class screening; (3) norms-based screening;(4) integration of ESG factors;( 5) sustainability-themed investing; (6) impact/community investing; and (7) corporate engagement and shareholder action.[27] Socially responsible investors can promote change in business practices through investment or divestment choices.

[22] *See generally* David Webber, The Rise of the Working-Class Shareholder: Labor's Last Best Weapon (2018).

[23] Suzanne L. Shier, *Responsible Investing: Making an Impact Prudently*, CV041 ALI-CLE 313 (2014).

[24] *Id.*

[25] *Id.*

[26] *Id.*

[27] Glob. Sustainable Inv. Alliance, Global Sustainable Investment Review 2014 (2015) http://www.ussif.org/Files/Publications/GSIA_Review.pdf; Ulrich Volz, *Fostering Green Finance for Sustainable Development in Asia* (ABDI Inst., ABDI working paper 814, 2018), https://www.adb.org/sites/default/files/publication/403926/adbi-wp814.pdf.

More mainstream money managers and institutional investors are using ESG criteria to assess whether an investment could be attractive for clients concerned about social and environmental issues following the precedent set by faith-based investors.[28] Some SRI investors believe that firms able to meet certain ESG criteria have superior management practices or present lower risk to investors and other stakeholders.[29]

In contrast to negative screens to exclude certain business enterprises, positive screens to capture certain types of commercial activities are attracting greater appeal as evidence mounts that responsible corporations increase shareholder value.[30] Modern SRI seeks to combine an investor's economic goals and values in a manner that does not dramatically reduce diversification or sacrifice financial performance in the long run.[31] A growing number of investors employ positive screening as an investment approach because, unlike negative screening, which merely excludes investment portfolios that contain companies with objectionable products, positive screening allows investors to "methodically support companies that set positive examples of environmentally friendly products or production methods and socially responsible business practices."[32] The development and sophistication of strategic approaches to SRI reflect a greater willingness among those most concerned to more actively manage their money in accord with their values, beyond financial returns.

Portfolio managers and research analysts have cited two main reasons for considering ESG factors when making investment decisions: to adequately manage risk and to satisfy client demand. In 2015, the CFA Institute, a professional association of investors, surveyed its membership and found a full 73 percent of survey respondents indicated they now routinely take ESG issues into account in their investment analysis and decisions, with governance being the most

[28] *See, e.g.*, Casey O'Connor & Sara Labowitz, NYU Stern Center for Business and Human Rights, *Putting the "S" in ESG: Measuring Human Rights Performance for Investors* (Mar. 2017); Ernst & Young, Tomorrow's Investment Rules: Global Survey of Institutional Investors on Non-Financial Performance (2014); PricewaterhouseCoopers, Sustainability Goes Mainstream: Insights into Investor Views (May 2014); Inst. for Hum. Rts. and Bus., Investing the Rights Way: A Guide for Investors on Business and Human Rights (2013); Common Fund Institute, From SRI to ESG: The Changing World of Responsible Investing (Sept. 2013); Bus. for Social Responsibility, Environmental, Social and Governance: Moving to Mainstream Investing? (June 25, 2008).

[29] US SIF: The Forum for Sustainable and Responsible Investment, The Impact of Sustainable and Responsible Investment 11 (2016), http://www.ussif.org/files/Publications/USSIF_ImpactofSRI_FINAL.pdf.

[30] *See, e.g.*, Leonardo Becchetti et al., *Corporate Social Responsibility and Shareholder's Value*, 65 J. Bus. Res. 1628–1635 (2012); Francesco Perrini et al., *Deconstructing the Relationship Between Corporate Social and Financial Performance*, 102 J. Bus. Ethics 59–76 (2011); Emma Sjöström, *Shareholders as Norm Entrepreneurs for Corporate Social Responsibility*, 94 J. Bus. Ethics 177–191 (2010).

[31] US SIF, *supra* note 29, at 21–22.

[32] A. Kempf & P. Osthoff, *The Effect of Socially Responsible Investing on Portfolio Performance*, 13(5) Eur. Fin. Mgmt. 908–922 (2007).

important issue, followed by environmental and social issues.[33] An additional 38 percent considered ESG performance a proxy for management quality. Fully 61 percent of respondents agreed that public companies should be required to report at least annually on a cohesive set of sustainability indicators in accordance with the most up-to-date reporting framework. Of the 27 percent of respondents who did not take ESG issues into account, the chief reason indicated was a lack of demand from their clients, at 47 percent. This demonstrates that the demands of clients can make a difference in how investments are assessed. The growing importance of ESG issues is driven largely by market demand.

Trends suggest that SRI should no longer continue to be minimized as a "niche" or novelty concern of investors with special interests taking ideological positions "at odds with the goal of achieving optimized risk adjusted returns," rather responsible investment is seen as consistent with higher returns and lower risk.[34] SRI is no longer solely for niche clients; it is fast becoming a social and financial force serving to shift traditional investment practices in the investment industry, driven in large part by the institutions and organizations purchasing the services of financial advisors. Indeed, Larry Fink, leader of Blackrock, the world's largest investment firm, made media headlines in 2019 when he penned a letter informing CEOs that corporate purpose must be understood to include making positive contributions to society. He also noted: "Stakeholders are pushing companies to wade into sensitive social and political issues—especially as they see governments failing to do so effectively."[35] Powerful traditional investors are identifying ESG issues as increasingly important due in part to pressure from their clients, shareholder advocates, and changing societal expectations.

A report by the Global Sustainable Investment Alliance projects that growth rates for global assets under SRI management could reach $53 trillion by 2025, which would represent approximately 20–30 percent of total assets under management globally in 2020.[36]

[33] CFA Inst., Environmental, Social & Governance (ESG) Survey (June 2015), https://www.cfainstitute.org/-/media/documents/survey/esg-survey-report-2015.ashx.

[34] Edward J. Finely & Andrew King, *Socially Responsible Investing*, WealthManagement.com (Sept. 9, 2013); Luc Renneboog, Jenke Ter Horst, & Chendi Zhang, *Socially Responsible Investments: Institutional Aspects, Performance, and Investor Behavior*, 32 J. Banking & Fin. 1723, 1723 (2008) ("Over the past decade, SRI has experienced an explosive growth around the world reflecting the increasing awareness of investors to social, environmental, ethical and corporate governance issues.") .

[35] Andrew Ross Sorkin, *World's Biggest Investor Tells C.E.O.s Purpose Is the Animating Force for Profits*, N.Y. Times (Jan. 1, 2019), https://www.nytimes.com/2019/01/17/business/dealbook/blackrock-larry-fink-letter.html.

[36] The Economist Intelligence Unit, *Women in Focus: Gender Diversity and Socially Responsible Investing*, Barclays, 7 (2015), https://www.investmentbank.barclays.com/content/dam/barclaysmicrosites/ibpublic/documents/investment-bank/global-insights/women-in-focus-gender-diversity-and-socially-responsible-investing-2.4mb.pdf.

## C. Shareholder Advocacy: Shareholder Proposals to Protect Rights

In addition to putting their money where their moral commitments are, some shareholders are exercising the rights that accompany ownership by participating in corporate governance and proposing changes to policies and procedures to ensure that business practices are in better alignment with human rights principles. Shareholder advocacy as distinct from "shareholder activism" endeavors to proactively influence for the better managerial decision-making that ethical investors believe will have a detrimental impact on society.[37] As Andrew Behar, CEO of As You Sow, a nonprofit shareholder advocacy organization, explains: "Shareholder activists are hedge fund guys who are trying to extract as much value out of a company as they can for their own personal gain." In contrast, "shareholder advocates are really advocating on behalf of all the stakeholders to make the company a better company to increase value as opposed to destroy value. So, we're actually at the opposite ends of the spectrum but using the same tools."[38]

Shareholder advocates have employed a variety of strategies to advance their issues. They have filed resolutions and presented proposals to educate the public with the aim of persuading corporate management to take a particular course of action. Sometimes their efforts attract media attention and raise the profile of particular issues. These actions often put additional pressure on corporations to conduct business in a way that comports with the values of ethical investors.[39]

### 1. The Shareholder Proposal Process and Proxy Statements

In the United States, publicly traded companies are required to make regular reports to shareholders, consistent with rules promulgated by the SEC. Among other requirements, public companies must file annual reports with the SEC and hold an annual meeting with shareholders. In connection with the annual meeting, a company's management must provide shareholders with a proxy statement disclosing material information about the company and explaining issues that are up for vote at the annual meeting.[40] Eligible shareholders can vote to ratify or reject issues contained in the company's proxy statement.[41]

[37] Michael Chamberlain, *Socially Responsible Investing: What You Need to Know*, FORBES (Apr. 24, 2013), http://www.forbes.com/sites/feeonlyplanner/2013/04/24/socially-responsible-investing-what-you-need-to-know/; Parthiban David, Matt Bloom, & Amy J. Hillman, *Investor Activism, Managerial Responsiveness, and Corporate Social Performance*, 28 STRAT. MGMT. J. 91–100 (2007).

[38] Telephone Interview with Andrew Behar, CEO, As You Sow (Jan. 11, 2019).

[39] *Id.*

[40] ANDREW BEHAR, THE SHAREHOLDER ACTION GUIDE: UNLEASH YOUR HIDDEN POWERS TO HOLD CORPORATIONS ACCOUNTABLE, 31 (2016); *see also* CONRAD MACKERRON, UNLOCKING THE POWER OF THE PROXY (2004).

[41] BEHAR, *supra* note 40, at 31 ("The proxy statement is the document used by companies seeking approval from shareholders on issues related to corporate governance. The name indicates that

The US proxy system is the most direct way for investors in US companies to influence corporate behavior.[42] It is often the principal means for shareowners and companies to communicate with one another and for shareowners to weigh in on important issues.[43] Filing shareholder resolutions is an important tool for advancing change at publicly traded companies for shareholder advocates.[44]

Under current SEC rules, a shareholder proposal that consistently gets the support of at least 10 percent of the shares voted can be refiled indefinitely, assuming it meets the overall requirements for proper subject matter. Investors now file more shareholder proposals on social and environmental issues than they did a decade ago.[45] Investors are primarily interested in "improving disclosure and oversight of corporate political spending, environmental policy—especially with regard to climate change—and overall sustainability."[46] The percentage of votes in favor of shareholder resolutions that raise social and environmental issues has grown in recent years.[47] Although a vote of support of over 50 percent remains rare for proposals raising social and environmental concerns, it is increasingly common for ESG proposals to receive up to 30–40 percent of the shares voted.[48]

According to SEC regulations, shareholders that have owned at least $2,000 worth of shares for one year may request that issues be included in the company's proxy and put forward for a vote.[49] Corporate management must include the proposals of eligible shareholders in the company's proxy statement, or management may object to the inclusion of proposals and seek approval from the SEC to exclude it. The SEC will issue a "no action" letter releasing management from the obligation to distribute a shareholder proposal in proxy materials only when there are sound legal grounds to exclude.

A shareholder's proposal must get a minimum number of votes to be included in a company's proxy materials each year.[50] A proposal must gain 3 percent of the total vote in the first year it appears in order to be presented again, 6 percent in the second year, and 10 percent each year in the years following.[51] Eligible

most shareholders will be voting remotely-by proxy-rather than in person at the company's annual meeting.").

42 Press Release, "SEC Votes to Seek Public Comment on U.S. Proxy System," *available at* http://www.sec.gov/news/press/2010/2010-122.htm.

43 *Id.*

44 Stuart L. Gillian & Laura T. Starks, *The Evolution of Shareholder Activism in the United States*, in INSTITUTIONAL INVESTOR ACTIVISM: HEDGE FUND & PRIVATE EQUITY, ECONOMICS AND REGULATION (William W. Bratton & Joseph A. McCarhert eds., 2015).

45 US SIF, *supra* note 29, at 24.

46 *Id.*

47 *Id.*

48 *Id.*

49 BEHAR, *supra* note 40, at 32.

50 *Id.* at 33 ("Shareholders can vote their proxies via regular mail, Internet, phone, by attending the annual meeting in person, or by having your broker or proxy service vote on your behalf").

51 *Id.*

shareholders in a company are entitled to vote for a proposal or against a proposal, abstain from voting on the proposal, or not vote.[52] The votes of shareholders who do not vote are automatically counted as votes in favor of management's position on a proposal.[53] In contrast, abstentions are counted neither in support of nor in opposition to a proposal.[54]

Ordinarily, shareholder resolutions are nonbinding, with votes serving as an indication of shareholder sentiment.[55] It is rare for any resolution to receive a majority of votes, as management usually opposes most shareholder proposals.[56] Many resolutions now receive votes within the 30–50 percent range because shareholders see resolutions as related to improving corporate performance.[57] Proponents are permitted to resubmit defeated resolutions within a specified time frame, provided that support for the proposal reaches a minimum-threshold percentage of the vote.[58]

Despite being nonbinding and frequently defeated in votes, shareholder resolutions nevertheless play an important role in corporate governance.[59] They have the potential to lead to improvements in corporate policies and serve to increase public awareness about issues related to corporate practices.[60] To that end, shareholder proposals are becoming an increasingly important part of environmental and human rights advocacy.[61]

As You Sow, under the leadership of Andrew Behar, is campaigning to encourage shareholders to vote based on values.[62] Shareholder advocacy is also helping to shape the ESG agenda. In 2018, a coalition of shareholder organizations comprised of asset managers, unions, and faith communities launched a new Investor Alliance for Human Rights to provide a "collective action" platform

[52] *Id.*

[53] *Id.*

[54] *Id.*

[55] *See* 17 C.F.R. § 240.14a-8(i)(1) (2018).

[56] *See generally* Yonca Ertimur et al., *Board of Directors' Responsiveness to Shareholders: Evidence from Shareholder Proposals*, 16 J. Corp. Fin. 53 (2005).

[57] *See* Julie Fox Gorte & Tim Smith, *The Value of the Shareholder Proposal Process*, Harvard Law School Forum on Corporate Governance and Financial Regulation (July 11, 2017).

[58] Rule 14a-8(i)(12).

[59] *See generally* Doron Levit & Nadya Malenko, *Nonbinding Voting for Shareholder Proposals*, 66 J. Fin. 1579–1614 (2011); *see also* Andrew K. Prevost & Ramesh P. Rao, *Of What Value Are Shareholder Proposals Sponsored by Public Pension Funds?*, SSRN Electronic J. (1999).

[60] A. Dhir, *Realigning the Corporate Building Blocks: Shareholder Proposals as a Vehicle for Achieving Corporate Social and Human Rights Accountability*, 43 Am. Bus. L.J. 365, 374 (2006).

[61] *Id.*; *see also* Miguel Rojas et al., *Bringing About Changes to Corporate Social Policy through Shareholder Activism: Filers, Issues, Targets, and Success*, 114(2) Bus. & Soc'y Rev. 217–252 (2009); Chang Hoon Oh, Jae-Heum Park, & Pervez N. Ghauri, *Doing Right, Investing Right: Socially Responsible Investing and Shareholder Activism in the Financial Sector*, 56 Bus. Horizons 703–714 (2013); Huimin Chung & Till Talaulicar, *Forms and Effects of Shareholder Activism*, 18(4) Corporate Governance: An International Review 253–257 (2010).

[62] Telephone Interview with Andrew Behar, CEO, As You Sow (Jan. 11, 2019); *see also* Behar, *supra* note 40, at 34.

to enable investors to seek stronger business and human rights policies through standard setting and advocacy.

The Interfaith Center on Corporate Responsibility (ICCR), the driving force behind the Investor Alliance, brings together institutional shareholders of various religious traditions to press public companies to change policies in order to promote social justice and to protect the environment.[63] According to data collected by the ICCR on annual shareholder resolutions, there has been a relatively steady increase in the total number of resolutions filed.[64] The number of shareholder resolutions filed in the United States rose after 2011, when the UN Guiding Principles on Business and Human Rights were unanimously endorsed by the UN Human Rights Council, and again in 2015, after the Paris Accord was adopted by the member states of the United Nations.[65] In 2011, there were just under two hundred shareholder resolutions filed.[66] By 2017, there were over three hundred shareholder resolutions filed.[67]

In 2018, investors made proposals seeking to change the policies and practices of public companies on issues ranging from diversity, corporate political contributions, gun safety, human trafficking, to corporate governance.[68] Climate-related shareholder resolutions outweighed all other social and environmental issues based on the number of proposals put forward.[69] There were sixty-one different climate-related resolutions filed by investors in 2018.[70] Figure 5.1 is a bar graph prepared by the ICCR and reflects the range of social and environmental issues shareholders raised during the 2018 proxy season organized by number of filings.

More than a third of the shareholder proposals submitted by ICCR members in 2019 resulted in changed policies and practices.[71] Figure 5.2 is a pie chart prepared by the ICCR that shows what portion of shareholder proposals on social and environmental issues resulted in successful engagement with the company or went to a vote in 2019.

63 *See* Interfaith Center on Corporate Responsibility, *About ICCR*, https://www.iccr.org/about-iccr (last visited Sept. 11, 2018) [https://perma.cc/TB84-VYF7]; *see also* Investor Alliance for Human Rights, *About the Investor Alliance for Human Rights*, https://investorsforhumanrights.org/about (accessed Mar. 25, 2020).

64 ICCR 2017 Shareholder Resolutions, https://www.iccr.org/reports-and-publications/iccrs-2017-shareholder-resolutions (last visited Oct. 2, 2018) [https://perma.cc/KQU4-NUMD].

65 2018 Proxy Season Wins and Challenges, https://www.iccr.org/2018-proxy-season-wins-and-challenges (last visited Sept. 11, 2018) [https://perma.cc/T9LM-ZSUW].

66 *Id.*

67 *Id.*

68 *See* https://www.ey.com/us/en/issues/governance-and-reporting/ey-2018-proxy-season-review.

69 *See* https://www.iccr.org/2018-proxy-season-climate-change-update.

70 *Id.*

71 Interfaith Center on Corporate Responsibility, *Catalyzing Corporate Change* (2019), https://www.iccr.org/catalyzing-corporate-change-2019.

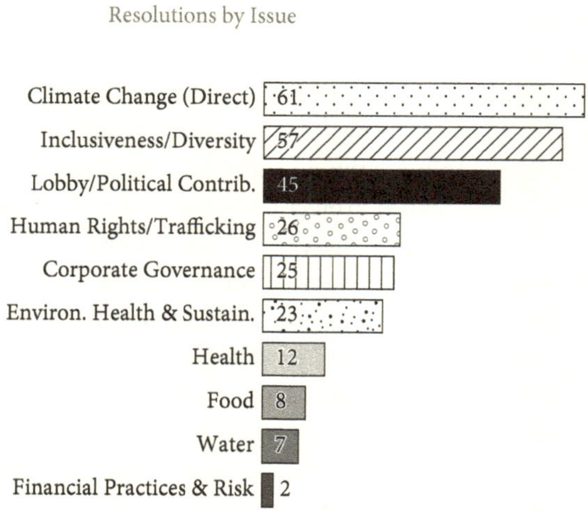


**Figure 5.1** ICCR Members Resolutions by Year: *Source* ICCR 2018 Proxy Season Wins and Challenges

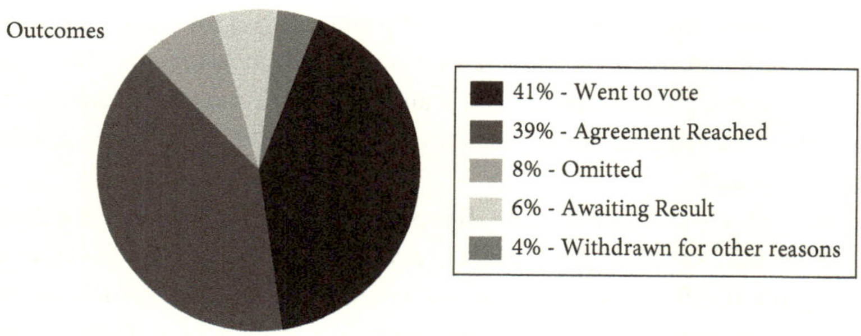


**Figure 5.2** Resolutions by Issue: *Source* ICCR 2018 Proxy Season Wins and Challenges

## 2. Shareholder Advocacy in Selected Industry Sectors: Activity and Efficacy

This section tracks the progress of the ethical investment movement and the potential efficacy of shareholder advocacy through proposals in selected industry sectors. To examine the trend toward demands for greater transparency with respect to ESG issues that could influence human rights performance, I researched recent proposals made between 2000 and 2015 by shareholders invested in leading transnational corporations in four different industry sectors. The sectors I studied include: (1) agriculture, food, and beverage; (2) apparel and footwear; (3) extractives (oil and gas); and (4) internet communications technology and electronics. These sectors were selected because the UN Special Representative

**Table 5.1** List of companies in the case study by sector.

| Agriculture, Food, and Beverage | Apparel | Extractives (Oil and Gas) | Internet Communications Technology |
|---|---|---|---|
| Coca-Cola | Gap | Chevron | Alphabet (Google) |
| Pepsi | Nike | Exxon | Apple |

on Business and Human Rights identified them as most often implicated by rights activists as involved in abuses or having an adverse impact on the enjoyment of human rights. The firms selected for study had been forced to publicly defend against allegations of complicity in human rights violations between 2000 and 2015. The companies reviewed are presented in Table 5.1.

I analyzed the content of all shareholder proposals that made explicit reference to human rights or labor rights. I tracked whether the proposals failed or prevailed, as well as the percentage of votes the proposals received over time. I found that the most common human rights–related proposals aimed to influence change in corporate governance. The most popular type of proposal called for the creation of a board-level committee on human rights. The next most popular proposals with respect to human rights issues called for the creation of policies on human rights and for reporting on human rights impacts. In many instances, proposals went beyond broad calls for policy commitments to calls for greater transparency. For certain industry sectors, specific issues related to operations risks in particular countries or particular human rights issues raised by acts or omissions of the firms appeared as common subjects for shareholders to raise in proposals. Across industry sectors it was common for the introductory or explanatory language in a shareholder proposal to provide detailed information about human rights impacts by referencing academic research or documentation of abuses by human rights organizations. In essence, the shareholder proposal is acting as an advocacy and ethical enforcement tool. The proposals are presented in a manner that appears calculated to educate other owners and to require a response or reform from the business enterprise.

### *a. Agriculture, Food, and Beverage Sector Shareholder Proposals*

Excerpts from representative proposals of the firms I studied in the agricultural, food, and beverage sector are presented as follows.

**i. Coca-Cola Shareholder Resolutions Related to Human Rights** The total number of shareholder resolutions specifically referencing human rights from 2000 to 2015 for the Coca-Cola Company was ten. The resolutions ranged in subject matter from seeking a greater voice in governance for shareholders to demanding the pursuit of an active human rights and corporate social responsibility (CSR) strategy in specific countries with troublesome human rights records, such as China and Colombia.

China operations first appeared as a concern for shareholders in proposals in 2002 and 2004. The 2002 proposal sought to put limits in place to curb the company's alleged complicity in creating risks to human rights and to implement "[p]olicies designed to protect human rights—civil, political, social, cultural and economic—consistent with respect for human dignity and International Labor Organizations' core labor standards."[72] The proposal also called for information on working conditions in China and the company's efforts to uphold basic freedoms be shared.[73] The 2004 resolution likewise sought the following commitment from the company: "We will not sell or provide products or technology in China that can be used to commit human rights violations or labor rights abuse."[74]

Prior to these general reform proposals seeking changes in board configuration to create special committees, shareholder advocates had emphasized the company's operations in specific country contexts. For example, in 2006 and in 2003, shareholders called for high-level oversight for operations in Colombia, due to allegations that the firm was complicit in abuses against union leaders and labor organizers.

A proposal from 2013 similarly sought a greater say in governance in order to give voice to shareholder concerns over human rights issues. The proposal pressed for a resolution to amend the firm's bylaws to create a board committee on human rights. The proposed board committee on Human Rights would be "authorized to review the implications of company policies, above and beyond matters of legal compliance, for the human rights of individuals in the US and worldwide" and "empowered . . . to solicit public input and to issue periodic reports to shareholders and the public, . . . above and beyond matters of legal compliance for the human rights of individuals in the US and worldwide."[75]

In a supporting statement, proponents of the resolution explained that the human rights controversies the Coca-Cola Company and its subsidiaries had

[72] Coca-Cola Co., Notice of 2002 Annual Meeting of Shareholders and Proxy Statement (Form DEF 14A), at 40 (Mar. 5, 2002).

[73] *Id.* at 42.

[74] Coca-Cola Co., Notice of 2004 Annual Meeting of Shareholders and Proxy Statement (Form DEF 14A), at 62–63 (Mar. 4, 2004).

[75] Coca-Cola Co., Notice of 2013 Annual Meeting of Shareholders and Proxy Statement (Form DEF 14A), at 95 (Mar. 11, 2013).

been associated with revealed management failures and that human rights issues needed to be elevated.[76] In defining "human rights," proponents recommended that the proposed committee use the US Bill of Rights and the Universal Declaration of Human Rights as nonbinding benchmarks or reference documents.[77]

For example, a 2015 resolution sought "a meaningful voice in nominating directors" to enhance accountability of the corporation's board.[78] Proponents of the resolution claimed that the board had "failed to insulate the company from regulatory pressure and reputational risks"[79] by ignoring human rights risks, such as worsening water conditions in certain countries.[80]

Significantly, similar proposals raising human rights issues has been put before the Coca-Cola shareholders for voting previously. A virtually identical proposal first appeared in 2008,[81] then again in 2009,[82] and as in 2013 and 2015, the board of directors had recommended a vote *against* the proposal.[83]

In this instance, in contrast to subsequent human rights–related resolutions proposed, the company offered a detailed explanation of the reasons for its recommendation. In its "Statement Against Shareowner Proposal Regarding a Board Committee on Human Rights," Coca-Cola explained that the company's board of directors had already established a committee with the authority to review the implications of company policies on human rights issues, specifying that the Public Issues and Diversity Review Committee was the body responsible for the task. In sum, it was the opinion of management that the measures already in place were sufficient to address any issues.

These proposals demonstrate expressions of dissent from a segment of Coca-Cola shareholders disappointed by the company's human rights performance. Taken together, the resolutions identify and explain pressing problems associated with management failure to sufficiently address risks, at least to the satisfaction of a concerned constituency of shareholders. There is specific reference to public input and periodic reporting in the proposals. Shareholder advocates want information about rights abuses and business risks.

[76] *Id.* at 95.

[77] *Id.* at 95–96 (the board recommended a vote against the shareowner proposal; the proposal received just 107, 460, 952 votes).

[78] Coca-Cola Co., Notice of 2015 Annual Meeting of Shareholders and Proxy Statement (Form DEF 14A), at 84 (Mar. 12, 2015).

[79] *Id.* at 84.

[80] *Id.* at 84.

[81] Coca-Cola Co., Notice of 2008 Annual Meeting of Shareholders and Proxy Statement (Form DEF 14A), at 93 (Mar. 3, 2008).

[82] Coca-Cola Co., Notice of 2009 Annual Meeting of Shareholders and Proxy Statement (Form DEF 14A), at 93–94 (Mar. 3, 2009) (the 2009 proposal received only 58,513, 021 votes in favor).

[83] This proposal received approximately 3% of shares voted.

**ii. PepsiCo Shareholder Resolutions Related to Human Rights** Coca-Cola's competitor, PepsiCo, has also been called upon to address concerns raised about human rights in shareholder resolutions. However, far fewer shareholder resolutions were made by Pepsi shareholders. From 2000 to 2015, just four of the many proposals put forward by shareholders referenced human rights issues. Pepsi shareholders proposed similar sorts of reforms as those proposed by Coca-Cola shareholders. As was the case with Coca-Cola, shareholder demands steadily escalated starting with calls for the corporation to address specific challenges, then later seeking systemic changes and information about the company's impacts on human rights.

In contrast to later proposals that sought structural reforms through the creation of board committees, earlier Pepsi proposals asked that the company address specific challenges. For example, a 2008 proposal urged that the company make a "commitment to the human right to water" and put a comprehensive policy in place to ensure respect for the right to water.[84]

> We believe that significant commercial advantages may accrue to our company by adopting a comprehensive Human Right to Water policy including: enhanced corporate reputation, improved employee recruitment and retention, improved community and stakeholder relations, and reduced risk of adverse publicity, consumer boycotts, divestment campaigns, and lawsuits.[85]

A 2014 proposal concerning executive compensation and retention of stock referred to Pepsi's relatively poor score on Oxfam's human rights rankings for its social and environmental practices. The proposal identified Pepsi's failure to connect compensation to performance on social and environmental matters as a factor contributing to the firm's poor performance on social indicators. Proponents of the resolution argued that the success of environmental and social initiatives should be linked to incentive pay for executives.[86]

The board of directors recommended that the shareholders vote against both proposals, albeit with some concession to the concerns expressed by the proponents. For example, the board agreed that executive officers should own a significant amount of company stock to align their interests with those of shareholders. However, the board argued that the proposal was unnecessary because Pepsi already had policies in place and actively engaged shareholders and stakeholders on environmental priorities and sustainability initiatives, including human rights.[87] In other words, no additional action was necessary.

[84] PepsiCo, Inc., Notice of 2008 Annual Meeting of Shareholders and Proxy Statement (Form DEF 14A), at 47 (Mar. 24, 2008).

[85] *Id.* at 47.

[86] PepsiCo, Inc., Notice of 2014 Annual Meeting of Shareholders and Proxy Statement (Form DEF 14A), at 70 (Mar. 21, 2014).

[87] *Id.* at 70.

A 2015 human rights–related resolution requested the creation of a sustainability committee at the board level, citing growing investor and consumer concern with public policy and sustainability-related initiatives, including human rights and public health matters such as nutritional standards and the use and labeling of genetically modified crops.[88] For example, one 2015 proposal focused on human rights impact assessments, requesting that the board of directors "prepare a public report about identifying and mitigating human rights risks related to the company's sugar supply sourcing."[89] Pepsi's board of directors recommended that stockholders vote against the proposal.[90]

My review of Coca-Cola and Pepsi proxy materials revealed that, most commonly, shareholder proposals in the food and beverage sector have sought to change governance through the creation of board committees devoted to human rights issues. Some proposals have called for the creation and implementation of policies to regulate conduct that could have an adverse impact on the enjoyment of a given right in a particular context. More recent proposals request that shareholders be informed about human rights–related risks and the impacts of business operations on human rights and the environment. Specific issues relevant to the industry sector include responsible sourcing concerns such as labor conditions on farms and in factories and the implications of resource use on access to clean water supplies.

Proposals raising human rights issues went into some detail presenting evidence in support of the reasons why these issues were indeed relevant to investors. It was not uncommon for proposals to cite studies by academics and reports from international human rights organizations or to cite international human rights law. Investors are incorporating rights into proxy materials to encourage corporations to align policies and practices with respect for human rights and the environment.

### *b. Apparel and Footwear Sector Shareholder Proposals*

Excerpts and analysis of human rights and environment-related proposals made by shareholders with interests in the apparel and footwear sector are presented as follows.

**i. Gap Shareholder Resolutions Related to Human Rights** Gap, Inc., is an American worldwide clothing and accessories retailer headquartered in San Francisco, California. The company operates six primary divisions: Gap (the namesake banner), Banana Republic, Old Navy, Intermix, Weddington Way, and

[88] PepsiCo, Inc., Notice of 2015 Annual Meeting of Shareholders and Proxy Statement (Form DEF 14A), at 74 (Mar. 25, 2015).

[89] Dr. Pepper Snapple Group, Inc., Notice of 2015 Annual Meeting of Shareholders and Proxy Statement (Form DEF 14A), at 19–20 (Mar. 30, 2015).

[90] The proposal was defeated with just 11,092,881 votes in favor and 130,128,759 votes against.

Athleta. Gap Inc. is the largest specialty retailer in the United States and is third in total international locations, behind Inditex Group and H&M.[91]

My review identified two human rights–related proposals included in Gap proxy materials between 2000 and 2018.

In 2012, a shareholder resolution proposed that the company cease doing business in Sri Lanka until the government ended abuses.[92] An extensive supporting statement detailed the impacts of Sri Lanka's long civil war that had claimed the lives of an estimated forty thousand Tamil civilians and maintained that the Sri Lankan government had acted in violation of international humanitarian law. The shareholder proposal cited reports from leading international human rights research and advocacy organizations documenting continuing violations in the country and noted that even the US Senate's Committee on Appropriations proposed that "international institutions vote against any loan, agreement or other financial support (except humanitarian aid) for Sri Lanka unless it complies with standards set by international law."[93] The supporting statement referenced the company's status as "one of the largest garment manufacturers in Sri Lanka" and expressed concern not only that Gap "will appear to endorse the crimes perpetrated by the Government of Sri Lanka, if it continues its trade with that country"[94] but also that the company was "providing Sri Lanka with the foreign exchange that keeps its massive military viable."[95]

Citing risks to return on investment, the supporting statement opined that not only would negative publicity and consumer protest damage the brand and hurt employee morale, it would negatively impact the company's investors.

> We believe that shareholders do not want to be connected to human rights violations, but through their investments in Gap Inc securities, they may inadvertently be funding such atrocities in Sri Lanka. In the face of human rights concerns, we see no compelling reason to invest in companies that fund human rights violations, particularly since Sri Lanka has failed to address human rights issues despite continued calls by the international community.

In conclusion, the supporting statement suggests that Gap "temporarily move its manufacturing base to other cost-effective regions" that do not pose the same risks.

[91] Graham Keeley & Andrew Clark, *Zara Overtakes Gap to Become World's Largest Clothing Retailer*, The Guardian (2008), https://www.theguardian.com/business/2008/aug/11/zara.gap.fashion (last visited Nov. 17, 2018).

[92] Gap Inc., Notice of 2001 Annual Meeting of Shareholders and Proxy Statement, 24–25 (Form DEF 14A) (May 15, 2012).

[93] *Id.*

[94] *Id.*

[95] *Id.*

In response, Gap's Statement Against the Shareholder Proposal is quite detailed. It responds directly to the points raised with an acknowledgment of the validity of the shareholders' concerns and reports that the board did consider the issues raised in the proposal but defends the decision to remain in Sri Lanka. Gap's Statement clarifies that the company does not in fact "engage in a trade partnership with the Sri Lankan government" directly. It points to the actions being taken by governments and intergovernmental entities such as the US government, the European Union, and the United Nations and expresses the view that these entities, not business enterprises, are "the best institutions to be engaging with the Sri Lankan government."[96]

Gap's Statement goes on to explain that apparel production provides employment to Sri Lankan citizens and that the company has taken steps to ensure a safe and nondiscriminatory work environment.[97] The statement cites the company's Code of Vendor Conduct and its Human Rights Policy and declares support for the principles contained in international rights agreements including: "the Universal Declaration of Human Rights; the UN Global Compact; the OECD Guidelines for Multinational Enterprises; and the fundamental labor principles that protect workers' rights, which are defined in the International Labour Organization's (ILO) Declaration on Fundamental Principles and Rights at Work (often referred to as the 'ILO Core Conventions')."[98]

Beyond codes and policies, Gap's Statement also lists a number of steps being taken to reduce human rights risks, including regular announced and unannounced factory audits, special assistance for refugees, and employment opportunities for Tamils. The statement also highlights Gap's philanthropic efforts in Sri Lanka, including the Personal Advancement and Career Enhancement program for female garment workers offered in both Tamil and Sinhala languages in factories throughout the country.[99]

Gap used its opposition statements to shareholder proposals to promote information about activities the company was involved in that were conceivably related to reducing risks to rights. The company also references international legal instruments. Significantly, Gap states a commitment to promote and advance rights within "sphere of influence" that is arguably rather expansive.

**ii. Nike Shareholder Resolutions Related to Human Rights** Nike, Inc., is an American multinational corporation that is engaged in the design, development, manufacturing, and worldwide marketing and sales of footwear and apparel. The

[96] *Id.*
[97] *Id.*
[98] *Id.*
[99] *Id.*

company is headquartered in Oregon and is the world's largest supplier of athletic shoes and apparel.[100]

My review identified five human rights–related proposals included in Nike proxy materials between 2000 and 2018.

As early as 2001, shareholders were concerned about the rights of workers in China. A resolution filed by the principal of an impact investment fund asked Nike to ensure that "no goods or products produced within our company's facilities or those of suppliers shall be manufactured by bonded labor, forced labor, within prison camps or as part of reform-through-labor or reeducation-through-labor programs."[101] The 2001 resolution sought assurances that Nike facilities and suppliers would pay a living wage for reasonable hours, keep employees safe from abuse of all sorts, guard against child labor, and ensure a healthy and safe working environment.[102]

The proposal also asks Nike to refrain from inviting police and military into factories to exercise control and impinge upon their rights to unionize, bargain collectively, or express themselves, among other rights.[103] In a supporting statement, the proponents explained the need for Nike to take the measures requested in the resolution as follows: "As U.S. companies import more goods, consumer and shareholder concern is growing about working conditions in China that fall below basic standards of fair and humane treatment. We hope that our company can prove to be a leader in its industry and embrace these principles."[104]

Nike's Statement in Opposition to the Proposal states that the company "supports the general intent of the [p]roposal" but observes that the company's existing Code of Conduct already addresses most of the issues raised in the resolution that the company could "legally comply with in China."[105] Nike's statement also objects on the grounds that that "there are elements of the proposal that are vague and so sweeping in nature that compliance would be difficult or impossible to measure."[106] Nike's statement goes on to note that it was among the first in the industry to set standards for labor practices and environmental responsibility in its countries of manufacture, pointing to its Code of Conduct, which contains requirements that "frequently exceed the requirements of local

[100] *The World's Most Valuable Brands: Nike*, FORBES, https://www.forbes.com/pictures/591c87fc31358e03e5593101/16-nike/#417577ce3bca (last visited Nov. 17, 2018).

[101] Nike Inc., Notice of 2001 Annual Meeting of Shareholders and Proxy Statement, 27–29 (Form DEF 14A) (Aug. 10, 2001).

[102] *Id.*

[103] *Id.*

[104] *Id.*

[105] *Id.*

[106] *Id.*

laws in many countries, and in many instances impose standards that are higher than those stated in the Proposal."[107]

Nike goes on to use its statement to point out flaws in the request and to contextualize the company's achievement, noting:

> [S]ince NIKE does not control the state in China, nor its police, the Company is not in a position to guarantee workers freedom from arrest or detention. Where rights of free association and collective bargaining are illegal, NIKE has successfully used worker opinion surveys conducted by independent non-governmental organizations to provide necessary information to NIKE and factory management about workers' needs and desires.[108]

Nike's response explaining its efforts to address issues raised by shareholders relies on a "business case" for doing better. The company emphasizes that it is going above and beyond customary standards in China. Nike maintains that it is already doing enough by doing more than local rules would require.

*c. Extractives Sector Shareholder Proposals*

Excerpts and analysis of human rights and environment related proposals made by shareholders with interests in the extractives sector are presented as follows.

**i. ExxonMobil Shareholder Resolutions Related to Human Rights and the Environment** The first substantive shareholder proposal calling for ExxonMobil to take action on climate issues was filed in 2009. Later the Tri-State Coalition for Responsible Investment, a nonprofit organization made up of Roman Catholic institutional investors based in New England would continue to press for change.[109] Proponents of shareholder resolutions requested that Exxon set goals on greenhouse gas (GHG) emissions, with reduction targets, and that the company report to shareholders on plans to achieve these goals.[110] The coalition compared Exxon to other firms taking action on risks and opportunities

[107] *Id.*

[108] *Id.*

[109] *See* Letter from Sister Patricia A. Daly, OP Corporate Responsibility Representative, Sisters of St. Dominic of Caldwell N.J., to Rex W. Tillerson, CEO, ExxonMobil Corp., at 14 (Dec. 12, 2011), https://www.sec.gov/divisions/corpfin/cf-noaction/14a-8/2012/sistersofstdominic021012-14a8.pdf.

[110] *See* Reduce Greenhouse Gas Emissions: ExxonMobil 2012, Sisters of St. Dominic of Caldwell N.J. (Dec. 12, 2011), at 15 https://www.sec.gov/divisions/corpfin/cf-noaction/14a-8/2012/sistersofstdominic021012-14a8.pdf ("Shareholders request that the Board of Directors adopt quantitative goals, based on current technologies, for reducing total greenhouse gas emissions from the

associated with a changing climate and found the company lagging.[111] The resolution gained the support of 29 percent of the shares voted.[112]

When the coalition filed its resolution again in 2011, asking that ExxonMobil adopt GHG reduction targets, the resolution received just 26.5 percent of the shares voting.[113] The coalition again argued that its repeated requests for GHG goals were aligned with the company's existing environmental business planning process[114] and acknowledged that there had been some improvements, such as "incremental investments in energy efficiency and flaring reductions."[115] Nevertheless, incremental investments were insufficient to address broader climate concerns in the absence of a clear strategy for dealing with the risks and opportunities associated with climate change.[116] "Investors expect ExxonMobil to take leadership in developing solutions to this global challenge as the company

Company's products and operations; and that the Company report to shareholders by November 30, 2012, on its plans to achieve these goals.").

[111] ExxonMobil, Notice of 2009 Annual Meeting of Shareholders and Proxy Statement (Form DEF 14A) (Apr. 13, 2009) ("[W]e believe ExxonMobil has done a poor job of articulating a cohesive business plan for dealing with climate risk and opportunity—especially regarding its products—or offered robust responses to the financial, regulatory, and technology impacts of the climate crisis . . . BP, Royal Dutch Shell, ConocoPhillips, and Chevron have made newsworthy investments in renewables and low-carbon technologies to reduce emissions, and/or have begun integrating the cost of carbon into planning and investments.").

[112] *See* 2009 Exxon Shareholder Resolution, Adopt GHG Reduction Targets (XOM, 2009 Resolution), CERES, https://engagements.ceres.org/ceres_engagementdetailpage?recID=a0l1H00000C4nVUQAZ (last visited Nov. 17, 2020)

[113] *See* 2011 Exxon Shareholder Resolution, Adopt GHG reduction targets (XOM, 2011 Resolution), CERES, https://engagements.ceres.org/ceres_engagementdetailpage?recID=a0lA0000002syg6IAA (last visited Nov. 17, 2020).

[114] In pertinent part the resolution explained the need for targets and reductions as follows:

a. Shareholders' repeated request for GHG reduction goals is consistent with ExxonMobil's own Environmental Business Planning process, which is used "to identify key environmental drivers, set targets in key focus areas, and identify projects and actions to achieve these targets." ExxonMobil has set specific targets for environmental performance in recent years, such as operations and refinery energy efficiency (10% by 2012), VOCs (5% reductions per year), upstream flaring volumes (23% cuts from 2008 baseline), and NOx and SO2 (70% reduction by 2012 from 2000 baseline).
b. Our Company has made incremental investments in energy efficiency and flaring reductions, the low-hanging fruit. But the time has clearly come for ExxonMobil to articulate a cohesive strategy for deeper emissions reductions. Proponents believe our Board has never sufficiently responded to shareholders in their request for a clear strategy for dealing with climate risk and opportunity, including articulating goals for reducing GHG emissions from ExxonMobil's products AND operations.
c. It is widely agreed that research has understated the enormity of the impact of GHG emissions. Investors expect ExxonMobil to take leadership in developing solutions to this global challenge as the company plays such a critical role in energy markets.

[115] Exxon Shareholder Resolution, *supra* note 113.

[116] *Id.* at 69.

plays such a critical role in energy markets."[117]

By 2017, sentiment had shifted, and a climate-related shareholder proposal by the New York State Comptroller passed among owners, over the objection of Exxon's board of directors.[118] The New York State Comptroller oversees the third-largest public pension plan in the United States, with an estimated value of over $206 billion in assets held in trust for over one million members, retirees, and beneficiaries.[119]

In the intervening years—between the first climate-related resolution proposed to the final resolution adopted—the global community had come to a consensus about the risks associated with climate change, culminating in the Paris Agreement.[120]

The New York State Comptroller's shareholder resolution calling for reporting on climate scenarios and strategy received 62.1 percent support.[121] The 2017 resolution was reminiscent of the proposals put forward several years earlier, raising similar issues and requesting similar actions on the part of Exxon.[122] The resolution requested detailed reporting on and analysis of "portfolio impacts of technological advances and global climate change policies."[123] Notably, it cites the Paris Agreement's stringent reporting and GHG reduction guidelines and Exxon's awareness of them but inaction on studying the effects implementing such guidelines might have.

**ii. Chevron Shareholder Resolutions Related to Human Rights and the Environment** My review of Chevron filings identified a total of ten shareholder resolutions from 2000 to 2015 referring to human rights. Before proposals seeking changes to board composition through the creation of human rights committees were proposed, Chevron shareholders had called for policy commitments on human rights. For example, proposals in 2008 and 2007 called

[117] *Id.*

[118] Office of the New York State, *NYS Comptroller DiNapoli: ExxonMobil Agrees to Assess Impacts of Climate Change*, OFF. OF THE N.Y. STATE COMPTROLLER, https://www.osc.state.ny.us/press/releases/dec17/121217.htm (last visited Nov. 17, 2020).

[119] *See* New York State Comptroller, *Pension Fund Overview*, https://www.osc.state.ny.us/pension/snapshot.htm (accessed June 13, 2018).

[120] U.N. Framework Convention on Climate Change, Adoption of the Paris Agreement, Dec. 12, 2016, U.N. Doc. FCCC/CP/2015/10/Add.1, *available at* http://unfccc.int/files/home/application/pdf/paris_agreement.pdf.

[121] *See* Climate and Sustainability Shareholder Resolutions Database, https://engagements.ceres.org/ceres_engagementdetailpage?recID=a0l1200000Bn9eLAAR (last visited May 24, 2018).

[122] Exxon Mobil Inc., Notice of 2017 Annual Meeting of Shareholders and Proxy Statement (Form DEF 14A), at 62–63 (Apr. 13, 2017).

[123] *Id.*

for the creation of a "comprehensive, transparent, verifiable human rights policy" to inform business practices.[124] The 2008 resolution explained the need for a policy by emphasizing the business case for change:

> Corporations operating in countries with civil conflict, weak rule of law, endemic corruption, poor labor and environmental standards face serious risks to reputation and shareholder value when they are seen as responsible for, or complicit in, human rights violations. Chevron operates in numerous areas that the U.S. State Department classifies as high-risk environments. Conditions in such areas continue to experience significant human rights violations, notably Burma and Nigeria.[125]

The resolution also referred to emerging business and human rights standards to further explain the prudence of adopting a policy commitment, citing the fact that "[t]he extractive sector—oil, gas, and mining—utterly dominate the sample of reported [human rights] abuses".[126]

Finally, the resolution requested that a report to be prepared at reasonable expense, omitting proprietary information.[127]

Chevron did eventually adopt a human rights statement. However, shortcomings still remained according to proponents of the human rights policy resolutions. The 2007 shareholder proposal elucidates:

> Social and economic developments are absent, but they are central to the UN Declaration on Human Rights and to the concerns of Chevron stakeholders; The Statement is also not transparent. It does not identify specific actions to prevent, investigate or mediate allegations against our Company, nor does it address responsibility and accountability for implementation. It does not identify the mechanism to monitor and evaluate the implementation of the values Chevron proclaims.[128]

Similar proposals seeking the formation of human rights committees were submitted in 2010[129] and 2009.[130] These proposals included a specific request

[124] Chevron, Notice of 2008 Annual Meeting of Shareholders and Proxy Statement (Form DEF 14A), at 70 (Apr. 17, 2008).

[125] *Id.*, citing http://www. state.gov/g/drl/rls/hrrpt/2006/.

[126] *Id.*, citing http://www.umn.edu/humanrts/business/RuggieReport2006.html.

[127] *Id.*

[128] Chevron, Notice of 2007 Annual Meeting of Shareholders and Proxy Statement (Form DEF 14A), at 48 (Mar. 17, 2007).

[129] Chevron, Notice of 2010 Annual Meeting of Shareholders and Proxy Statement (Form DEF 14A), at 82 (Apr. 15, 2010).

[130] Chevron, Notice of 2009 Annual Meeting of Shareholders and Proxy Statement (Form DEF 14A), at 82 (Apr. 13, 2009).

for individuals with experience in China to be appointed as members of a board-level committee. For example, the 2010 resolution stipulates, "This Committee will follow the Universal Declaration of Human Rights and will include high-level officials of Chevron, and respected outside human rights experts (especially with knowledge of China's human rights situation) to help Chevron understand the human rights impacts of Chevron business abroad."[131] For example, a 2011 resolution proposed the creation of a board committee on human rights to review and assess, "beyond matters of legal compliance," the impact of company operations and security practices on human rights.[132] The proposed board committee would provide oversight and be authorized to "solicit public input and to issue periodic reports to shareholders and the public."[133]

In 2013, a similar proposal was presented, calling for country selection guidelines because of Chevron's involvement in countries with troubling human rights records. The text of the proposal emphasized the importance of "transparency and accountability" and specifically expressed concern about the company's acquisitions in Burma and potential to inherit human rights risks because by "purchasing Unocal, Chevron acquired Unocal's investment in Burma including its legal, moral, and political liabilities."[134] A series of proposals regarding country selection guidelines started in 2012 with a request for development and disclosure of standards which would, among other things, inform withdrawal from specific high-risk countries, including in particular Burma, now Myanmar.[135]

A 2014 proposal called for the development and disclosure of country-selection criteria. Because Chevron does business in other countries with "controversial human rights records," shareholders requested the Board report on Chevron's criteria for: "(i) investment in; (ii) continued operations in; and, (iii) withdrawal from specific high-risk countries."[136] The resolution also contained qualifying language concerning the costs of disclosure and the consequences of disclosure for protecting confidentiality where necessary.

While proposals from 2012 to 2015 sought the specification of criteria, earlier proposals had sought to secure basic policy commitments and structural changes to the board of directors.

[131] Chevron, Notice of 2010 Annual Meeting of Shareholders and Proxy Statement (Form DEF 14A), at 82 (Apr. 15, 2010).

[132] Chevron, Notice of 2011 Annual Meeting of Shareholders and Proxy Statement (Form DEF 14A), at 76 (Apr. 14, 2011).

[133] *Id.*

[134] Chevron, Notice of 2013 Annual Meeting of Shareholders and Proxy Statement (Form DEF 14A), at 88 (Apr. 11, 2013).

[135] Chevron, Notice of 2012 Annual Meeting of Shareholders and Proxy Statement (Form DEF 14A), at 80 (Apr. 12, 2012).

[136] Chevron, Notice of 2014 Annual Meeting of Shareholders and Proxy Statement (Form DEF 14A), at 72 (Apr. 10, 2014).

Chevron shareholders appear to have successfully used resolutions to move the company toward making policy commitments that are more consistent with international human rights standards.

A comparative review of the substantive content of proposals made by shareholders in Exxon and Chevron shows a pattern of escalating social and environmental performance expectations on the part of a wider range of investors linking adverse social and environmental impacts to economic risks for the businesses. The shareholder advocacy in the extractives sector arguably invites innovation. There is evidence demonstrating that shareholder advocacy through proposals can influence corporate conduct. For example, a 2006 unsuccessful shareholder proposal—in that it did not secure a majority of votes—was brought by Chevron investors to request that the board adopt a human rights policy. By 2007, Chevron had a draft policy, and the firm adopted a human rights statement. In the next proxy season, the shareholder proposal reviewed Chevron's statement as insufficient and recommended adding reports on the firm's human rights performance. The instance of Chevron demonstrates a form of dialogue through the proxy process bringing human rights into the conversation and positioning it to be material. In the instance of Exxon, shareholders successfully shifted the company's position on reporting its climate impacts.

### *d. Internet Communications Technology Sector Shareholder Proposals*

My review of proposals made by shareholders of leading companies in the internet communications technology industry sector revealed concerns over the effects on human rights of products and polices related to privacy, freedom of expression, and access to information.[137] Excerpts and analysis of selected shareholder proposals raising issues relevant to human rights are presented as follows.

**i. Google (Alphabet) Shareholder Resolutions Related to Human Rights** Between 2000 and 2015, a total of five human rights–related shareholder proposals appeared in Google proxy materials. As early as 2007, shareholders recognized the risks associated with Google's products and services. For example, a 2007 proposal on "Internet Censorship" filed by the Office of the Comptroller of New York City as the custodian and trustee of a number of pension funds in the New York City Employees' Retirement System called on Google

[137] Facebook Inc., Notice of 2015 Annual Meeting of Shareholders and Proxy Statement, 57 (Form DEF 14A) (Apr. 25, 2015) (requesting that Facebook reveal its process for analyzing the human rights effects of Facebook's privacy policy); Disney, Notice of 2019 Annual Meeting of Shareholders and Proxy Statement, 68 (Form DEF 14A) (Jan. 11, 2019) (requesting that the board publish a report assessing the feasibility of improving their cybersecurity).

to "institute policies to help protect freedom of access to the Internet."[138] The proposal appeared in Google proxy materials again in 2008 and in 2009 including recommended "minimum standards" for the creation of policies to protect freedom of access, as follows:

1. Data that can identify individual users should not be hosted in internet-restricting countries, where political speech can be treated as a crime by the legal system.
2. The company will not engage in proactive censorship.
3. The company will use all legal means to resist demands for censorship. The company will only comply with such demands if required to do so through legally binding procedures.
4. Users will be clearly informed when the company has acceded to legally binding government requests to filter or otherwise censor content that the user is trying to access.
5. Users should be informed about the company's data-retention practices, and the ways in which their data is shared with third parties.
6. The company will document all cases where legally binding censorship requests have been complied with, and that information will be publicly available.[139]

In supporting statements, shareholder proposal sponsors pointed to international human rights law, noting the failure of technology companies to develop adequate standards of protection. Presumably, an adequate standard must at minimum not deviate from international human rights standards. Specifically, relying on Article 19 of the Universal Declaration of Human Rights in proposals filed in 2007, 2008, and 2009 shareholders argued that "freedom of speech and freedom of the press are fundamental human rights, and free use of the Internet is protected in Article 19 of the Universal Declaration of Human Rights, which guarantees freedom to 'receive and impart information and ideas through any media regardless of frontiers.' "[140]

In a 2010 shareholder proposal asking Google to establish a board-level (confirmed) human rights committee, proponents registered concerns over the "misuse of information technology."[141] The proposal pointed to China in particular as significant cause for concern, citing the Chinese government's misuse of

[138] Google Inc., Notice of 2008 Annual Meeting of Shareholders and Proxy Statement, 29 (Form DEF 14A) (Mar. 28, 2008).
[139] *Id.*
[140] Google Inc., Notice of 2007 Annual Meeting of Shareholders and Proxy Statement, 30 (Form DEF 14A) (Apr. 6, 2007).
[141] Google Inc., Notice of 2010 Annual Meeting of Shareholders and Proxy Statement, 38 (Form DEF 14A) (Mar. 29, 2010).

technology to surveil and restrict electronic communications, sometimes leading to arrest and punishment.[142] According to the proponents of the proposal, because Google was "doing business in China in ways that could contribute to these abuses,"[143] the company had "special responsibilities and obligations."[144]

The proposed human rights committee would serve as a check and balance for any actions the company might take that would affect human rights.[145] The proposed committee would be staffed by "high level officials of Google" as well as "respected outside human rights experts who are in a position to help Google understand the human rights impacts of their activities abroad, and frame approaches that will assure that Google does not contribute to human rights abuses by foreign governments."[146] The 2010 call for a human rights committee followed an earlier 2008 proposal that had also sought to establish a board committee on human rights, "authorized to review the implications of company policies, above and beyond matters of legal compliance, for the human rights of individuals in the U.S. and worldwide."[147]

In sum, the series of shareholder proposals filed against Google were motivated by well-founded concerns on the part of investors that "technology companies in the United States have failed to develop adequate standards by which they can conduct business with authoritarian governments while protecting human rights to freedom of speech and freedom of expression."[148]

Management opposed all human rights–related proposals recommending that shareholders vote against the changes. Before 2009, Google's response was limited to a simple boilerplate statement: "Our board of directors recommends a vote AGAINST the stockholder proposal." In 2010, Google appeared to have realized that a more responsive reply to shareholder proposals related to human rights was now required. In response to a shareholder proposal that would address censorship and violations of privacy perpetrated by the Chinese government, Google stated that it was "already following strong and specific standards to protect its users and promote global free expression."[149]

**ii. Apple Shareholder Resolutions Related to Human Rights** Between 2000 and 2015 there were five proposals related to human rights and environmental

[142] *Id.*
[143] *Id.*
[144] *Id.*
[145] *Id.*
[146] *Id.*
[147] Google Inc., Notice of 2008 Annual Meeting of Shareholders and Proxy Statement, 31 (Form DEF 14A) (Mar. 28, 2008).
[148] Google Inc., Notice of 2007 Annual Meeting of Shareholders and Proxy Statement, 30 (Form DEF 14A) (Apr. 6, 2007).
[149] Google Inc., Notice of 2010 Annual Meeting of Shareholders and Proxy Statement, 38 (Form DEF 14A) (Mar. 29, 2010).

issues included in Apple's proxy materials. In 2009, a shareholder proposal co-sponsored by the Green Equity Fund asked Apple to prepare a sustainability report covering climate change, GHG emissions, and safety of products and for employees, among other concerns.[150] In a supporting statement accompanying the proposal, investors explained that "taking early action to calculate emissions and prepare for standards could provide competitive advantage, while inaction risks exposing companies to regulatory and litigation risk and reputational damage."[151] The supporting statement recommended that Apple use the Global Reporting Initiative's Sustainability Reporting Guidelines to prepare the sustainability report as well as the Carbon Disclosure Project's standards to report on its GHG emissions and reduction efforts.[152]

In 2010, another proposal regarding sustainability reporting was put forward by As You Sow, co-sponsored by Calvert Asset Management Company.[153] A 2013 proposal, repeated again in 2014, sought the creation of a board committee on human rights to review the impact of company policies on human rights worldwide. The proposed committee would be tasked with "assessing the impacts of company operations and supply chains on resources and public welfare in host communities."[154] In a supporting statement explaining the need for a committee, sponsors of the proposal highlighted the fact that Apple had been implicated in highly visible controversies about human rights issues, both in terms of products and supply chains, in China as well as in other places.[155] The investor's supporting statement also pointed to problems due to the growing pressure to eliminate the use of so-called "conflict minerals" in Apple products that could be connected to substantially prolonging the armed conflict in the Congo, leading to death, human rights abuses, and environmental destruction as another reason to have board-level leadership and expertise on human rights.[156] Apple responded that establishing a committee would "would distract the Board from its other responsibilities to the Company and its shareholders, while adding little value to the Company's existing commitment to human rights and social responsibility."[157]

[150] Apple Inc., Notice of 2009 Annual Meeting of Shareholders and Proxy Statement, 51 (Form DEF 14A) (Jan. 7, 2009).

[151] *Id.*

[152] *Id.*

[153] Apple Inc., Notice of 2010 Annual Meeting of Shareholders and Proxy Statement, 51 (Form DEF 14A) (Jan. 12, 2010).

[154] Apple Inc., Notice of 2013 Annual Meeting of Shareholders and Proxy Statement, 47 (Form DEF 14A) (Jan. 10, 2013); *see also* Apple Inc., Notice of 2014 Annual Meeting of Shareholders and Proxy Statement, 58 (Form DEF 14A) (Jan. 10, 2014).

[155] Apple Inc., Notice of 2014 Annual Meeting of Shareholders and Proxy Statement, 58 (Form DEF 14A) (Jan. 10, 2014).

[156] Apple Inc., Notice of 2013 Annual Meeting of Shareholders and Proxy Statement, 47 (Form DEF 14A) (Jan. 10, 2013).

[157] *Id.*

Apple opposed each of the shareholder proposals. However, by 2014, even Apple's board began to reference widely recognized international human rights principles in response to shareholder proposals. For example, Apple asserts its Supplier Code of Conduct is based on human rights principles recognized by the UN and the International Labour Organization. Even though it opposes the shareholder proposal to create a human rights committee, the board cites instances where changes are being made to address issues raised by investors. For instance, Apple explains that its auditing program has "expanded significantly over the past several years,"[158] and went on to detail Apple's status as the first electronics company to become a member of the Fair Labor Association, a multi-stakeholder factory auditing organization, which, at Apple's invitation in 2012, had inspected and published findings about Apple's suppliers. The response goes on to say that Apple began to support training for new employees of suppliers to make them aware of their rights and protections as well as the Code of Conduct for suppliers, touting that "[m]ore than one million workers have been educated on their rights as part of this initiative."[159]

### 3. Comparing Investor Concerns across Industry Sectors

While not as common as resolutions related to the environment and climate change, human rights resolutions are on the rise. Today, the typical human rights resolution calls for a human rights risk or impact assessment of the sort described in the UN Guiding Principles (UNGPs).[160] My review found that rights resolutions evolved over time to ask more of business enterprises. Shareholder proposals related to human rights issues have become more specific and sophisticated.

Far and away the most common resolution demanded across industry sectors during the time period I reviewed was the creation of a board-level human rights committee. Shareholder proposals show how, over time, the expectations of some investors increased and the types of reforms requested escalated. Shareholders first sought policy reforms by asking a company to create standards. Next, the shareholders strove to have institutional structures created to oversee human rights developments.

These shareholder proposals were consistent with the guidelines for a business's responsibility to maintain human rights set forth in the UNGPs. Principle 16 stipulates that a business enterprise should express its commitment to meeting the responsibility to respect human rights by making a statement of

[158] *Id.*

[159] Apple Inc., Notice of 2013 Annual Meeting of Shareholders and Proxy Statement, 47 (Form DEF 14A) (Jan. 7, 2013). Apple subsequently left the FLA.

[160] *See* United Nations, Guiding Principles on Business and Human Rights 17 (2011) [hereinafter UNGPs] Guiding Principle 18.

policy that has been approved at the highest level of the enterprise[161] and is communicated publicly.[162] Principle 18 provides that companies "should identify and assess any actual or potential adverse human rights impacts with which they may be involved either through their own activities or as a result of their business relationships."[163] Guiding Principle 18 also provides that human rights risk assessments should draw on internal as well as independent human rights expertise. In fact, several shareholder proposals sought to include independent input on human rights impacts. UNGP Principle 21 calls for companies to explain how they will address human rights impacts through formal reports that "provide information that is sufficient to evaluate the adequacy" of their responses to the particular human rights risk presented by their operations.[164]

Taken together, the shareholder proposals I have examined here are consistent with the substantive content of the business responsibility to respect human rights set forth in the UNGPs.

### 4. Protecting Shareholder Voice to Promote Change

In 2019, the SEC proposed revisions to Rule 14a-8, which allows shareholders who have held $2,000 worth of stock for at least one year to file a resolution. The proposed revisions would extend the amount of time a shareholder must own shares before submitting a resolution, increase the dollar amount of shares an owner must hold in order to file a resolution, and raise the threshold of support required for resubmitting a proposal. These changes would restrict the ability of investors to access the corporate proxy and inform other owners about issues. Raising the threshold would risk the exclusion of smaller investors.

The proposed change could curtail one of the few avenues for concerned shareholders to shape business policies and priorities to better align with respect for human rights and reduce risks to rights. Small investors in the United States have raised significant salient human rights–related issues in recent years, as my review of proposals shows. A 2014 cross-country study of how the legal rights and protections provided to shareholders influence a company's public reputation found that in societies where shareholders enjoy a high degree of legal rights, the stock market returns on corporate reputation is positively correlated.[165]

As private companies increasingly influence a range of public institution and, in the United States, pouring money into politics, this exercise of shareholder voice through the proposal process has provided a small but not insignificant

161 *Id.* at 16, Guiding Principle 16(a).
162 *Id.*, Guiding Principle 16(d).
163 UNGPs, *supra* note 160, at 21 Guiding Principle 18.
164 *Id.* at 23, Guiding Principle 21(b).
165 Abrahim Soleimani, William D. Schneper, & William Newburry, *The Impact of Stakeholder Power on Corporate Reputation: A Cross-Country Corporate Governance Perspective*, 25(4) Org. Sci., 991–1008 (2014).

avenue for the investing public to have a voice and share concerns with those leading governance of publicly traded companies. There has been an increase in shareholder proposals concerned about social impacts. These investors are advocates providing input, not as a distraction to management but as means for management to understand which issues matter. These SEC regulatory changes are being proposed just as very serious environmental and social issues such as climate change, gun safety, immigration, global health—along with risks of causing or contributing to adverse human rights impacts—are increasingly being raised by company shareholders and stakeholders alike.

## II. Global Policy Initiatives: Information Access to Advance Respect for Human Rights

International policy instruments recognize the important role that investors can play in contributing to change for good or ill. Newer initiatives aim to advance the good. Global guiding principles and projects are calling upon investors to be more active and make choices that are better aligned with respect for human rights.

### A. UN Guiding Principles on Responsible Investment

In April 2006, the United Nations announced a set of international sustainable and responsible investment principles.[166] Where the accepted aim of investment is to advance the financial interests of the investor, the Principles for Responsible Investment (PRIs) acknowledge an obligation to invest with the aim of advancing broader societal interests as well. This commitment is stated as follows in the preamble to the PRIs:

> We have a duty to act in the best long-term interests of our beneficiaries. In this fiduciary role, we believe that environmental, social, and corporate governance issues can affect the performance of investment portfolios (to varying degrees across companies, sectors, regions, asset classes and through time).[167]

This commitment captures the practical concern that ESG issues may have implications for investment performance. To that end, the PRIs articulate a series

[166] Responsible Investing: Making an Impact Prudently, CV041 ALI-CLE 313; *see also* Gail E. Henderson, *Making Corporations Environmentally Sustainable: The Limits of Responsible Investing*, 13 German L.J. 1412 (2012).
[167] *Id.*

of measures to be taken in order to advance both the long-term interests of beneficiaries and broader societal interests, including among others:[168]

- We will incorporate ESG issues into investment analysis and decision-making processes;
- We will be active owners and incorporate ESG issues into our ownership policies and practices;
- We will seek appropriate disclosure on ESG issues by the entities in which we invest;
- We will promote acceptance and implementation of the Principles within the investment industry.[169]

The PRI Principles have hundreds of signatories, including the California Public Employees' Retirement System, the New York State Teachers' Retirement System, the Canada Pension Plan, and the Norwegian Government Pension Fund.[170] Since 2005, the number of signatories to the PRIs has grown steadily, with signatories collectively representing over $70 trillion in assets under management in 2017.[171] According to the PRI, the number of new signatories has increased worldwide with a significant percentage adopting a responsible investment strategy policy.[172] US signatories include public, private, and union pension funds, including CalPERS, CalSTRS, AFL-CIO funds, and Connecticut, Illinois, and New York state pension funds, as well as prominent asset managers, such as JP Morgan Asset Management and TIAA-CREF.[173] This recent growth in PRI participation largely confirms David Webber's research on retirement system shareholders in the US demonstrating that when pension funds become more active on issues directly related to the labor rights of the working-class shareholders they represent, real change results.[174]

## B. The Global Reporting Initiative

The Global Reporting Initiative (GRI) is a multistakeholder forum dedicated to providing guidance on sustainability reporting. GRI guidelines are regarded as

[168] *Id.*

[169] *What are the Principles for Responsible Investment?*, PRI https://www.unpri.org/about/the-six-principles.

[170] *About the PRI*, PRI, https://www.unpri.org/pri/about-the-pri (last visited Nov. 18, 2020) (providing and Excel spreadsheet of signatories).

[171] *PRI Reporting Framework 2017 Snapshot Report*, https://app.powerbi.com/view?r=eyJrIjoiZjA2OTA5MWUtMzc4OC00MTZhLWIyZDYtYTc3NDMzOGE1OGFjIiwidCI6ImZiYzI1NzBkLWE5OGYtNDFmMS1hOGFkLTEyYjEzMWJkOTNlOCIsImMiOjh9 (last visited Nov. 20, 2020).

[172] UN PRI, Annual Report 7, 11 (2019), https://d8g8t13e9vf2o.cloudfront.net/Uploads/t/j/z/priannualreport2019_901594.pdf.

[173] *About the PRI*, *supra* note 170.

[174] Webber, *supra* note 22.

"the de facto global standard" for voluntary sustainability disclosure.[175] The GRI was founded in 1997 with an aim to develop a business reporting framework that encompassed environmental, social, economic, and governance information with investors as the framework's original target.[176] The GRI's stated mission is "to empower decisions that create social, environmental and economic benefits for everyone."[177]

The GRI aims to aid businesses and governments all over the world to better understand and communicate the impacts that they have on sustainability, human rights, climate change, human well-being, and governance.[178] To serve these aims, the GRI has developed sustainability standards, which have been adopted by 75 percent of the world's largest 250 corporations.[179] Nearly half of the Bloomberg 50 and 315 of the FT Europe 500 use the GRI to report on sustainability.[180]

The GRI relies heavily on collaborative partnerships and has developed long-standing relationships with the Organisation for Economic Co-operation and Development, the UN Environment Program, CDP (formerly the Carbon Disclosure Project), International Organization for Standardization's ISO 26000, International Finance Corporation, the UN Conference on Trade and Development, and the Earth Charter Initiative among others.[181]

The GRI tracks over four hundred fifty policy instruments in seventy-seven countries and regions that drive sustainability disclosures. Additionally, fifty-eight capital market instruments in thirty-eight countries now mandate disclosures on sustainability issues.[182] According to the GRI, this wide distribution of the standards, combined with high rates of voluntary reporting, adds to the supply of sustainability information to the benefit of stakeholders.[183] The

[175] Rüdiger Hahn & Regina Lülfs, *Legitimizing Negative Aspects in GRI-Oriented Sustainability Reporting: A Qualitative Analysis of Corporate Disclosure Strategies*, 123 J. Bus. Ethics 401, 402 (2014).

[176] *See GRI's History*, Global Reporting Initiative, https://www.globalreporting.org/information/about-gri/gri-history/Pages/GRI's%20history.aspx.

[177] *About GRI*, Global Reporting Initiative, https://www.globalreporting.org/information/about-gri/Pages/default.aspx.

[178] *Id.*

[179] *Id.* (citing a 2017 study conducted by KPMG on corporate responsibility reporting).

[180] Global Reporting Initiative, Annual Report 2016–2017, at 21.

[181] *Id.* at 31; *see also* Cynthia A. Williams, *The Global Reporting Initiative, Transnational Corporate Accountability, and Global Regulatory Counter Currents*, 1 UC Irvine J. Intl. Trans. & Comp. 75 (2016).

[182] Global Reporting Initiative, Annual Report 2016–2017 at 6.

[183] *Id.*; *see also* Chloe Ghoogassian, *Evading the Transparency Tragedy: The Legal Enforcement of Corporate Sustainability Reporting*, 112 Hasting Bus. L.J. 361 (2015).

quality of information provided by businesses improves in response to disclosure demands from stakeholders.[184]

The European Directive—which requires large firms (greater than five hundred employees) to publish a nonfinancial statement containing information on the impact of the firm's activity on environmental, social, and human rights issues—has benefited from the GRI, which provides specifications to assist European firms in developing compliant reporting.[185] The GRI has also informed sustainability reporting among corporations and governments by providing reporting frameworks that make disclosure easier and more uniform. GRI standards for reporting have even been codified by governments to facilitate reporting in compliance with local laws. However, absent investor or public scrutiny, there are essentially no adverse consequences for organizations that report infrequently or that produce inaccurate reporting.

## III. Government Regulation: Information Access to Advance Respect for Human Rights

Beyond the responsibility to respect human rights to which all business enterprises are beholden, all states must regulate to protect human rights. This responsibility to regulate to protect human rights extends to all areas of law, including corporate and securities law. As outlined by the UN Special Representative on the issue of Human Rights and Transnational Corporations and other Business Enterprises, transparency in capital markets is consistent with the obligations all governments have to protect human rights.[186] For instance, Guiding Principle 3(d) offers that states should "encourage, and where appropriate require, business enterprises to communicate how they address their human rights impacts." It clearly supports the development of reporting requirements for human rights: "Financial reporting requirements should clarify that human rights impacts in some instances may be 'material' or 'significant' to the economic performance of the business enterprise."[187]

[184] Belen Fernandez-Feijoo, Silvia Romero, & Silvia Ruiz, *Effect of Stakeholders' Pressure on Transparency of Sustainability Reports within the GRI Framework*, 112 J. Bus. Ethics 53–63 (2014).

[185] *Id.* at 117.

[186] *See* International Corporate Accountability Roundtable, "Knowing and Showing" Using US Securities Laws to Compel Human Rights Disclosures, (2013).

[187] *Id.* (citing Ruggie Report § 3(d) & (cmt). "The commentary to the draft Guiding Principles released in November 2010 was even more explicit on this point: 'Financial reporting requirements should clarify that human rights impacts in some instances may be 'material' or 'significant' from the investors' point of view and indicate when they should be disclosed.' " *See Draft Guiding Principles for the Implementation of the United Nations 'Protect, Respect and Remedy' Framework, available at* http://www.reports-and-materials.org/Ruggie-UN-draft-Guiding-Principles-22-Nov-2010.pdf, § 5 (cmt)).

## A. Capital Markets: Material Information and Mandatory Reporting

In the aftermath of the 1929 market crash that led the world into the Great Depression, Congress enacted the Securities Act of 1933.[188] Because misstatements, omissions, and other fraud on the part of securities issuers contributed to the crash, the Securities Act requires companies, upon the issuance of new securities, to disclose certain information about themselves to protect investors and prevent fraud.[189] The Securities Exchange Act of 1934 (Exchange Act) further expanded not only the circumstances under which information disclosures are mandatory but also the nature of the information that must be disclosed to address similar perceived information asymmetries relating to securities purchased and sold in capital markets.[190] The disclosure requirements of the Securities Act and the Exchange Act govern mandatory disclosure for statements, reports, and schedules filed with the SEC.[191] Financial transparency is fundamental to the function of US capital markets. Today, to access capital markets through listings on stock exchanges anywhere in the world, businesses must issue financial reports on an annual basis at minimum, and often quarterly. Financial reports must be consistent with generally accepted accounting principles.

Disclosures made in mandatory filings to the SEC are subject to a "materiality" test, which sets a basic benchmark for the information firms are required to report.[192] The materiality requirement arises from gap-filling and antifraud rules contained in the Securities Act and the Exchange Act to ensure that disclosures made are not misleading. Information that is not required by the mandatory disclosure provisions contained in the Securities Act and the Exchange Act, or

[188] Securities Act of 1933, 15 U.S.C § 77 *et seq.*

[189] For a comprehensive discussion of the history of securities regulation and origins of the SEC, *see generally* Joel Seligman, The Transformation of Wall Street: A History of the Securities and Exchange Commission and Modern Corporate Finance (2003); *see also* Daniel M. Firger, Note, *Transparency and the Natural Resource Curse: Examining the New Extraterritorial Information Forcing Rules in the Dodd-Frank Wall Street Reform Act of 2010*, 41 Geo. J. Int'l L. 1043, (2010) (emphasizing the importance of congressional intent "to insist that every issue of new securities to be sold in interstate commerce shall be accompanied by full publicity and information, and that no essentially important element attending the issue shall be concealed from the buying public" (citing 77 Cong. Rec. 937 (1933)).

[190] Securities Exchange Act of 1934, 15 U.S.C. § 78 *et seq.*; *see also* Joan MacLeod Heminway, *Materiality Guidance in the Context of Insider Trading: A Call for Action*, 52 Am. U.L. Rev. 1131, 1170–1171 (2003) (discussing the key legislative, regulatory and judicial rationales supporting disclosure under the 1934 act).

[191] *See* SEC, Adoption of Integrated Disclosure System, Securities Act Release No. 33-6383 (1982), *available at* http://www.sec.gov/rules/final/33-8591.pdf.

[192] Williams, *supra* note 7; *see also* Marcia L. Narine, *Living in Material World—From Naming and Shaming to Knowing and Showing: Will New Disclosure Regimes Finally Drive Corporate Accountability for Human Rights?*, in The Business and Human Rights Landscape: Moving Forward, Looking Back (Jena Martin & Karen E. Bravo eds., 2016); Bennett Freeman, *Investors and Human Rights: Values, Risk and Materiality* in Business and Human Rights: From Principles to Practice (Justine Nolan & Dorothée Baumann-Pauly, eds. 2016).

other information that does not meet the materiality benchmark, is deemed immaterial and need not be disclosed. The US Supreme Court has held that "there must be a substantial likelihood that the disclosure of [an] omitted fact would have been viewed by the reasonable investor as having significantly altered the 'total mix' of information made available" by the issuer in order for information to be deemed material and meet the benchmark.[193] Where there is a substantial likelihood that a reasonable investor would consider information important in making a voting or investment decision, the information is material. Under the theory of efficient capital markets, absent the disclosure of mandated information and any additional "material" information, investors would be unable to value securities properly or take measures to protect against fraud, waste, or mismanagement by corporate management.[194] It is important that human rights be understood as material. The increase in rights-related shareholder proposals and socially responsible investors interested in ESG performance suggests that human rights certainly matter.

### 1. Leveraging Securities Law to Promote Corporate Social Responsibility and to Protect Human Rights

There is a powerful opportunity for concerned investors to leverage securities laws to ensure that business policies and practices are better aligned with respect for human rights by requiring reporting related to human rights risks.[195] In July 2010, President Obama signed the Dodd-Frank Wall Street Reform and Consumer Protection Act (Dodd-Frank) into law.[196] Specific provisions of Dodd-Frank amended the Exchange Act to require firms to produce information on the extent to which, if any, their commercial activities could be associated with either conflict or corruption. The new disclosure regime contained in Dodd-Frank, in effect, made matters that pertain to human rights material recognizing that reasonable investors consider information about rights to be relevant when making investment decisions.

[193] *T.S.C. Indus., Inc. v. Northway, Inc.*, 426 U.S. 438, 449 (1976); *see also Basic Inc. et al. v. Levinson*, 485 U.S. 224, 232 (applying materiality standard set forth in *T.S.C. Indus.* in the merger context).

[194] The Efficient Capital Markets hypothesis holds that stock prices reflect available information relevant to their values. *See* Lynn A. Stout, *The Unimportance of Being Efficient: An Economic Analysis of Stock Market Pricing and Securities Regulation*, 87 Mich. L. Rev. 613, 619 (1988); Ronald J. Gilson & Reinier H. Kraakman, *The Mechanisms of Market Efficiency*, 70 Va. L. Rev. 549, 564–565 (1984).

[195] Erika George, *Influencing the Impact of Business on Human Rights: Corporate Social Responsibility Through Transparency and Reporting*, in Corporate Accountability for Human Rights Impacts: New Expectations and Paradigms (American Bar Association, Lara Blecher, Nancy Kaymar-Stafford, & Gretchen Bellamy eds., 2014); Galit A. Sarfaty, *Human Rights Meets Securities Regulation*, 54 Va. J. Int'l L. 97, 118–119 (2013).

[196] The Dodd-Frank Wall Street Reform and Consumer Protection Act, Pub. L. No. 111-203, 124 Stat. 1376 (2010) [hereinafter the Dodd-Frank Act]. *See also* Helene Cooper, *Obama Signs Overhaul of Financial System*, N.Y. Times (July 21, 2010), *available at* http://www.nytimes.com/2010/07/22/business/22regulate.html.

*a. Curbing Conflict and Section 1502*

Section 1502 of Dodd-Frank amends Section 13 of the Securities Exchange Act of 1934 (15 USC 78m) and requires disclosures, largely on corporate due diligence procedures, relating to conflict minerals that originate in the Democratic Republic of the Congo (DRC) and its adjoining countries.[197] Appreciating the urgent need to address the human rights abuses associated with the ongoing violence in the DRC, fueled in significant part by the proceeds from the illicit trade in conflict minerals by armed groups in the eastern region, provisions pertaining to the trade of DRC conflict minerals were included in Dodd-Frank.[198] The broad aim of the provision was to disrupt the connection between violent conflict and commercial activity.[199] Section 1502 of Dodd-Frank was the first legally binding regulatory initiative in the United States intended to curtail commercial complicity in human rights violations.[200]

Section 1502 requires publicly traded companies that utilize certain conflict minerals to report the due-diligence steps they have taken to determine the source of their minerals. The goal of this provision is to ensure that companies demonstrate that links along their product supply chains are not, in effect, providing further financial support for the violent conflict in the DRC, or otherwise contributing to the country's emergency humanitarian situation.[201] To serve these ends, issuers must annually disclose whether "conflict minerals" necessary for any of their manufactured products originated in the DRC or a country that shares an internationally recognized border with the DRC.[202] "Conflict

[197] Dodd-Frank Act, § 1502, 124 Stat. 2213-18 (2010) (to be codified at 15 U.S.C. § 78m(p)).

[198] The conflict minerals provision in the Dodd-Frank Act was approved by a voice vote on an amendment proposed by Senator Sam Brownback (R-KS). In a statement issued after the vote, Senator Russ Feingold (D-WI), who co-sponsored the amendment, explained that their aim was to address reports issued by the UN Group of Experts in support of UN S.C. Res. 1857 (2008), which called upon member states to take measures "to ensure that importers, processing industries and consumers of Congolese mineral products under their jurisdiction exercise due diligence on their suppliers and on the origin of the minerals they purchase." *See* Lucinda A. Low et al, *FCPA Self-Reporting and the Effects of the Dodd-Frank Whistleblower Provisions: A New Calculus*, Practicing Law Institute (May 5, 2011).

[199] *See* 145 Cong. Rec. S3816-17 (daily ed. May 17, 2010) (statement of Sen. Durbin) (Section 1502 "encourages companies using [conflict] minerals to source them responsibly" and also seeks to "address where the armed groups are receiving their funding").

[200] For legislative history of Section 1502, *see* Conflict Minerals, 75 Fed. Reg. 80948, 80950–75 (proposed Dec. 23, 2010), *available at* http://www.gpo.gov/fdsys/pkg/FR-2010-12-23/pdf/2010-31940.pdf; 156 Cong. Rec. S3976 (daily ed. May 19, 2010) (statement of Sen. Feingold). In his statement before Congress, Senator Feingold described Section 1502 as a unique contribution to securities regulation in that it is intended to ensure "greater transparency around how international companies are addressing issues of foreign corruption and violent conflict that relate to their business." 156 Cong. Rec. S3976.

[201] *See* Dodd-Frank Act, *supra* note 196 at § 1502(a). Due diligence standards are also contained in the UNGPs on human rights endorsed in 2011 by the UN Human Rights Council. However, the two due diligence frameworks are quite different, as will be discussed later.

[202] *Id.* §1502(b). Angola, Burundi, the Central African Republic, the Republic of Congo, Rwanda, South Sudan, Tanzania, Uganda, and Zambia border the DRC.

minerals" are defined to include columbite-tantalite (coltan), cassiterite (tin), wolframite (tungsten) and gold, or their derivatives, which are limited to tantalum, tin, and tungsten.[203]

Section 1502 imposes a duty on corporations using conflict minerals from the DRC or its neighbors to submit a report to the SEC detailing measures taken to exercise due diligence with respect to determining the source and chain of custody of its minerals.[204]

According to the UN Group of Experts on the DRC, Section 1502 had "a massive and welcome impact" requiring "the world to take due diligence and conflict financing seriously."[205] This Group of Experts reports a reduction in the level of conflict financing as commercial actors seeking conflict-free status have stopped purchasing from suspect sources and have demonstrated interest in taking ownership over greater lengths of the supply chain to create a closed system of custody over minerals from production to export.[206]

Some commentators cautioned that an unintended consequence of Section 1502 could be the creation of a de facto embargo on minerals from the DRC, costing civilians their livelihood.[207] The National Association of Manufacturers, the Chamber of Commerce of the United States of America, and the Business Roundtable sued to challenge the SEC's final rule.[208]

At the conclusion of the Obama administration, the SEC reversed its position, indicating that the agency would no longer enforce provisions requiring reporting on the source and chain of custody of conflict minerals.[209] Some

[203] Conflict Minerals, 77 Fed. Reg. 56274, 56285 (Sept. 12, 2012) (to be codified at 17 C.F.R. pts. 240 and 249b).

[204] Conflict Minerals, 77 Fed. Reg. at 56320.

[205] Letter from Fred Robarts, Coordinator Group of Experts on the DRC re-established pursuant to Resolution 1952 (2010), to Mary Schapiro, Chairman Securities and Exchange Commission (Oct. 21, 2011), *available at* http://www.sec.gov/comments/s7-40-10/s74010-346.pdf.

[206] U.N. Group of Experts on the Democratic Republic of the Congo, Rep., transmitted by letter dated Nov. 18, 2011, from the Chair of the Security Council Comm. established pursuant to Resolution 1533 (2004) concerning the Democratic Republic of the Congo addressed to the President of the Security Council, paras. 368–370, U.N. Doc. S/2011/738 (Dec. 2, 2011), *available at*https://www.un.org/ga/search/view_doc.asp?symbol=S/2011/738.

[207] *See, e.g.*, Laura Seay, *What's Wrong with Dodd-Frank 1502?: Conflict Minerals, Civilian Livelihoods, and the Unintended Consequences of Western Advocacy*, 11–16 (Center for Global Development, Working Paper No. 284), *available at* http://www.cgdev.org/content/publications/detail/1425843; Jonny Hogg, *Congo Miners Suffer as Traceability Rule Bite*, REUTERS (May 5, 2011), http://www.reuters.com/article/2011/05/05/congo-democratic-minerals-idUSLDE7431UG20110505; Christiana Ochoa & Patrick J. Keenan, *Regulating Information Flows, Regulating Conflict: An Analysis of United States Conflict Minerals Legislation*, 3(1) GOETTINGEN J. INT'L L. 129–154 (2011); Celia R. Taylor, *Conflict Minerals and SEC Disclosure Regulation*, HARV. BUS. L. REV. ONLINE (2012).

[208] *See* Nat'l Ass'n of Mfrs. v. Sec. Exch. Comm'n, 956 F. Supp. 2d 43, 43 (D. DC 2013); *see also* Jeff Schwartz, *The Conflict Minerals Experiment*, 6 HARV. BUS. L. REV. 129 (2016) (proposing improvements to Section 1502 reporting requirements).

[209] Michael S. Piwowar, *Statement of Acting Chairman Piwowar on the Court of Appeals Decision on the Conflict Minerals Rule*, SEC (Apr. 7, 2017), https://www.sec.gov/news/public-statement/piwowar-statement-court-decision-conflict-minerals-rule.

commentators have interpreted SEC statements as the SEC's "firm indication"[210] that the agency will no longer enforce the Conflict Minerals Rule.[211]

*b. Combating Corruption and Section 1504*

Section 1504 of Dodd-Frank amends Section 13 of the Securities Exchange Act of 1934 to require disclosures by issuers engaged in resource extraction.[212] A resource extraction issuer has a duty to disclose under the section if it is ordinarily required to file an annual report with the SEC and if it engages in the "commercial development of oil, natural gas, or minerals."[213] Commercial development includes exploration, extraction, processing, and export, or the acquisition of a license for any such activity.[214]

Resource extraction issuers covered by Section 1504 must report to the SEC any payments made directly, through a subsidiary, or through an entity under its control to a foreign government or the federal government.[215] Covered corporations—those required to file an annual report with the SEC and are engaging in commercial development of oil, natural gas, or minerals—must report on a country-by-country and project-by-project basis how much they pay foreign governments and how they make payments to further the commercial development of oil, natural gas, or minerals or to improve infrastructure whether through: taxes, royalties; fees; production entitlements; bonuses; or dividends.[216]

The American Petroleum Institute, concerned that the costs of compliance will have negative effects on the profits of its members, has opposed such disaggregated reporting.[217] The coalition campaign group Publish What You Pay is a proponent of the measure and counters that disclosure of detailed information is essential for civil society efforts to monitor corporate and government interactions.[218] Oxfam America, a member of the Publish What You Pay

[210] Marc Butler, *Why the Conflict Minerals Rules Refuses to Die*, INTELLIGIZE (June 21, 2018), https://www.intelligize.com/why-the-conflict-minerals-rule-refuses-to-die/.

[211] Jennifer Horvath, *Latest Updates in Conflict Minerals Law*, BRAUMILLER LAW GROUP (Nov. 20, 2017), https://www.braumillerlaw.com/latest-updates-conflict-minerals-law/.

[212] Dodd-Frank Act, *supra* note 196, § 1504 (amending Section 13 of the Securities Exchange Act of 1934 (15 U.S.C. 78m).

[213] Disclosure of Payments by Resource Extraction Issuers, 77 Fed. Reg. 56365, 56374-375 (Sept. 12, 2012) (to be codified at 17 C.F.R. pts. 240 and 249).

[214] Disclosure of Payments by Resource Extraction Issuers, 77 Fed. Reg. at 56374.

[215] Disclosure of Payments by Resource Extraction Issuers, 77 Fed. Reg. at 56385.

[216] Disclosure of Payments by Resource Extraction Issuers, 77 Fed. Reg. 56379.

[217] Revenue Watch, *Costs & Criticisms: The Facts about Disclosure Rules* (Sept. 7, 2011), http://www.revenuewatch.org/publications/fact_sheets/costs-criticisms-facts-about-disclosure-rules.

[218] THE BROOKINGS INSTITUTION, *Transparency, Conflict Minerals and Natural Resources: Debating Sections 1502 and 1504 of the Dodd-Frank Act* (Dec. 20, 2011), http://www.brookings.edu/opinions/2011/1220_debating_dodd_frank_kaufmann.aspx.

coalition, filed suit against the SEC seeking to compel the agency to issue a Final Rule pursuant to Section 1504, citing unreasonable and unlawful delay.[219]

When the SEC issued the Final Rules, the American Petroleum Institute, the Chamber of Commerce of the United States of America, the Independent Petroleum Association of America, and the National Foreign Trade Council challenged those rules. They argued, among other things, that the rules violate the First Amendment by "compelling speech on a controversial matter in order to influence political affairs."[220] They also contended that the Rules were "arbitrary and capricious and a violation of the Commission's statutory duty to consider its rules' effects on efficiency, competition, and capital formation."[221] Oxfam America and other civil society organizations intervened in the litigation as interested investors.

Acting under the Congressional Review Act, a newly installed Republican Congress and president repealed the rule.[222] As a result, the reporting requirement now has "no force or effect."[223] Accordingly, "[t]he result for affected issuers is clear: the existing rule is gone."[224]

These new duties to disclose are not without detractors. Indeed, these legally binding transparency initiatives have confronted a common set of criticisms concerning costs and institutional capacity. For example, some commentators argued such reporting requirements are improper interventions motivated by public policy concerns rather than concern for shareholders or potential investors being misled (in other words, the proper purpose of reporting to the SEC).[225] Critics also questioned the institutional competence of the SEC for managing social, as distinct from financial, reporting.[226] For some observers, information requirements mark an unwarranted departure from the SEC's mission to "protect investors, maintain fair, orderly and efficient markets and facilitate capital formation."[227]

[219] *See* Complaint at paras. 21–31, 39–45, Oxfam America, Inc. v. S.E.C., (D. Mass. 2012) (No. 12-10878).

[220] Brief for Petitioner at 2, Am. Petroleum Inst. v SEC, (No. 12-1398), 2012.

[221] *Id.* at 3.

[222] H.R.J. Res. 41, 115th Cong. (2017), https://www.congress.gov/115/plaws/publ4/PLAW-115publ4.pdf.

[223] *Id.*

[224] Nicholas Grabar & Sandra L. Flow, *Congress Rolls Back SEC Resource Extraction Payments Rule*, Harvard Law School Forum on Corporation Governance & Finance Regulation (Feb. 16, 2017), https://corpgov.law.harvard.edu/2017/02/16/congress-rolls-back-sec-resource-extraction-payments-rule/.

[225] *See* David M. Lynn, *The Dodd-Frank Act's Specialized Corporate Disclosure: Using the Securities Law to Address Public Policy Issues*, 6 J. Bus. & Tech. L. 327, 330–331 (2011).

[226] *Id.*

[227] *Id.* at 330.

### 2. Emerging Mandatory Nonfinancial Reporting Requirements and Human Rights: Incorporating Moral Concerns

Arguments that financial regulators should not be involved in social issues notwithstanding, in major global markets there is a move toward more mandatory disclosure of information incorporating social and environmental issues. Certain stock exchanges now require some form of nonfinancial disclosures from listed corporations. The Shanghai Stock Exchange offers preferential treatment in the Shanghai Corporate Governance Sector selection process to listed corporations that provide information on sustainability performance.[228] The London Stock Exchange requires listed companies to disclose any relevant nonfinancial information in annual reports.[229] The Johannesburg Stock Exchange now requires integrated reporting such that all listed firms must provide financial and nonfinancial information in one report.[230]

As early as 2003, the European Union approved rules requiring corporations to provide information on social and environmental performance indicators in annual reports.[231] Some EU member states that did not already have mandatory reporting requirements have since promulgated voluntary guidelines to encourage compliance with EU directives on disclosure.

Several European nations have mandated social and environmental impact disclosures. France now requires all listed corporations to include disclosures on social and environmental impacts in annual reports.[232] Denmark requires larger firms, as well as institutional investors, to include social and environmental disclosures in financial reports to regulators.[233] All business entities subject to Danish regulations must "report or explain" such that disclosures provided to regulators describe the firm's ESG efforts or discuss the challenges confronted in undertaking ESG efforts.[234]

In 2010, South Africa introduced an integrated reporting requirement that in order to list on the Johannesburg Stock Exchange, all firms must submit a single integrated report containing information on financial performance and on ESG performance. The architect of integrated reporting in South Africa, Professor Mervyn King, aims to provide the public with an appreciation of the connection

[228] *See* Press Release, Global Reporting Initiative, Investing in a Sustainable Future: The Role of the Shanghai Stock Exchange in the Uptake of Sustainability Reporting Initiatives in China (Sept. 5, 2012).

[229] Companies Act, 2006, c.46, Section 417 (U.K.).

[230] Inst. of Dirs. S.Afr., King Code of Governance for South Africa 10 (2009).

[231] Council Directive 2003/511/EC, of the European Parliament and of the Council of June 18, 2003, amending Directives 78/660/EEC, 83,349,EEC, 86/635/EEC, and 91/674/EEC on the Annual and Consolidated Accounts of Certain Types of Companies, Banks and Other Financial Institutions and Insurance Undertakings, art. 1(14), 2003 O.J. (L 178) 16.

[232] Code de Commerce [C. Com] Art. L225-102-1 (Fr.) (2001).

[233] Danish Financial Statements Act, Section 99a (2008)(Den.).

[234] *Id.*

between material financial information and issues that influence sustainability. To access South Africa's capital markets, companies now must put financial results in perspective by reporting on "how a company has both positively and negatively, impacted on the economic life of the community in which it operated during the year under review; and how the company intends to enhance those positive aspects and eradicate or ameliorate the negative aspects in the year ahead."[235]

In 2011, the Indian Securities and Exchange Board also required businesses listed with the Exchange to issue business responsibility reports presenting actions taken in accordance with the National Voluntary Guidelines on Social, Environmental and Economic Responsibilities.[236] In 2011, China made it mandatory for state-owned enterprises to submit sustainability reports.[237]

Opposition to Sections 1502 and 1504 as a departure from the purpose of the SEC notwithstanding, there are examples of the SEC reaching into the realm of social concerns with respect to security threats and climate change. For example, the SEC established the Office of Global Security Risk within its Division of Corporation Finance to develop procedures to identify all listed companies operating in "terrorist-sponsoring states" as identified by the US Department of State.[238] The commission has also issued interpretive guidance to companies about reporting the impact of climate change on their businesses.[239]

There are subject-specific areas, like trafficking and modern slavery, about which governments have required reporting. In 2010, California enacted the first state law requiring manufacturers and retail companies to publicly disclose their policies to eradicate slavery, forced labor, and human trafficking within their supply chains.[240] The California Transparency in Supply Chains Act (CTSCA) requires all retailers and manufactures that do business in California and have over $100 million in annual gross receipts to disclose on their company website any efforts the company is making to eradicate slavery and human trafficking from its supply chain.[241] As the world's ninth largest economy after the United States, China, Japan, Germany,

[235] King Code of Governance for South Africa (2009), cited in Robert G. Eccles & Daniela Saltzman, *Achieving Sustainability through Integrated Reporting*, STAN. SOC. INNOVATION REV. at 57 (Summer 2011).

[236] *See* Press Release, Sec. & Exch. Bd. of India, SEBI Board Meeting, PR No. 145/2011 (Nov. 24, 2011).

[237] State-Owned Assets Supervision & Admin. Comm'n of the State Council (SASAC), Guidelines to the State-Owned Enterprises Directly Under the Central Government on Fulfilling Corporate Social Responsibilities (2011) (China).

[238] Amy Deen Westbrook, *What's in Your Portfolio? U.S. Investors Are Unknowingly Financing State Sponsors of Terrorism*, 59 DEPAUL L. REV. 1151, 1195–1221 (2010) (describing and analyzing the effectiveness of the Office of Global Security Risk), *available at* http://www.washburnlaw.edu/faculty/westbrook-amy-fulltext/2010-59depaullawreview1151.pdf.

[239] *See* John M. Broder, *S.E.C. Adds Climate Risk to Disclosure List*, N.Y. TIMES (Jan. 28, 2010), at B1.

[240] CAL. CIV. CODE § 1714.43 (West 2012) [hereinafter Cal. Supply Chain Act].

[241] Cal. Supply Chain Act § 1714.43(a)(1), (b).

France, the United Kingdom, Italy, and Brazil,[242] California passed the CTSCA to leverage the substantial economic power of California consumers in order to promote social responsibility in the business community and prevent the use of forced and trafficked labor.[243] Since passage of the CTSCA, the governments of the United Kingdom and Australia have passed similar reporting requirements intended to curb modern slavery and human trafficking.

These legislative changes to require ESG reporting in various jurisdictions on various issues are also likely to have extraterritorial effects whether or not similar measures are taken in other countries.[244] For example, all US and foreign corporations registered with the SEC must report pursuant to governing regulations.[245] Companies outside the United States that want to develop business relationships with SEC-listed companies will also need to meet the reporting standards to remain attractive potential partners in the United States and elsewhere.[246]

To be sure, the quality of ESG reporting is presently poor, according to observers.[247] Critics claim that mandatory ESG reporting would be too costly and would not make a significant difference. Nevertheless, the growing expectation that information about human rights and environmental impacts will be shared with the public is moving the business community in the right direction. Mandatory reporting has required companies to investigate sourcing practices and as a result some companies have identified and addressed problems through industry and multistakeholder initiatives to promote change and improve conditions.

Consistent with the demands of conscious consumers, corporations down the supply chain that are not demonstrably conducting business in a manner that supports respect for human rights could become disfavored. Retailers may increase efforts to source from suppliers with better business practices in order to avoid reputational risks associated with disclosures that could link a brand with conflict or slavery.[248]

[242] 2010 California Economy Rankings, *available at* http://www.ccsce.com/PDF/Numbers-Jan-2012-CA-Economy-Rankings-2010.pdf; *California Economy Ranking in the World*, ECONOMIC POST (Feb. 3, 2011), *available at* http://econpost.com/californiaeconomy/california-economy-ranking-among-world-economies.

[243] George, *supra* note 195.

[244] *See* FOREIGN & COMMONWEALTH OFFICE (UK), LEGALLY BINDING PROCESS, http://www.fco.gov.uk/en/global-issues/conflict-minerals/legally-binding-process/.

[245] *See* FOREIGN & COMMONWEALTH OFFICE (UK), DODD-FRANK SECTION 1504: TRANSPARENCY LEGISLATION, http://www.fco.gov.uk/en/global-issues/conflict-minerals/legally-binding-process/dodd-frank-act-section-1504.

[246] *See* FOREIGN & COMMONWEALTH OFFICE (UK), LEGALLY BINDING PROCESS, *supra* note 244.

[247] *See, e.g.*, MICHELLE LANGLOIS, SHIFT, HUMAN RIGHTS REPORTING: ARE COMPANIES TELLING INVESTORS WHAT THEY NEED TO KNOW? (2017); ASSOCIATION OF CHARTERED CERTIFIED ACCOUNTANTS, WHAT DO INVESTORS EXPECT FROM NON-FINANCIAL REPORTING? (June 2013).

[248] For discussions of how a corporation's approach to social and environmental issues can affect its reputation and long-term financial performance, *see, e.g.*, DELOITTE RESEARCH, DISCLOSURE OF LONG-TERM BUSINESS VALUE: WHAT MATTERS? 2–3 (2012), *available at* http://www.deloitte.com/assets/Dcom-UnitedStates/Local%20Assets/Documents/us_scc_materialitypov_032812.pdf;

## B. Integrated Reporting and Investment Performance

Accompanying the rise of CSR and sustainability reporting, companies and investors alike have recently recognized that integrated reporting provides a more accurate picture of the value and social impacts of various organizations. Some stock exchanges and governments have started to require integrated reporting for a company to be listed. Integrated reporting requirements are consistent with the UNGPs and could aid business enterprises in making responsible human rights and environmental decisions.

There are three basic types of corporate reporting: financial, sustainability/responsibility, and integrated. The three types differ in their goals, their intended audience, and the practices associated with each.[249] Investors are the intended audience for financial information, and laws mandated that firms disclose such information as a condition for accessing public capital markets. Stakeholders are the intended audience for "non-financial" information such as sustainability reports, which remain for the most part entirely voluntary in most jurisdictions. Integrated reporting recognizes that a range of information is relevant to investors such that salient issues arise that matter to both shareholders and stakeholders alike.

Integrated reporting has received increasing attention in recent years. The simplest definition of integrated reporting is the integration of a financial report and a sustainability or CSR report.[250] One explanation of the aims of incorporating social concerns into financial returns provided by the International Integrated Reporting Council (IIRC) offers: "the primary purpose of an integrated report is to explain to providers of financial capital how an organization creates value over time, including employees, customers, suppliers, business partners, local communities, legislators, regulators and policy-makers."[251] While sustainability reporting usually exacts change through pressure from civil society on the company to disclose information, integrated reporting is advanced as a way to foster

UNEP Finance Initiative, *Environmental and Corporate Governance Issues to Equity Pricing: 11 Sector Studies by Brokerage House Analysts at the Request of the UNEP Finance Initiative Asset Management Working Group*, 7 (2004), *available at* http://www.unepfi.org/fileadmin/documents/amwg_materiality_equity_pricing_report_2004.pdf.

[249] Robert G. Eccles & Birgit Spiesshofer, *Integrated Reporting for a Re-Imagined Capitalism*, Harvard Business School General Management Unit Working Paper No. 16-032 (2015). See generally, Amol Mehra & Sara Blackwell, *The Rise of Non-Financial Disclosure: Reporting on Respect for Human Rights*, in Business and Human Rights: From Principles to Practice (Justine Nolan & Dorothée Baumann-Pauly, eds. 2016).

[250] Thomson Reuters, *Why Investors Should Care About Integrated Reporting* (Mar. 24, 2015), https://blogs.thomsonreuters.com/answerson/investors-integrated-reporting/.

[251] Ernst & Young, IIRC Integrated Reporting Framework—Executive Summary, at 2.

"integrated thinking" so that the company takes account of material ESG issues by operating in a holistic way.[252]

The IIRC is dedicated to the goal of urging the adoption of integrated reporting on an international basis "as a means to improve communication about value creation, advance the evolution of corporate reporting, and make a lasting contribution to financial stability and sustainable development."[253] The long-term vision of the IIRC is "a world in which integrated thinking is embedded with mainstream business practice in the public and private sectors, facilitated by integrated reporting as the corporate reporting norm."[254] The IIRC is comprised of business and reporting entities, providers of financial capital, policymakers, regulators, reporting framework developers, civil society, and academia.[255] The IIRC provides guidelines, the "IR" Framework, as a template for companies that wish to prepare reports responsive to a growing market demand.[256]

Like sustainability reporting, integrated reporting was until recently an entirely voluntary exercise. Over the past several decades, however, mandatory corporate reporting has begun a move beyond only financial disclosure to include social and environmental impacts of business.[257] For instance, in 2009, the Johannesburg Stock Exchange began requiring companies to produce an annual integrated sustainability report as a condition to listing on the exchange.[258]

Disclosure of company compliance with environmental regulations is also becoming a more common governmental regulation. For example, Australia requires companies to report on their compliance with the nation's environmental regulations.[259] More countries are requiring disclosure of "material" nonfinancial information in annual company financial reports.[260]

The popularization of ESG disclosures among companies has prompted interest in the effect of transparency on financial performance. Study results remain

[252] *Id.* at 7; *see also* Narine, *supra* note 192; Adam Sulkowski & Sandra Waddock, *Beyond Sustainability Reporting: Integrated Reporting Is Practiced, Required and More Would Be Better*, 10(4) U. St. Thomas L.J. (2014).

[253] IIRC, *Structure of the IIRC*, http://integratedreporting.org/the-iirc-2/structure-of-the-iirc/.

[254] IIRC, *The International Framework* (2013), at 2, *available at* http://integratedreporting.org/wp-content/uploads/2015/03/13-12-08-THE-INTERNATIONAL-IR-FRAMEWORK-2-1.pdf.

[255] *Id.*

[256] *See generally Procedures Handbook IIRC Pronouncements and Other Communications*, *available at* http://integratedreporting.org/wp-content/uploads/2016/06/IIRC_Procedures_HandbookApr06_16.pdf.

[257] Ruth Jebe, *Sustainability Reporting and New Governance: South Africa Marks the Path to Improved Corporate Disclosure*, J. Int'l & Comp. L. 233, 237 (2015).

[258] *Id.*

[259] *Id.* (the regulation in question is cited in the countries Corporation Act).

[260] *See* David Monsma & Timothy Olson, *Muddling Through Counterfactual Materiality and Divergent Disclosure: The Necessary Search for a Duty to Disclose Material Non-Financial Information*, 26 Stan. Envtl. L.J. 137, 147 (2007)

mixed. Some empirical studies on the relationship between financial performance and corporate social responsibility have found a positive relationship between the two—responsible corporations do better financially.[261] Other studies have shown a negative link, emphasizing that CSR reporting can be costly and may inhibit a company's competitiveness.[262] Still other scholars argue that there is a neutral or no relationship between CSR and financial performance,[263] especially when variables such as investment in research and product development are controlled for.[264] In sum, information offers opportunity for improvement.

## IV. Ethical Consumption to Advance Respect for Rights

Private investors are not the only economic actors with influence in the market. Increasingly, public institutions, powerful purchasers, and concerned segments of consumers have chosen to put their money where their morals are. In the following I present examples of entities exerting economic influence in ways that align business practices with respect for human rights.

### A. Public Institutions: Government Procurement Initiatives to Promote Rights Protection

Public procurement programs use contractual choices to promote economic development and social justice.[265] Public procurement ordinances frequently give preference to particular types of businesses for awarding bids on public projects.[266] On occasion, however, local government contracting choices have

261 *See* Patrice Laroche & José Allouche, *A Meta-Analytical Investigation of the Relationship Between Corporate Social and Financial Performance*, 57 REV. GEST. DES RESSOURCES HUM. 18–41 (2005); *see also* A. Najah & A. Jarboui, *The Social Disclosure Impact on Corporate Financial Performance: Case of Big French Companies*, 3 INT'L J. MANAG. BUS. RES. 337, 339 (2013).

262 Najah & Jarboui, *supra* note 261, at 340.

263 *Id.*

264 Abagail McWilliams & Donald Siegel, *Corporate Social Responsibility and Financial Performance: Correlation or Misspecification*, 21 STRATEG. MANAG. J. 603, 608 (2000).

265 For an examination of how governments use contracting to promote social justice, *see generally* CHRISTOPHER MCCRUDDEN, BUYING SOCIAL JUSTICE: EQUALITY, GOVERNMENT PROCUREMENT AND LEGAL CHANGE (2007); *see also* Carol Cravero, *Socially Responsible Public Procurement and Set-Asides: A Comparative Analysis of the US, Canada, and the EU*, 8 ARCTIC REV. L. & POL. 174 (2017).

266 *See* California Small Business Procurement and Contract Act, Cal. Gov't Code §§ 14835–14847 (West 2012). Public procurement ordinances allow governments to prefer certain producers when procuring goods over producers. Developing countries often use public procurement as a way to strengthen infant industries, and public procurement policies have been shown to have a meaningful impact on development. Victor Mosoti, *The WTO Agreement on Government Procurement: A Necessary Evil in the Legal Strategy for Development in the Poor World?*, 25 U. PA. J. INT'L ECON. L. 593, 599 (2004). At the state level, procurement ordinances like California's allow the state government to give preference to companies that are either registered in or have their principle place of

been used to impact global issues by structuring incentives to create changes in social policies.[267] For example, public authorities in the United States and Europe used procurement practices to protest apartheid by threatening corporations operating in South Africa with the loss of government contracts.[268]

Some governments make it a policy to regularly evaluate the social consequences of their procurement; the United Kingdom recently overhauled its process for awarding public procurement contracts to require businesses to prove their track record in addressing injustices.[269]

Public procurement promises to be an important avenue for influencing corporate conduct, as sustainable and social procurement concepts gain ground and government authorities exercise such preferences. In the United States, public procurement accounts for an estimated 9 percent of the GDP.[270] The United States and the European Union possess enormous influence in various markets and industries. Larger states in the United States can wield substantial market influence.[271] For example, California used its economic leverage to influence issues. The Los Angeles school district considers health and nutrition, environmental stability, labor rights, and support of local economies when making food procurement choices for public schools.[272] Reflecting the significance of public procurement on the industries that bid on government contracts, California also considers the broader market impact of its food purchases.[273]

In the European Union, purchases by public authorities account for approximately 14 percent of GDP.[274] The European Commission has long acknowledged the potential social dividends public procurement policies in the EU

business in California when purchasing goods for government use. *See* Small Business Procurement and Contract Act Cal. Govt. Code §§ 14835–47.

[267] Christopher McCrudden, *Using Public Procurement to Achieve Social Outcomes*, 28 Natural Resources Forum, 257, 263 (2004).

[268] *See* McCrudden, *supra* note 265, at 9–10.

[269] Sarah Shearman, *UK Govt Insists Businesses Tackle "Evil Practices" to Win Contracts*, Reuters (Mar. 10, 2019), https://www.reuters.com/article/britain-contracts-social-idUSL8N20X0XF.

[270] OECD, Government at a Glance, at 173 (2017).

[271] NASBO, State Expenditure Report: Examining Fiscal 2014–2016 State Spending, at 8 (2016).

[272] California Strategic Growth Council, California State Government Food Procurement Policies and Practices, at 10 (2016).

[273] *Id.*

[274] Christopher Bovis, *Where Does the Regulation of Public Procurement and Public Private Partnerships Take the Member States of the EU*, 2 Eur. Pub. Private Partnership L. Rev. 53, 53 (2011); *European Semester Thematic Factsheet: Public Procurement*, Eur. Comm'n, (Nov. 22, 2017), https://ec.europa.eu/info/sites/info/files/file_import/european-semester_thematic-factsheet_public-procurement_en_0.pdf ("Every year public authorities in the EU spend around 14% of GDP on public procurement."); *Public Procurement in a Nutshell*, Eur. Comm'n, https://ec.europa.eu/trade/policy/accessing-markets/public-procurement/ (last updated Nov. 22, 2019) ("In the EU, in 2017, the public purchase of goods and services was estimated to be worth some €2 trillion or 13.3% of GDP.").

member states could pay in promoting corporate respect for human rights and environmental protection.[275] The European Parliament has asked the European Commission to explore how social and environmental considerations could be integrated into public procurement and to educate public purchasers about the opportunities for greater integration of these considerations in their purchasing decisions.[276] The Commission has also issued an interpretive communication on European Community law relevant to public procurement.[277] Therefore, it is clear that governments are leveraging their dual role in the market as regulators and purchasers through procurement programs that take account of social criteria.

## B. Powerful Purchasers: Strategic Sourcing to Reduce Rights Risks

Powerful purchasers in the private sector can also exert influence to improve conditions. The Fair Food Program provides a case in point. The program is: "worker driven," "consumer powered," and "market enforced." The program's Fair Food Standards Council oversees the Fair Food Code of Conduct. Given the leverage and market power of corporate buyers where the Fair Food Program is in place and implemented, workers have been able to reverse downward wage pressure and increase demand from buyers that growers protect worker rights.

Most certification schemes are voluntary in that certified firms and farms can usually opt in and out of compliance standards without legal consequences because commitments are not binding and are largely not enforceable. Moreover, there may be relatively few market consequences for firms and farms that fail to comply with certification standards and lose certification status. The Fair Food Program's Agricultural Justice Project label is a notable exception among social justice certification labels because it incorporates a valuable enforcement model that uses market-based mechanisms and contractual terms to support compliance.

[275] *See* Jan Wouters & Leen Chanet, *Corporate Human Rights Responsibility: A European Perspective*, 6 Nw. J. Int'l Hum. Rts. 262, 290 (2008); Peter Kunzlik, *Making the Market Work for the Environment: Acceptance of (Some) "Green" Contract Award Criteria in Public Procurement*, 15 J. Envtl. L. 175, 189 (2003).

[276] *See* Wouters & Chanet, *supra* note 275, at 290 n.198 (citing Parliament Resolution 2002/278 on the Commission Green Paper on Promoting a European Framework for Corporate Social Responsibility (COM (2001) 366-C5-0161/2002/2069 (COS) of 30 May 2002, 2003 O.J. (C 187 E), Preamble, Recital J.)).

[277] *Commission Interpretative Communication on the Community Law Applicable to Public Procurement and the Possibilities for Integrating Social Considerations into Public Procurement*, COM (2001).

The Fair Food Program uses contract law to ensure commitments and has focused on large produce buyers like McDonald's and Subway, so has benefited from the social pressure that can brought to bear on brands. Protests at restaurant chains helped to promote change. For example, after activists protested against the McDonald's and Taco Bell chains, the brands became Fair Food Program members.

While there is growing evidence that consumers care and that the market for fair trade goods continues to grow, it is not clear that average retail consumers can mount a sustained and durable demand for justice. However, consumer demand can be mobilized to move businesses to make commitments that worker-centered, multistakeholder structures such as the Fair Food Program can build upon. For example, student movement allies helped to advance the cause of fair food by demanding their universities source responsibly.[278]

## C. Private Individuals: Certification, Choice, and the Concerned Connected Consumer

Consumers could contribute to the promotion of more ethical business conduct through choosing products and purchasing from companies that take the responsibility to respect human rights seriously. To take the conventional wisdom that "the customer is always right" to heart increasingly will mean having a strategy to assess and address human risks. More customers care about human rights today than ever before and increasingly have the capability to seek information and to support or oppose certain products or practices through personal procurement choices.[279] Aside from controlling costs, the profitability of most major corporations depends on selling products or services to buyers.

Recent research suggests that there is a direct positive relationship between consumer attitudes toward a business enterprise and the CSR activities of the business.[280] Under certain conditions, CSR initiatives can influence consumer

[278] *See, e.g.*, Charlie Daffron, *Marchers Push to Remove Wendy's from UF*, Gainesville Sun (Mar. 14, 2019), https://www.gainesville.com/news/20190314/marchers-push-to-remove-wendys-from-uf; *and* Ava Erfani, *Why You Should Boycott Wendy's*, Carolina Political Review, (Feb. 27, 2019), https://www.carolinapoliticalreview.org/editorial-content/2019/2/27/why-you-should-boycott-wendys; *see also* Noam Scheiber, *Why Wendy's Is Facing Campus Protests (It's About the Tomatoes)*, N.Y. Times (Mar. 7, 2019), https://www.nytimes.com/2019/03/07/business/economy/wendys-farmworkers-tomatoes.html; and Molly Mina, *Students and Farmworkers Are Teaming Up to Boot Wendy's Off Their Campuses*, The Nation (Mar. 29, 2017), https://www.thenation.com/article/students-and-farmworkers-are-teaming-up-to-boot-wendys-off-their-campuses/.

[279] *See* Raphel Bemporad & Mitch Baranowski, *Conscious Consumers are Changing the Rules of Marketing. Are You Ready?* Highlights from the BBMG Conscious Consumer Report (Nov. 2007); Guido Palazzo, *Felicitas Morhart & Judith Schrempf-Stirling, Shopping for a Better World: How Consumer Decisions Can Help to Promote Sustainability and Human Rights* in Business and Human Rights: From Principles to Practice (Justine Nolan & Dorothée Baumann-Pauly, eds. 2016).

[280] Sankar Sen & C.B. Bhattacharya, *Does Doing Good Always Lead to Doing Better? Consumer Reactions to Corporate Social Responsibility*, 38 J. Marketing Res. 225 (2001).

conduct and activist groups can influence corporate social change.[281] For companies operating in "advertising-intensive" environments, CSR activities can influence consumer choices.[282] Because CSR is so broad, the range of behaviors considered to be driving this positive correlation varies with respect to different issues and in different industry sectors.

That consumption appears to be self-constituting in some measure is reaffirmed by research on the effects of CSR on consumer choices. For example, a study by Ellen, Mohr, and Webb found that consumer response to cause-related product marketing depended on both the particular cause and the "consumer's" attributions regarding their own motivations and that of the retailer.[283] Consumers further differentiated between companies' strategic and egoistic motives, and values-driven and stakeholder-driven motives.[284] Consumers regarded CSR effort most positively when they believed it was driven by both the business's sincere values and strategic interests.[285] Considerations like length of commitment to a CSR initiative had significant influence in how consumers perceived those efforts.[286] Other researchers have found that consumer choices are more likely to be informed by a general sense or overall impression of a company than by specific issues that influence a consumer's assessment of a company and whether to buy its products.[287]

Research experiments conducted by Sankar Sen and C.B. Bhattacharya found that CSR initiatives operated to the benefit of a business best when there was a "self-company congruence."[288] Consumers that perceive a congruity with brands may form deeper bonds with the associated company.[289] Sen and Bhattacharya found that in evaluating corporations, consumers were much more attuned to information about poor CSR performance or unethical practices than the positive contributions of a corporation.[290]

In a competitive marketplace, congruence between a consumer's values and a company's ethical commitments could provide incentives for businesses to

[281] *Id.*; *see also* Frank Den Hond & Frank G.A. De Bakker, *Ideologically Motivated Activism: How Activist Groups Influence Corporate Social Change Activities*, 32(3) ACAD. MGMT. REV. 901–924 (July 2007); TIM BARTLEY & CURTIS CHILD, SHAMING THE CORPORATION: SOCIAL MOVEMENT PRESSURE AND CORPORATE SOCIAL RESPONSIBILITY (2010).

[282] Henri Servaers & Ane Tamayo, *The Impact of Corporate Social Responsibility on Firm Value: The Role of Consumer Awareness*, 59 MGMT. SCI., 1045, 1058 (2013).

[283] Pam Scholder Ellen et al., *Charitable Programs and the Retailer: Do They Mix?*, 76 J. RETAILING 393 (2000).

[284] Pam Scholder Ellen et al., *Building Corporate Associations: Consumer Attributions for Corporate Socially Responsible Programs*, 34 J. ACAD. MARKETING SCI. 147 (2006).

[285] *Id.*

[286] *Id.* at 154.

[287] T.J. Brown et al., *The Company and the Product: Corporate Associations and Consumer Product Responses*, 61 J. MARKETING 68 (1997).

[288] Sen & Bhattacharya, *supra* note 280, at 238.

[289] *Id.*

[290] *Id.*

improve social and environmental performance. Projecting a positive image by respecting rights or protecting the environment would be important for business enterprises that must appeal to image conscious buyers who are interested in ethical business practices. Image conscious consumers affiliate themselves with brands that are reputed to be responsible and avoid brands that are perceived to be unethical.

Research has found that the benefits consumers derive by patronizing ethical business enterprises could easily be disrupted by damaging information about unethical conduct on the part of the business.[291] While virtually all consumers react to negative information about poor CSR performance, only the most committed consumers register positive information.[292] Studies have shown that consumers are more likely to punish unethical companies than they are to reward ethical companies.[293]

There are drawbacks and shortcomings to ethical consumerism as a strategy to advance corporate accountability. For example, one study found that consumers make inferences on CSR performance based on little information or inaccurate information and, in most instances, based primarily on information provided by the firm.[294] Companies could engage in "greenwashing" or otherwise manipulate information to influence consumer perceptions.[295] Different contexts may limit the flexibility consumers have to make choices consistent with their moral motivations or expressed ethical values.[296] Research has also documented a gap between consumer attitudes and actions with respect to ethical consumption choices.[297] Many consumers remain cynical about the ethical integrity of

[291] *Id.* at 238.

[292] *Id.*

[293] Remi Trudel & June Cotte, *Does it Pay to Be Good?* 50 MIT Sloan Mgmt. Rev. 61, 62 (2009).

[294] *See* Todd Green & John Peloza, *How Do Consumers Infer Corporate Social Responsibility? The Role of Organisation Size*, 13 J. Consumer Behav. 282 (2014) ("[C]onsumers are also largely unaware of CSR activities of firms and often use available information to infer."); N. Craig Smith et al., *Consumer Perceptions of Corporate Social Responsibility: The CSR Halo Effect*, INSEAD Social Innovation Centre 16–17 (2010) (Faculty & Research Working Paper) (on file with author) (consumers make inferences about corporate social performance based on limited information); Victor Fleischer, *Brand New Deal: The Branding Effect of Corporate Deal Structures*, 104 Mich. L. Rev. 1581, 1634 (2006) ("Consumers purchasing integrity products rely on information specialists such as corporate social responsibility (CSR) groups, experts, or others who have already invested the time to gather the relevant information.").

[295] Smith *supra* note 294 at 17.

[296] *See* Neeru Paharia, et al., *Sweatshop Labor is Wrong Unless the Shoes are Cute: Cognition Can Both Help and Hurt Moral Motivated Reasoning*, 121 Organizational Behavior and Human Decision Processes 81, 87 (2013); Archon Fung et al., The Political Economy of Transparency: What Makes Disclosure Policies Effective? (Cambridge, MA: Ash Inst. for Democratic Governance and Innovation, John F. Kennedy School of Government, 2004); Erika George, Transformation through Transparency: Human Rights and Corporate Responsibilities in the Global Food System in Power, Participation, and Private Regulatory Initiatives: Human Rights Under Supply Chain Capitalism (Daniel Brinks, Julia Dehm, Karen Engle & Kate Taylor, eds. forthcoming 2021).

[297] Marylyn Carrigan & Ahmad Attalla, *The Myth of the Ethical Consumer: Do Ethics Matter in Purchase Behaviour?*, 18 J. Consumer Marketing 564 (2001).

business enterprises.[298] Providing consumers with actionable and accurate information could reduce skeptism and narrow the gap between consumer commitment to ethical products and consumer purchasing practices.

According to a 2012 survey by Nielsen's Global Corporate Citizenship Unit, more than half of consumers believe companies should support the environment and almost half of consumers around the world responded that they were willing to reward socially responsible companies.[299] Nielsen surveyed 28,000 internet users in fifty-six countries, a sophisticated and desirable base of respondents. More than half of global consumers surveyed reported they would be willing to pay more for the products and services of a company that has programs which contribute to society in 2014.[300] The majority of survey respondents indicated that within the past six months they purchased products from at least one businesses reputed to be socially responsible.[301]

Studies have shown that many consumers do want companies to behave more responsibly and are willing to pay a premium price to improve conditions for workers.[302] Consumers are indicating greater interest in information about production processes.[303] However, the information environment is complicated, as is consumer behavior.

Research shows that consumers who express a preference for socially conscious products and services are more likely than others to use social media to aid in making purchasing decisions.[304] Millennials—consumers born between 1985 and 1999—tend to be more receptive than older consumers to ethical appeals when selecting products and services to purchase.[305] This generation has been born into a world of international interdependence and networked communications technology.[306] They will boycott brands that violate social or environmental norms.[307] Millennials believe they can contribute to making social change in the world seeing beyond particular transactions to encompass a broader perspective.[308] While price and quality are central considerations when

[298] *Id.* at 575.

[299] NIELSEN, THE GLOBALLY SOCIALLY-CONSCIOUS CONSUMER, 3 (2012).

[300] NIELSEN, DOING WELL BY DOING GOOD 2 (2014).

[301] *Id.*

[302] P.H. Howard & P. Allen, *Consumer Willingness to Pay for Domestic "Fair Trade": Evidence from the United States*, 23 RENEWABLE AGRICULTURE & FOOD SYSTEMS, 235, 240 (2008).

[303] Douglas A. Kysar, *Preferences for Processes: The Process/Product Distinction in the Regulation of Consumer Choice*, 118 HARV. L. REV. 525, 579–587 (2004).

[304] Chad Brooks, *Shopper Willing to Pay More to Socially Responsible Companies*, BUSINESS NEWS DAILY (Mar. 29, 2012), https://www.businessnewsdaily.com/2273-shoppers-pay-socially-responsible-companies.html.

[305] Tania Bucic et al., *Ethical Consumers Among the Millennials: A Cross-National Study*, 110 J. BUS. ETHICS 113, 114 (2012).

[306] *Id.*

[307] *Id.* at 115.

[308] *Id.*

purchasing products, many millennials also view ethical considerations as significant.[309] Millennials are far from monolithic in their consumer preferences and consumption patterns, but only a small minority "never" evaluate the ethical implications of purchases.[310] The size and purchasing power of this generation has the potential to shape the global marketplace.[311]

Consumers, and especially millennials, are likely to reward ethical companies with brand loyalty and repeat patronage.[312] They may use such apps as "Buycott" to not only avoid products owned by companies who violate or oppose their values but also to prioritize purchasing products that support those values.[313] A growing body of research supports the benefits a business can derive from ethical business practices from loyal consumers who are willing to purchase the company's products and promote a brand.[314] Researchers have identified a growing group of people engaged in "socially responsible consumer behavior" (SRCB) who view purchasing in personal terms and seek information about corporate social and environmental performance because they believe consumer choices can impact society.[315] This community of consumers can contribute to advancing corporate accountability to better align business practices with respect for human rights.

## V. Incorporating Rights

In this chapter we have considered how the enforcement of corporate commitments to respect human rights can occur through the provision of actionable information to concerned constituencies of investors and consumers. We discussed competitive pressures being brought to bear on particular industries due to greater transparency, reporting requirements, and the connected nature of communication enjoyed by a significant segment of consumers. A connected and concerned community of investors and consumers can leverage concerns about social issues into social change.

[309] *Id.* at 120.
[310] *Id.* at 128.
[311] *Id.* at 114.
[312] *Id.* at 126.
[313] *See* Karin Eli et al., *Mobile Activism, Material Imaginings, and the Ethics of the Edible: Framing Political Engagement through the Buycott App*, 74 GEOFORUM 63–73 (2016); Clare O'Connor, *New App Lets You Boycott Koch Brothers, Monsanto and More by Scanning Your Shopping Cart*, FORBES (May 14, 2013), https://web.archive.org/web/20130515033004/http://www.forbes.com/sites/clareoconnor/2013/05/14/new-app-lets-you-boycott-koch-brothers-monsanto-and-more-by-scanning-your-shopping-cart/.
[314] See Shuili Du, et al., *Maximizing Business Returns to Corporate Social Responsibility (CSR): The Role of CSR Communication*, 12 INT'L J. MGMT. REVIEWS 8, 9 (2010).
[315] Lois A. Mohr, et al., *Do Consumers Expect Companies to be Socially Responsible? The Impact of Corporate Social Responsibility on Buying Behavior*, 35 J. CONSUMER AFFAIRS 45, 67 (2001).

The expectations that activists, investors, and consumers place on business enterprises are increasing—as are requests for information relevant to social and environmental impacts. My review of shareholder proposals revealed a progression of demands made for more responsible business conduct, with investors demanding policy commitments and versions of impact assessments. When capital markets and consumer choices start to be aligned with rewarding responsible business conduct, an economic incentive to prioritize avoiding adverse human rights impacts and complicity in abuses is created.

Access to actionable information would allow investors to aid in enforcing the now-established norm that a business enterprise must fulfill its obligation to respect human rights through its operations wherever it operates. In the face of present political obstacles to advance a treaty to regulate business conduct at international level, insisting on access to information may be the best option for advancing the business and human rights agenda. Sharing information is easy for sophisticated actors with access to communications technology. The collective influence of interested stakeholders sharing information about corporate ESG performance enables them to reach a larger audience and have a potentially larger impact on outcomes. The GRI and other voluntary reporting frameworks have laid a foundation for progress and could compliment emerging mandated financial disclosures if backed by government enforcement.[316]

These developments point toward a trend to expand the meaning of what is "material" to better reflect what matters to a growing group of investors. Coupled with the recent proliferation of mandatory social reporting requirements, evolving market trends make social criteria more important to investors and hold promise for making the responsibility of businesses to respect human rights obligatory.

To be sure, voluntary reporting seems to consistently suffer from a lack of consistency, with companies free to underreport any metric that might be troubling to potential investors. Reporting isn't always viewed favorably. Some critics view CSR reporting as "window dressing," arguing that it is simply a marketing ploy.[317]

Still, a company's reputation among shareholders and stakeholders remains the main mechanism by which good companies are rewarded and bad companies are punished. This makes monitoring CSR claims to protect consumers from false or misleading information an important concern. Companies face pressure for transparency from "non-market stakeholders, such as NGOs, policymakers, or the media."[318] To that end, "the disclosure of certain sustainability information can be an instrument for generating favorable impressions

[316] Ruth Jebe, *Corporate Sustainability Reporting and "Material Information": An Empirical Study of Materiality Under the GRI and IR Frameworks*, 33 Conn. J. Int'l L. 95, 126 (2017).

[317] Jegoo Lee & Sylvia Maxfield, *Doing Well by Reporting Good: Reporting Corporate Responsibility and Corporate Performance*, 120 Bus. & Soc. Rev. 577, 579 (2015).

[318] Hahn & Lülfs, *supra* note 175, at 404.

of an organization's sustainability performance, thus preserving organizational legitimacy."[319] Moreover, the "stock market views activities of publishing these reports not as strategic investment, not purely cost."[320] Research suggests that responsible business enterprises enjoy reduced agency costs and that providing information to the public induces goodwill.[321] The positive link between CSR and financial performance implies that good companies are rewarded. Information can aid enforcement of the ethical commitments companies are making in codes of conduct.

The next chapter traces changes in corporate reporting on social and environmental performance with a focus on human rights. It also tracks the incorporation of codes of conduct into public communications and supplier contracts.

319 *Id.*
320 Lee & Maxfield, *supra* note 317, at 600.
321 *Id.* at 601.

# 6

# From Voluntary to Obligatory

## Corporate Reporting and Codes of Conduct to Promote Respect for Human Rights

### Introduction

This chapter examines what corporations are doing to address the human rights risks before and after alleged involvement in human rights abuses due to particular business practices. It offers an overview of the different strategies used by transnational business enterprises to respond to concerns expressed by investors, consumers, and affected communities. Among the self-regulation strategies used by businesses examined are the promulgation of codes of conduct and the publication of sustainability reports. This chapter presents the findings from a comparative discourse analysis of the corporate social responsibility (CSR) reporting and codes of conduct created by competing corporations in selected industry sectors over specific time periods when human rights issues involving these business enterprises received increased public attention. I assess the extent to which sustainability reports and codes of conduct have come to incorporate reference to international human rights standards both over time and in response to conflicts with constituencies interested in or impacted by the human rights performance of the corporations. Corporate responses to allegations of complicity in human rights abuses are also analyzed.

Based on my findings, I argue that the discursive frame asserted by corporate responsibility rhetoric incorporating human rights issues increasingly treats compliance with norms that are "voluntary" as though these norms were obligatory. Codes of conduct and communication about corporate conduct through sustainability reporting are now essential for maintaining a "social license" to operate for large companies and, sometimes by extension, suppliers to large companies. I argue that the creation of codes of conduct can provide insights into transnational legal processes that may influence and inform law and may provide a measure of protection in areas where law has been less effective for ensuring that human rights are not violated.

In this chapter, I demonstrate that codes of conduct and corporate reporting are changing to meet the escalating expectations placed on business enterprises by a growing portion of the public interested in social and environmental issues.

*Incorporating Rights*. Erika George, Oxford University Press. © Erika George 2021.
DOI: 10.1093/oso/9780199941483.003.0007

It is in this changing context that I argue that "soft law" standards and voluntary corporate codes of conduct may be understood as obligatory. Where references to codes of conduct are incorporated into contractual provisions, codes must be understood as enforceable "hard law" with the potential to contribute to transnational private ordering and new governance.

CSR and sustainability initiatives have become an increasingly important part of many business models. A growing number of corporations have voluntarily incorporated social and environmental issues in their business models and daily operations by adopting corporate policies and codes of conduct.[1] Recent international policy initiatives call for responsible business conduct and look to the policies and practices a business has in place to avoid adverse human rights impacts.[2] Still, without an overarching international institution with the power to enforce compliance with international human rights obligations, enforcement remains a challenge for international law and policy. The regulatory gap is particularly pronounced where private actors, such as business enterprises, are concerned. Globalization increases the importance of corporate self-regulation through codes of conduct and communications with the public.

Because some governments are unwilling or unable to regulate the social impacts of transnational business enterprises, while consumers and investors increasingly are interested in the social impacts of business, the forms of voluntary corporate self-regulation that have arisen in the absence of effective state regulation merit greater attention. Increasingly, consumers are seeking more information about the manufacturing processes of the products they consume, and investors are requesting information on social, environmental, and governance issues. Overall, the demand for greater business transparency appears to be increasing. It is in this context of increasing reputational risks to brands and rising interest in the impact of business on society that more business enterprises are devising strategies to manage reputational risks and to better understand the impact of particular business practices on human rights. Communications on social and environmental impacts have become an important risk-management strategy for corporations.

Section I of this chapter discusses provisions of the UN Guiding Principles on Business and Human Rights relevant to human rights policy commitments and

[1] Robert G. Eccles, Ioannis Ioannou, & George Serafeim, *The Impact of Corporate Sustainability on Organizational Processes and Performance*, NAT'L BUR. ECON. RES. 2 (2012).

[2] *See, e.g., Report of the Special Representative of the Secretary-General on the issue of human rights and transnational corporations and other business enterprises, John Ruggie, Guiding Principles on Business and Human Rights: Implementing the United Nations "Protect, Respect and Remedy" Framework*, U.N. Doc. A/HRC/17/31 (Mar. 21, 2011) [hereinafter *Guiding Principles on Business and Human Rights*]; Olivier De Schutter (Special Rapporteur on the right to food), *Promotion and Protection of All Human Rights, Civil, Political, Economic, Social and Cultural Rights, Including the Right to Development*, U.N. Doc. A/HRC/12/31 (July 21, 2009).

corporate communications on human rights impacts. Section II presents original qualitative empirical findings based on my analysis of corporate representations concerning human rights issues. Section III provides a survey of selected general codes of conduct intended to provide guidance to corporations. It presents selected human rights relevant provisions of industry-level codes of conduct created through multistakeholder initiative partnerships.

I compare representative corporate reports and codes of conduct across different industry sectors for selected corporations that have confronted allegations of complicity in human rights abuses to demonstrate the evolving approaches of business enterprises to address human rights challenges. In the process, I present insights into the trends of an emerging transnational regulatory regime that relies on greater corporate transparency in response to changing community expectations to govern the social and environmental impacts of business enterprises. Corporate reports often use the concept of "sustainability" to capture the human rights and environmental issues activists have raised over the years.

## I. Policy Commitments and Public Reporting to Promote Human Rights

The 2008 Framework for Business and Human Rights makes clear that business enterprises have a responsibility to respect human rights. The 2011 UN Guiding Principles (UNGPs) contain provisions that pertain to codes of conduct and corporate communications about social performance. Corporate responsibility, as detailed in the UNGPs, involves avoiding infringing on the human rights of others and addressing adverse human rights impacts in which the corporation is involved.[3] There are three things a business should ensure that they have in place to respect rights:

1. A policy commitment to meet their responsibility to respect human rights;
2. A human rights due-diligence process to identify, prevent, mitigate, and account for how they address their impacts on human rights; and
3. Processes to enable the remediation of any adverse human rights impacts they cause or to which they contribute.[4]

Corporate codes of conduct and corporate sustainability reporting both can aid the promotion of human rights protections by reducing the risk of a company's involvement in adverse human rights impacts.

[3] *Guiding Principles on Business and Human Rights*, *supra* note 2, at 13.
[4] *Id.* at 15.

## A. Policy Commitments: The UN Guiding Principles on Business and Human Rights

Responsible business conduct must start with a commitment to respect human rights. Commitment can drive change. Principle 16 of the UNGPs provides:

> As the basis for embedding their responsibility to respect human rights, business enterprises should express their commitment to meet this responsibility through a statement of policy that:
>
> (a) Is approved at the most senior level of the business enterprise;
> (b) Is informed by relevant internal and/or external expertise;
> (c) Stipulates the enterprise's human rights expectations of personnel, business partners and other parties directly linked to its operations, products or services;
> (d) Is publicly available and communicated internally and externally to all personnel, business partners and other relevant parties;
> (e) Is reflected in operational policies and procedures necessary to embed it throughout the business enterprise.[5]

The interpretative commentary that accompanies Principle 16 provides that the policy statement of commitment should be publicly available and provided to all parties the business enterprise contracts with, such as security providers, or that are connected to business operations, such as investors. The commentary also calls on companies to communicate its policy commitment externally to potentially affected stakeholders in instances where business operations present significant human rights risks.[6] Internal communications of company policy commitments and procedures regarding human rights should "make clear what the lines and systems of accountability will be."[7] Individuals in relevant business functions should receive support and training in order to promote conduct consistent with the policy commitment.

The commentary emphasizes the importance of policy coherence. To that end, the entire business enterprise should align the policies and procedures governing general business activities and relationships with the responsibility to respect human rights. In sum, incorporating human rights should be a priority

[5] *Id.* at 16.
[6] *Id.*
[7] *Id.*

for business enterprises and "embedded from the top of the business enterprise through all its functions."[8]

### 1. Corporate Codes of Conduct as Policy Commitments

Codes of ethics are increasingly prevalent among large transnational corporations.[9] The majority of large US corporations have some form of a code of ethics.[10] Several transnational corporations have created codes of conduct, or have endorsed industry association codes, or codes as supply-chain regulatory strategies. These codes serve to structure relationships with business partners and to set expectations for suppliers. Some corporate codes of conduct contain a policy commitment to respect human rights, and many corporations have developed a separate human rights policy guidance.

## B. Communication: The UN Guiding Principles on Business and Human Rights

The UNGPs also contain provisions that pertain to corporate reporting and communications. The principles contemplate that reporting related to human rights should be of a form and frequency sufficient to empower an interested audience to assess the effectiveness of how a business enterprise addresses its human rights impacts. In pertinent part, Principle 21 of the UNGPs provides:

In all instances, communications should:

1. Be of a form and frequency that reflect an enterprise's human rights impacts and that are accessible to its intended audiences;
2. Provide information that is sufficient to evaluate the adequacy of an enterprise's response to the particular human rights impact involved;
3. In turn not pose risks to affected stakeholders, personnel, or to legitimate requirements of commercial confidentiality.[11]

The interpretative commentary accompanying Principle 21 offers further clarification for business enterprises about communicating human rights concerns. Beyond developing a human rights policy, the responsibility to respect human rights demands that a corporation can also demonstrate that it respects human

[8] *Id.* at 16.
[9] Mark S. Schwartz, *A Code of Ethics for Corporate Codes of Ethics*, 41 J. Bus. Ethics 27, 28–29 (2002).
[10] *Id.*
[11] Ruggie, *supra* note 6, at 20.

rights in practice. As the commentary to Principle 21 puts it, a company should have policies and processes in place through which it can "know and show" respect for human rights.[12] The commentary explains that showing "involves communication, providing a measure of transparency and accountability to individuals or groups who may be impacted and to other relevant stakeholders, including investors."[13] According to the commentary, communication may take many forms, including "in-person meetings, online dialogues, consultation with affected stakeholders, and formal public reports."[14] The commentary observes that formal corporate reporting continues to evolve and offers corporate responsibility, corporate sustainability reports, and integrated financial reports as examples of advances beyond traditional annual reports.

Most communications by corporations about social and environmental issues are not required and are not regulated, and what corporations report varies widely. The commentary to Principle 21 offers guidance:

> The reporting should cover topics and indicators concerning how enterprises identify and address adverse impacts on human rights. Independent verification of human rights reporting can strengthen its content and credibility. Sector-specific indicators can provide helpful additional detail.[15]

The commentary also makes clear that reporting by enterprises is "expected where risks of severe human rights impacts exist, whether this is due to the nature of the business operations or operating contexts."[16]

Significantly, the commentary to Principle 21 encompasses potential audiences beyond shareholders to include stakeholders, and in particular calls for individuals or groups likely to be impacted by the practices or policies of the enterprise to have access to information. It is important that the commentary recognizes a range of ways communications can occur, including direct in-person meetings and dialogues. It envisions corporate engagement on human rights beyond pro forma mention in a formal sustainability report or securities filing. Active participation in a multistakeholder initiative offers an opportunity to share information and to gather knowledge about human rights impacts and improving practices.

### 1. Public Sustainability and Social Responsibility Reporting

Like codes of conduct, business enterprises have voluntarily elected to issue sustainability and CSR reports.

[12] *Id.*
[13] *Id.*
[14] *Id.*
[15] *Id.*
[16] *Id.*

## II. Rights and Responsibility Rhetoric in Corporate Reporting

This section presents the methods and procedures that I used to test the thesis that voluntary CSR codes evolve to complement existing human rights norms as shareholder and stakeholder interest in allegations of corporate complicity in human rights abuses increases. I discuss the research design, case selection, data-collection procedures, data analysis, and key general findings. I outline the methods used to evaluate and interpret the data. To gain insight into the impact of the emerging regulatory soft law standards at the international and industry levels in response to allegations of corporate complicity in human rights abuses, I conducted a critical discourse analysis of how transnational corporate actors address issues of human rights, ethics, and CSR in their codes of conduct and in sustainability reports. The objective of my analysis was to identify trends and common terms in corporate rhetoric on social responsibility and human rights for purposes of cross-comparison between specific companies, across particular industry sectors, and in relation to recent developments in law and policy that pertain to incorporating human rights concerns into business conduct.

### A. Research Design

I used a qualitative empirical research design to examine changes that corporations incorporate in rights-and-responsibilities-related discourse after "crises" related to allegations of their involvement in human rights abuses. For the purpose of my analysis, crisis events include litigation or allegations of corporate complicity in human rights violations reported in global media outlets. In order to fully understand the mechanisms at play in the phenomenon of pressure exerted and elevated expectations and changes that corporations make in the aftermath, I used a series of case studies of the human rights challenges that corporations in different industry sectors have confronted in recent years. A multiple case study design was the most appropriate method to adopt for this research, as it provided an opportunity to study patterns and trends with respect to when, whether, and how corporations change the rhetoric they use to discuss human rights and corporate responsibility in the context of crises.

Discourse analysis is a research methodology that investigates how social power is produced and reproduced in various texts taken in social, economic, and political context.[17] In critical discourse analysis, rhetoric is more than a mere

[17] *See* Lolita Buckner Inniss, *Sisters Underneath Their Skin* 82 (2011) (unpublished dissertation on file with author); Teun A. Van Dijk, *Critical Discourse Analysis*, in 1 THE HANDBOOK OF DISCOURSE ANALYSIS 466, 466–467 (Deborah Tannen, Heidi E. Hamilton, & Deborah Schiffrin eds., 2015).

messaging of particular content; it is an "action made upon a reader" to produce a particular effect in service of the strategic intent of the author.[18] Accordingly, texts must be examined for more than the meaning of a given message, as well as for the way the text performs.[19] For example, legal texts including international human rights treaties perform to produce normative authority. Legal discourses can shape social discourses while also being subject to social discourses that generate a reciprocal relationship in that there is an exchange between stakeholders that serves to inform content and meaning.[20] Critical discourse analysis locates its origins in linguistics, yet it is an interdisciplinary approach that understands language to constitute social practice.[21] Meaning is discursively constructed and social issues are shaped in large part by discourses.[22] Among the operative analytical tools available for discourse analysis are metaphor and word—or phrase-level concepts that allow for classification and the interpretation of connotation.[23] For example, in discussions of immigration, the decision to use the term "illegal alien" rather than "undocumented" assumes a particular view of immigrant identities. Classifications are how an author elects to name and label people, places, things, or phenomena, while connotations are the associations and nuances of meaning beyond the words used to label and classify. Social processes motivate the creation of a text, and social structures create the confines within which individuals and institutions create meaning in interaction with texts. Through a close reading and analysis of different discourses, whether textual, oral, or visual, it is possible to gain insight into the manner in which meaning evolves.

What does it mean for business to have a "responsibility to respect human rights"? To understand, I take corporate communications as texts that contribute to the social meaning of corporate responsibility where human rights may be at risk.[24] I use corporate sustainability reports not to test their truth or falsity but to examine their contributions to an ever-evolving understanding of

[18] Stanley Fish, *Literature in the Reader Affective Stylistics*, 2 New Literary History No. 1, at 123, 124.

[19] *Id.*

[20] *See* Johanna Niemi-Kiesilainen, Paivi Honkatukia, & Minna Ruuskanen, *Legal Texts as Discourses*, in Exploiting the Limits of Law 69 (Ava Gunnarson, Evan-Maria Svensson, & Margaret Davies, eds., 2007).

[21] Ruth Wodak & Michael Meyer, Methods of Critical Discourse Analysis 2 (2001).

[22] Ruth Wodak, *Critical Linguistics and Discourse Analysis*, in Discursive Pragmatics 50, 51–52 (Jan-Ola Ostman, Jef Verschueren, & Jan Zienkowski eds., 2011).

[23] *See, e.g.*, George Lakoff & Mark Johnson, Metaphors We Live By (1980); Sara Mills, Discourse 8 (2004).

[24] *See, e.g.*, Ruth Breeze, Corporate Discourse 29 (2013); Jerry M. Carlton & Nancy B. Kurland, *A Theory of Stakeholder Enabling: Giving Voice to an Emerging Postmodern Praxis of Organizational Discourse*, in Postmodern Management and Organizational Theory (David M. Boje, Robert P. Ghepart, & Tojo Joseph Thatchenkery eds., 1996); Frank De Bakker et al, *Tracing the Evolution of Corporate Discourse on Corporate Social Responsibility: A Longitudinal, Lexicological Study in Managing Corporate Social Responsibility* in Action: Talking, Doing, Measuring (Frank de Bakker, Frank den Hond, & Professor Peter Neergaard eds., 2016); Frank den Hond et al, *Managing Corporate Social*

the social obligations of business and the contrasting cultures of different industry sectors. My discourse analysis aims to assess the extent to which there is an incorporation of human rights concepts in the corporate codes of ethics and sustainability reporting that shapes a business enterprise's understanding of corporate responsibility and obligations to respect human rights. My analysis examines the manner in which discourse is deployed by business enterprises when confronted with pressure from shareholders and external stakeholders.

### 1. Data Selection

The codes of conduct for leading companies in industry sectors identified by human rights advocates as confronting human rights challenges, and against whom allegations of complicity in abuse were made with the most frequency, were the material I analyzed. The sectors I selected for analysis included apparel and textiles; extractives; food, beverage, and agriculture; and consumer-electronics technology. The cases I selected for this study came from companies with both numerous voluntary CSR initiatives and numerous allegations of involvement in human rights abuses. Table 6.1 shows the specific company brands in each of these targeted sectors.

I selected the following terms for analysis across all industry sectors: *human rights*, *ethics*, *values*, *corporate social responsibility*, *sustainability*, *customers/users*, *investors/shareholders/stakeholders*, *employees/labor*, *law*, and *legal*. I went on to search for reference to the proper titles of international human rights policy instruments that make reference to human rights obligations, such as the UN Guiding Principles on Business and Human Rights and the OECD Guidelines. I also searched for terms specific to the types of human rights issues salient in each industry sector. For example, *security* in the extractives sector and *privacy* in the technology sector.

**Table 6.1** List of companies in the case study by sector.

| Agriculture, Food, and Beverage | Apparel | Extractives (Oil and Gas) | Technology |
|---|---|---|---|
| Coca-Cola | Adidas | Chevron | Apple |
| Nestle | Gap | ExxonMobil | Facebook |
| PepsiCo | Nike | Shell | Microsoft |

*Responsibility in Action: Reconciling Rhetorical Harmony and Practical Dissonance* in MANAGING CORPORATE SOCIAL RESPONSIBILITY IN ACTION: TALKING, DOING, MEASURING (Frank de Bakker, Frank den Hond, & Professor Peter Neergaard eds., 2016).

2. Data Collection

The codes of conduct and the sustainability reports were obtained from the publicly available website of each business. My data collection proceeded in three phases. First, a crisis event of alleged complicity in human rights abuses was identified for a leading corporation in a given industry sector. Media reports of the alleged incident were then reviewed. Next, the company's code of conduct was reviewed. Then, available CSR—or sustainability reports—were collected from three different points in time: (1) pre-allegation; (2) post-allegation; and (3) present. A review of these public representations—made just prior to the allegations of abuse became known, just after the exposure of abuse allegations, and latest available report—was conducted. Finally, the codes and reports of competing companies in that industry sector were reviewed for common terms as points of comparison in order to assess whether different companies approached corporate responsibility and human rights issues in different ways.

3. Data Analysis

I read the selected company codes of conduct and sustainability reports to gain a deeper understanding of the substantive content of representations of responsibility and avoiding human rights risks before I conducted a detailed analysis of the data. This review enabled me to identify words that were related to crises events, those that occurred frequently in the sustainability reports prior to the crisis events, and those that appeared after the crises events. I hypothesized that more responsible companies would change what they disclosed about human rights after advocacy organizations had exposed human rights issues. Put another way, I sought to test whether the way a corporation or an industry sector addressed human rights issues would be altered after confronting major crisis events involving allegations of their involvement in human rights abuse. To gain insight into whether soft law standards set by the UN Framework and Guiding Principles on Business and Human Rights and the extent to which reputational risk associated with allegations of complicity in abuses or unethical actions create incentives for corporate actors to change policies, I conducted a close analysis of how business enterprises talk about human rights, sustainability, corporate responsibility, and ethics.

I conducted my detailed content analysis of the rhetoric used in corporate codes of conduct and sustainability reports using the software NVivo, a platform that supports qualitative, mixed methods research. I used the platform to code corporate reports for the frequency with which human rights–related issues are reflected in the information presented to the public. I ran word-frequency queries for the first one hundred frequently used words in the reports. I also queried terms relevant to human rights and corporate responsibility in the content of the document and in the context of crisis incident. I narrowed these searches by restricting them to words of more than four letters in length. Using Microsoft Excel's search query and the words I had selected, I then compared the word frequencies from the sustainability reports prior to the crisis period to the word frequency from the sustainability reports after the crisis period. I also included words that that were not part of the list but appeared often in the word-frequency list and were related to crisis events.

Next, I reviewed the weighted percentage use of the words to analyze whether words differed prior to the challenge or crisis and after the challenge or crisis. Weighted percentages better reveal the relative frequency with which terms are used than a numerical count of the number of times a word appears in a text. Weighted percentages were my preferred basis of comparison, because comparing the actual word counts would have been misleading—sustainability reports varied in length and total word count for each year.

In addition to the word frequencies, I also ran text searches for the keywords and extracted "word clouds" and "word trees" in order to further analyze the context within which words were used in the sustainability reports. Word clouds show terms used most frequently in a text in larger fonts and other less frequent but significant terms in smaller font. Word clouds visually represent salient concepts contained in a text. Word trees display the context in which a term appears and visually represents the relationship between different concepts. I reviewed the data with a view toward counting references to terms that are relevant to CSR and human rights issues, thus most salient or material, for that particular sector.

I analyzed the data for evidence of an evolving understanding of what responsible business conduct requires where international human rights are at issue. I then compared the data collected and analyzed with what specific companies are saying and what they are doing to manage the perceptions of investors, consumers, and other stakeholders.

My review was aimed at conducting a comparative content analysis of common terms significant for the sector as identified by human rights activists. I then compared policy content with known practice as reported in public forums to assess whether different companies of approach similar issues in different ways. I considered whether some corporations were doing better than their competitors with respect to policy commitments and performance, and then assessed the codes for how they compared to standards being set by global policy initiatives on business and human rights and developed through industry multistakeholder initiatives.

To test and better understand how emerging voluntary CSR codes of conduct may appropriately be seen as obligatory compacts with activist investors and conscious consumers, I looked for rhetoric related to responsibility or requirement. My review of the codes considered whether there had been any progress or change over time in the content of policy statements and corporate reporting with respect to human rights impacts. The codes were assessed for the extent to which corporations came to give more or less attention to CSR and human rights issues over the time period. All of these findings were then compared with the competing rankings and indices in the industry sector created by activists or investors.

My findings inform answers to the following questions:

- *Has investor, consumer, and community pressure related to human rights abuses contributed to corporate responsibility progress?*
- *Has there been progress or change over time in the content of corporate policy statements and sustainability reporting with respect to human rights impacts? Has progress, if any, been permanent?*
- *Have leading corporations given more or less attention to human rights issues over time?*
- *Are some corporations doing better than their competitors in the industry sector addressing issues relevant to human rights?*
- *Have CSR initiatives addressed articulated constituency concerns?*
- *Do corporate responsibility policy and reported human rights performance measure up to emerging international standards?*

## B. Human Rights Challenges and Corporate Responsibility Reporting

### 1. Agriculture, Food, and Beverage

Corporations in the food and beverage industry face similar human rights challenges that often intersect with environmental issues and inequality. Labor rights abuses on farms and in factories as well as conflicts over the use of land and water resources are especially salient concerns for the sector. In some instances companies have been connected to placing human rights at risk, on other occasions companies have been complicit in abuses, sometimes a company's conduct causes violations. Expectations for large companies to address these issues have increased as evidenced by shareholder proposals, bad publicity, boycotts, and stated consumer preference for "green" and responsible brands.

#### *a. PepsiCo Human Rights Challenges*

Like other global food and beverage companies, PepsiCo has been implicated in contributing to adverse human rights impacts. For example, a

2008 shareholder proposal raised concerns about the company's impacts on water resources.[25] In 2015, a shareholder proposal sought information about potential rights risks associated with the sugar supply chain.[26] In 2016, one of PepsiCo's largest suppliers of palm oil, IndoAgri, was accused of child labor and abusive worker conditions on their Indonesian plantation sites.[27]

PepsiCo's sustainability reports reveal that the company became more responsive to rights-related risks raised by concerned stakeholders over time. I reviewed a decade of reports to detect patterns in communicated policy changes and practices relevant to human rights issues raised by investors, consumers, and activists. My quantitative review revealed that the term "human rights" never appeared in PepsiCo's 2006 report. The word "water" appeared 61 times in the 2006 report at a weighted percentage of 0.18. By 2007, after activists alleged PepsiCo's business operations put water at risk, the number of times the word "water" appeared in the company's report increased significantly from the prior year with 168 references at a weighted percentage of 0.38, more than double the amount of attention given to the issue just one year earlier. PepsiCo's 2007 report also includes 10 references to the term "human rights" at a weighted percentage of 0.04. By 2017, the weighted percentage of the term "human rights" appearing in PepsiCo's report increased to 0.11 percent with the amount of coverage given to water remaining constant.

**i. Content Change: Human Rights and CSR Reports** PepsiCo's 2006 CSR report titled "Performance with Purpose" is introduced with a letter to shareholders co-signed by Steven Reinemund, the Executive Chairman and Chairman of the Board, and Indra Nooyi, Chairman Elect and Chief Executive Officer.[28] The 2006 report appears to address shareholders, not stakeholders. For example, the introductory letter leads with overview information about the firm's financial returns instead of social impacts.[29] The letter explains that the report will show how the company strikes a "balance" between strong returns on investments and delivering "Performance with Purpose" through "giving back" to the communities

[25] PepsiCo, Inc., Notice of 2008 Annual Meeting of Shareholders and Proxy Statement (Form DEF 14A), at 47 (Mar. 24, 2008).

[26] Dr. Pepper Snapple Group, Inc., Notice of 2015 Annual Meeting of Shareholders and Proxy Statement (Form DEF 14A), at 19–20 (Mar. 30, 2015).

[27] Beh Lih Yi, *Pepsi Cuts Ties with Palm Oil Supplier over Labor Abuse Claims*, Reuters (Jan. 25, 2018), https://www.reuters.com/article/us-indonesia-palmoil-labour/pepsico-cuts-ties-with-palm-oil-supplier-over-labor-abuse-claims-idUSKBN1FD1UE.

[28] PepsiCo, PepsiCo 2006: Performance with Purpose 2–3 (2006), https://www.pepsico.com/docs/album/annual-reports/2006-Annual-English.pdf.

[29] *Id.* at 2.

the company serves.[30] The letter from Pepsi leadership does not refer to human rights; instead it discusses "human sustainability," a concept related to consumer health and product nutritional balance.

PepsiCo published a combined report for the years 2007–2008, titled "Our Sustainability Journey," continuing variations on the company's "Performance with Purpose" theme. Instead of a signed statement from the CEO, there is a "Q&A," in which CEO Indra Nooyi answers questions such as "How does the Performance with Purpose mission tie in with our business?" and "How is the company addressing water issues?"

The 2007–2008 report presents an overview that proclaims: "In a world that continues to experience unprecedented economic, environmental and social challenges, PepsiCo-one of the world's largest food and beverage companies-recognizes our *responsibilities* to help make a difference."[31] There is less discussion of charity and philanthropy and more discussion of responsibility. The rhetoric of the report signals a significant shift indicating that addressing environmental, social, and governance issues is not just voluntary but increasingly necessary.

The report explains that the company is moving "towards developing and enhancing metrics to more meaningfully reflect PepsiCo's global performance."[32] It offers that, while this will take time, PepsiCo is committed to bringing a "sharper focus to achieving demonstrable progress and to integrating sustainability goals more fully," and announces that PepsiCo now follows the guidelines of the Global Reporting Initiative.

In contrast to the 2006 report, which was clearly addressed to shareholders, the 2007–2008 report intends to reach a broader audience: the company represents: "employees, customers, consumers, shareholders, analysts and other non-governmental (NGO) groups interested in PepsiCo and sustainability."[33] The 2007–2008 report lists the company's sustainability achievements and awards. This is significant because, as commonly acknowledged in the business community, "what gets measured gets managed" and could portend a path toward managing human rights risks though impact assessments and due diligence that could prevent violations. Indeed, as human rights rankings could prove an effective way of elevating human rights as a priority. This rhetorical shift demonstrates that for public perception and brand reputation it is now important for Pepsi to seem to be succeeding in social performance.

Still, Pepsi's report remains relatively thin on human rights references. Human rights are only referenced in the context of "talent sustainability" and workplace

[30] *Id.*

[31] PEPSICO, 2008 ANNUAL REPORT: WE ARE PERFORMANCE WITH PURPOSE 2 (2008), https://www.pepsico.com/docs/album/annual-reports/2008-annual-english.pdf?sfvrsn=2fe2d333_4.

[32] *Id.*

[33] *Id.*

policies.[34] The report highlights the introduction of the new "PepsiCo Human Rights Workplace Policy." However, it is not clear whether the firm's new human rights policy contemplates addressing adverse human rights impacts beyond the company's workplace, but the report provides that the company's partners, suppliers, contractors, and vendors are encouraged to share PepsiCo's "commitment to human rights."[35]

The report also includes a very brief mention of "Stakeholder Collaboration," and states that PepsiCo is a signatory in to the UN Global Compact and that the company is committed to collaborating with its various constituents to ensure their health and safety.[36]

In its 2017 "Performance with Purpose" report, PepsiCo outlines an approach to sustainability in a letter from Chairman and CEO Nooyi.[37] The 2017 report organizes PepsiCo's sustainability discussion around "products," "planet," and "people," reframing what the company had originally referred to as human sustainability, environmental sustainability, and talent sustainability.[38] Following PepsiCo's CEO letter, there is a Q&A with the company's Vice Chairman and Chief Scientific Officer of Global Research and Development conducted by the CEO and president of Ceres, a sustainability nonprofit organization that works with institutional investors.[39] The exchange explores questions such as "How are you using transparency and disclosure as tools for getting results?"[40] This shows Pepsi's engagement with investors; the company is in conversation to communicate with investors and share information speaking to concerns about social and environmental impacts.

The 2017 report more clearly demonstrates an understanding that human rights issues extend beyond workplace diversity. For example, a "Perspectives" section of the report features a Q&A outtake with Oxfam America's Senior Advisor on Land Rights and Markets commenting on questions such as "What is the biggest human rights challenge for the food and beverage industry to address?"[41] This exchange shows engagement with the concerns raised by civil society activists.

PepsiCo has also expanded its discussion of human rights by highlighting how both the company and the PepsiCo Foundation are now working to "leverage" scale and external partnerships to ensure that the human rights of all people in the company's value chain are respected.[42] The report features a section titled

34 *Id.* at 40.
35 *Id.* at 41.
36 *Id.* at 40.
37 PEPSICO, 2017 ANNUAL REPORT: PERFORMING WHILE TRANSFORMING 1–3 (2017), https://www.pepsico.com/docs/album/annual-reports/pepsico-inc-2017-annual-report.pdf [hereinafter PEPSICO, 2017 REPORT].
38 *Id.* at 2–3.
39 *Id.* at 4; *see also About Us*, CERES, https://www.ceres.org/about-us (last visited Mar. 5, 2020).
40 PEPSICO, 2017 REPORT, *supra* note 37, at 4.
41 *Id.* at 27.
42 *Id.* at 28.

"Promoting Human Rights Around the World," outlining the standards PepsiCo uses to regulate conduct concerning human rights issues and introducing the company's Sustainable Sourcing Program, Sustainable Farming Program, and its Global Labor Human Rights Assessment Program.[43] The report announces the launch of a new agricultural grievance mechanism process that allows third parties to raise concerns about environmental and social risks in PepsiCo's value chain. PepsiCo has also introduced a "Speak Up!" hotline to receive reports about human rights concerns. This indicates that the company is attempting to create space for other voices to raise issues and that the firm will use its position to reduce adverse social and environmental impacts.

PepsiCo has announced that its approach to respecting the human rights of workers and local communities throughout its operations and value chain is now informed by the UN Guiding Principles on Business and Human Rights. The report also references the International Bill of Human rights and the International Labour Organization (ILO) Declaration on Fundamental Principles and Rights at Work. To promote human rights, PepsiCo reports that it has prioritized:

- Embedding respect for human rights throughout our business
- Conducting due diligence to proactively identify, address and track potential human rights impacts in our value chain
- Engaging with stakeholders, including rights holders, to inform our programs and approach
- Providing effective grievance mechanisms and access to remedy in the event we may have caused or contributed to adverse human rights impacts.[44]

Analysis of word trees affirms that PepsiCo's communication concerning human rights has become more sophisticated over the years in response to external pressure for change. For instance, Figure 6.1 shows a word tree of PepsiCo's 2006 sustainability report and Figure 6.2 shows a word tree of PepsiCo's 2017 sustainability report. Together, these visual representations demonstrate an increased use of the term "human rights" in relationship to a wider range of issues as branches of the 2017 word tree extends beyond the company's workplace health and safety policies to reach the promotion of human rights around the world. The word trees show how PepsiCo has grown to understand human rights performance information as important to share with stakeholders. The stylistic inclusion of other voices through outtakes and the Q&A format interviews with company leadership gives the feel of an exchange or dialogue responsive to

[43] *Id.* at 29.
[44] *Id.*

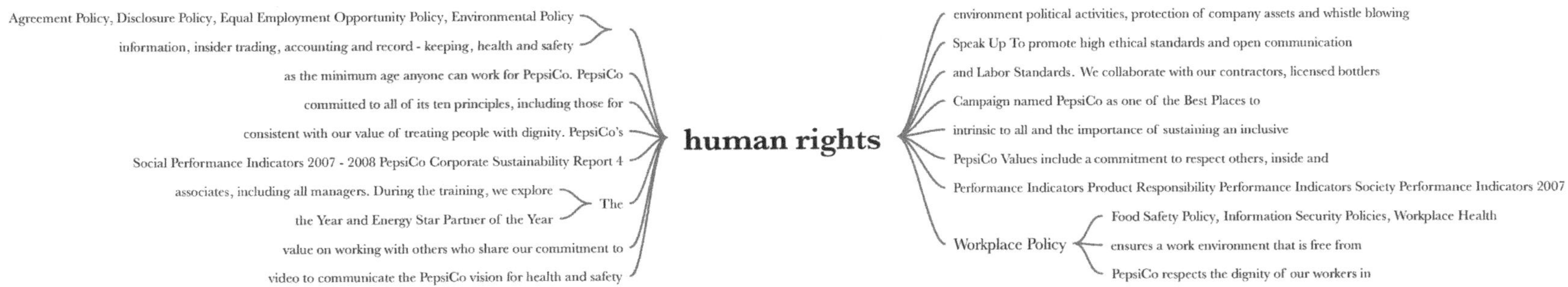


**Figure 6.1** Pepsi (2006)

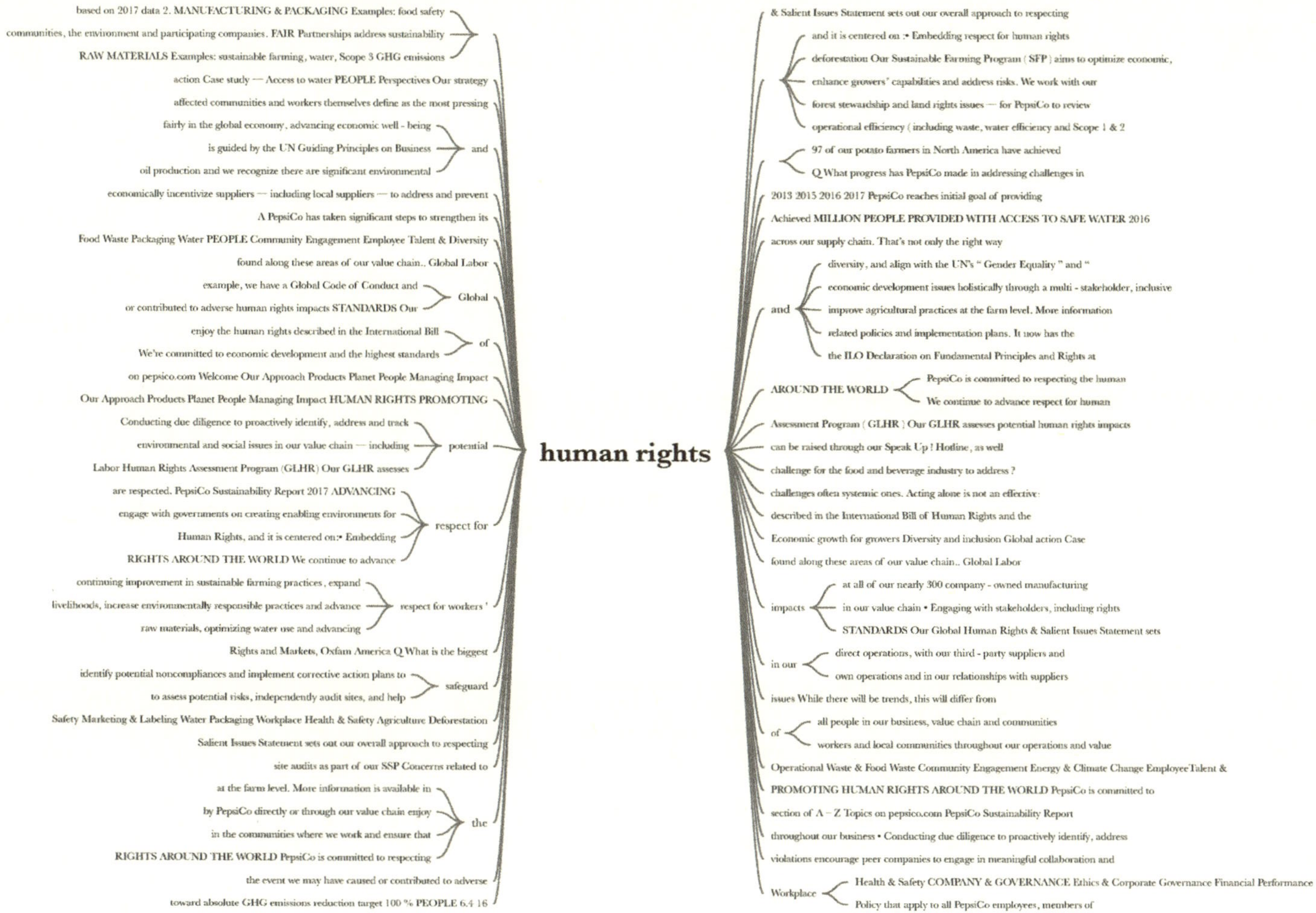


**Figure 6.2** Pepsi (2017)

questions raised that concerned constituencies have about PepsiCo's social and environmental impacts.

**ii. Conduct Change: PepsiCo Before and After Human Rights Challenges** In 2013, PepsiCo launched a Sustainable Farming Program aimed to improve its human rights practices.[45] From 2013 to 2017, the Sustainable Farming Program was implemented in thirty-eight countries and helped PepsiCo "identify potential noncompliances and implement corrective action plans to address human rights issues."[46] In 2017, PepsiCo "conducted or recognized over 1,000 on-site audits for [its] first-tier suppliers through [the] Sustainable Sourcing Program"[47] and identified two forced-labor-related noncompliances.[48] The noncompliances were addressed through corrective action plans, which set a time frame for remediation and tracked the suppliers' progress.[49] As a result of the identified noncompliances, PepsiCo updated its supplier code of conduct.[50] A follow-up audit of the sites identified that the sites had remediated the issues.[51]

PepsiCo also introduced a "grievance mechanism" to improve its approach to human rights concerns raised by third parties in 2017.[52] PepsiCo used this grievance mechanism to address child labor and worker exploitation allegations against Indofood Agri Resources (IndoAgri),[53] resulting in PepsiCo issuing a moratorium in 2018 on all sourcing of palm oil from IndoAgri.[54]

Along with formal grievance mechanisms, PepsiCo engages with external stakeholders to address "issues they raise on behalf of individuals in [the] value chain."[55] In 2016, the International Union of Food, Agricultural, Hotel, Restaurant, Catering, Tobacco and Allied Workers' Associations (IUF) alleged that one of PepsiCo's snack plants in Pakistan was not in compliance with local

45 PepsiCo, *Corporate Sustainability Report* (2017), *available at* https://www.pepsico.com/docs/album/sustainability-report/2017-csr/pepsico_2017_csr.pdf (last visited Nov. 7, 2019).
46 PepsiCo, *Pepsico Statement on Modern Slavery and Human Trafficking* (2017), *available at* https://www.pepsico.com/docs/album/esg-topics-policies/pepsico-modern-slavery-and-human-trafficking-statement.pdf?sfvrsn=eee2fdfd_10 (last visited Nov. 7, 2019).
47 *Id.* at 7.
48 *Id.* at 7.
49 PepsiCo, *Human Rights: Our Goal* (2019), *available at* https://www.pepsico.com/sustainability/human-rights (last visited Nov. 7, 2019).
50 PepsiCo, *supra* note 45, at 7.
51 *Id.* at 7.
52 PepsiCo, *PepsiCo Grievance Mechanism for Our Agricultural Supply Chain* (2017), *available at* https://www.pepsico.com/docs/album/esg-topics-policies/agricultural-supply-chain-grievance-mechanism-summary.pdf?sfvrsn=8d8bccf3_6 (last visited Nov. 7, 2019).
53 Lih Yi, *supra* note 27.
54 PepsiCo, *Sourcing of Palm Oil from Indonesia* (Jan. 2018), *available at* https://www.pepsico.com/docs/album/esg-topics-policies/pepsico-palm-oil-indonesia-sourcing.pdf (last visited Nov. 7, 2019).
55 PepsiCo, *supra* note 46.

standards and pointed to similar problems in other countries.[56] PepsiCo acknowledged the allegations and responded with an explanation of the company's policies and an offer to facilitate a meeting between union leaders and local management with an external Pakistani labor expert.[57]

In 2018, PepsiCo stated its commitment to work with Oxfam's FAIR Company-Community Partnerships project in Indonesia to address sustainability and human rights.[58] In 2018, PepsiCo instituted a Palm Oil Traceability Protocol, providing guidelines to external parties on how to verify the traceability data of PepsiCo's suppliers. Since launching the protocol, twenty-six suppliers reported traceability to plantation.[59] There has been an increase in traceability to the mill from 65 percent in 2015 to 97 percent at the end of 2017, and 22 percent of direct suppliers' self-reported mill data can be independently verified.[60]

## 2. The Apparel Industry Sector and Human Rights

Companies in the apparel sector confront similar social and environmental challenges. There are labor rights risks both on farms and in factories. Reports of forced and child labor taints Uzbek and Egyptian cotton.[61] Working conditions in factories are often discriminatory, hazardous, and sometimes deadly as the well-documented deaths of thousands of Bangladeshi women crushed underneath the rubble of their unsafe workplace as they made clothes for popular global brands demonstrated.

### *a. Adidas and Human Rights Challenges*

Like Nike, Adidas has been criticized for operating sweatshops, in Indonesia, India, China, and Myanmar.[62] Workers in factories supplying Adidas allege they

[56] The International Union of Food, Agricultural, Hotel, Restaurant, Catering, Tobacco and Allied Workers' Associations (IUF) is an international trade union federation based in Geneva, Switzerland composed of 387 trade unions in 120 countries representing over 10 million workers. For IUF's allegations against PepsiCo, *see* IUF PEPSICO INVESTOR UPDATE, A DISTURBING PATTERN OF HUMAN RIGHTS VIOLATIONS, Oct. 10, 2016, *available at* https://media.business-humanrights.org/media/documents/files/documents/PepsiCoInvestorUpdate10092016-e.pdf (last visited Nov. 20, 2020).

[57] For PepsiCo's response to abuse allegations, *see* PEPSICO'S RESPONSE TO IUF'S ALLEGATIONS OF RIGHTS VIOLATIONS 2, *available at* https://www.business-humanrights.org/en/latest-news/pepsicos-response/ (last visited Nov. 20, 2020).

[58] Shift, *PepsiCo's Participation in Oxfam's FAIR Company-Community Partnerships*, *available at* https://www.shiftproject.org/sdgs/land-rights/pepsico/ (last visited Nov. 7, 2019).

[59] PepsiCo, *Palm Oil Progress Report* (2018), at 4, *available at* https://www.pepsico.com/docs/album/esg-topics-policies/palm-oil-progress-report-2018.pdf?sfvrsn=69379f0c_2 (last visited Nov. 7, 2018).

[60] *Id.* at 4.

[61] Vikram Parekh, *Underage and Unprotected: Child Labor in Egypt's Cotton Fields*, HUM. RTS. WATCH (Jan. 2001); Namratha Somayajula, *Forced Labor Lives on in Uzbekistan's Cotton Fields*, HUM. RTS. WATCH (Apr. 16, 2019), https://www.hrw.org/news/2019/04/16/forced-labor-lives-uzbekistans-cotton-fields; *Patricia Jurewicz, Reducing Child Labor in Uzbekistan: Lessons Learned and Next Steps*, 21 U.C. Davis J. Int'l L. & Pol'y 191 (2014).

[62] Andrew Osborn, *Adidas Attacked for Asian "Sweatshops,"* THE GUARDIAN (Nov. 22, 2000), https://www.theguardian.com/world/2000/nov/23/.

were fired for demanding back pay and fair wages.[63] According to rights activists, Adidas maintained production contracts with factories with poor human rights records.[64]

United Students against Sweatshops started a campaign calling for universities to cut contracts with Adidas.[65] In 2012, rights researchers found that the predominantly female workforce in the Bangladeshi and Chinese factories supplying Adidas were subjected to sexual harassment and unrealistic production targets and were required to work in extremely unsafe conditions.[66]

My quantitative review revealed that in 2005 the term "human rights" occurred only once in Adidas's CSR report, at less than .01 percent coverage. However, by 2016, there were twenty-three references to the term "human rights" in Adidas's CSR report, at .09 percent coverage. References to related terms such as "suppliers" and "factories" also appeared more frequently in Adidas's sustainability reporting after stakeholders and activists expressed concerns, at .74 percent and .49 percent, respectively, in the company's 2016 report.

**i. Content Change: Adidas Before and After Human Rights Challenges** In its 2005 *Social and Environmental Report*, Adidas announced a new approach to its CSR reporting: "reports should help readers understand our approach to issues they are concerned about, so they can form their own view about how well we are doing."[67] According to Adidas, "a corporate report must reflect both the nature and circumstances of the company and the concerns of its stakeholders."[68] Adidas states that it will provide detailed sustainability information and Global Reporting Initiative data on its website. It also invites reader input by providing an email address for questions and comments.

While the term "human rights" does not appear in his letter introducing the 2005 report, Adidas CEO and Chairman Herbert Hainer does highlight that the company's compliance program earned Fair Labor Association accreditation. He also cites recognition from the Dow Jones Sustainability Index, the

63 *Id.*

64 Osborn, *supra* note 62.

65 Alison Shapiro, *Students against Sweatshops Asking Erickson to Cut Adidas Contract*, THE DAILY COLLEGIAN (Feb. 27, 2013), https://www.collegian.psu.edu/archives/article_aab3662d-282f-5fcd-af52-6f7d0d3bd5a5.html (last visited Mar. 5, 2020).

66 Gethin Chamberlain, *Olympic Brands Caught in Abuse Scandal, While Adidas, Nike and Puma Make Millions out of the Games Their Employees Are Claiming Exploitation*, THE OBSERVER (Mar. 3, 2012), https://www.theguardian.com/business/2012/mar/03/olympic-brands-abuse-scandal (last visited Mar. 5, 2020); Emily Dugan, *Forced Labor Claims Dent Image of London 2012*, THE INDEPENDENT (May 6, 2012), https://www.independent.co.uk/sport/olympics/forced-labour-claims-dent-image-of-london-2012-7717615.html (last visited Mar. 5, 2020).

67 ADIDAS GROUP, SOCIAL AND ENVIRONMENTAL REPORT 2005: CONNECTED BY FOOTBALL 4 (2005), https://www.adidas-group.com/media/filer_public/2013/08/26/connected_by_football_social_and_environmental_report_2005.pdf [hereinafter ADIDAS GROUP, 2005 REPORT].

68 *Id.* at 2.

FTSE4GOOD Index, and Ethibel's ESI Europe Index.[69] He reports on changes to CSR at Adidas, including integrating supplier compliance into core operations, establishing indicators to measure the efficacy of actions taken by suppliers to meet the company's social compliance and operational standards, and participating in multistakeholder initiatives to promote long-term improvements in the industry's social and environmental performance.[70] The company's reference to its standing rankings indicates an interest in speaking to a growing segment of the marketplace interested in social and environmental impacts. To the extent that accreditations and rankings can capture human rights impacts and improvements in human rights performance, business can be conducted in a way that is better aligned with respect for the rights of workers.

Beyond celebrating successes, Hainer's letter also shares the company's struggles. For instance, the letter discloses that the company had not met all of its goals, explaining, "[w]e failed to issue comprehensive guidelines on worker-management communications and guidance for small and medium-sized enterprises on health and safety."[71] Hainer's letter references founder Adi Dassler's "passion and dedication to performance" and pledges to bring that type of "teamgeist" to "the challenges of responding to stakeholder concerns and being a responsible business."[72] Adidas appeals to history and heritage and the values of the firm's founder. The report also acknowledges failure, goals were set and not met. Consumer research suggests that firms are forgiven for failures if difficulties are disclosed.

In a section of the 2005 report titled "Challenges and Responses," Adidas identifies a wide array of stakeholders and says that the information the company shares speaks to concerns raised by stakeholders[73] Adidas directs readers to the company website for information about meetings with its stakeholders, including its customers, its employees, its shareholders, its board of directors, trade associations, unions, its suppliers, and supply chain laborers. Professional athletes, retailers, distributors, and "opinion formers," including journalists, community members, and special interest groups are also identified as important Adidas stakeholders.[74]

Adidas explains that as "a highly visible brand that operates in a dynamic competitive environment and sources from a multilayered supply chain," it confronts particular challenges.[75] Among the challenges acknowledged by Adidas was "building credibility and trust" amid stakeholder concerns about the company's

[69] *Id.* at 4.
[70] *Id.*
[71] *Id.*
[72] *Id.* at 3.
[73] *Id.* at 8.
[74] *Id.* at 13.
[75] *Id.*

internal supply chain monitoring efforts. Indeed, concerned stakeholders are generally skeptical about the independence and impartiality of internal monitoring. Adidas acknowledges concerns about sourcing from certain countries—with poor working conditions or where freedom of association is legally restricted.[76]

Adidas addresses stakeholder concerns by summarizing the company's approach to "transparency, disclosure and collaboration."[77] Adidas explains that it practices "full disclosure" in response to specific requests for information from nongovernmental organizations, trade unions, and researchers, citing its disclosure of factory names and addresses to local affiliates of the International Textile, Garment, and Leather Workers Federation in Indonesia. Adidas also provided detailed information about collegiate licensed suppliers to universities in the United States.[78]

The 2005 report references "human rights" in a discussion of the challenges related to remaining both "competitive and customer-focused," explaining Adidas's Standards of Engagement (SOE), the company's code of conduct. Adidas reports that its SOE are "based on" ILO and UN conventions on human rights and employment practices.[79] According to Adidas, its SOE are "an integral part of the Global Operations cumulative factory rating system and ensures that customer demands and competitive advantages are achieved in a responsible environment."[80]

The SOE form the basis of Adidas' relationship with its suppliers and is treated as a "contractual obligation" such that all suppliers must be able to show compliance with Adidas's SOE before they can become authorized business partners.[81] Here, Adidas is acting as a regulator and could potentially push respect for human rights through structured contracting to ensure consequences for supplier failure to respect worker rights.

Adidas's Social and Environmental Affairs (SEA) team is responsible for monitoring supplier compliance with the SOE and for managing CSR for the entire business enterprise. The SEA team "collaborates closely" with Adidas's Global Operations team responsible for product development and sourcing.[82] The SEA team reports to the general counsel and the executive board of the company.[83]

[76] *Id.* at 8.
[77] Adidas Group, 2005 Report, *supra* note 67, at 8.
[78] *Id.* at 8.
[79] *Id.* at 10.
[80] *Id.*
[81] *Id.*
[82] *Id.*
[83] *Id.*

The 2005 report also makes explicit reference to "shareholder rights" and makes clear that as a publicly listed company, Adidas is "obligated to fulfil" the rights of shareholders related to receiving business information.[84] Adidas explains that representatives of the financial community are now making more detailed requests for information about how the company is managing risks, and points to the Global Reporting Initiative to promote corporate transparency, referencing the rise of transparency benchmarks and ratings.[85]

Reference to the term "human rights" does appear in the CEO letter introducing the 2016 Adidas Sustainability Progress Report titled *Calling All Creators*. Adidas's new CEO Kasper Rorsted offers: "Sports needs a space to exist . . . these spaces are increasingly endangered due to various threats to our world such as increased industrial pollution and its effect on the environment and our planet's climate, the violation of *human rights* such as forced labour . . . to name a few."[86] Rorsted asserts that Adidas will "aim to protect these spaces that have a direct link to our business," by targeting strategic priorities that center "people and product."[87] To that end, he announces that the company has set "ambitious, tangible and measurable goals" to achieve by 2020.[88]

Where past CEO statements introducing sustainability, the report recognized the common challenges the industry must confront highlighting collaborations in multistakeholder initiatives, there is a decidedly competitive in tone in Rorsted's letter and throughout the report emphasizing Adidas's achievements relative to others in the industry. For example, he states: "We do not only see sustainability as an opportunity to get a competitive advantage. We see it as an *obligation* for us as a global company to do business in a responsible and sustainable way."[89] Touting Adidas as one of few companies integrating sustainability into business operations, he said, "we are proud we are seen as being honestly committed to sustainability and a *leader* in our industry."[90] He credits Adidas's sustainability efforts with generating excitement about the company:

> Our focus on sustainability is not only recognized by investors, experts and consumers. It also excites our 60,000 employees and is a major reason why young people from all over the world would like to work for us. They want to be part of a company that has a clear mission.[91]

[84] *Id.* at 9.
[85] *Id.*
[86] Adidas Group, 2016 Sustainability Progress Report: Calling all Creators 5 (2016), https://www.adidas-group.com/media/filer_public/08/7b/087bf055-d8d1-43e3-8adc-7672f2760d9b/2016_adidas_sustainability_progress_report.pdf [Adidas Group, 2016 Report].
[87] *Id.*
[88] *Id.*
[89] *Id.*
[90] *Id.*
[91] *Id.*

As evidence of the company's leadership, the 2016 report points to Adidas's inclusion in global sustainability indices such as the Dow Jones Sustainability Index and the recognition for excellence it received as a "Gold Class and Industry Mover" from RobecoSAM,[92] the world's first asset-management firm focused exclusively on sustainability investment.[93] Adidas's North American organization earned a "perfect 100 point score" on the Human Rights Campaign Foundation's Corporate Equality Index, a benchmark on business policies and practices related to LGBTQ employees.

In a section devoted to discussing human rights, titled "How We Learn from our Partners: Thought Leadership in Protecting Human Rights," the report highlights Adidas's leading performance on human rankings, including the Corporate Human Rights Benchmark, which rates the human rights practices of companies and KnowTheChain (KTC), which rates companies on forced labor eradication.[94] Adidas earned the top spot among the global apparel and footwear industry from KTC for efforts to end forced labor, including its "Modern Slavery Outreach Program," its supply chain risk-mapping disclosures, and its willingness to work with partners in high-risk countries to curb modern slavery.[95] The company couches its rankings against these external metrics as "an important validation" of efforts to address human rights challenges.[96] The report states that the company will use ranking results to identify areas for improvement with respect to human rights.[97]

Adidas's explanation of its understanding of its social obligations with respect to human rights in the 2016 report is wholly consistent with concepts set forth in Pillar II of the UNGP, though the report doesn't make explicit reference to the standard it uses same terms and concepts as those contained in the UNGPs. For example:

> [W]e recognise our *responsibility to respect human rights* and the importance of showing that we are taking the necessary steps to fulfil this social obligation as a business. We do this by striving to operate responsibly along the entire value chain, safeguarding the rights of our own employees and those of our suppliers through our "Workplace Standards," and applying our influence

[92] *We are Sustainable Investing*, ROBECOSAM https://www.robecosam.com/en/about-us/ ("RobecoSAM is a sister company of Robeco, the Dutch investment management firm founded in 1929. Both entities are subsidiaries of ORIX Corporation Europe N.V., the center of asset management expertise for ORIX Corporation.").

[93] ADIDAS GROUP, 2016 REPORT, *supra* note 86, at 5.

[94] *Id.* at 10.

[95] *Id.*

[96] *Id.*

[97] *Id.*

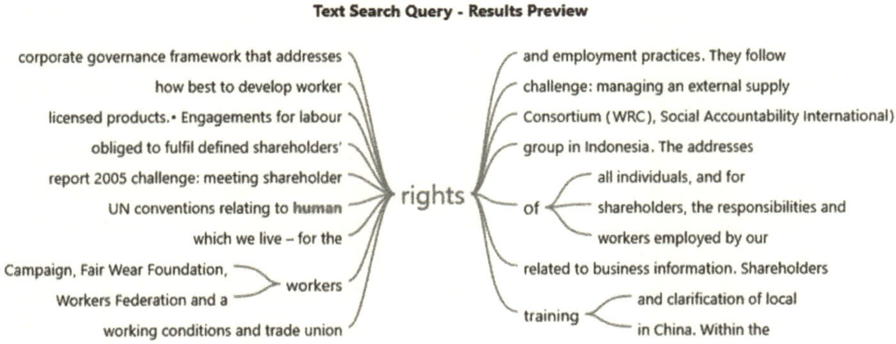


**Figure 6.3** Adidas (2005)

> to affect change wherever human rights issues are linked to our business activities.[98]

The report states that Adidas is still "seeking to understand and define the most *salient* issues to address as a company, to learn from them and use that knowledge."[99]

In a section titled "It Starts with Listening," the 2016 report explains the company's efforts to "empower workers" through implementation of the Adidas Workplace Standards. The company treats its supply chain code of conduct as "contractually binding rules" for factories to ensure worker health and safety.[100] Adidas reports that its code of conduct is informed by international law, ILO conventions, and the World Federation of Sporting Goods Industry model code of conduct.

Word trees of Adidas's CSR reports spanning time before, during, and after upticks in abuse allegations and the international community's endorsement of the UNGPs demonstrate that Adidas is incorporating rights. For instance, Figure 6.3 is a word tree of the term "human rights" as it appears in Adidas's 2005 CSR report connects the concept of human rights to working conditions and employment practices. Figure 6.4 shows a word tree of the company's 2016 report with branches from the term "human rights" reaching a broader range of issues beyond working conditions to reference responsibility, worker rights, benchmarks, audits, and monitoring. Taken together, Figures 6.3 and 6.4 illustrate the growing influence of human rights in Adidas's sustainability reporting.

[98] *Id.* at 10.
[99] *Id.* at 10.
[100] *Id.* at 40.

**Figure 6.4** Adidas (2016)

**ii. Conduct Change: Adidas Before and After Human Rights Challenges** Beyond meeting its responsibility to respect rights, Adidas's publication of a separate report, "Approach to Human Rights Defenders," suggests the company is willing promote the protection of human rights.[101] Adidas pledges to petition governments on behalf of at-risk rights defenders.[102] When reports of Syrian war refugees working in Turkey surfaced,[103] even though Adidas did not identify any Syrian refugee labor in its supply chain, acknowledging the larger humanitarian issue, Adidas joined BEST—Building Effective Solutions Together, a public-private collaboration with the Turkish Ministry of Labor and the Fair

[101] Adidas Group, The Adidas Group and Human Rights Defenders (2016), https://www.adidas-group.com/media/filer_public/f0/c5/f0c582a9-506d-4b12-85cf-bd4584f68574/adidas_group_and_human_rights_defenders_2016.pdf [hereinafter The Adidas Group and Human Rights Defenders]; *Policies and Standards*, Adidas Group, https://www.adidas-group.com/en/sustainability/reporting/policies-and-standards/.

[102] The Adidas Group and Human Rights Defenders, *supra* note 101, at 3.

[103] Patrick Kingsley, *From War to Sweatshop for Syria's Child Refugees*, The Guardian (May 6, 2016), https://www.theguardian.com/world/2016/may/06/war-to-sweatshop-for-child-refugees; Didem Talli, *As Refugees Pour in, Child Labor Booms in Turkey*, Al Jazeera America (Jan. 6, 2016), http://america.aljazeera.com/articles/2016/1/4/as-refugees-pour-in-child-labor-booms-in-turkey.html.

Labor Association. Adidas trained its suppliers in Turkey on the impact of illegal workers and the importance of legal and fair recruitment.[104] Adidas also created materials to inform Syrian refugees about their employment rights and established a bilingual Arabic and Turkish language hotline for workers.[105]

### 3. The Extractives Industry Sector and Human Rights

Companies in the extractive industry sector from oil and gas exploration and drilling to mining for rare earth minerals face similar human rights challenges and can present risks for the communities in which they operate by causing or contributing to adverse social and environmental impacts. The companies must operate where the resources exist. Unlike an apparel brand, these companies cannot easily relocate, and where firms have failed to negotiate with area affected communities conflicts have arisen. Significant capital investment may be required to locate resources. The costs of disrupted operations can also be high, costing the company money and environmental activists their lives. There have been documented instances of clashes with security forces hired to protect company property pillaging villages and killing peaceful protesters. Environmental damage and the changing climate have led to displacement and have been linked to the business activities of extractives companies.

#### *a. ExxonMobil and Human Rights Challenges and Communications*

ExxonMobil Corporation is the largest of the world's "Big Oil" companies, or "supermajors" and the largest refiner in the world, with thirty-seven oil refineries in twenty-one countries.[106] In 2001, the International Labor Rights Fund sued the company on behalf of villagers from Aceh in Indonesia, who reported human rights abuses by security forces hired by ExxonMobil.[107] The suit alleged that ExxonMobil employed military troops to secure its operations and that the company aided and abetted human rights violations through financial and other material support to the security forces.[108]

My review of ExxonMobil CSR reports before, during, and after the introduction of the UNGPs, human rights litigation, and activist climate change campaigns targeting the company revealed increased coverage of social and environmental issues of interest to activists and shareholder advocates. For example, my quantitative review revealed that in 2010 the term "human rights" was

[104] ADIDAS GROUP, 2016 REPORT, *supra* note 86, at 56.
[105] *Id.*
[106] *Big Oil*, WIKIPEDIA, https://en.wikipedia.org/wiki/Big_Oil (last visited Mar. 5, 2020).
[107] Complaint at 2, *John Doe v. Exxon Mobil Corp.* (2001), http://iradvocates.mayfirst.org/sites/default/files/06.11.01%20Exxon%20complaint.pdf.
[108] *Id.*

weighted 0.15 and occurred 55 times. In 2017, it was weighted 0.22 and occurred 28 times. In 2010, the term "climate change" was weighted 0.05 and occurred 14 times. In 2017, it was weighted 0.38 and occurred 42 times. Similarly, the term "community" increased in weighting from .23 pre-abuse allegations in 2010 to .58 post-abuse allegations. Company attention to these issues, at least with respect to communications, increased.

Since 2006, ExxonMobil has conducted annual "materiality assessments" to identify issues with the potential to significantly affect sustainability performance. For example, in its 2017 report, ExxonMobil evaluated key metrics informed by IPIECA reporting guidance, input from external stakeholders, a benchmark of peer company reports, and a media review.[109]

**i. Content Change: ExxonMobil Before and After Abuse Allegations** The 2010 ExxonMobil Corporate Citizenship Report titled "Taking on the World's Toughest Energy Challenges" is introduced by a letter from CEO Rex Tillerson. While there is no reference to "human rights" in his letter, he does mention "the critical importance of corporate accountability and responsibility" and repeatedly refers to "risks" and "challenges."[110] Tillerson notes that the company's experience after the Exxon Valdez oil spill "fundamentally shaped the way [ExxonMobil] understands and manages risks."[111] Tillerson recognizes that shareholder returns require managing risks. For example, he explains: "The sustainability of our business is based on our ability to apply consistent processes and systems in our daily operations to ensure that risk is identified, planned for, and successfully managed."[112] He asserts that the company's success depends on adherence to high safety and ethical standards and "embedding" environmental performance and community engagement in all aspects of its activities.[113]

In the report, ExxonMobil points to its Standards of Business Conduct as promoting values of human rights, labor standards, the environment, and anticorruption as outlined in the UN Global Compact.[114] The company's suppliers and contractors are expected to comply with local laws and regulations as well as ExxonMobil's policies and procedures with respect to human rights. Suppliers must meet prequalification requirements, and suppliers that fail to comply with ExxonMobil's Standards of Business Conduct are deemed to be in breach of

[109] ExxonMobil, 2017 Sustainability Report Highlights 7, 21, 30 (2017), https://corporate.exxonmobil.com/en/~/media/Global/Files/sustainability-report/publication/2017-Sustainability-Report.pdf [hereinafter ExxonMobil, 2017 Report].

[110] ExxonMobil, 2010 Corporate Citizenship Report 3 (2010), https://corporate.exxonmobil.com/-/media/Global/Files/sustainability-report/publication/2010-ccr.pdf.

[111] *Id.*

[112] *Id.*

[113] *Id.*

[114] *Id.* at 22.

contract. Contractors or suppliers "may be subject to contractual and legal remedies, including, in some cases, denial of access to [ExxonMobil] facilities and termination of the contract."[115]

The 2010 report devotes an entire section to "Community Engagement and Human Rights."[116] In it, ExxonMobil emphasizes that 75 percent of private security personnel contracts were revised to incorporate human rights concerns, that briefing sessions were conducted with security forces in Nigeria, and that ninety-five preconstruction surveys were conducted in Papua New Guinea.[117] ExxonMobil reports that its approach to managing impacts on local communities includes elements such as adherence to "corporate policies and expectations" and "national laws and universally recognized principles."[118]

In a subsection titled "Respecting Human Rights," ExxonMobil states: "We respect human rights in our operations not just because doing so fosters a stable business environment, but more importantly because it is the right and responsible thing to do."[119] The company also shares that it has participated in consultation processes leading to the creation of the UNGPs.[120] ExxonMobil states that while its approach is "consistent with the basic components" of the UNGPs, policies and processes will be assessed for consistency with the UN Special Representative's final report, and a computer-based human rights training module will be developed for distribution.[121]

The "socioeconomic management" portion of ExxonMobil's report encompasses "human rights, labor and workplace rights, economic development, cultural heritage, land use, social and environmental considerations, treatment of communities and indigenous peoples, security and relationships with host-country governments."[122]

ExxonMobil reports that it conducts impact assessments in order to mitigate negative impacts, recognizing its activities can affect host communities and other stakeholders. ExxonMobil Environmental, Socioeconomic, and Health Assessments (ESHIA) are conducted at the outset of a project and throughout the project lifecycle. The ESHIA process is informed by public consultation. ExxonMobil reports that it has introduced a Best Practices in External Affairs initiative. ExxonMobil's Operations Integrity Management System uses the company's Upstream Socioeconomic Management Standard, which provides

[115] *Id.* at 22.
[116] *Id.* at 44–47.
[117] *Id.* at 44.
[118] *Id.* at 45.
[119] *Id.* at 46.
[120] *Id.*
[121] *Id.* at 44.
[122] *Id.* at 45.

guidance on "key socioeconomic issues that should be identified and addressed throughout the upstream resource development life cycle."[123]

In addition to describing ExxonMobil's approach to managing community impacts and socioeconomic matters through an operations integrity mechanism, the human rights portion of the company's report discusses consultation and engagement with respect to Indigenous peoples and cultural heritage. ExxonMobil explains it has a "Cultural Heritage Management Plan," which aims to: (1) "avoid those sites which are to be protected from disturbance," and (2) "establish the process for the compensation, management, clearance, and salvage of sites that are authorized by the government for disturbance."[124]

The report also includes discussions of "Land Use and Resettlement" and "Addressing Security Concerns." ExxonMobil represents that it is committed to respect for property rights in its efforts to implement "free, prior and informed consultation of impacted communities" before operations start[125] and that it is "committed to safeguarding company personnel and property in a manner that respects human rights and fundamental freedoms."[126] The company claims that its resettlement activities are conducted consistent with international best practice as set forth in the International Finance Corporation Performance Standards on Social and Environmental Sustainability to restore the livelihoods of persons displaced by its projects.[127] The 2010 report references the Voluntary Principles on Security and Human Rights and the company's own Framework on Security and Human Rights that it designed to facilitate implementation of the Voluntary Principles cross referencing subjects covered with standards, IPIECA/API and the Global Reporting Initiative (GRI).[128] It also notes that security challenges in Nigeria and Papua New Guinea are being systematically addressed and regularly reviewed, and the company is conducting trainings for security forces protecting its assets.[129]

In 2017, ExxonMobil transitioned from a "corporate citizenship report" to a "sustainability report."[130] ExxonMobil's 2017 Sustainability Report Highlights is introduced by Chairman and CEO Darren Woods. His letter does reference "human rights," stating:

> For more than 135 years, ExxonMobil has strived to meet society's evolving needs. We work to meet growing demands for energy and chemical products

[123] *Id.*
[124] *Id.*
[125] *Id.* at 46.
[126] *Id.* at 47.
[127] *Id.* at 46.
[128] *Id.* at 47.
[129] *Id.*
[130] ExxonMobil, 2017 Report, *supra* note 109, at 6.

> while advancing other priorities such as economic growth, environmental protection, education, poverty reduction, health, security and human rights.[131]

His letter invites feedback on the report and provides a link to a website address.

The 2017 report lists the six key areas that anchor ExxonMobil's sustainability approach; among them, "Managing the risks of climate change" and "Community engagement and human rights." The 2017 sustainability report also collapses multiple concerns previously identified as central, such as "shareholder trust," "employee loyalty," "license to operate," and "consumer confidence" into one central category: "sustainability."

The 2017 report contains a statement from ExxonMobil's External Advisory Panel, whereas the 2010 report simply stated that an external advisory panel existed but did not share the advice provided by the panel. The panel's statement qualifies its comments, explaining: "This letter is not an official endorsement of ExxonMobil's sustainability report, the corporation, or its policies or strategies."[132] The letter is an evaluation of "the quality and progress made in ExxonMobil's sustainability reporting and transparency."[133] Because ExxonMobil is a leader that others in the energy industry will follow, the panel encourages the company and its management to be "more bold and transparent in all aspects of sustainability performance."[134]

The panel addresses human rights in the context of climate change: "We hope that the company will take further steps to demonstrate how climate change, the SDGs, human rights and other sustainability-related challenges link directly with corporate investments and programs central to its long-term business strategy."[135] The panel asks ExxonMobil to do more: "Due to the possible negative impacts climate change poses to business operations, human rights and economic development around the world, we urge further integration of climate change into the core of ExxonMobil's business strategy."[136] The panel acknowledges that the company's approach is consistent with the UNGPs and advises ExxonMobil to provide "greater specificity about practices and performance" on human rights to better align with "societal and industry expectations of best practices."[137] For instance, the company could increase efforts to identify potential adverse impacts and explain its procedures for identifying rights risks and processes for mitigating risks.[138]

As in 2010, a portion of the 2017 report is dedicated to "Community Engagement and Human Rights."[139] ExxonMobil's "Respecting Human Rights" discussion is more

[131] *Id.* at 3.
[132] *Id.* at 6.
[133] *Id.*
[134] *Id.* at 7.
[135] *Id.* at 6.
[136] *Id.*
[137] *Id.* at 7.
[138] *Id.*
[139] *Id.* at 23–25.

abbreviated but does reference international human rights instruments, including the Universal Declaration of Human Rights, the UNGPs, and the ILO Declaration on Fundamental Principles and Rights at Work.[140] The 2017 version also mentions the company's participation in the Voluntary Principles on Security and Human Rights. The company reports that more than five thousand ExxonMobil-contracted and host government security staff from twelve higher-risk countries were trained on the Voluntary Principles in 2017.[141] An "Explore More" section refers readers to the company website for details about a grievance procedure initiative in Indonesia and various philanthropic efforts, including childhood education, women's empowerment, and malaria prevention.[142] The 2017 report concludes with table of performance tends and directs readers to a link with an additional information on the company's sustainability reporting consistent with IPIECA, GRI, and the UN's Agenda 2030 Sustainable Development Goals (SDGs). The word trees in Figures 6.5 and 6.6 show how use of the term "human rights" has changed from Exxon's 2010 sustainability report (Figure 6.5) to its 2018 report (Figure 6.6).

**ii. Conduct Change: ExxonMobil Before and After Crisis Incidents** ExxonMobil has taken some steps to exert influence on the companies it works with to prevent human rights abuses by contractors following criticism for substantial human rights abuses committed by its security contractors.[143] Starting in 2013, the company started requiring security contractors to complete a training focused on protecting human rights.[144] Additionally, ExxonMobil began adding language to all of its private security contracts, requiring security personnel to uphold human rights.[145]

Additionally, ExxonMobil has taken steps to ensure that its supply chain is free of human rights abuses. In 2016, ExxonMobil implemented a review process for all materials sourced from countries where the US Department of Labor's lists a high probability included in the US Department of Labor's List of Goods Produced by Child Labor or Forced Labor.[146] In 2016, this process identified about three hundred purchases for further review; however, ExxonMobil found that none of these purchases were at risk of being produced using these practices.[147]

ExxonMobil has also taken some substantial steps to address climate change in its operations. The vast majority of these changes, meant to combat the effects of climate

[140] *Id.* at 24.
[141] *Id.* at 24.
[142] *Id.* at 25.
[143] ExxonMobil, Business and Human Rights Resource Centre, https://www.business-humanrights.org/en/exxonmobil-0 (last accessed Nov. 7, 2019) (interviewing ExxonMobil Public & Government Affairs Office).
[144] *Id.*
[145] *Id.*
[146] *Respecting Human Rights: Human Rights and the Supply Chain*, ExxonMobil, https://corporate.exxonmobil.com/en/community-engagement/sustainability-report/community-engagement-and-human-rights/respecting-human-rights#humanRightsInTheSupplyChain (last accessed Nov. 7, 2019).
[147] *Id.*

**Figure 6.5** ExxonMobil (2010)

**rights**

- These focus areas span the length and breadth
  - a forum for discussion and information - sharing among extractive industry
  - and the
    - need for improved access to effective remedy mechanisms.
    - status of implementation of the Framework in the
  - as well as the principles of our Standards of Business
  - labor
    - and workplace rights, economic development, cultural heritage, land use,
    - practices, financial and operational qualifications, export restrictions, and security
    - standards, the environment, and anti-corruption as outlined in
  - the
    - Fund for Peace, and consultations with John Ruggie, United
    - requirements of our Framework on Security and Human Rights,
  - All requests for quotations include clauses relating to the prohibition
  - Each session also includes information on the Voluntary Principles on
  - Professor Ruggie's 2008 report set forth a widely accepted policy
  - Since 2002, we have been an active participant in the
- abuses by third parties, the corporate responsibility to respect human
- Addressing security concerns
  - ENV3, ENV4, ENV5, ENVA8 ENVA8 SOCA1 SOC8,
  - SOC2, SOC6 SOC3, SOCA1 ENV6, H & S1
- and
  - Business Customers Suppliers Millions of consumers and industrial customers
  - fundamental freedoms. Framework on Security and Human Rights. Since
  - security training has been completed in 16 countries over
  - the 1998 Declaration on Fundamental Principles and Rights at
- arena as well as to incorporate feedback from trainees. The
- awareness training Percent of private security contracts with enhanced language
- by government security personnel, as well as by private security
- challenges
  - based on distinct yet complementary responsibilities for governments and
  - facing our industry and specific operations. to addressing security
- Community impacts and relationships Consultation and engagement Respecting human rights
- concerns
  - 2010 Corporate Citizenship Report ExxonMobil's community relationships are
  - Human rights is a priority in our Nigerian operations.
  - into existing business operations What we did in 2010
- conferences and working groups, as well as consultations with U.N.
- pre - construction surveys finalized in Papua New Guinea
- in our operations, not just because doing so fosters a
- involves due diligence, having policies in place, conducting impact assessments,
- is
  - a
    - priority in our Nigerian operations. There have been
    - recurring component in both quarterly LCM communications 2010
  - supported by the policies in our Standards of Business
- materials through regular, systematic communications Participated in several social and
- Number of countries in which affiliates received dedicated human rights
- policies and practices exxonmobil.com / humanrights Papua New Guinea liquefied natural
- provides expectations for our majority-owned operating affiliates. The Framework
- through selfassessments and other processes Engage in international dialogues such
- training
  - in priority countries
    - and assess follow - up needs for
    - Distributed security and human rights materials
  - is based on ExxonMobil guidelines, practices, and priorities, and
  - module for efficient, wider availability Update the Upstream Socioeconomic
  - Our human rights training is based on ExxonMobil guidelines,
  - to
    - appropriate staff Further implement our Framework on Security
    - key affiliates and staff, including lead country managers
- We respect human rights in our operations, not just because
  - Continue to integrate human rights concerns into existing business operations
  - Labor practices Security IPIECA/GRI Content Index Safety, Health,
  - National content plan development and implementation Workforce development Supplier development

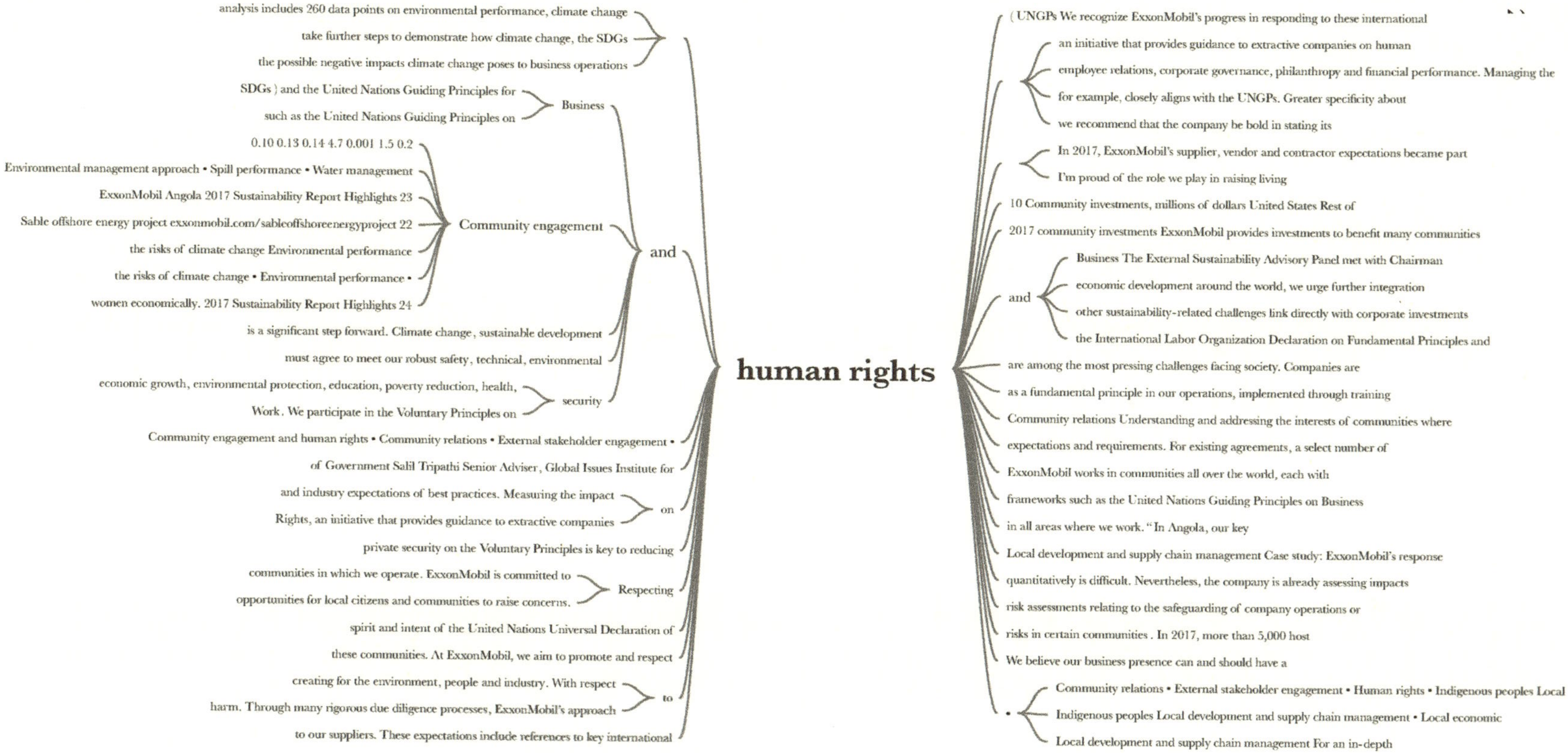


**Figure 6.6** ExxonMobil (2018)

change, have involved emissions reductions at its existing facilities.[148] ExxonMobil has also spent resources on research of alternative energies. In 2017, the company reported that it avoided emitting 23.4 metric tons of greenhouse gas emissions.[149] These reductions are largely the result of increases in the efficiency of existing operations like reductions in flaring and methane escape from natural gas operations.[150] Additionally, ExxonMobil started expansion of a carbon-capture facility in 2010; it is now one of the largest of its kind in the world.[151] Yet it was under the leadership of former ExxonMobil CEO Rex Tillerson as US secretary of state that the United States left the Extractives Industry Transparency Initiative, a multistakeholder regulatory regime reinforcing the importance of publishing payments to curb corruption in many of the countries where ExxonMobil has a presence.

### 4. The Technology Sector and Human Rights

Companies in the tech sector confront a range of human rights challenges, from protecting user privacy to preventing the dissemination of disinformation and manipulation through misinformation while promoting freedom of expression.[152] Technology is also an increasingly powerful and influential economic sector impacting many aspects of human life such that access to technology is increasingly recognized as essential in many regions of the world.[153] Indeed, it is said that "data is the new oil."[154]

[148] ExxonMobil 2017 Report, *supra* note 109, at 18.

[149] *Id.*

[150] *Id.*

[151] Mike Lee & Jenny Mandel, *Big Oil Looks to CCS, but Will It Really Help the Climate?*, E&E News (June 19, 2019), https://www.eenews.net/stories/1060626447

[152] *See e.g.*, *Harmful Content: The Role of Internet Platform Companies in Fighting Terrorist Incitement and Politically Motivated Disinformation*, NYU Stern: Ctr. for Bus. and Hum. Rts. (Nov. 2017); Erika George, *Corporate Social Responsibility and Social Media Corporations: Incorporating Human Rights Through Rankings, Self-Regulation and Shareholder Resolutions*, 28 Duke J. of Comp. & Int'l L. 521–538 (2018).

[153] *See* Haochen Sun, The Fundamental Right to Technology, 48 Hofstra L. Rev. 445 (2019) (arguing technology is important for human dignity and equality understanding access to technology as fundamental right will promote equitable distribution of technological benefits and prevent harmful applications of technologies); John Garrity, *Getting Connected: The Internet and Its Role as a Global Public Good*, 18 Geo. J. Int'l Aff. 6 (2017) (considering technology as a necessity); *see also*, *Digital Economy Report 2019*, Un Conf. on Trade and Dev. (Sept. 4, 2109) (Digital economy ranges from 4.5 to 15.5 percent of the world GDP), https://unctad.org/en/PublicationsLibrary/der2019_overview_en.pdf; Measuring the Digital Economy, Int'l Monetary Fund (Feb. 28, 2018), https://www.imf.org/~/media/Files/Publications/PP/2018/022818MeasuringDigitalEconomy.ashx.

[154] *The World's Most Valuable Resource Is No Longer Oil, but Data*, The Economist (May 6, 2017), https://www.economist.com/leaders/2017/05/06/the-worlds-most-valuable-resource-is-no-longer-oil-but-data; Kiran Bhageshpur, *Data Is The New Oil—And That's A Good Thing*, Forbes (Nov. 15, 2019), https://www.forbes.com/sites/forbestechcouncil/2019/11/15/data-is-the-new-oil-and-thats-a-good-thing/?sh=28b70a3b7304; The Great Hack (The Others 2019) ("Data is the most valuable asset in the world"); *see also*, Shoshana Zuboff, The Age of Surveillance Capitalism 377 (2020) (comparing data to ivory and technology companies engaged in surveillance capitalism to poachers of human behavior: "not unlike the monstrous slaughter of elephants for ivory. . . . you are the abandoned carcass. The "product" derives from the surplus that is ripped from your life.").

*a. Microsoft and Human Rights Challenges*

In 2013, Microsoft was implicated in abusing the privacy rights of its users when Edward Snowden, a former US National Security Association (NSA) and Central Intelligence Agency contractor, disclosed documents that showing Microsoft was the first tech company to provide user information to the NSA pursuant to the PRISM project, a government mass surveillance program that collected data from internet communications technology companies.[155] The full extent of Microsoft's cooperation with government surveillance remains contested.[156]

My quantitative review of Microsoft Corporate Sustainability Reports published between 2009 and 2017—before, during, and after the company came under criticism for participation in government surveillance initiatives alleged to violate user privacy review—revealed that in 2010 the term "human rights" was weighted .05 percent and occurred 12 times. In 2017, the term "human rights" occurred 51 times and was weighted at .40 percent. The term "privacy" and was weighted at .34 percent in 2010. By 2017, "privacy" was weighted at .48 percent.

**i. Content Change: Microsoft Before and After Human Rights Challenges** In its 2009 report, titled "Corporate Citizenship @ Microsoft Report: Addressing Societal Needs in the Global Economy," the company celebrates having a "culture of business integrity, accountability and transparency" in its approach to corporate governance.[157] A letter from CEO Steven A. Ballmer introduces Microsoft's 2009 report. While he does not refer to "human rights" or "privacy," he does emphasize Microsoft's role in "helping to advance social and economic opportunities" as the world's largest software company.[158] He also highlights the importance of working with a range of different constituencies, from governments to civil society organizations, to "transform communities" through providing the

[155] Barton Gellman & Laura Poitras, *U.S., British Intelligence Mining Data from Nine U.S. Internet Companies in Broad Secret Program*, Washington Post (June 7, 2013), https://www.washingtonpost.com/investigations/us-intelligence-mining-data-from-nine-us-internet-companies-in-broad-secret-program/2013/06/06/3a0c0da8-cebf-11e2-8845-d970ccb04497_story.html.

[156] Laura K. Donohue, *NSA Surveillance May Be Legal—But It's Unconstitutional*, Washington Post (June 21, 2013), https://www.washingtonpost.com/opinions/nsa-surveillance-may-be-legal--but-its-unconstitutional/2013/06/21/b9ddec20-d44d-11e2-a73e-826d299ff459_story.html?utm_term=.399baa19745c (arguing that PRISM is an unconstitutional program); Elizabeth Dwoskin, *Rand Paul Recruits for a Class Action Against NSA*, Bloomberg (June 13, 2013), https://www.bloomberg.com/news/articles/2013-06-13/rand-paul-recruits-for-a-class-action-against-nsa (arguing that merely knowing that you are monitored by the government may not be harmful enough to gain standing to sue).

[157] Microsoft, Corporate Citizenship @ Microsoft: Addressing Societal Needs in the Global Community 7 (2009), https://www.microsoft.com/en-us/corporate-responsibility/reports-hub (to locate the report, navigate to "Archived reports" and search "2009" within the "Microsoft CSR Annual Reports" field).

[158] *Id.*

"training, infrastructure and technology" necessary to promote sustainable economic growth and prosperity.[159]

The report notes that Microsoft has endorsed the UN Global Compact, aligning its business operations and strategies with the ten compact principles, including human rights. Microsoft states that it "works to be a responsible leader across a range of policy areas and programs, including environmental sustainability, human rights, disaster response and humanitarian relief, protecting consumers' privacy and security, and building more interoperable technologies."[160] The 2009 report includes a dedicated section on "Preserving Freedom of Expression." Here, Microsoft discusses its support for basic human rights as essential to building healthy communities and declares that communications technologies must provide a platform for "open, diverse and unimpeded content and commerce."[161]

Microsoft clarifies that risks associated with use of communication technologies will require regulation, acknowledging that issues arise that "often justify government attention, especially on matters of privacy, national security and the protection of children."[162] The company calls on governments to fulfill the duty to protect human rights, as follows: "governments around the world make differing judgements about the legal standards and policy trade-offs appropriate to their own cultures and national circumstances. In doing so, governments should act in a manner that fulfills their duty to protect internationally recognized human rights, such as the rights of privacy and freedom of expression."[163]

Microsoft's 2009 report points out the importance of partnerships. For example, the company explains its role in founding the Global Network Initiative (GNI), which helps the company respond in a principled manner to regulatory demands for user data and respect freedom of expression and privacy as part of responsible business decision making.[164] Through the GNI, Microsoft collaborates with other companies in the tech sector and stakeholders to "promote laws, policies and practices that respect freedom of expression and privacy, and to develop credible systems of accountability among participants in the initiative."[165]

In its 2010 "Corporate Citizenship" report, Microsoft discusses "Operating Responsibly" and devotes entire sections to "Online Privacy and Safety" and "Responsible Sourcing."[166] CEO Ballmer's letter introducing the 2010 report does refer to privacy. While earlier reports stated Microsoft's commitment to human rights standards contained in the UN Global Compact, the 2010 report itemizes the company's progress in key areas related to human rights. For

159 *Id.* at 2.
160 *Id.* at 7.
161 *Id.* at 8–9.
162 *Id.* at 9.
163 *Id.*
164 *Id.*
165 *Id.*
166 *Id.* at 28–29.

example, the report outlines Microsoft's "Privacy & Freedom of Expression" commitment to "empower individuals to manage their information confidently and safely." Microsoft states it will extend these same principles to its operations in China and to markets where the company stores customer data.[167]

A section of the 2010 report on "Freedom of Expression Online" represents that Microsoft understands "respecting and reconciling" fundamental rights as central to good corporate citizenship and essential for advancing innovation, economic development, academic inquiry, and well-being.[168]

The freedom of expression discussion in the 2010 report summarizes the company's progress on its commitment to addressing issues raised by its business practices and the ways in which it has made changes. For example, Microsoft explains:

> We consider free expression and privacy when determining the markets where we will store customer data. Before certain types of personal information can be hosted in a particular country, Microsoft undertakes a risk assessment process. This includes an examination of the country concerned, including a review of its overall human rights situation and the rule of law, as well as specific laws, policies, and practices. Senior executive leadership reviews this assessment before approving a decision to locate the personal information in the country.[169]

In addition, the report addresses the issues the company confronts in the Chinese market and explains its presence in China fosters "free access to information, promotes the role of information technology in society, and advances rule of law."[170]

The 2010 report even credits an investigation by the National Labor Committee, an international NGO focused on labor rights, that documented abuses at a Microsoft supplier factory in Dongguan, China, for pressing Microsoft to "take a hard look at our existing standards and how we implement them."[171] In a section of the 2010 report devoted to "Responsible Sourcing" Microsoft explains that its Vendor Code of Conduct sets workplace and human rights standards and that it conducts informal and formal risk-based third-party monitoring for compliance with its code of conduct based on standards set forth by the Electronics Industry Citizenship Coalition's Code of Conduct (EICC). The EICC is a group of electronics companies that convene to create industry social and environmental standards.[172] Microsoft says that it continues to "look for

[167] *Id.* at 29.
[168] *Id.* at 51.
[169] *Id.* at 51.
[170] *Id.* at 51–52.
[171] *Id.* at 44.
[172] *Id.*

ways to enhance [its] Code of Conduct and monitoring processes to ensure the fair treatment of all workers in [its] supply chain."[173]

A section of the 2010 report devoted to "Online Privacy and Safety" discusses Microsoft's commitment to "improve the online ecosystem and generate good integration among policy goals" and describes new products and services the company has released to "promote" privacy and safety.[174] Looking forward to future challenges, Microsoft points to the problem of "aligning legal and social policies on security and privacy in a global environment"[175] and pledges that it "will work to initiate dialogue among governments and other stakeholders to work toward achieving more alignment on legal and social policies."[176]

The 2010 report also describes Microsoft's approach to government demands for data as follows:

> While we must adhere to local laws to which we are subject, legal compliance does not necessarily require absolute or reflexive deference to local authorities. If we disagree with governments, we try to find the most constructive and pragmatic approach to sustain a principled stand. Sometimes that involves public statements of our views; other times we may find it more constructive to engage directly with the government.[177]

To that end, Microsoft explains that it has now "integrated support and responsibility for human rights, free expression and privacy into [its] business operations."[178] A team of senior leaders from across the company coordinates oversight responsibility of rights.

The 2017 Microsoft Corporate Social Responsibility Report devotes still more attention to human rights and privacy rights in particular. Previous reports positioned human rights later in text, but the 2017 report gives rights a more prominent position early in the document. However, the introductory letter from CEO Satya Nadella makes no reference to human rights, privacy, or freedom of expression.[179]

The 2017 report sets out how Microsoft CSR governance works and introduces the firm's approach to "transparent reporting" on CSR issues, in which human rights figures prominently. Significantly, it explains Microsoft's efforts to align its

173 *Id.* at 45.
174 *Id.* at 46–50.
175 *Id.* at 50.
176 *Id.*
177 *Id.* at 51.
178 *Id.*
179 MICROSOFT, 2017 CORPORATE SOCIAL RESPONSIBILITY REPORT 4–9 (2017) https://www.microsoft.com/en-us/corporate-responsibility/reports-hub (to locate the report, navigate to "Archived reports" and search "2017" within the "Microsoft CSR Annual Reports" field).

CSR commitments to reporting with the Global Reporting Initiatives' Sustainability Reporting Guidelines. Microsoft also points to its position as one of the first companies to align its human rights work with the UN Guiding Principles on Business and Human Rights and to adopt the UNGP Reporting Framework.[180] The report goes on to explain how reporting guidelines have informed Microsoft's approach to CSR.[181]

Among the top issues identified through Microsoft's materiality assessment in 2017 were human rights and data privacy and security. Microsoft reports plans to conduct "best-in-class human rights impact assessments" to make decisions that are "rights aware" through an integrated approach to human rights. Microsoft reports it will proactively engage through public statements advocating the promotion of human rights and to lead on transparency through "increased disclosure and engagement."[182] Figure 6.7 shows a word tree of Microsoft's 2010 sustainability report and Figure 6.8 shows a word tree of Microsoft's 2018 sustainability report. A comparison of these visual representations of the company's social responsibility and sustainability vocabulary reveals that the reach of the term "human rights" has extended and become more integrated.

**ii. Conduct Change: Microsoft Before and After Human Rights Challenges** At Microsoft, the Technology and Corporate Responsibility Team (TCR) works with leaders across the company's business and operations to lead system-wide approaches to core CSR issues. The head of TCR reports directly to Microsoft's president and chief legal officer, who in turn reports directly to the company's CEO.[183] Microsoft has created a Regulatory and Public Policy Committee on its corporate board charged with the responsibility to "review and provide guidance to the board and management about the company's policies and programs that relate to corporate social responsibility including human rights, environmental sustainability, responsible sourcing and philanthropy."[184]

Microsoft updated its Global Human Rights Statement and now provides training for employees. The company continues to conduct human rights impact assessments of artificial intelligence (AI). The company has issued reports on the data requests it receives from governments. In global policy meetings on business and human rights, Microsoft executives have called for standards to regulate AI and facial recognition technology.

[180] *Id.* at 13–15.
[181] *Id.*
[182] *Id.*
[183] *Id.* at 10–13.
[184] *Id.*

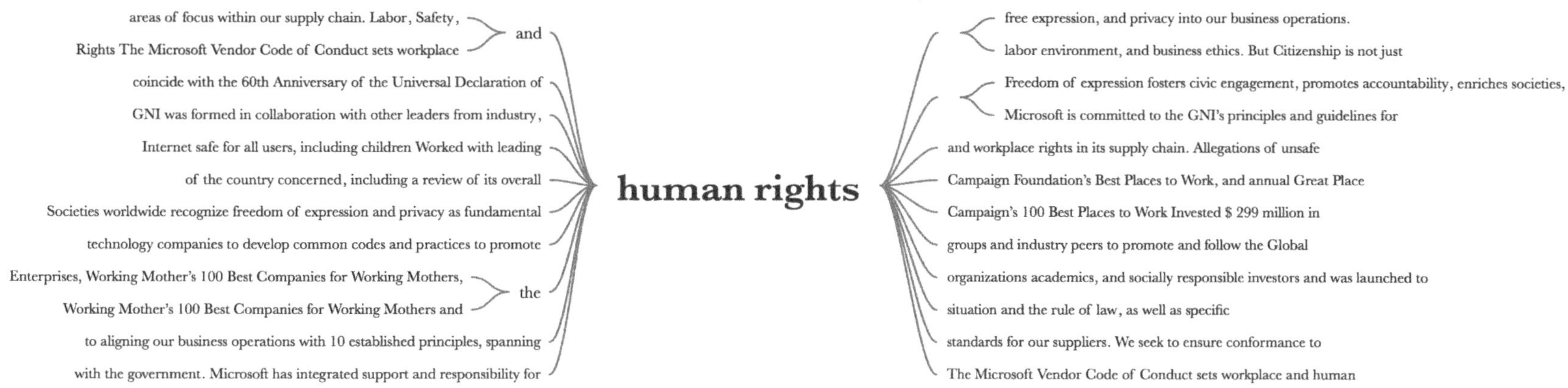


**Figure 6.7** Microsoft (2010)

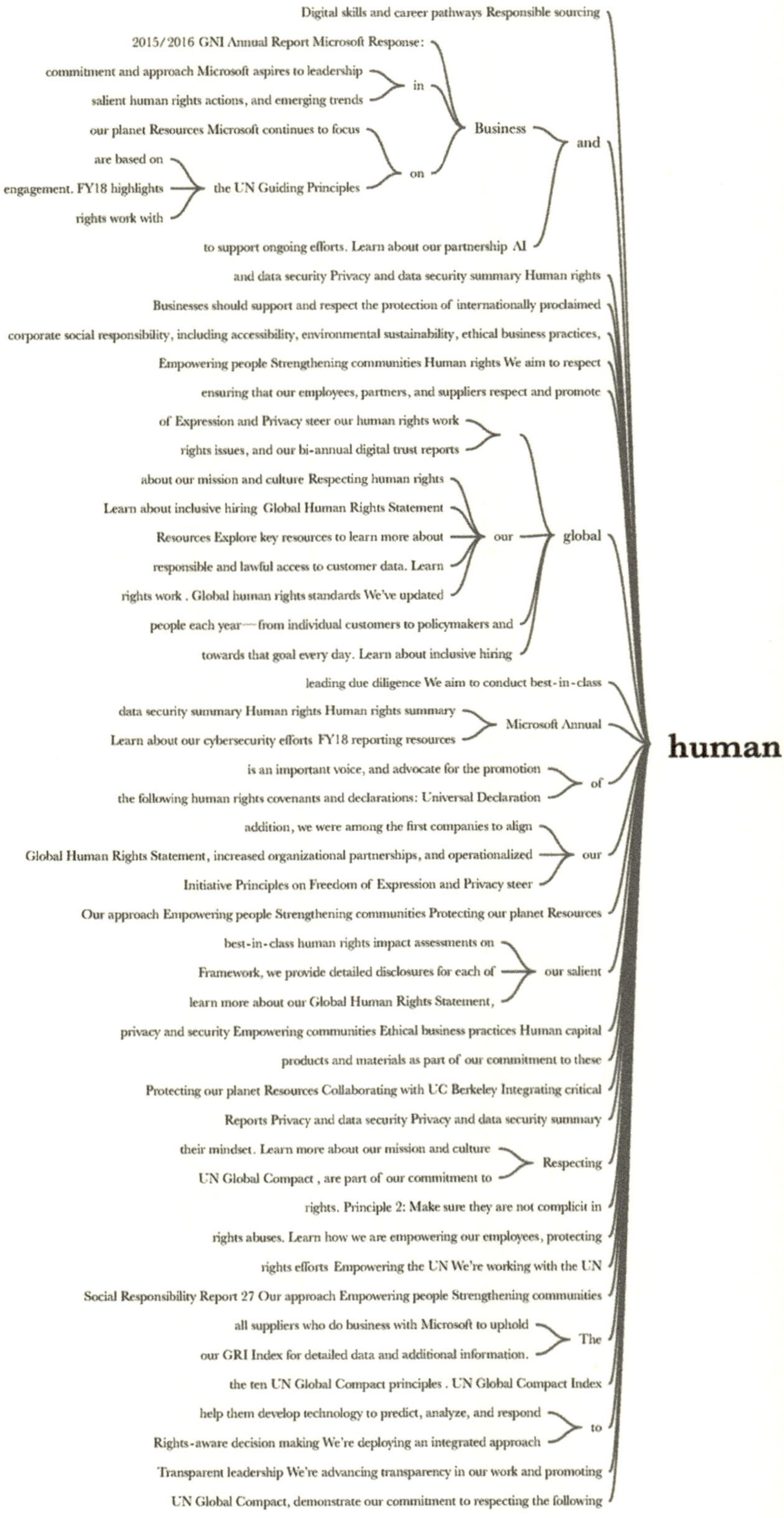


**Figure 6.8** Microsoft (2018)

**rights**

- and
  - acts as a catalyst for others who are participating
  - ensuring the responsible sourcing of all our products and
  - that technology plays a positive role across the globe.
  - to serve as a catalyst for action by others—
- labor health and safety, environmental, and business ethics practices prescribed
- philanthropy privacy and cybersecurity, and responsible sourcing. At Microsoft, our
- - related disclosures are based on the UN Guiding Principles on
- Principle 2: Make sure they are not complicit in human
- Rights aware decision making We're deploying an integrated approach to
- Transparent leadership We're advancing transparency in our work and promoting
- Our employees
  - Microsoft 2018 Corporate Social Responsibility Report
  - Strengthening communities Empowering nonprofits Humanitarian
- abuses Learn how we are empowering our employees, protecting human
- actions and emerging trends in business and human rights. Rights-
- and
  - the Global Network Initiative Principles on Freedom of Expression
  - to adopt the UN Guiding Principles Reporting Framework. We're
- Artificial intelligence (AI) can improve life in many ways and
- Campaign HRC) Corporate Equality Index ™ IMicrosoft received a 100% rating
- commitments through employee training and other due diligence activities. We've
- covenants and declarations
  - Review the statement Employee stories Explore the
  - Universal Declaration of Human Rights International Covenant
- decision making across key aspects of Microsoft. Proactive engagement We
- efforts Empowering the UN We're working with the UN Human
- Human rights summary Microsoft Annual Human Rights Report Microsoft
- impact assessments on our salient human rights actions, and emerging
- in the way we do business, and to advance those
- issues
  - and
    - activities through a downloadable report. GNI Assessment 2015/
    - our bi-annual digital trust reports. Global Human
  - directly into education can generate innovative approaches to managing
- Office to help them develop technology to predict, analyze, and
- Our Global Human Rights Statement, and participation as a signatory
- Principle 1: Businesses should support and respect the protection of
- principles Resources Microsoft 2018 Corporate Social Responsibility Report
- Report
  - Microsoft Report on the GNI Independent Assessment 2015/
  - Using the United Nations Guiding Principles Reporting Framework,
- Reporting Framework (RAFI). In addition, this report serves as the
- Resource Center Empowering our employees Empowering our employees summary EEO-
- Responsible sourcing and device lifecycle impacts Applying technology for environmental
- situations We're also collaborating on joint projects and have provided
- specialists We bring outside perspectives into the company and inform
- standards We've updated our Global Human Rights Statement, increased organizational
- Statement
  - and participation
    - as a signatory to the UN Global
    - in the UN Global Compact, are part
  - increased organizational partnerships, and operationalized our human rights commitments
  - our
    - Global Human Rights Statement and participation in the
    - salient human rights issues, and our bi-annual
  - We have committed to ensuring that our employees, partners,
- summary Microsoft Annual Human Rights Report Microsoft Report on
- through increased disclosure and engagement. FY18 highlights The UN Guiding
- We aim to respect human rights in the way we
- work
  - Global human rights standards We've updated our Global Human
  - with the UN Guiding Principles on Business and Human
- International Covenant on Civil and Political Rights International Covenant on

## C. Consistency with Global Standards and Contrasts between Competitors

According to operational principles contained in the UN Guiding Principles on Business and Human Rights, companies should make policy commitments to respect human rights that are approved at the most senior level of the enterprise; that are informed by internal and external expertise; that set and state expectations for personnel, business partners, and other parties connected to the products, services, or operations of the enterprise; that are communicated to the public; and that are embedded throughout the business enterprise.[185] Companies should conduct due diligence and human rights impact assessments. Companies should also provide grievance mechanisms to resolve disputes.

The CSR reports from the companies studied were all introduced by senior high-level executives. Companies explained the process by which issues were identified and the extent to which stakeholder input contributed. CSR policy and reported human rights performance are increasingly aligned with emerging international standards incorporating their responsibility to respect human rights; however, results remain mixed. Some firms make explicit reference to international human rights instruments and the UNGPs, and reports contain discussions of policy commitments to "respect human rights." Many use the Global Reporting Initiatives' template for reporting, which is aligned with the UNGPs. Some reports explain or mention the company's human rights due diligence process and note that human rights impact assessments are conducted. A few companies mention grievance mechanisms.

I see patterns and some progress. There are rhetorical patterns of responsibility sharing, "journey," competition, leadership, and diversity. Diversity, when paired with equity and inclusion, could be an important gateway for broader discussions about a range of different human rights as many abuses originate in discriminatory treatment.

Investor consumer community pressure has contributed to the progress made to date as evidenced by CSR reports that are reacting to the human rights issues made urgent by activists and later recognized by global policymaking authority through international human rights standards. There has been change over time in the content of corporate policy statements and sustainability reporting on human rights impacts. Reference to human rights is up all over as have mechanisms to monitor also proliferated in terms of rankings and shareholder proposals. On the whole, leading companies have given more attention to human rights over time. Next, is to have more business enterprises follow these leaders. But it is important to appreciate the challenges of shifting burdens on small businesses that are less able to bear them.

[185] *Guiding Principles on Business and Human Rights*, *supra* note 2, at 15.

### D. Remaining Challenges: Access to Remedy and Sustaining Reforms

While there has been considerable progress on paper, at least with respect to sustainability reporting, the extent to which the reporting is making a difference in the real world and in the lives of would be victims of rights violations remains an open question. For example, there is increased attention given to an issue by companies once it becomes acute and the public appears to be paying attention, but the risk remains that once public attention fades, an issue could fall further down the list of a company's priorities. Moreover, while my research demonstrates that business processes and procedures to mitigate risk to rights are becoming better as more sophisticated and detailed corporate reporting consistent with voluntary global standards, mandatory disclosures, and the rise of rankings benchmarks, this does not demonstrate victims of rights violations are better off. Indeed, access to remedy for victims of human rights violations involving business enterprises has in many jurisdictions become more, not less, difficult. That said, there should be fewer future victims should new and improving processes and procedures to detect and mitigate risks to human rights be sustained and strengthened. For example, a number of business executives, while concerned about the cost and time it took to comply with mandatory reporting requirements, shared that the process of putting reports together welcomed the early identification of potential problem areas. Rights activists, investors, and consumers have the power to strengthen corporate commitments and improve corporate conduct. Things are headed in the right direction and things are driven in large measure by the work of those rights activists best able to frame issues identified as salient by stakeholders and concerned investors.

## III. Codes of Conduct as Policy Commitments: From Voluntary to Obligatory

Along with communicating commitments to respect human rights, leading business enterprises have adopted codes of ethical conduct detailing responsibilities and expectations. Frequently, elements of codes of conduct are incorporated into the contracts a corporation enters into with its suppliers and business partners. These forms of voluntary corporate self-regulation have arisen in response to the relative absence of effective state regulation to address human rights abuses and to the presence of effective campaigns pressing for change. Accordingly, voluntary corporate self-regulation through codes of conduct merits greater attention.

This section defines and discusses corporate codes of conduct. It then compares representative codes of conduct across selected industry sectors subjected to scrutiny by human rights activists and shareholder advocates.

I survey the substantive policy content of these codes and the practices put in place by corporations to ensure code compliance. I also assess the extent to which the content of corporate codes speak to activist calls for reform, victim demands for remedy, investor interest in reducing human rights risks, and global standards that corporations respect human rights. For review, I selected the codes of leading corporations in industry sectors that activists and shareholder advocates most often identify as having potentially adverse impacts on the enjoyment of certain human rights. Codes covered include industry sector standards and individual company policies that outline expectations for business relationships with employees, suppliers, and stakeholders.

Increasingly, codes of conduct, like sustainability reporting, incorporate rights. The prevention of human rights violations could be strengthened if the standards contained in codes were properly put into practice and affected stakeholders were invited to participate in processes to create codes and monitor compliance. Codes of conduct can provide insights into the transnational processes of norm creation that may influence the policy commitments, communications, and performance of business enterprises—especially in those areas where laws have been underenforced or ineffective for ensuring protections. Corporate codes of conduct often echo or evolve into standards of conduct that become binding and should be looked at to understand what may come to constitute a new form of "soft law" strong enough to close existing global social and environmental governance gaps and to create a new transnational private governance informed and influenced by public pressure.

## A. Codes of Conduct and Corporate Social Responsibility

There are various forms and formulations of corporate codes of conduct. Sometimes referred to as codes of ethics, codes of conduct are often normative in nature.[186] Many codes emphasize not only legal compliance but also conduct that, while not legally mandated, may be advisable ethically.

To address human rights challenges, several transnational corporations have created codes of conduct. Often a company's code is informed by an industry association code, a code created by an international organization, or a subject matter–specific code created through multistakeholder consultations. Corporate codes of conduct can operate as regulatory strategies to structure relationships with partners and suppliers, and they often serve as components of basic CSR programs. My review of CSR reports found that most leading companies referred

[186] Mark S. Schwartz, *Universal Moral Values for Corporate Codes of Ethics*, 59 J. BUS. ETHICS 27, 27 (2005).

to their codes of conduct in their reporting as contractually binding and forming the basis for business relationships with a range of different partners and entities in a company's supply chain.

In business ethics literature, codes are described as formal written instruments that include the moral standards meant to set expectations for the behavior of the corporation and its management and employees toward stakeholders.[187] A code of conduct in the business context is usually a set of standards that aims to inform how an organization will conduct business. Codes act to set expectations. A code of conduct can influence the culture of an organization. To be a part of an organization, to represent an organization, to be engaged with it in some way, or to merit affiliation or association with it may be conditioned on compliance with its code of conduct. At minimum, codes of conduct set baseline expectations for behavior.

Codes can serve both internal and external functions by clarifying relationships with and commitments to stakeholders. Codes of conduct are also public expressions of a corporation's core values, related to ethics in operations. They often encompass responsibilities to protect the environment and to respect human and labor rights. Codes of conduct can reach the far periphery of global sourcing; for example, many multinationals have separate codes regulating human rights specifically geared to suppliers.

There are a range of different types of codes of conduct on a variety of topics. The level of generality and specificity in content varies between codes. There are global standards contained in international instruments that have been crafted to clarify shared standards of practice. There are industry-sector codes that address common challenges to reduce risks industry-wide. Finally, there are codes made by specific corporations that consider particular business context and constituencies. Individual corporations increasingly incorporate reference to international or industry guidelines when addressing human rights obligations. I discuss examples of these different types of codes in turn as follows.

## B. International Codes and Corporate Responsibility

The proliferation of instruments that seek to address the role of global business in the international community heralds a significant shift in expectations. International "soft law" instruments, such as the OECD Guidelines for Multinational Enterprises and the ILO Tripartite Declaration of Principles Concerning Multinational Enterprises, are recognized as supporting the concept that business enterprises have

[187] *Id.* at 27; *see also* Muel Kaptein, *Business Codes of Multinational Firms: What Do They Say?*, 50 J. BUS. ETHICS 13, 13 (2004).

social responsibilities. The UN Global Compact asks that corporations joining the compact commit to respect human rights. The UN Guiding Principles on Business and Human Rights clarify that businesses have a responsibility to respect human rights and provide ways businesses should operationalize policy commitments to promote respect for rights. Understanding the ways in which these instruments are being incorporated into business operations and sustainability reporting demonstrates the growing strength of soft law.

## C. Industry Sector Instruments and Individual Company Codes

Codes that aim to regulate the conduct of business enterprises are not limited to general global guidance. Some industry sectors have created their own codes to address challenges relevant to rights issues in specialized instances. Among those industries under considerable pressure from human rights activists, and identified by the Special Representative of the Secretary General on Business and Human Rights as often implicated in abuses, are agriculture, apparel, extractives, and electronics. Instruments intended to reduce risks to human rights now exist in each of these industry sectors.

At the industry level, the most salient codes have been the result of consultative processes with different stakeholder constituencies. The creation of industry codes came in response to shared challenges and after activists took action to raise awareness. External scrutiny generated a greater impetus to improve the policies and practices of corporations in different industries. The codification of standards that incorporate human rights concerns is due in significant part to the efforts of these activists who raised the profile of risks to rights and put pressure on corporations.

### 1. The Voluntary Principles on Security and Human Rights as Obligatory

The Voluntary Principles on Security and Human Rights (VPSHRs, or Voluntary Principles) offer one of the earliest examples of efforts to use a code of conduct to aid and inform compliance with a common set of standards across different countries with disparate legal cultures governing the use of force by law enforcement or security providers. In the aftermath of high-profile atrocities committed against environmental and Indigenous activists by security forces paid to protect company property, the UK and US governments convened a series of stakeholder conversations that led to the creation of a uniform standard to regulate security.[188] The Voluntary Principles were designed for implementation in

[188] Interview with Arvind Ganesan, Director, Human Rights Watch Business Division (Nov. 20, 2018); interview with Bennett Freeman, former US Deputy Assistant Secretary of State for Democracy, Human Rights and Labor (Jan. 14, 2019).

complicated social contexts where local laws were unenforced or inconsistent with internationally accepted standards. In such a situation, a code can provide a baseline for conduct and be used to promote better practices.

The Voluntary Principles call for companies to conduct risk assessments and to contract responsibly when entering into agreements with security providers to protect operations. According to the Voluntary Principles, an effective risk assessment entails the identification of factors that may heighten risks of future conflict or violence, including, among other things, the human rights records of a nation's public security forces, paramilitaries, and law enforcement authorities, as well as the reputations of private security service providers and the capacity of the local authorities to legally prosecute abuses.[189] Companies are advised to consider the risks associated with equipment transfers to security providers and to take measures to prevent misappropriation by putting controls in place where resources could be diverted and used to abuse rights.

The Voluntary Principles counsel that "civil society, home and host government representatives, and other sources should be consulted to identify risks presented by the potential for violence."[190] In addition, the VPSHRs provide that "companies should consult regularly with the host governments and local communities about the impact of their security arrangements on those communities."[191] Beyond consultation, the Voluntary Principles speak to communication as follows: "companies should communicate their policies regarding ethical conduct and human rights to public security providers, and express their desire that security be provided in a manner consistent with adequate and effective training."[192] The Voluntary Principles also provide that company responses to human rights abuses should involve pressing for a proper investigation and resolution of credible allegations of abuse by security forces.

The Voluntary Principles reference other international guidelines on the use of force, including the UN Principles on the Use of Force, Firearms by Law Enforcement Officials, and the UN Code of Conduct for Law Enforcement Officials. While the Voluntary Principles predate the UNGPs, they do call for conduct consistent with the responsibility to respect human rights. For instance, the identification of risks and implementing responses to rights abuses necessarily requires conducting human rights due diligence and assessing the likelihood of adverse human rights impacts as contemplated by the Principle 17 and Principle 18 of the UNGPs.

[189] The Voluntary Principles Initiative, Voluntary Principles on Security and Human Rights 2–3 (2000), http://www.voluntaryprinciples.org/wp-content/uploads/2019/12/TheVoluntaryPrinciples.pdf.

[190] *Id.* at 2.

[191] *Id.* at 3.

[192] *Id.* at 3–4.

A former BP sustainability employee explained that having a global industry standard of principles in place to point to when working in countries where military security was required by the government gave the company an opportunity to engage security forces on human rights obligations more effectively.[193] A former Chevron executive shared:

> [W]e've seen fewer security incidents, nothing like the security incidents that our industry had seen in the past—despite some tense protest situations. I think we've also been able to us what the UNGPs call leverage with other companies. We refer to the voluntary principles on security, and we say our expectation is that you're following these, you have to do training on them and evaluations on them. We have IFC resettlement principles too. It gives us a chance to explain and try to change their understanding, change their behavior.[194]

The Director of the Business Program and Human Rights Watch, describing the origins of the VPSHRs, explained: "it was very clear at the outset that there wasn't an appetite within the government to create regulations . . . it was very clear from industry that they wouldn't accept regulations."[195]

Since the formulation of the VPSHRs, industry trade associations have further developed resources to provide companies with guidance on human rights issues. For example, IPIECA published "Human Rights and Ethics in the Oil and Gas Industry." The World Gold Council issued a "Conflict-Free Gold Standard."[196] Individual companies have also promulgated principles to govern business activities. I review an example as follows.

*a. Selected Self-Regulation Instruments: Shell*

In a letter titled "Living by Our Principles," CEO Ben van Beurden introduces the Shell General Business Principles (SGBP) and explains:

> We are judged by how we act. Our reputation will be upheld if we act in accordance with the law and the Business Principles. We encourage our business partners to live by them or by equivalent principles. It is the responsibility of management to lead by example, to ensure that all employees are aware of these

[193] Christine Bader, Human Rights Advisor BSR, Remarks at the Business for Social Responsibility Conference, Leadership in Action (Nov. 5, 2013).

[194] Jeff Collins, Presentation at Business and Human Rights Seminar, University of Utah (Mar. 12, 2015) (transcript on file with author).

[195] Telephone interview with Arvind Ganesan, Jan. 19, 2019.

[196] World Gold Council, Conflict Free Gold Standard 1 (2012), https://www.gold.org/sites/default/files/documents/Conflict_Free_Gold_Standard_English.pdf ("A common approach by which gold producers can assess and provide assurance that their gold has been extracted in a manner that does not cause, support or benefit unlawful armed conflict or contribute to serious human rights abuses or breaches of international humanitarian law.").

principles, and behave in accordance with the spirit as well as with the letter of this statement. In turn, it is the responsibility of Shell employees to report suspected breaches of the Business Principles to Shell.[197]

Shell's General Business Principles govern how all the companies that comprise the Shell Group must conduct affairs. There are eight general business principles: (1) economics; (2) competition; (3) business integrity; (4) political activities; (5) health, safety, security, and the environment; (6) local communities; (7) communication and engagement; and (8) compliance.[198]

Shell's General Business Principles provide that Shell Group companies have certain duties as responsible corporate members of society to discharge with respect to shareholders, customers, employees, business partners, and society, including complying with applicable legal rules and regulations and supporting fundamental human rights consistent with the legitimate role of business.[199]

Shell's code of conduct is also introduced by the CEO and contains a section on human rights in which it explains that "conducting our activities in a way that respects human rights is a business imperative . . . and supports our license to operate."[200] Shell also has a separate human rights policy.[201] Significantly, the application of Shell's principles are supported by "a comprehensive set of assurance procedures" designed to ensure that Shell employees understand them and that Shell management provides employees with "safe and confidential channels to raise concerns and report instances of non-compliance."[202]

Shell extends its principles of conduct to others outside of the business enterprise, indicating that it expects contract staff as well as contactors and consultants working on behalf of or in the name of a Shell company to act in accordance with its code.

Because the code cannot provide "specific advice for every situation, dilemma or decision," Shell provides an "Integrity Check," which lists questions for individuals to consider when weighing a course of action.[203] In addition to whether or not a contemplated course of action is legal, among questions Shell's integrity check asks individuals to consider are:

- "Is what I am doing ethical and in line with the SGBP, our code of conduct, and supporting manuals?"

[197] Royal Dutch Shell, Shell General Business Principles 1 (2014), https://www.shell.com/about-us/our-values/_jcr_content/par/relatedtopics.stream/1572622107415/f3e59c06223516799f4a2d5fe63b824839f3a4f3/shell-general-business-principles-2014.pdf.

[198] *Id.* at 2.

[199] *Id* at 4.

[200] *Id.* at 11.

[201] Royal Dutch Shell, Code of Conduct 11 (2015), https://www.shell.com/about-us/our-values/_jcr_content/par/relatedtopics_1339962475.stream/1572621199415/2e554716a2fb77d4048b4338387fac946178699d/codeofconduct-english-2015.pdf.

[202] *Id.* at 1.

[203] *Id.* at 5.

- "Have I thoroughly understood the potential risks, including the risks to Shell's reputation?"
- "If this becomes public knowledge, will I still feel I have done the right thing?"

The company's policy commitment to human rights through codes of conduct to support self-regulation is reinforced in its sustainability reporting. For example, in its 2010 report, Shell cites its support for a number of voluntary codes and points to its participation in the UN Global Compact's LEAD Program.[204] Shell's 2017 sustainability report shares that the company now includes VPSHR clauses in contracts with its private security contractors and that it contracts with third-party human rights organizations to provide human rights training to Shell's operational teams in countries where there are identified threats of infraction.[205]

In contrast to Shell, there appears to be a disconnect between the content of the ExxonMobil's policies and its published reporting on social performance. For example, in its 2012 Corporate Citizenship Reports, ExxonMobil represents that the company's Standards of Business Conduct "uphold values related to human rights, labor, the environment and anti-corruption."[206] Yet the term "human rights" simply does not appear in ExxonMobil's Standards of Business Conduct. Nor are the VPSHRs mentioned in the Standards, though ExxonMobil's 2017 "Sustainability Report Highlights" notes that more than five thousand host government security and ExxonMobil-contracted security staff were trained on the VPSHR in twelve higher risk countries.[207]

Chevron's Business Conduct and Ethics Code now incorporates the company's Human Rights Policy.

### 2. The Fair Labor Association Workplace Code of Conduct and Compliance Benchmarks

The Fair Labor Association's (FLA's) Workplace Code of Conduct sets forth labor standards that aim to achieve decent and humane working conditions. A series of Compliance Benchmarks accompanies the code. The standards contained in the FLA Code are based on ILO standards and are widely accepted international

[204] Royal Dutch Shell, PLC Sustainability Report 2010, at 31 (2010), https://www.shell.com/investors/financial-reporting/annual-publications/annual-reports-download-centre/_jcr_content/par/tabbedcontent_f645/tab/textimage.stream/1519790790787/1051284bed71f7eb4af6976a1d67d0c40461e530/shell-sustainability-report-2010.pdf.

[205] Royal Dutch Shell, PLC Sustainability Report 63 (2017), https://reports.shell.com/sustainability-report/2017/servicepages/downloads/files/shell_sustainability_report_2017.pdf.

[206] ExxonMobil, 2012 Corporate Citizenship Report 13 (2012), https://corporate.exxonmobil.com/-/media/Global/Files/sustainability-report/publication/2012-ccr.pdf.

[207] ExxonMobil, 2017 Report, *supra* note 109, at 24.

best practices. As a multistakeholder organization with certifying authority, the FLA works to establish best practices for the ethical treatment of workers and safe and healthy workplaces.[208]

The FLA's Workplace Code of Conduct covers nine topics to support continuous improvement in labor conditions, including: (1) employment relationship; (2) nondiscrimination; (3) harassment or abuse; (4) forced labor; (5) child labor; (6) freedom of association and collective bargaining; (7) health, safety, and environment; (8) hours of work; and (9) compensation. Participating companies commit to adopt and adhere to rules of employment that respect worker rights and to provide a safe and healthy workplace.[209]

*a. Selected Self-Regulation Instruments: Nike*

Nike CEO Philip Knight introduces "Inside the Lines," the Nike Code of Ethics, by explaining, "We play hard, we play to win, and we play by the rules of the game."[210] The Code of Ethics is addressed to employees and applies to the company's subsidiaries worldwide. It instructs:

> NIKE's good name and *reputation* result in large part from our collective actions. That means the work-related activities of every employee must reflect standards of honesty, loyalty, trustworthiness, fairness, concern for others and accountability. We are expected to be sensitive to any situations that can adversely impact NIKE's *reputation* and are expected to use good judgment and common sense in the way we all conduct business.[211]

The text makes clear that social expectations and reputational risk are important to Nike. Employees are asked to exercise care to identify issues that could compromise the company's reputation and are expected to promote compliance with the code.[212]

Nike's code sets high expectations for its suppliers, providing: "NIKE is committed to socially responsible sourcing practices. We are driven to do not only what is required by law, but also what is expected of a leader. We expect our business partners to do the same."[213] The company expects its business partners, such as distributors, consultants, representatives, attorneys, agents, and independent contractors, to observe the same standards of conduct as Nike

208 *FLA Workplace Code of Conduct and Compliance Benchmarks* 3, Fair Labor Association, https://www.fairlabor.org/our-work/code-of-conduct (last visited Mar. 8, 2020).

209 *Id.*

210 Nike, Inside the Lines The Nike Code of Ethics: Defining the Nike, Inc Playing Field and the Rules of the Game 3 (2011).

211 *Id.*

212 *Id.*

213 *Id.*

employees.[214] The text seeks to extend ethical obligations beyond employees and to encourage company partners to conduct business in a manner that exceeds legal requirements.

In 2017, Nike updated its code of conduct to "further align with the expectations of key stakeholders."[215] It sets out the minimum standards expected of supplier factories using the exact same language as the FLA code on working hours and the right to freedom of association.[216] The code states that Nike's sourcing strategy "prioritizes and favors suppliers who show demonstrable leadership in corporate responsibility and sustainability and who seek to move beyond minimum standards."[217] In its 2016–2017 Sustainable Business Report, Nike recognizes that "consumers increasingly demand ethical production and sustainable sourcing from business."[218] Nike credits the UNGPs for making human rights "an integral part of how business is done and reported."[219]

### 3. The Fair Food Code of Conduct

The Fair Food Program's Fair Food Code of Conduct (FFCC) is the result of continuing negotiations among farmworkers, farms, and buyers. It sets out "minimum requirements" for employment practices that farms and buyers must abide by to participate in the Fair Food Program.[220] The program is unique in that it explicitly uses market mechanisms to enforce labor rights protections.[221] Farms participating in the Fair Food Program that can demonstrate compliance with the FFCC enjoy priority within the supply chains of participating buyers.[222] Buyers participating in the program agree to give preference to farms that meet or exceed the program standards.[223] Buyers include grocery retailers such as Whole Foods, Trader Joe's, and Walmart, as well as fast food chains such

[214] *Id.*

[215] *Code of Conduct*, NIKE, https://sustainability.nike.com/code-of-conduct (last accessed Sept. 14, 2018).

[216] *Id.*

[217] *Id.* at 10.

[218] NIKE, INC., FY16/17 SUSTAINABLE BUSINESS REPORT: MAXIMUM PERFORMANCE MINIMUM IMPACT 39 (2017), https://purpose-cms-production01.s3.amazonaws.com/wp-content/uploads/2018/05/18175102/NIKE-FY1617-Sustainable-Business-Report_FINAL.pdf.

[219] *Id.*

[220] *Code of Conduct*, FAIR FOOD STANDARDS COUNCIL, www.fairfoodstandards.org/resources/fair-food-code-of-conduct/ (last visited Mar. 9, 2020) [hereinafter FAIR FOOD, *Code of Conduct*].

[221] FAIR FOOD PROGRAM, 2018 UPDATE 11 (2018), https://www.fairfoodprogram.org/wp-content/uploads/2019/10/Fair-Food-Program-2018-SOTP-Update-Final.pdf; Greg Asbed & Steve Hitov, *Preventing Forced Labor in Corporate Supply Chains: The Fair Food Program and Worker-Driven Social Responsibility*, 52 WAKE FOREST L. REV. 497, 526 (2017).

[222] FAIR FOOD, *Code of Conduct*, *supra* note 220.

[223] *Id.*

as McDonald's, Burger King, and Subway.[224] The Fair Food Program created its code of conduct to provide a "platform upon which to build a truly sustainable agriculture industry."[225] The Fair Food Standards Council (FFSC) oversees implementation of the Fair Food Program.

The FFCC is designed to increase wages and to improve the conditions of work for farmworkers. Participating growers agree to a set of workplace practices regulating wages and benefits, working hours and conditions, and worker safety standards contained in the FFCC. For example, participating farms must pass a portion of the premium that is paid by participating buyers for their produce on to farm workers.[226] Pursuant to the FFCC, participating growers must provide workers with protective equipment, shade, and sufficient work breaks.[227] Where a grower provides housing, residence in the provided housing must be voluntary.[228] Participating growers agree to work with the Coalition of Immokalee Workers, a farmworker organization that creates and carries out a worker health and safety process that provides workers the opportunity to give the grower input on issues in a systematic way.[229] Finally, participating farms must inform farmworkers of their rights and their right to access the complaints-resolution procedure operated by the FFSC.[230]

There are clear consequences for farms that violate provisions of the code that escalate in proportion to the nature of the infraction. Certain violations, such as infractions that involve forced labor or illegal child labor, can result in automatic suspension of a participating farm from the program for a designated time period.[231] Other violations—involving threats of violence; sexual harassment involving physical contact; discrimination; retaliation against workers asserting or aiding others to assert labor rights protections; or failing to fully cooperate with monitoring, audits, or complaint-resolution procedures established by the code—can require a participating farm to take specified remedial actions to avoid suspension or probation. Other violations require implementation of an approved "Corrective Action Plan." Steven Hitov, General Counsel for the CIW explained the FFSC's success as follows: "Corporate social responsibility is a mechanism for buyers dealing with the public relations fallout from unwanted behavior that happens in their supply chain. What we have created is worker driven social responsibility, not corporate social responsibility. What's the best

[224] *Participating Buyers*, FAIR FOOD PROGRAM, https://www.fairfoodprogram.org/partners/ (last visited Mar. 9, 2020) [hereinafter *Participating Buyers*].
[225] FAIR FOOD, *Code of Conduct*, *supra* note 220.
[226] *Id.*
[227] *Id.*
[228] *Id.*
[229] *Id.*
[230] *Id.*
[231] *Id.*

way to protect your brand when atrocities come to light? Don't have any atrocities, and they can't come to light. We have prevented all the behavior that they used to have to figure out how to deal with. They have figured out that, that is far cheaper to buy the penny a pound than it is to pay their PR people. Anybody who thinks any one of these corporations, even the most "liberal" among them, is doing this because it's the right thing, doesn't understand the market. This is business, plain and simple. We have just channeled the market so that it now addresses human rights abuses, as opposed to ignoring them."[232]

*a. Selected Self-Regulation Instruments: McDonald's*

McDonald's has been a Fair Food Program participating buyer since 2007.[233] On its website, McDonald's has a human rights policy commitment that applies to the corporation and its wholly owned subsidiaries worldwide. McDonald's also acknowledges that the level of human rights enforcement varies significantly around the world and in countries where the company operates. Where national and international standards conflict, the company states that it will "adhere to the applicable national or local law, while seeking ways to respect international human rights principles."[234]

The McDonald's Human Rights Policy is informed by the UN Guiding Principles on Business and Human Rights, the International Bill of Human Rights, and the principles set out in the ILO's Declaration on Fundamental Principles and Rights at Work. Echoing the responsibility language contained in the UNGPs, McDonald's maintains: "we take seriously our responsibility to respect and promote human rights and to act with due diligence to avoid infringing on the human rights of others and addressing any impacts on human rights if they occur."[235] The policy is signed by the president and CEO of McDonald's Corporation.[236]

McDonald's instructs that its Human Rights Policy should be read in conjunction with other relevant company policies and guidance, including the supplier code of conduct. The McDonald's 2012 supplier code of conduct contains four areas of focus: (1) human rights; (2) workplace environment; (3) environmental management; and (4) business integrity. As an introduction to its code, McDonald's explains that it "aspires to *protect the Brand* and live our values."[237]

232 Telephone interview Stephen Hitov, General Counsel Coalition of Immokalee Workers, March 11, 2015.

233 *Participating Buyers*, *supra* note 224; *see also*, Bob Langert, The Battle to Do Good: Inside McDonald's Sustainability Journey, 131–142 (2019) (offering an account of the company's earliest engagement with the Coalition of Immokalee Workers to provide better wages for farm workers).

234 *Respecting Human Rights: Human Rights Policy*, McDonalds (2018). https://corporate.mcdonalds.com/content/dam/gwscorp/nfl/scale-for-good/McDonalds_Human_Rights_Policy.pdf.

235 *Id.*

236 *Id.*

237 McDonald's, McDonald's Supplier Code of Conduct 2 (2012), https://corporate.mcdonalds.com/content/dam/gwscorp/nfl/corporate-governance-content/codes-of-conduct/Supplier_Code_of_Conduct.pdf.

The McDonald's supply chain is long, and linkages are not as direct as those in other nonfranchise business models. Recognizing this fact, McDonald's code contains the following:

> We recognize that our suppliers are independent businesses and the exclusive employers of their employees. However, the actions of our business partners can be attributed to McDonald's, affecting our reputation and the level of trust we have earned from customers and others. We appreciate that suppliers operate in different legal and cultural environments throughout the world. At a minimum, we require that all suppliers and their facilities meet the standards and promote the principles outlined in this Code, which are intended to advance McDonald's commitment to all aspects of sustainability (ethical, environmental, and economic).[238]

While the human rights portion of the McDonald's supplier code does not make explicit reference to the FFCC, it does cite the Universal Declaration of Human Rights. The supplier code states that McDonald's suppliers "shall" be expected to conduct activities in a manner consistent with respect for human rights, including, among other things, the rights of workers to freely associate and to be free from discrimination and harassment.[239] The code also calls on suppliers to create grievance mechanisms to handle reports of workplace problems.[240] These expectations are consistent with those contained in the FFSC code.

Beyond presenting its policy commitments, McDonald's provides information on how the company is carrying out its commitments through programs and partnerships. For example, McDonald's explains its Supplier Workplace Accountability (SWA) program as a way to improve human rights performance built on education and continued improvement through verifying compliance with its supplier code of conduct. In 2017, McDonald's had 3,733 suppliers participating in its SWA program.[241] To become a McDonald's supplier, aspiring suppliers now must complete SWA program requirements, including trainings on company expectations, regular self-assessment of systems and practices, audits and inspections, and plans to address instances of noncompliance.[242]

Among other things, McDonald's human rights web page discusses promoting human rights in is supply chain through due-diligence and grievance mechanisms.[243] The prevention of forced labor and the company's UK Modern

[238] *Id* at 4.
[239] *Id.* at 5.
[240] *Id.* at 6.
[241] *Human Rights*, McDonald's, https://corporate.mcdonalds.com/corpmcd/scale-for-good/our-people-and-communities/respecting-human-rights.html (last visited Mar. 8, 2020).
[242] *Id.*
[243] *Id.*

Slavery Act statement are also presented in a brief summary.[244] The company professes its support for the SDGs, specifically five on gender equality and inclusive workplaces, eight on decent work and economic growth, sixteen on peace justice and strong institutions, and seventeen on partnerships to accelerate progress.[245]

McDonald's is "partnering for progress." For example, in 2018, the company worked with Versik Maplecroft, a risk analysis research consulting firm, to conduct a human rights impact assessment of key supply chain commodities and identify the "most salient human rights issues" to improve risk management procedures and increase awareness. McDonald's reports that it is participating in the Human Rights Working Group of Business for Social Responsibility to ensure that its supplier program is able to address emerging human rights risks.

4. The Responsible Business Alliance

The Responsible Business Alliance (RBA), formerly the Electronic Industry Citizenship Coalition (EICC), was founded in 2004 by eight major electronics brands and their first-tier suppliers to "drive positive change and increase efficiency" through the creation of an industry-wide standard to regulate the ethical, environmental, and social issues that arise in the supply chains of electronics corporations.[246] The founding members formed the EICC to facilitate the creation of a unified approach to ensuring that suppliers were held to common standards across the sector. In 2020, more than 150 electronics, retail, auto, and toy companies with combined annual revenues of over $5 trillion, directly employing over six million people were RBA members up from just eight founding member companies in 2004.[247] Influential RBA members in the technology industry include Apple, Amazon, Cisco, Dell, Facebook, GE, Hewlett Packard, and Microsoft, among others.[248]

Though not specifically keyed to any one law or set of laws, the RBA Code of Conduct is informed by many regulatory instruments.[249] It contains a list of references citing, among other instruments, the Dodd-Frank Act, the ILO Codes of Practice in Safety and Health and International Labor, the OECD Due Diligence Guidance for Responsible Supply Chains, and the OECD Guidelines for Multinational Enterprises.[250] The substance of the RBA Code references the

[244] *Id.*
[245] *Id.*
[246] *History: The Founding Members of the Responsible Business Alliance Saw an Opportunity to Drive Positive Change and Increase Efficiency*, Responsible Business Alliance, http://www.eiccoalition.org/about/history/ (last visited Mar. 8, 2020).
[247] *See Members*, Responsible Business Alliance, http://www.responsiblebusiness.org/about/members/ (last visited Nov. 15, 2020).
[248] *Id.* (providing a full list of subscribers).
[249] *See generally* Responsible Business Alliance, Code of Conduct 6.0 (2018), http://www.responsiblebusiness.org/media/docs/RBACodeofConduct6.0_English.pdf.
[250] *Id.* at 14.

UNGPs. The RBA Code incorporates rights in that the substantive provisions contained in the Code stem from fundamental international human rights standards, including the ILO Declaration on Fundamental Principles and Rights at Work and the Universal Declaration of Human Rights.[251]

The RBA Code "encourages Participants to go beyond legal compliance, drawing upon internationally recognized standards, in order to advance social and environmental responsibility and business ethics."[252] The Code also provides that where participants confront regulatory conflicts in the form of "differing standards between the RBA Code and local law, RBA defines [Code] conformance as meeting the strictest requirements."[253]

RBA members are required to adhere to a core set of requirements contained in the RBA Code of Conduct. The Code contains five sections. Three sections set forth standards for labor, health, safety, and the environment. The fourth section sets standards for business ethics, and the final section outlines the features of an "acceptable" systematic process to monitor Code compliance. Among other things, the business ethics section speaks to "integrity," transparency, and the responsible sourcing of minerals.

RBA members are expected to ensure that their suppliers also comply with the Code and must undertake assessments to show compliance. Because the RBA casts such a wide net in requiring that member-businesses extend their commitments to their entire supply chain, the RBA Code of Conduct has tremendous reach, and to the extent that members commit to the principles, they are ostensibly committing every entity in their supply chain to Code standards. RBA's self-assessment process entails questionnaires, audits, and corrective action where deemed necessary.[254]

*a. Selected Self-Regulation Instruments: Apple*

Apple places its code of conduct at the center of supplier responsibility. It "outlines" the company's "expectations for supplier conduct regarding labor and human rights, health and safety, environmental protection, ethics and management practices."[255] Apple states that its code "goes beyond compliance with applicable laws" and that "when differences arise between standards and legal requirements, the stricter standard shall apply, in compliance with applicable law." With respect to "Labor and Human Rights," Apple's supplier code

[251] *Id.* at 1.
[252] *Id.* at n.1 (noting "the code is not intended to create new and additional third-party rights, including for workers.").
[253] *Id.* at 1.
[254] *Standards and Accountability*, RESPONSIBLE BUSINESS ALLIANCE, http://www.responsiblebusiness.org/standards/accountability/ (last visited Mar. 8, 2020).
[255] APPLE, APPLE SUPPLIER RESPONSIBILITY STANDARDS 1 (2019), https://www.apple.com/supplier-responsibility/pdf/Apple-Supplier-Responsible-Standards.pdf.

says: "Apple believes all workers in our supply chain deserve a fair and ethical workplace. Workers must be treated with the utmost dignity and respect."[256] To that end, the code states: "Apple suppliers shall uphold the highest standards of human rights."[257] Apple's supplier code also speaks to the prevention of involuntary labor and human trafficking and underage labor.[258] The code calls on suppliers to exercise due diligence to identify risks and take to take appropriate steps to mitigate them to promote responsible sourcing.[259]

The code applies to Apple suppliers and their subsidiaries, affiliates, and subcontractors providing goods or services to the company for use in or with Apple products.

Much like Apple's code, among other issues, Microsoft's supplier code also covers legal and regulatory compliance practices including asking that suppliers observe the standards of conduct set forth in the US Foreign Corrupt Practices Act and the anticorruption and anti–money laundering laws of the countries in which it operates.[260] Like Apple, Microsoft is an RBA member and consistent with RBA industry standards it devotes an entire section to labor practices and human rights, in which it sets out expectations that suppliers use only voluntary labor and respect worker rights to freedom of association and collective bargaining.[261] Microsoft asserts: "we expect our suppliers and their employees, agents, and subcontractors to adhere to the same standards of conduct and behavior that we expect from our own employees while they are on Microsoft property or doing business with Microsoft." Microsoft explains that the company has established standards of business conduct that apply to all employees, directors, and officers. By extension, the company expects its suppliers to share a "commitment to integrity by complying with and training its employees on the Microsoft Supplier Code of Conduct."[262]

The code provides that Microsoft may require the "immediate removal of any supplier representative(s) or personnel who behave in a manner that is unlawful or inconsistent with [the] Code of Conduct or any Microsoft policy."[263] While Microsoft suppliers are expected to self-monitor their compliance, the code explains that Microsoft may audit or inspect facilities to verify compliance. Suppliers "must" promptly inform Microsoft when any situation develops that cause a code violation or a violation of the standards of business conduct. Suppliers must repay any fees that workers may have paid to third-party

256 *Id.* at 2.
257 *Id.*
258 *Id.*
259 *Id.* at 4.
260 Microsoft, Standards of Supplier Conduct (2016), https://www.microsoft.com/en-us/procurement/supplier-conduct.aspx?activetab=pivot%3aprimaryr7.
261 *Id.* at 3–4.
262 *Id.* at 1.
263 *Id.* at 1.

recruitment agencies.[264] The code concludes with contact information and instructions on how to report "questionable behavior" or a possible violations, and Microsoft states that it will not tolerate retaliation against individuals that provide information and that it will maintain confidentiality of those who seek advice or who report possible violations.[265]

## IV. From Voluntary to Obligatory: The Risks and Rewards of Conduct Codes and Corporate Reporting

Business enterprises that adopt and implement codes enjoy practical advantages.[266] Codes can supplement and strengthen legal compliance and enhance the reputation of a business in a number of ways.[267] A code can serve to clarify the objectives of an organization internally. A company's code often articulates the values and sets normative standards that can then be extended throughout the organization.[268] Codes can guide compliance with norms, and adherence to a code of conduct might reduce the risk of adverse incidents by virtue of members in or affiliated with a business organization being more cognizant of and having a commitment to a given course of conduct.[269] A code could encourage conduct that meets the expectations of stakeholders, engendering greater confidence in the corporation on the part of stakeholders.[270] Finally, codes signal to suppliers and business partners the prerogative and practices of the organization.

Codes play a role in promoting human rights by raising awareness, placing issue on agenda as a priority, signaling expectations and information about who business is and how it operates. Ideally, the relationship between codes of conduct, CSR, and respect for human rights is mutually reinforcing. Codes are referenced in CSR and sustainability reports. Codes are in conversation with corporate reporting and contracting.

### A. The Rewards and Risks of Codes and Corporate Reporting

Adopting and enforcing a code of ethics could enhance the reputation of a corporation and improve the image of a brand as ethical or sustainable. Reputation

[264] *Id.* at 3.
[265] *Id.* at 5.
[266] Ada-Iuliana Popescu, *In Brief: Pros and Cons of Corporate Codes of Conduct*, 9 J. Pub. Admin., Fin. & L. 125, 127 (2016).
[267] *Id.*
[268] *Id.* at 128.
[269] Schwartz, *supra* note 9, at 27, 28–29.
[270] *Id.* at 36.

remains a valuable asset for consumer brands. As calls for corporate accountability increase and supply chain sustainability is appreciated as imperative for continued profitability, using codes of conduct to align business practices with respect for human rights principles could help protect against reputational risk of association with abuses. Arguably, the risk of reputational harm could be reduced by businesses reducing the likelihood of contributing to adverse human rights impacts.

Where business enterprises are operating in contexts where local laws are underdeveloped or unenforced, or otherwise inconsistent with internationally recognized human rights standards, a code of conduct can contribute to the creation of constructive change by providing regulatory order in weaker or conflict affected regions.

To be sure, some commentators have raised concerns about the reliance on codes to ensure ethical business conduct. There are concerns over the risks presented to business of being held liable for failure to live up to commitments. For example, Cavanagh has observed: "in American litigious society, corporate lawyers advise business executives that to sign a compact or pledge increases exposure of a firm to law suits; a firm might be sued if it does not appear to be acting as it pledges in a code."[271]

The early normative critiques of codes published in the 1980s drew attention to the relatively narrow scope of several corporate codes. For example, some commentators have argued that corporate codes remain insular and inward-looking, addressed to individuals within the company.[272] Others commentators have argued that corporate codes of conduct remain primarily concerned with the well-being of the company and not with external stakeholder constituencies. Later, normative critiques of international codes of ethics charged that these instruments adopted largely American management strategies on corporate ethics.[273]

Others charge that codes are inadequate and the victims of rights violations remain vulnerable. For example, the RBA has been accused of being completely "toothless" and falling far short of being a "real" regulator by any measure[274] because "there is no record of any manufacturing facility losing business, permanently or temporarily, for failing to live up to the group's code of conduct."[275]

[271] Gerald F. Cavanagh, *Global Business Ethics: Regulation, Code, or Self-Restraint*, 14 Bus. Ethics Q. 625, 636 (2004).

[272] Schwartz, *supra* note 186, at 29 (citing D. Cressey and A Moore, *Managerial Values and Corporate Codes of Ethics*, 25 California Mgmt R. 53–77 (1983)).

[273] *Id.* (citing G.R. Weaver, *Ethics Programs in Global Business: Culture's Role in Managing Ethics*, 30 J. Bus. Ethics 3–15 (2001)).

[274] Alexis C. Madrigal, *Why Other Electronics Companies Aren't Following Apple's Lead on Factory Audits*, The Atlantic (Feb. 27, 2012), https://www.theatlantic.com/technology/archive/2012/02/why-other-electronics-companies-arent-following-apples-lead-on-factory-audits/253691/.

[275] *Id.* (quoting former Infinera CEO Tom Fallon (internal quotation marks omitted)).

Another major criticism of the RBA is that the self-reporting or third-party audits of member organizations often fail to uncover human rights abuses. In 2017, Samsung attempted to discredit forty-five female whistle-blowers who accused the company of health and safety violations in its factories by, among other things, pointing to the fact that third-party audits approved by the RBA had failed to uncover the alleged abuse.[276]

Codes are changing and improving in response to the expectations of stakeholders.

### B. From Voluntary to Obligatory: Strengthening Soft Standards

Corporate codes of conduct crafted by multinational corporations are like international soft law in that they are not binding. Yet corporate codes may be even stronger for the purposes of advancing human rights because the consequences for failure to comply could result in the loss of economic or employment opportunities. Harm to reputation such that others are unwilling to do business with the entity anymore could be a result of persistent poor performance relative to code commitments.

Codes are voluntary in the sense that the government is not making or mandating that a business have one. A code of conduct does not need to be filed with any government regulatory authority as a condition of incorporation or access to capital markets. Yet codes are obligatory in that corporations are acting as if they are indeed bound. Increasingly code provisions are being incorporated into supplier contracts. Contract law introduces the understanding that code provisions with respect to human rights are binding because contracts can be enforced. Consequences for failure to perform or to improve performance could come at the cost of losing a business relationship.

## V. Incorporating Rights

Here I have demonstrated that corporate responsibility rhetoric incorporating human rights issues increasingly treats compliance with voluntary international standards as obligatory. For example, mandatory reporting is limited to what is deemed "material" to investors, and now the voluntary sustainability reporting

[276] The Business and Human Rights Resource Center published a response to Samsung's effort to stifle reporting on the subject in 2017. *Letter from Pham Thi Minh Hang, Vice Director, Research Center for Gender, Family, and Environment in Development*, Business and Human Rights Resource Center (Dec. 18, 2017), https://www.business-humanrights.org/sites/default/files/documents/Response%20to%20Samsung%20BHRRC%2018%20Dec%202017.pdf.

of leading corporations uses the term "material" to identify what matters to report. Human rights performance has been deemed material information by some companies in some industry sectors as demonstrated by increased reference to rights in sustainability reporting.

Codes and communications are essential for maintaining a "social license" to operate in some industry sectors. The creation of codes by corporations in the case of the RBA, by multistakeholder initiatives like the VPSHRs, or by stakeholder constituencies in the case of the Fair Food Program offer insights into processes that may influence and inform law and may provide an added measure of protection in areas where law has been less effective for ensuring that human rights are not violated.

The rhetoric of responsibility and materiality contained in corporate codes and sustainability reports could be made real, provided investors and consumers have sufficient information to assess human rights performance and to guide purchasing decisions and act as a form of enforcement. Codes of conduct and reporting are changing to meet the escalating expectations placed on business enterprises by constituencies concerned about human rights.

# Conclusion

## Incorporating Rights: Bridging the Human Rights Regulatory Gap

A wide array of actors beyond states must be recognized as possessing the potential to participate in the creation of policies to regulate transnational business practices with respect to human rights. Traditional business practices and traditional understandings of international law are not sufficient to protect and promote human rights where multinational business enterprises are involved. It is no longer descriptively accurate to imagine states to be sole powers with the potential to affect the enjoyment of human rights. A pragmatic approach to rethinking the role of business enterprises in the international system could help create stronger protections for human rights. Change is underway.

Conflicts over corporate complicity in alleged abuses served to catalyze the creation of the different industry-specific multistakeholder initiatives, and international policy frameworks are gaining traction as authoritative among those stakeholders best situated to address or avoid human rights abuses involving business—businesses. Ranking and ratings evaluating the conduct of transnational corporate actors are serving as regulatory tools with potential to bridge a global governance gap that places human rights at risk. In the ecology of global governance, new business and human rights indicators, rankings, and benchmarks now provide rights advocates with greater power and the ability to inform and influence investors. Taken together, this mix of strategies has the potential to play an important role in solidifying emerging soft law standards and strengthening future regulation. The commitments contained in voluntary codes of conduct to respect human rights are becoming obligatory through being incorporated into supplier contracts that link global supply chains. Greater competitive pressures could be brought to bear on particular industries by virtue of greater transparency, including the connected nature of communication enjoyed by a significant segment of investors and consumers. A connected and concerned community of consumers and investors could leverage concerns into change.

My analysis of the content of codes created by competing corporations in selected industry sectors demonstrated that over time the extent to which codes incorporate reference to human rights standards has increased. Similarly, the

*Incorporating Rights.* Erika George, Oxford University Press. © Erika George 2021.
DOI: 10.1093/oso/9780199941483.003.0008

rhetorical framing used in corporate sustainability reporting is incorporating rights and increasingly treats voluntary standards as de facto obligatory for maintaining a "social license" to operate.

More and more corporations are voluntarily assuming commitments to protect human rights and to promote economic development. Corporations are voluntarily incorporating human rights into codes of conduct. Corporations are voluntarily reporting on more than financial matters. Corporate sustainability reports now address environmental and social performance. These private initiatives are positive developments for public international law and human rights protection. Responsible business practices and corporate codes of conduct consistent with the responsibility to respect international human rights will serve to create a body of soft law to supplement the human rights regime and strengthen protections. Domestic laws in some countries are incorporating the concepts contained in international standards. For example, domestic legal efforts to combat human trafficking and the trade in conflict commodities through transparency requirements are evidence of a trend to increase information that businesses and stakeholders can use to promote human rights protections.

This mix of standards and strategies to actually operationalize respect for human rights in business enterprises is likely to be a more promising avenue for progress than promulgating still more international human rights treaties. This is not to say that there is no place for law. Rather, I argue that more than law will be required to bridge the human rights regulatory gap.

## Incorporating Rights: Commitment, Communication, and Change

Given the enforcement problems already inherent in public international law and the existing incentives embedded in corporate law, a new approach to corporate social responsibility in the international arena may be the best option for improving standards and practices and assuring corporate conduct consistent with the existing international human rights law already applied to states. Indeed, a broader business ethic, one that embraces human rights, is imperative. Significantly, corporate culture and committed leadership are important in driving change.

I have shown how voluntary standards, soft law norms, and corporate social responsibility initiatives are evolving to actually influence the business operations of leading companies. Many leading companies are becoming better attuned to the importance of demonstrating respect for fundamental human rights and basic human dignity. By tracing how certain initiatives have hardened and become more significant, I have shown that change is currently occurring in certain industry sectors.

Still, there is a long way to go. In the absence of a binding international regulatory regime to govern corporate conduct with respect to human rights, an "order without law" is emerging. This evolving transnational regulatory regime is serving to advance human rights protections by reducing risks to rights where corporate reputation is at risk. However, accountability remains a challenge.

This book examined the incorporation of human rights into corporate social responsibility and sustainability initiatives. A growing portion of the commercial sector has voluntarily stepped into the global regulatory gap to promulgate corporate social responsibility codes and to pledge support for global policy initiatives like the UN Guiding Principles and the UN Sustainable Development Goals. This book also examined governance developments in corporate social responsibility and human rights. I have explored and explained how social pressure from activists and investors have influenced corporate communications and in some instances conduct with respect to human rights claims that business enterprises are connected to, contribute to, or have caused violations.

From my qualitative empirical field research among stakeholders, including interviews with activists, lawyers, policymakers, professionals, and investors, and ethnographic field research among corporate social responsibility professionals and policymakers examining how external and internal pressures are promoting positive change and a stronger form of "soft law," I learned the following:

- The UN Guiding Principles on Business and Human Rights have indeed proved to be the "authoritative focal point" intended by Professor John Ruggie. His "principled pragmatism" has contributed to progress providing policy guidance. Clarifying the business responsibility to respect human rights has served as a significant policy contribution to catalyze change.
- The activities of human rights and labor rights activists and researchers to expose abuses have been essential in placing human rights on the policy agenda for business enterprises globally. The efforts of civil society have served to give substantive content to the business responsibility to respect human rights to promote change. The business and human rights movement now enjoys growing attention in academic literature and policy arenas.
- The development of sound indicators that inform credible public rankings and ratings of business enterprises based on human rights performance have been gaining influence with business enterprises and audiences of investors interested in reducing reputational risks. By extension, this impetus to evaluate human rights performance could lend support to activist demands for demonstrated respect for rights on the part of business

enterprises, especially publicly traded corporations that must compete for market share.

- The increased interest of investors in environmental and social issues holds untapped potential to propel the business and human rights movement forward. Purchasing and investing with purpose are not being sufficiently utilized to underscore the importance of the business responsibility to respect rights. Shareholder proposals are serving to educate a broader base of investors about important issues. More investors are asking questions about social, environmental, and governance issues.
- The role of multistakeholder initiatives in leading to lasting change and leveraging influence to institute reforms in an industry sector can truly be significant. While some initiatives are stronger and more effective than others for a range of reasons, those that reach root causes and combine policies and practice and provide connections between where decisions are made with where rights may be at risk work best for business and rights.
- Aligning economic incentives with respect for rights can provide effective protection.
- There is an ongoing interplay between a range of different stakeholders that is serving to change the stakes for conducting global business emanating from local actors. Shareholder proposals increasingly show evidence of incorporating priorities of rights and labor activists. Research questions used to rank the human rights performance of corporations are becoming questions that business enterprises must ask and answer. Corporate codes of conduct increasingly incorporate standards contained in international human rights instruments. Corporate sustainability reporting incorporates references to codes of conduct.
- Successfully incorporating rights will require engaging all parts of the ecosystem that informs governance to make the responsibility to respect rights real.

To be sure, much still needs to be done to better align business conduct with respect for human rights, and a healthy skepticism about the potential for these strategies to prevail in promoting real sustained change remains. The treaty effort is a testament to the work that remains. Even were a binding treaty to be ratified, more than law will be required to bring business conduct into alignment with respect for human rights. Rights must be incorporated in an integrated way in business and operationalized such that sourcing is connected to corporate social responsibility and sustainability, not just to a corporation's marketing department. The push and pull of performance metrics and internal and external pressures can aid the press for change.

The corporation is an evolving entity. Business enterprises can evolve under the right conditions to be more cognizant of the moral imperative to respect human rights and alter conduct accordingly, particularly where there is also a market imperative to inspire action. I am encouraged that there is an opportunity should we come to appreciate how to leverage the facts that corporations evolve, that the corporation is not an "atomistic" individual but rather is made of up of different individuals, and that the strong shareholder profit maximization assumptions are not sufficiently robust to describe what goes on in a corporation and do not fully capture influential features like leadership and culture. While corporate law has constituted the corporate person as a single unitary individual, most corporations are more aptly understood as institutions made up of individuals who have their own interests and goals. These individuals may be party to groups or subgroups within the institution with different perspectives on how to do business responsibly. Recent high-profile instances of employees in technology companies like Google, Facebook, and Microsoft, raising issues about the human rights impacts of products designed and services provided by their employers have highlighted differences of opinion within business organizations.

Corporate social responsibility (CSR) and sustainability measures that recognize respect for human rights must become material to the market. Respect for human rights must be and will be monetized or must be made to cost corporations that cause or contribute to abuses. If we accept the premise that the principal purpose of business is to make profits, it must become less profitable to violate human rights. The costs and consequences of violating human rights must be increased. The costs of conducting business in a manner at odds with respect for human rights will increase as information about rights impacts reaches the market and consumers.

It is essential that we rethink and understand as obligatory what has been characterized as voluntary. Governments frequently do not have the resources to enforce in the conventional sense. The Securities and Exchange Commission is reportedly underresourced relative to the scope of its enforcement authority. The US Department of Labor similarly does not have the capacity to cover every workplace under its authority to investigate violations. Other countries face similar if not worse resource constraints. Accordingly, other enforcement alternatives must be strengthened to support respect for human rights.

I propose a different way of understanding the drivers and dynamics of voluntary global standards and the sustainability of the business and human rights movement—as potentially generative of social norms to influence corporate conduct in a manner consistent with many norms of international human rights law. To the extent that CSR initiatives incorporating rights are informed by and are emerging from a process of communication and from cycles of conflict resolution between corporations, states, and civil society stakeholders, all of these actors are shaping expectations about appropriate and inappropriate conduct for the responsible business enterprise. This interplay between stakeholders can serve to give substantive content to the business responsibility to respect rights rooted in the international human rights legal regime.

Even in the absence of binding international law to regulate business conduct with respect to human rights, through the interplay of interest convergence and increasing information access on the part of investors and consumers where corporations will necessarily seek the respect of the consumer community and wish to avoid reputational risk. There is growing evidence that new norms of conduct consistent with respect for human rights are emerging and may evolve to become binding on businesses. Certain voluntary codes of conduct could become binding on corporations, if not in a strictly legal sense, then in a sense that makes pragmatic sense to corporate leaders.

What appears to be voluntary self-regulation on the part of corporations is more appropriately seen as obligatory. The proliferation of principles, standards, and frameworks serves to create compacts between new nonstate actors in the international arena: corporations and concerned investors, workers, consumers, and communities. There is untapped potential to make progress through coordination to increase policy convergence and coherence, institutional interactions, market competition, procedural mechanisms, and access to information in service of increasing respect for human rights.

A mix of actors are involved in the co-creation of norms and expectations for corporate behavior. The new norm of business responsibility to respect human rights can be enforced, provided that material information about corporate social impacts is made accessible to concerned stakeholder constituencies. Greater transparency holds promise for giving power to a shared responsibility to avoid adverse human rights impacts as investors and consumers could choose to reward business enterprises that address issues of human rights effectively and avoid complicity in human rights abuses. Realizing the business responsibility to respect rights will require the efforts of an ecosystem of activists, investors, consumers, employees, and communities impacted by business operations.

It is critical that we expand our understanding of private nonstate actors in international law because of the norm-generating power these actors wield. Under present conditions, the exchange between nonstate actors—corporations, communities, and consumers—may be the most promising possibility for closing the global governance gap into which the unregulated conduct of multinational corporations often falls.

My research is intended to contribute to the growing business and human rights literature by emphasizing the role of concerned and informed constituencies as potential "enforcers" or "regulators" of corporate behavior. Too often, these efforts are invisible, marginalized, or seen as irrelevant to "hard" legal processes such as courtroom advocacy or binding international accords. It is my hope that this research will encourage further strategic and analytical inquiry into how concerned and informed communities can influence the progressive development of corporate governance and international standards in the absence of agreement on a binding international instrument. The increasing prominence of private nonstate actors internationally presents unique challenges, but it may also provide an opportunity to globalize norms of social and environmental justice. Incorporating rights into business policies and process remains an urgent imperative.

# Epilogue

## A Reckoning for Corporate Responsibility and Human Rights

*Another world is not only possible, she is on her way.*

—Arundhati Roy

*It always seems impossible until it is done.*

—Nelson Mandela

As this book goes to print, the world continues to confront the uncertainty caused by the novel coronavirus (COVID-19), compounded by the unrest accompanying popular uprisings against racism around the world. These recent upheavals make clear that a return to business as usual will not be sufficient to meet the changes and challenges we now confront. More is required. Some companies are rising to these challenges, others are not.

## The Global Coronavirus Pandemic: Corporate Communications and Conduct

Government response to COVID-19 has been slow and inadequate in some countries, when gauged by rapidly rising rates of infection and mortality, as in the United States, for instance. The coronavirus shock to the global economy is projected to be seismic, and a prolonged economic slowdown is expected. Still, several businesses have demonstrated a desire to be seen as responsible corporate citizens consistent with stakeholder expectations that the business community contribute to meeting societal needs—voluntarily. Responding to supply shortages, some businesses repurposed regular manufacturing operations to produce much-needed personal protective equipment for healthcare providers and also medical equipment. Tesla engineers designed a prototype ventilator, using parts adapted from electric vehicles, and car companies collaborated with medical device manufacturers to accelerate production and increase the supply of devices. Recognizing the economic hardships caused by public health measures such as shutdowns to slow the spread of the virus, some companies pledged to pay workers unable to come to the workplace. For example, the member-owned cooperative outdoor sports retailer REI announced plans to continue to pay its employees during temporary store closures. Some supermarket chains have set aside special shopping hours for senior citizens and customers understood to be at higher risk for coronavirus complications. Some internet service providers in the United States signed a pledge with the government's communications regulatory agency agreeing to make free Wi-Fi hotspots available as well as to waive fees and avoid service interruptions for people unable to pay for services. Facebook created a $100 million small-business grant program offering funding along with free advertising. A "Corporate Responders" ranking has been published by *Forbes* that assesses how the largest US public companies responded to the public health crisis.

While some corporations have been commended for stepping up, other business enterprises have been condemned for failing to adequately protect workers. When countries entered quarantine, some workers were deemed essential to perform important social functions, such as people employed in healthcare and people working in factories, on farms, in fast food restaurants, and in grocery stores, as well as people working in the delivery and transportation industries. Although recognized as essential, these workers have been treated as expendable. Infection outbreaks have plagued meatpacking plants, where health and safety measures have been inadequate. Labor rights activists in the United States have criticized fast food chain McDonald's for failure to have paid sick and family leave policies adequate to protect its largely low-paid and minority workforce. Shares in UK-based fashion brand Boohoo slumped after allegations of unsafe sweatshop labor conditions in its supply chain surfaced, prompting online retailers like Amazon.com to remove the company's products from their websites. Companies in the food and fashion industries are not the only businesses implicated in coronavirus complexities. Disinformation about the nature of the novel disease continues to spread on social media, arguably making public health measures to contain the virus more difficult to implement.

The COVID-19 pandemic has served to surface underlying structural and systemic inequalities. Historically and currently subjected to discriminatory treatment, disfavored racial and ethnic minority groups have borne a disproportionate impact of the suffering associated with the disease globally, potentially exacerbating existing inequalities into the future. For example, in the United States, Black and Latinx people comprise a significant portion of the essential workforce often exposed to higher risk of infection. The pandemic has also unearthed the harsh reality of racism—inequality has become more difficult to ignore due to significant racial disparities in COVID-19 death rates and discriminatory enforcement of pandemic-related movement restrictions.

## The Global Protests: Corporate Communications and Conduct

Despite the global pandemic and physical distancing, around the world thousands of people joined anti-racism protests to demand accountability for human rights abuses. These protests first erupted in the United States after cellphone video footage capturing a White police officer casually kneeling on the neck of a handcuffed Black man named George Floyd for nearly nine minutes went viral online. The civil unrest that followed Floyd's death quickly spread with solidarity demonstrations in Paris, Nairobi, Berlin, London, and other global capitals. Protestors denounced the racist legacy of colonialism and demanded reparations and the removal of monuments celebrating racist historical figures. Independent experts of the Special Procedures of the UN Human Rights Council issued a joint statement condemning "systemic racism" and "state sponsored racial violence" in the United States and cautioning the government against the threatened use of military force to put down protests as replicating the type of injustice that prompted protests in the first instance.

A broad section of the business community has reacted to the civil unrest with responses ranging from solidarity statements, procurement practices to prefer more minority businesses, hiring practices, philanthropy, and introducing antiracist education into diversity training. Many corporations rushed to reevaluate their role in racism and pledged reforms. Some brands rushed to embrace the previously untouchable #BlackLivesMatter movement. Business leaders expressed renewed interested in doing diligence to determine the ways their policies and practices serve to promote or perpetuate racism.

Several of the corporations discussed in this book have communicated an intention to make changes in the aftermath of the uprisings following George Floyd's death in response to the protest movement. For example, Microsoft announced it would stop providing facial recognition technology to law enforcement due to racial bias until legal protections were put in place. Amazon issued a self-imposed moratorium on the use of its facial recognition products by police. Google announced a hiring initiative to increase diversity in its leadership ranks and vowed to use its YouTube platform to amplify content from Black creators. IBM, a company that provided the tracking technology used by Nazis to facilitate crimes against humanity during World War II, has now gone on record opposing the use of its technology for mass surveillance and racial profiling as violations of basic human rights and freedoms inconsistent with the company's stated values of trust and transparency. Facebook has come under fire for its failure to #StopTheHate as many major brands and retailers have recently removed ads from the platform in solidarity with civil rights leaders concerned about the company's role in spreading and amplifying hate speech and disinformation.

Food and beverage sector firms have also found ways to answer growing calls to reckon with racism. For example, PepsiCo retired brands rooted in racist stereotypes criticized as nostalgic for chattel slavery. Apparel and sportswear firms are especially sensitive to brand image and have been pressed to acknowledge the need to do better given the debt these businesses owe to the Black athletes, artists, and consumers who have contributed culturally to enhancing brand image. When Adidas issued a public statement about diversity, some of the company's Black employees took to social media to share their previously private stories of racial discrimination experienced in the workplace. Black employees noted the inconsistency between the company's internal culture and external image. In response, Adidas promised more Black representation within the company and more funding for programs to address racial disparities.

## A Changing Conversation

Growing social movements that are gaining public support may serve to accelerate some of the reforms sought by socially responsible investors, the authors of human rights indicators, and other conscious capitalists interested in integrating shareholder and stakeholder value that I have discussed in this book. More than ever before businesses are talking about racism as the #BlackLivesMatter movement demands an end to injustice. Businesses are engaging in conversations about sexism as the #MeToo movement calls for an end to sexual harassment and gender discrimination. Businesses are talking about environmental impacts as mass youth protests and school strikes have served to elevate the issue of climate change. We are seeing stakeholders stand with frontline communities and youth in the fight for environmental justice. We are seeing a public that wants to know more about what companies are doing to eradicate racism and how companies are treating employees.

The "B Corporation" movement is growing. Rooted in the recognition that corporations must benefit a broader segment than shareholders, the B Corp movement maintains that businesses must benefit society more broadly. Internal pressures from employees and external pressure from consumer boycotts to questions from investors and other commercial partners are now providing more incentives for corporations to improve social and environmental performance.

COVID-19 has uncovered underlying structural and systemic inequalities, exacerbated by acts or omissions of decision makers in public institutions and private enterprise. Social movements are demanding substantive change and are increasingly challenging the status quo as unsustainable. Businesses are beginning to demonstrate understanding that short-term profit maximization is no longer sustainable and the reputation of business has suffered as a result of the coronavirus pandemic.

The coronavirus crisis is forcing a much-needed and long-overdue rethink of corporate responsibility, sustainability, and human rights. Solidarity statements are nice but not sufficient. Stakeholders and social movements are calling for more than marketing. All of us are called on to create a more just and equitable world. While the conversations concerning rights, race, and the role of the corporation in society are welcome, whether businesses will walk the talk remains to be seen.

## Answering Calls for Action

Any path forward toward a more just and equitable world must incorporate human rights, protect the environment, and promote peace. The UN 2030 Agenda for Sustainable Development is an ambitious plan of action that seeks to promote peace and prosperity. It contains Sustainable Development Goals (Global Goals) that are to be achieved by 2030. Among the Global Goals are ensuring healthy lives and promoting well-being; achieving gender equality; promoting sustained, inclusive, and sustainable economic growth, full and productive employment and decent work for all; reducing inequality within and among countries; taking urgent action to combat climate change and its impacts; and promoting peaceful and inclusive societies by providing access to justice for all and building effective, accountable, and inclusive institutions at all levels. Agenda 2030 also calls for strengthening global partnerships. The Global Goals are "integrated and indivisible" and seek to balance the economic, the social, and the environmental aspects of sustainability.

The UN Working Group on Business and Human Rights recently launched the UNGPs+10 initiative to celebrate the tenth anniversary of the unanimous endorsement of the Guiding Principles on Business and Human Rights (UNGPs) by the UN Human Rights Council in 2021 and to chart a course action for implementing the UNGPs more widely and broadly between now and 2030.

The pandemic and the protest movements make partnerships to promote peace and prosperity for everyone, everywhere all the more urgent. We have a real opportunity to reset and recommit to these global priorities and rights protections. Leaders in government and business must recommit to reaching the goals and putting the principles into practice.

The present moment provides an opportunity to push ourselves to move beyond business as usual—we must reimagine more equitable and inclusive ways of structuring economic, social, and political life.

## Reimagining Responsibility: Incorporating Rights

A more just way of doing business means we must reimagine corporate social responsibility and sustainability in ways that take calls for economic justice, environmental justice, racial justice, and gender justice seriously. Imagine. What if our technological innovations were used to analyze patterns of inclusion and exclusion to help expose and eradicate bias rather than to promulgate bigotry and hatred? What if corporate purpose was better aligned with playing a beneficial role in society? What if we truly treated economic, social, and environmental issues as interrelated and interdependent?

Whether these movements will make a lasting difference in the relationship between business and human rights and whether the present moment will mark a departure from the past remain to be seen, but I believe enough is different about our current moment to make change possible. This book has shown the potential of investor, consumer, and community pressure to promote corporate responsibility. Early corporate responses to the current challenges confronting business accompanying the coronavirus pandemic and protest movements confirm my research findings related to the power of public pressure to reorder and to expand business priorities. This book has documented some of the significant changes that have taken place since 2011 to promote the responsibility of businesses to respect human rights. Now we are seeing a growing critical mass of the public calling for systemic change and structural long-term solutions.

To be sure, the risk of global economic recession is high, and human suffering is real. The rising tide of authoritarianism and nationalism in some countries also presents real risks. Yet it is precisely these challenging conditions that make it critically important for the business community to conduct the human rights due diligence necessary to better understand how business practices and policies impact the enjoyment of human rights, to address any adverse impacts, and to reimagine better ways of doing business in ways that respect and promote human rights. My research reveals how important it is for each of us to exert the influence we do possess to insist that business leaders do better if we are to see sustained progress on business and human rights issues.

It is unlikely that the world will return to business as usual. Our world will be different and perhaps forever changed. When I took on this book project years ago, I could not have imagined that a global pandemic would cause such upheaval in our lives and cost so many lives. Nor could I have foreseen that one

Black man's murder would spark mass mobilizations against racism around the world. Author Arundhati Roy has observed that pandemics force humanity "to break with the past and imagine their world anew." She invites us to see the pandemic as a doorway to something different. We have a powerful opportunity to think differently and to do things differently. We have a responsibility to reimagine a better new world.

# APPENDIX A

# Selected Sustainability Reports

The following images are word clouds of the sustainability reports published by selected corporations published before and after human rights abuse allegations and the endorsement of the UN Guiding Principles on Business and Human Rights by the UN Human Rights Council. These images show changes in corporate rhetoric on social responsibility and human rights for purposes of cross comparison between specific companies, industry sectors, and in relation to developments in law and policy that pertain to linking business and human rights. These images visually represent the salient concepts in the reports. The size of a word reflects the number of times it is referenced in relation to others.

## Agriculture, Food, and Beverage

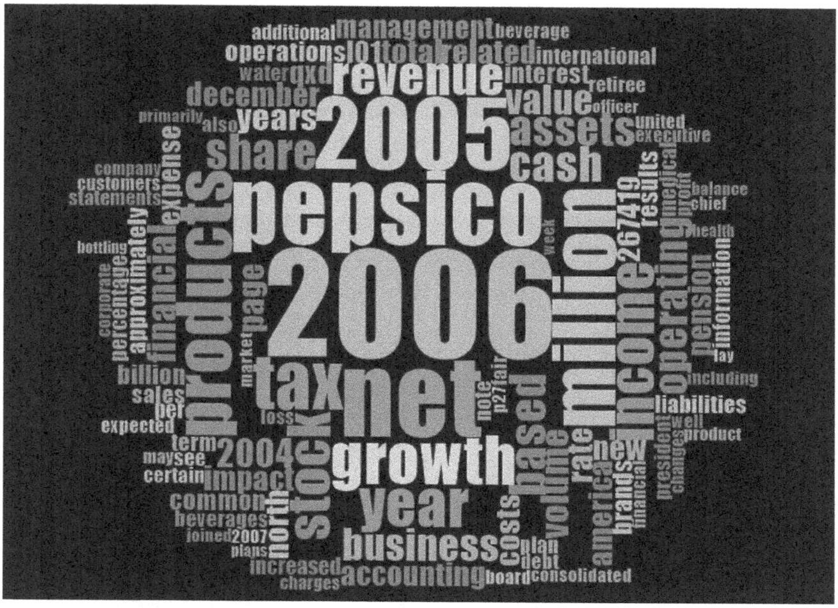


Figure 1 PepsiCo Word Cloud 2006

Figure 2 PepsiCo Word Cloud 2018

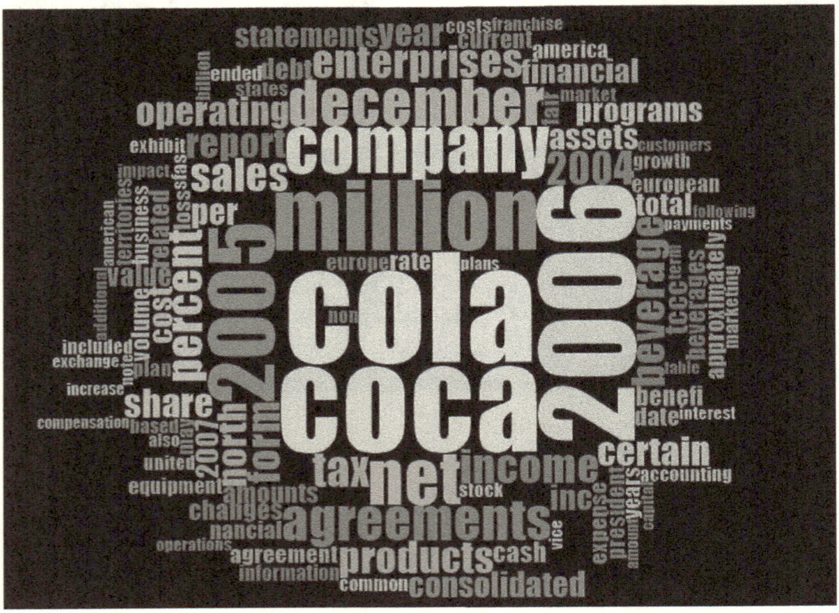


Figure 3 Coca Cola Word Cloud 2006

Figure 4 Coca Cola Word Cloud 2018

## Apparel

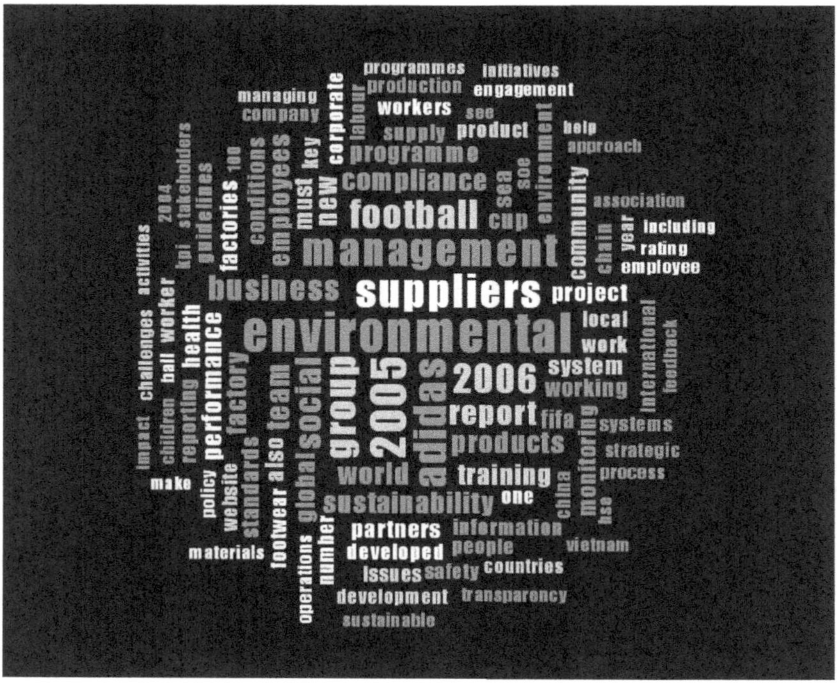


Figure 5 Adidas Word Cloud 2005

**Figure 6** Adidas Word Cloud 2015

**Figure 7** Nike Word Cloud 2006

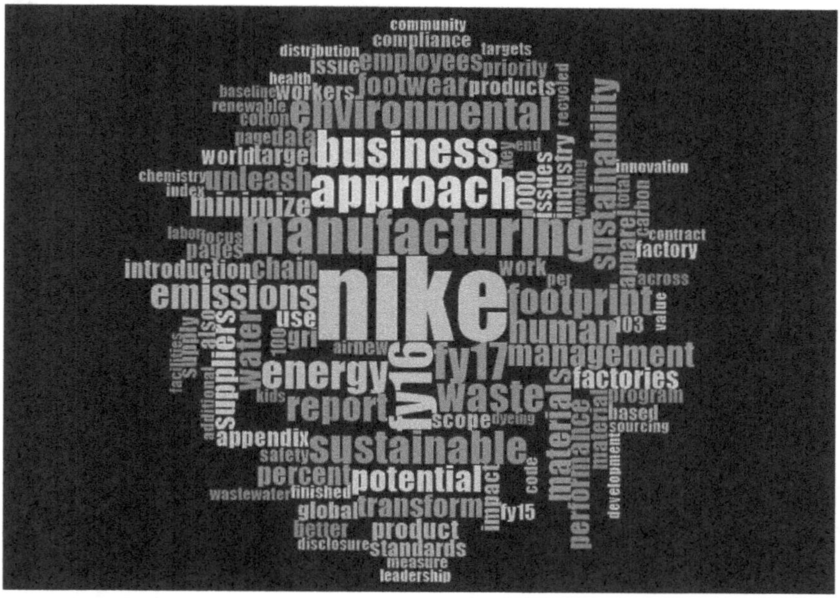


Figure 8 Nike Word Cloud 2016

## Energy, Oil, and Gas

Figure 9 Shell Word Cloud 1997

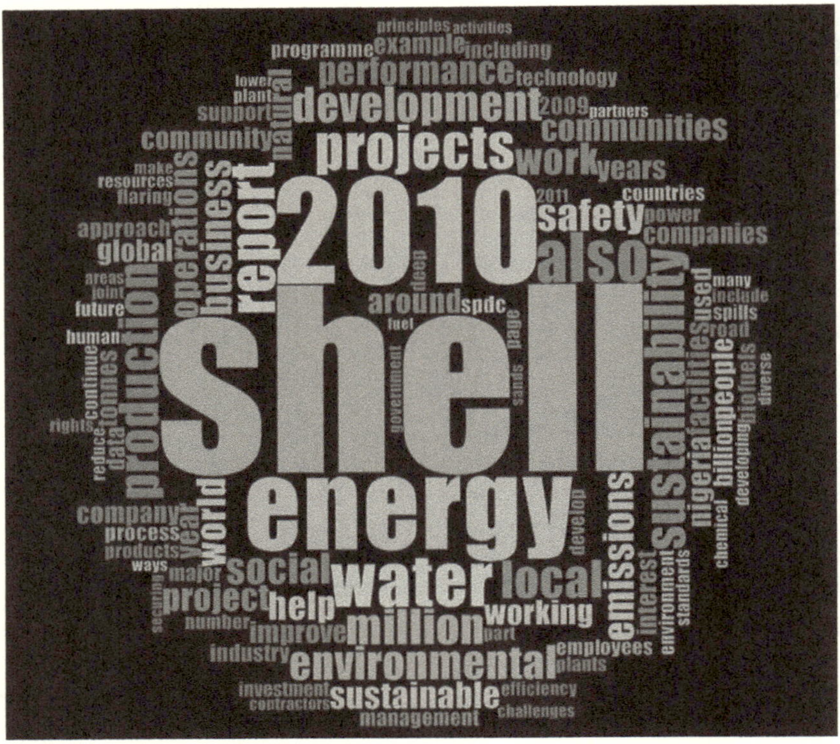


Figure 10 Shell Word Cloud 2010

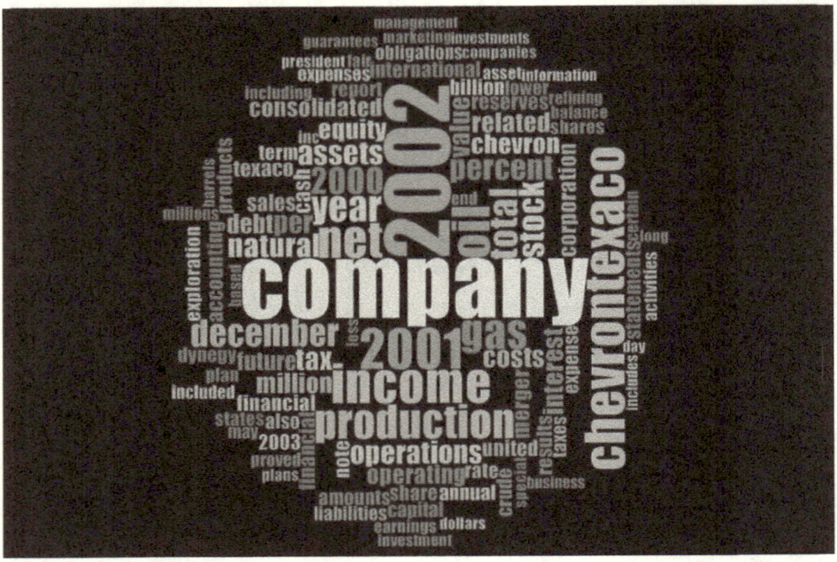


Figure 11 Chevron Word Cloud 2002

Figure 12 Chevron Word Cloud 2011

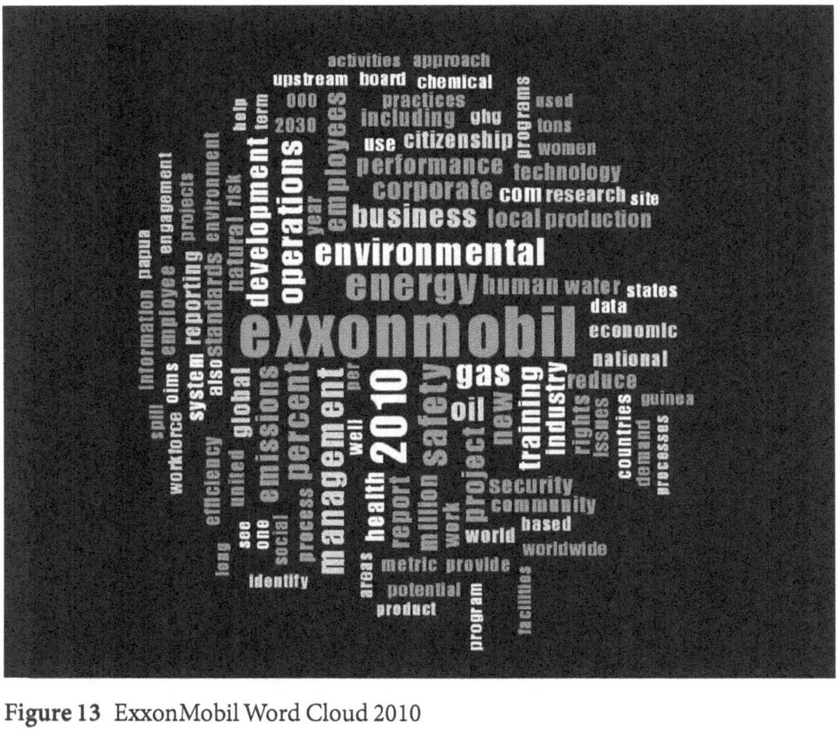


Figure 13 ExxonMobil Word Cloud 2010

Figure 14 ExxonMobil Word Cloud 2018

## Information Communications Technology

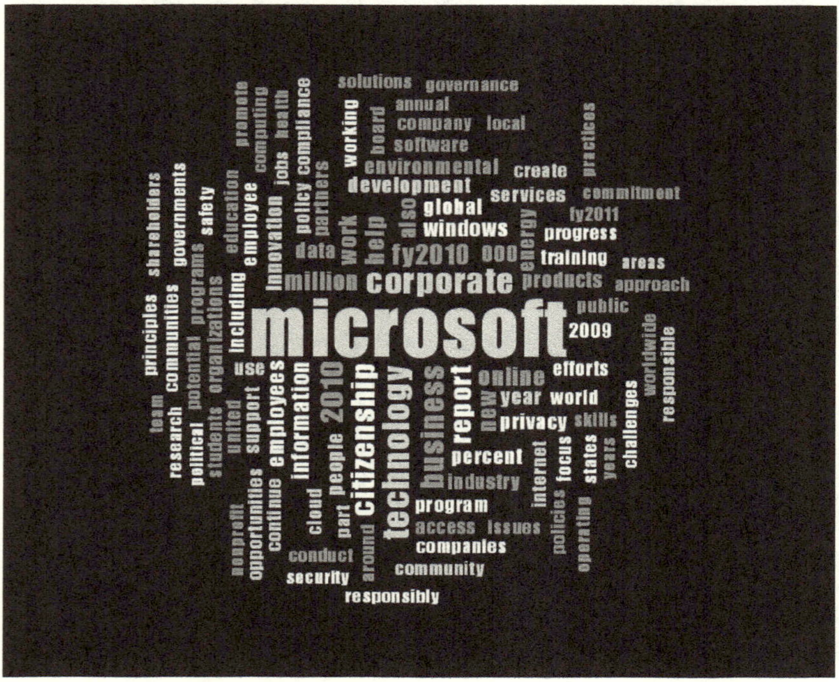

Figure 15 Microsoft Word Cloud 2010

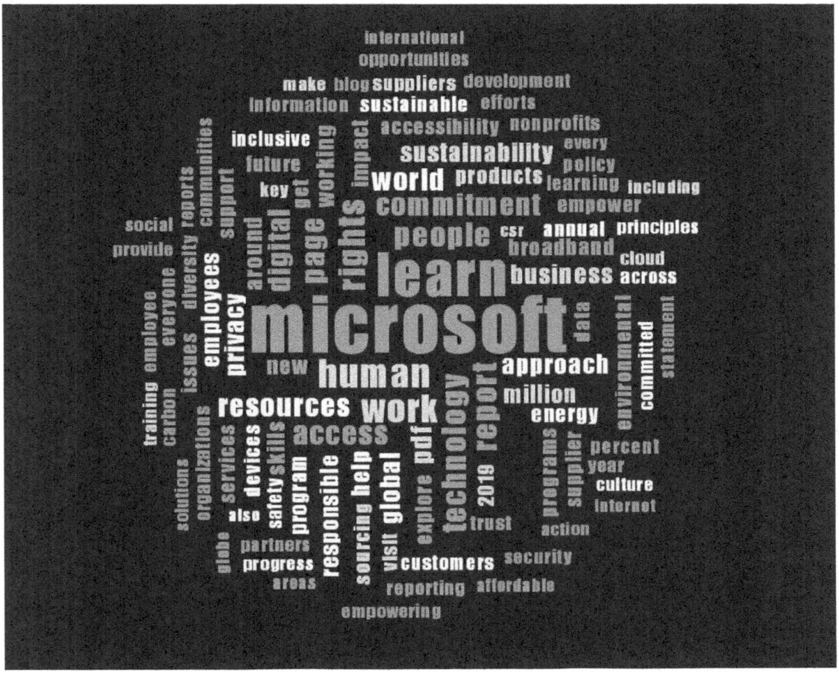


Figure 16 Microsoft Word Cloud 2019

Figure 17 Apple Word Cloud 2013

**Figure 18** Apple Word Cloud 2018

# APPENDIX B

# Selected Codes of Conduct

The following images are word clouds of the codes of conduct from selected corporations. These images show the salient concepts in the codes. The size of a word reflects the number of times it is referenced in relation to others.

## Agriculture, Food, and Beverage

**Figure 1** Coca Cola Word Cloud 2009

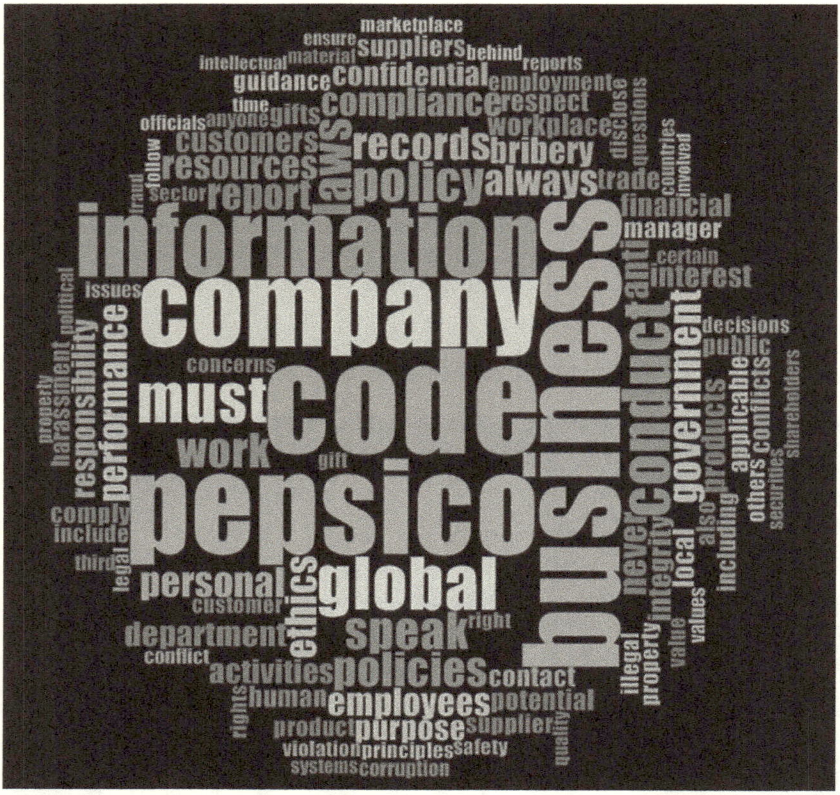


**Figure 2** PepsiCo Word Cloud 2012–2014

## Information Communications Technology

Figure 3 Apple Word Cloud 2015

Figure 4 Facebook Word Cloud 2016

Figure 5 Google Word Cloud 2015

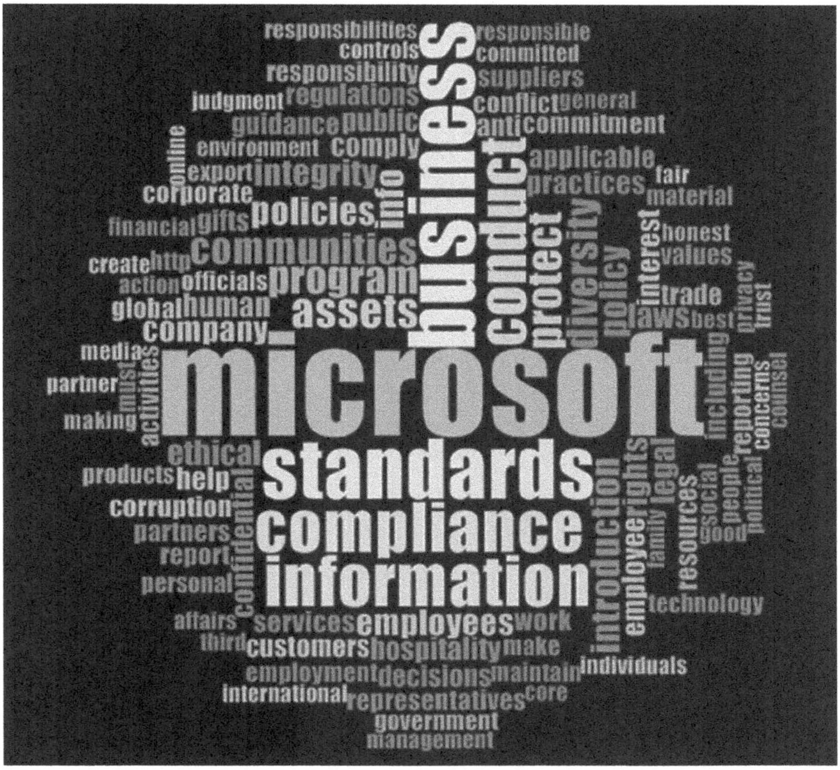


**Figure 6** Microsoft Word Cloud 2014

# Selected References

## Books


Addo, M., (ed.), *Human Rights Standards and the Responsibility of Transnational Corporations* (The Hague: Kluwer, 1999).

Alston, P. (ed.), *Non-State Actors and Human Rights* (New York: Oxford University Press, 2005).

Anghie, Antony, *Imperialism, Sovereignty and the Making of International Law* (Cambridge: Cambridge University Press, 2005).

Berle, A., & Gardiner, M., *The Modern Corporation and Private Property* (New York: Macmillan 1932).

Blair, J., Dickson, M.A., & Miller D. (eds.), *Workers' Rights and Labor Compliance in Global Supply Chains: Is a Social Label the Answer?* (New York: Routledge, 2014).

Blecher, L., Kaymar Stafford, N., & Bellamy, G.C., *Corporate Responsibility for Human Rights Impacts: New Expectations and Paradigms* (United States: American Bar Foundation, 2014).

Blumberg, P., *The Multinational Challenge to Corporation Law: The Search for a New Corporate Personality* (New York: Oxford University Press, 1993).

Bowen, H.R., *Social Responsibilities of the Businessman* (New York: Harper & Row, 1953).

Braithwaite, J., & Drahos, P, *Global Business Regulation* (Cambridge: Cambridge University Press, 2000).

Brownlie, I., *Principles of Public International Law* (Oxford: Oxford University Press, 5th ed. 1998).

Černič, J.L., *Human Rights Law and Business: Corporate Responsibility for Fundamental Human Rights* (Netherlands: Europa Law Pub., 2010).

Chaudhuri, K.N., *The Trading World of Asia and the English East India Company 1660–1760* (New York: Cambridge University Press, 1978).

Clapham, A., *Human Rights Obligations of Non-State Actors* (Oxford: Oxford University Press, 2006).

Clarke, T., "Introduction: Theories of Governance—Reconceptualizing Corporate Governance Theory After the Enron Experience." In *Theories of Corporate Governance: the Philosophical Foundations of Corporate Governance* (T. Clarke ed., New York: Routledge, 2004).

Dashwood, H., "Corporate Social Responsibility and the Evolution of International Norms." In *Hard Choices, Soft Law: Voluntary Standards in Global Trade, Environment and Social Governance* (John Kirton & Michael Trebilcock eds., Aldershot: Ashgate, 2004).

Davis, K.E., Fisher, A., Kingsbury, B., & Engle Merry, S. (eds.), *Governance by Indicators: Global Power through Quantification and Rankings* (Oxford: Oxford University Press, 2012).

Deva, S., *Regulating Corporate Human Rights Violations: Humanizing Business* (New York: Routledge, 2012).

Deva, S., & Bilchitz D. (eds.), *Human Rights Obligations of Business: Beyond the Corporate Responsibility to Respect?* (Cambridge: Cambridge, 2013).

De Schutter, O. (ed.), *Transnational Corporations and Human Rights* (Oxford: Oxford University Press, 2006).

Dilling, O., Herberg, M., & Winter, G., (eds.) *Responsible Business: Self-Governance and Law in Transnational Economic Transactions* (Portland, OR: Hart, 2008).

Duruigbo, E., *Multinational Corporations and International Law: Accountability and Compliance Issues in the Petroleum Industry* (New York: Transnational Publishers, 2003).

Engle Merry, S., Davis K.E., & Kingsbury, B. (eds.), *The Quiet Power of Indicators: Measuring Governance, Corruption and the Rule of Law* (New York: Cambridge University Press, 2015).

Flynn, J.J., "The Jurisprudence of Corporate Personhood: The Misuse of a Legal Concept." In *Corporations and Society Power and Responsibility* (Samuels W.J., & Miller A.S., eds., Westport, CT: Greenwood Press, 1987).

Friedman, M., *Capitalism and Freedom* (Chicago: University of Chicago Press, 1962).

Greenfield, K., *Corporations are People Too: (And They Should Act Like It)* (United Kingdom: Yale University Press, 2018).

Hans, V.P., *Business on Trial: The Civil Jury and Corporate Responsibility* (United Kingdom: Yale University Press, 2000).

Hemmati, M. (ed.), *Multi-Stakeholder Processes for Governance and Sustainability: Beyond Deadlock and Conflict* (London: Earthscan, 2002).

Ijalaye, D., *The Extension of Corporate Personality In International Law* (Leiden: Oceana, 1978).

Jagers, N., *Corporate Human Rights Obligations in Search of Accountability* (Utrecht: Intersentia, 2002).

Jagers, N., "The Legal Status of the Multinational Corporation Under International Law." In *Human Rights Standards and the Responsibility of Transnational Corporations* (Michael K. Addo ed., The Hague: Kluwer, 1999).

Jessup, P.C., *A Modern Law of Nations* (New York: Macmillan, 1948).

Joseph, S., & Castan, M., *The International Covenant on Civil and Political Rights: Cases, Materials, and Commentary* (Oxford: Oxford University Press, 2013).

Joseph, S., *Corporations and Transnational Human Rights Litigation* (United Kingdom: Bloomsbury Academic, 2004).

Jungk, M., "A Practical Guide to Addressing Human Rights Concerns for Companies Operating Abroad." In *Human Rights Standards and the Responsibility of Transnational Corporations* (M.K. Addo ed., The Hague: Kluwer 1999).

Kamminga, M., & Zia-Zarifi, S. (eds.), *Liability of Multinational Corporations under International Law* (The Hague: Kluwer International Law, 2000).

Kinley, D., *Civilising Globalisation: Human Rights and the Global Economy* (Cambridge: Cambridge University Press, 2009).

Kirton, J.J., & Trebilcock, M. (eds.), *Hard Choices, Soft Law: Voluntary Standards in Global Trade, Environment and Social Governance* (Aldershot: Ashgate, 2004).

Kobrin, S., "Multinational Corporations, the Protest Movement, and the Future of Global Governance." In *Leviathans Multinational Corporations and the New Global History* (A. Chandler & B. Mazlish eds., Cambridge: Cambridge University Press, 2005).

Li, C., & Bernoff, J., *Groundswell: Winning in a World Transformed by Social Technologies* (Boston: Harvard Business Press, 2008).

MacKinnon, R., *Consent of the Networked: The Worldwide Struggle for Internet Freedom,* (New York: Basic Books, 2012).

Mares, R. *The UN Guiding Principles on Business and Human Rights: Foundations and Implementation* (Leiden: Brill Academic, 2012).

Martin, J. & Bravo, K. (eds.), *The Business and Human Rights Landscape Moving Forward, Looking Back* (Cambridge: Cambridge University Press, 2015).

McBarnet, D., Voiculescu, A., & Campbell, T. (eds.), *The New Corporate Accountability: Corporate Social Responsibility and the Law* (Cambridge: Cambridge University Press, 2007).

Micklethwaith, J. & Wooldridge, A., *The Company: A Short History of Revolutionary Idea* (Modern Library, 2003).

Muchlinski, P., *Multinational Enterprises and the Law* (Oxford: Blackwell, 1995).

Muthu, S., *Enlightenment Against Empire* (Princeton: Princeton University Press, 2003).

Nolan, J., & Baumann-Pauly, D. (eds.), *Business and Human Rights: From Principles to Practice* (United Kingdom: Taylor & Francis, 2016).

Noortmann, M. & Ryngaert, C., "Non-State Actor Dynamics" *in International Law: From Law-Takers to Law-Makers* (United Kingdom: Ashgate, 2010).

Richter, J., *Holding Corporations Accountable: Corporate conduct, International Codes and Citizens Action* (New York: Zed Books, 2001).

Robins, Nick, *The Corporation that Changed the World: How the East India Company Shaped the Modern Multinational* (United Kingdom: Pluto Press, 2006).

Ruffing, L. & Hamdani, K., *United Nations Centre on Transnational Corporations: Corporate Conduct and the Public Interest* (United Kingdom: Taylor & Francis, 2015).

Ruggie, J., *Just Business: Multinational Corporations and Human Rights* (New York: W.W. Norton & Company Ltd., 2013).

Samuels, W.J., & Miller A.S. (eds.), *Corporations and Society: Power and Responsibility* (Westport, CT: Greenwood Press, 1987).

Samuels, W.J., "The Idea of the Corporation as a Person: On the Normative Significance of Judicial Language." In *Corporations and Society: Power and Responsibility* (Samuels W.J., & Miller A.S., eds., Westport CT: Greenwood Press, 1987).

Schilling, D., "Making Codes of Conduct Credible." In *Global Codes of Conduct: An Idea Whose Time Has Come* (Williams O., ed., Notre Dame: Notre Dame University Press, 2000).

Shelton, D. (ed.), *Commitment and Compliance: The Role of Non-Binding Norms in the International Legal System* (New York: Oxford University Press, 2000).

Sikkink, K., & Keck, M. E., *Activists Beyond Borders: Advocacy Networks in International Politics* (United Kingdom: Cornell University Press, 2014).

Sinden, A., "Power and Responsibility: Why Human Rights Should Address Corporate Environmental Wrongs." In *The New Corporate Accountability: Corporate Social Responsibility and the Law* (McBarnet, D., Vioculescu A., & Campbell T., eds., Cambridge: Cambridge University Press, 2007).

Smith, Adam, *An Inquiry into the Nature and Causes of the Wealth of Nations* (Edwin Cannan ed., 1977).

Steinhart, R., "Corporate Responsibility and the International law of Human Rights: The New Lex Mercatoria." In *Non-State Actors and Human Rights* (P. Alston ed., Oxford, 2005).

Stevens, Beth, "Corporate Accountability: International Human Rights Litigation Against Corporations in US Courts." In *Liability of Multinational Corporations under International Law* (M. Kamminga & S. Zia-Zarifi eds., The Hague: Kluwer International Law, 2000).

Stout, L., *The Shareholder Value Myth: How Putting Shareholder First Harms Investors, Corporations and the Public* (San Francisco: Berrett-Koehler, 2012).

Webber, D., *The Rise of the Working-Class Shareholder: Labor's Last Best Weapon* (United States: Harvard University Press, 2018).

Williams, O. (ed.), *Global Codes of Conduct: An Idea Whose Time Has Come* (Notre Dame: University of Notre Dame Press, 2000).

Winkler, A., *We the Corporations: How American Businesses Won Their Civil Rights* (United States: W.W. Norton & Co, 2018).

Yanacopulos, H. & Voiculescu, A., *The Business of Human Rights: An Evolving Agenda for Corporate Responsibility* (London: Zed Books Ltd., 2011).

Zerk, J., *Multinationals and Corporate Social Responsibility: Limitations and Opportunities in International Law* (Cambridge: Cambridge University Press, 2006).

## Articles

Abbot, K., & Snidal, D., "Strengthening International Regulation Through Transnational New Governance: Overcoming the Orchestration Deficit," 42 *Vand. J. Transnat'l L.* 501. (2009).

Akhtarkhavari, A., "The Global Compact, Environmental Principles, and Change in International Environmental Politics," 38 *Denv. J. Int'l L. & Pol'y* 227 (2010).

Arielle, Joy Albert, "Good for the Bottom Line: Incentivizing Private Companies to Join the Global Network Initiative," 11 *J. Int'l Bus. & L.* 379 (2012).

Alston, Philip, "'Core Labour Standards' and the Transformation of the International Labour Rights Regime," 15 *Eur. J. Int'l L.* 457 (2004).

Alvarez, José E., "Are Corporations 'Subjects' of International Law?," 9 *Santa Clara J. Int'l L.* 1 (2011).

Anghie, A., "Finding the Peripheries: Sovereignty and Colonialism in Nineteenth-Century International Law," 40 *Harv. Int'l L.J.* 1 (1999).

Aponte, Miranda L., "The Hybrid State-Corporate Enterprise and Violations of Indigenous Land Rights: Theorizing Corporate Responsibility and Accountability Under International Law," 11 *Lewis & Clark L. Rev.* 135 (2007).

Auld, G. et al., "The New Corporate Social Responsibility," 33 *Annual Review Environmental Resources* 413–435 (2008).

Backer, L., "Multinational Corporations, Transnational Law: The United Nations' Norms on the Responsibilities of Transnational Corporations as a Harbinger of Corporate Social Responsibility in International Law," 37 *Colum. Hum. Rts. L. Rev.* 287 (2005–2006).

Bales, Kevin, & Cornell, Becky, "The Next Step in the Fight Against Human Trafficking: Outlawing the Trade in Slave-Made Goods," 1 *Intercultural Hum. Rts. L. Rev.* 211 (2006).

Barnett, M.L., "Stakeholder Influence Capacity And The Variability Of Financial Returns To Corporate Social Responsibility," 32 *Acad. Mgmt. Rev.* 794–816 (2007).

Bartley, T., & Child, C., "Shaming the Corporation: Social Movement Pressure and Corporate Social Responsibility" (unpublished on file with author draft, 2010).
Baumann-Pauly, Dorothee et al., "Industry-Specific Multi-Stakeholder Initiatives that Govern Corporate Human Rights Standards."
Baur, Dorothea, & Hans Peter Schmitz, "Corporations and NGOs: When Accountability Leads to Co-Optation," 106 *J. Bus. Ethics* 9 (2012).
Baworowsky, Julie Marie, "From Public Square to Market Square: Theoretical Foundations of First and Fourteenth Amendment Protection of Corporate Religious Speech," 83 *Notre Dame L. Rev.* 1713, 1728 (2008).
Baxi, U., "Market Fundamentalisms: Business Ethics at the Alter of Human Rights," 5 *Hum. Rts. L. Rev.* 1 (2005).
Bhattacharya, C.B., Korschun, D., & Sen, S., "Strengthening Stakeholder–Company Relationships Through Mutually Beneficial Corporate Social Responsibility Initiatives," 85 *J. Bus. Ethics* 257–272 (2009).
Bhattacharya, C.B., & Sen, S. "Doing Better at Doing Good: When. Why, and How Consumers Respond to Corporate Social Initiatives," 47 *Cal. Mgmt. Rev.* 9–24 (2004).
Bird, Robert C. et al., "Corporate Voluntarism and Liability for Human Rights in A Post-Kiobel World," 102 *Ky. L.J.* 601, 603 (2014).
Blair, S., & Chernev, A., *Doing Well by Doing Good: The Benevolent Halo of Social Goodwill.* Working paper, Kellogg School of Management, Northwestern University (2014).
Blaire, Margaret M., "Of Corporations, Courts, Personhood, and Morality," 25 *Society for Business Ethics* 415–431 (2015).
Blumberg, P., "The Corporate Entity in an Era of Multinational Corporations," 15 *Del. J. Corp. L.* 283 (1990).
Borzel, Tanja A., & Honke, Jana, *From Compliance to Practice: Mining Companies and the Voluntary Principles on Security and Human Rights in the Democratic Republic of Congo*, Governance in Areas of Limited Statehood—Governance Working Paper Series (Oct. 2011).
Bunn, I., "Global Advocacy for Corporate Accountability: Transatlantic Perspectives From the NGO Community," 19 *Am. U. Int'l L. Rev.* 1265 (2003–2004).
Campopiano, G., De Massis, A., & Cassia, L., "The Relationship Between Motivations and Actions in Corporate Social Responsibility: An Exploratory Study," 13 *Int'l J. Bus. & Soc'y* 391–425 (2012).
Carrol, Archie B., & Shabana, Kareem M., "The Business Case for Corporate Social Responsibility: A Review of Concepts, Research and Practice," 12 *Int'l J. Mgmt. Rev.* 97–99 (2010).
Carroll, A., "Corporate Social Responsibility: Evolution of a Definitional Construct," 38 *Bus. & Soc'y* 268–295 (1999).
Chander, A., "Googling Freedom," 99 *Cal. L. Rev.* 1–45 (2011).
Chen, Stephen, & Bouvain, Petra, "Is Corporate Responsibility Converging? A Comparison of Corporate Responsibility Reporting in the USA, UK, Australia, and Germany," 87 *J. Bus. Ethics* 299 (2009).
Chilton, Adam S., & Sarfaty, Galit A., "The Limitations of Supply Chain Disclosure Regimes," 53 *Stan. J. Int'l L.* 1 (2017).
Chinkin, C.M., "The Challenge of Soft Law: Development and Change in International Law," 38 *Int'l & Comp. L.Q.* (1989).
Chung, H., & Talaulicar, T., "Forms and Effects of Shareholder Activism," 18 *Corp. Gov.: An Int'l Rev.* 253–257 (2010).

Cohen Maryanov, Debra, "Sweatshop Liability: Corporate Codes of Conduct and the Governance of Labor Standards in the International Supply Chain," 14 *Lewis & Clark L. Rev.* 397 (2010).

Collingsworth, Terry, "Corporate Social Responsibility, Unmasked," 16 *St. Thomas L. Rev.* 669 (2004).

Conway, Madeleine, "A New Duty of Care? Tort Liability from Voluntary Human Rights Due Diligence in Global Supply Chains," 40 *Queen's L.J.* 741 (2015).

Dam, L., & Scholtens, B., "Does Ownership Type Matter for Corporate Social Responsibility?," 20 *Corp. Gov.: An Int'l Rev.* 233–252 (2012).

Davis, K.E., Kingsbury, B., & Engle Merry, S., "Indicators as a Technology of Global Governance," 46 *L. & Soc'y Rev.* 71–104 (2012).

Den Hond, F., & De Bakker, F.G., "Ideologically Motivated Activism: How Activist Groups Influence Corporate Social Change Activities," 32 *Acad. Mgmt. Rev.* 901–924 (2007).

Deva, S., "Article: Global Compact: A Critique Of The U.N.'S 'Public-Private' Partnership For Promoting Corporate Citizenship," 34 *Syracuse J. Int'l L. & Com.* 107 (2006).

Deva, S., "Corporate Complicity in Internet Censorship in China: Who Cares for the Global Compact or the Global Online Freedom Act," 39 *Geo. Wash. Int'l L. Rev.* 255 (2007).

Deva, S., "Human Rights Violations By Multinational Corporations and International Law: Where from Here," 19 *Conn. J. Int'l L.* 1 (2003–2004).

Deva, S., "'Yahoo! For Good' and the Right to Privacy of Internet Users: A Critique," 11 *J. Internet L.* 3 (Mar. 2008).

Dewey, John, "The Historic Background of Corporate Legal Personality," 35 *Yale L.J.* 655 (1926).

Dhir, Aaron A., "The Politics of Knowledge Dissemination: Corporate Reporting, Shareholder Voice and Human Rights," 47 *Osgoode Hall L.J.* 47 (2009).

Dhir, Aaron A., "Realigning the Corporate Building Blocks: Shareholder Proposals as a Vehicle for Achieving Corporate Social and Human Rights Accountability," 43 *Am. Bus. L.J.* 2 (2006).

Dhir, Aaron A., "Shareholder Engagement in the Embedded Business Corporation: Investment Activism," *Hum. Rts. & TWAIL Discourse, Bus. Ethics Q.* 99–118 (Jan. 2012).

Dodd, M.D., & Supa, D.W., "Understanding the Effect of Corporate Social Responsibility on Consumer Purchase Intention," 5 *Public Relations J.* 1–19 (2011).

Drimmer, Jonathan, "Human Rights and the Extractive Industries: Litigation and Compliance Trends," 3 *J. World Energy L. & Bus.* 121–139 (2010).

Drucker, P.F., "The New Meaning of Corporate Social Responsibility," 26 *Cal. Mgmt. Rev.* 53–63 (1984).

Du, S., Bhattacharya, C.B., & Sen, S., "Maximizing Business Returns to Corporate Social Responsibility (CSR): The Role of CSR Communication," 12 *Int'l J. Mgmt. Rev.* 8–19 (2010).

Du, S., & Vieira Jr., E.T., "Striving for Legitimacy Through Corporate Social Responsibility: Insights from Oil Companies," 110 *J. Bus. Ethics* 413–427 (2012).

Duruigbo, Emeka, "Corporate Accountability and Liability for International Human Rights Abuses: Recent Changes and Recurring Challenges," 6 *Nw. J. Int'l Hum. Rts.* 222, 229–247 (2008).

Eccles, Robert G., Ioannis, Ioannou, & Serafeim, George, *The Impact of Corporate Sustainability on Organizational Processes and Performance* (Nat'l Bureau of Econ. Research, Working Paper No. 17950, 2012).

Eccles, Robert G., & Serafem, George, "The Performance Front Line: Innovating for a Sustainable Strategy," *Harv. Bus. Rev.* 50 (2013).

Egels-Zandén, N., "TNC Motives for Signing International Framework Agreements: A Continuous Bargaining Model of Stakeholder Pressure," 84 *J. Bus. Ethics* 529–547 (2009).

Elhauge, Einer, "Sacrificing Corporate Profits in the Public Interest," 80 *NYU L. Rev.* 733 (2005).

Engle, Eric, "What You Don't Know Can Hurt You: Human Rights, Shareholder Activism and SEC Reporting Requirements," 57 *Syracuse L. Rev.* 63 (2006).

Farrell, Kristen, "Corporate Complicity in the Chinese Censorship Regime: When Freedom of Expression and Profitability Collide," 11 *J. Internet L.* 1 (Jan. 2008).

Franks, Daniel M. et al., "Conflict Translates Environmental and Social Risk into Business Costs," 111 *PNAS* (May 27, 2014).

Fransen, L., "Multi-stakeholder Governance and Voluntary Programme Interactions: Legitimation Politics in the Institutional Design of Corporate Social Responsibility," 10 *Socio-Economic Rev.* 163–192 (2012).

Fransen, L.W., & Kolk, A., "Global Rule-Setting for Business: A Critical Analysis of Multi-Stakeholder Standards," 14 *Organization* 667–684 (2007).

Fransen, Luc W., & Kolk, Ans, "Global Rule-Setting for Business: A Critical Analysis of Multi-Stakeholder Standards," *Organization* 667 (2007).

Freeman, Bennett et al., "A New Approach to Corporate Responsibility: The Voluntary Principles on Security and Human Rights," 24 *Hastings Int'l & Comp. L. Rev.* 423 (2001).

Garrett, Allison D., "The Corporation as Sovereign," 60 *Me. L. Rev.* 129 (2008).

Gasser, Urs, "Regulating Search Engines: Taking Stock and Looking Ahead," 8 *Yale J.L. & Tech.* 201 (2006).

Genasci, M. & Pray, S., "Extracting Accountability: The Implications of the Resource Curse for CSR Theory and Practice," 11 *Yale Hum. Rts. & Dev. L.J.* 37 (2008).

George, E., "Tweeting to Topple Tyranny, Social Media and Corporate Social Responsibility: A Reply to Anupam Chander," 2 *Cal. L. Rev. Circuit* 23–29 (2011).

Gerber, Daniel W., & Biggie, Brian R., "The Global Supply Chain: Understanding, Measuring, Mitigating and Managing Exposure in a Supply Chain Dependent Globalized Market," 79 *Def. Couns. J.* 412, 413 (2012).

Greenwood-Daniel, J.H., "Greenwood, Markets and Democracy: The Illegitimacy of Corporate Law," 74 *UMKC L. Rev.* 41 (2005).

Groulx Diggs, E., Regan, M., & Parnace, B., "Business and Human Rights as a Galaxy of Norms," 50 *Georgetown J. Int'l L.* 309 (2019).

Hahn, Rüdiger & Lülfs, Regina, "Legitimizing Negative Aspects in GRI-Oriented Sustainability Reporting: A Qualitative Analysis of Corporate Disclosure Strategies," 123 *J. Bus. Ethics* 401 (2014).

Hainsfurther, Jennifer S., "A Rights-Based Approach: Using Cedaw to Protect the Human Rights of Migrant Workers," 24 *Am. U. Int'l L. Rev.* 843 (2009).

Harper Ho, Virginia, "Of Enterprise Principles and Corporate Groups: Does Corporate Law Reach Human Rights," 52 *Colum. J. Transnat'l L.* 113 (2013).

Harris, Theresa, "Settling a Corporate Accountability Lawsuit without Sacrificing Human Rights: Wang Xiaoning v. Yahoo!," 15 *Hum. Rts. Brief* 10 (Winter, 2008).

Hendriks, Mary Ross, "Modern Slavery and the Production of Consumer Goods in a Global Economy: Consumer Choice-Not Law-Will Trigger the Next Diaspora," 20 *T.M. Cooley L. Rev.* 431 (2003).

Hess, David, "The Transparency Trap: Non-Financial Disclosure and the Responsibility of Business to Respect Human Rights," 56 *Am. Bus. L.J.* 1, 5–53 (2019).

Hess, D., "Combatting Corruption through Corporate Transparency: Using Enforcement Discretion to Improve Disclosure," 21 *Minn. J. Int'l L.* 42 (2012).

Hovenkamp, Herber, "The Classical Corporation in American Legal Thought," 76 *Geo. L.J.* 1593, 1641 (1988).

Hung, H., "Directors' Roles in Corporate Social Responsibility: A Stakeholder Perspective," 103 *J. Bus. Ethics* 385–402 (2011).

Jackson, K., "Global Corporate Governance: Soft Law And Reputational Accountability," 35 *Brook. J. Int'l L.* 41 (2010).

Jerbi, Scott, "Assessing the Roles of Multi-Stakeholder Initiatives in Advancing the Business and Human Rights Agenda," 94 *Int'l Rev. Red Cross* 1027 (2012).

Jessup, Philip C., "The Subjects of a Modern Law of Nations," *Mich. L. Rev.* 45 (1947).

Jochnick, C., & Rabaeus, N., "Business and Human Rights Revitalized: A New UN Framework Meets Texaco in the Amazon," 33 *Suffolk Transnat'l L. Rev.* 413 (2010).

Jonassen, Frederick B., "A Baby-Step to Global Labor Reform: Corporate Codes of Conduct and the Child," 17 *Minn. J. Int'l L.* 7 (2008).

Kaeb, Caroline, "Emerging Issues of Human Rights Responsibility in the Extractive and Manufacturing Industries: Patterns and Liability Risks," 6 *Nw. J. Int'l Hum. Rts.* 327–353 (2008).

Kaeb, Caroline, "Putting the 'Corporate' Back into Corporate Personhood," 35 *Nw. J. Int'l L. & Bus.* 591–653. (2015).

Kamminga, M.T., Company Responses to Human Rights Reports: An Empirical Analysis (unpublished manuscript on file with author-published in BHR journal now?).

Kelly, Claire R., "Enmeshment as a Theory of Compliance," 37 *N.Y.U. J. Int'l L. & Pol.* 303 (2005).

Kenny, Katherine E., "Code or Contract: Whether Wal-Mart's Code of Conduct Creates a Contractual Obligation Between Wal-Mart and the Employees of its Foreign Suppliers," 27 *Nw. J. Int'l L. & Bus.* 2, 453 (2007).

Khamsi, Kathryn, "International Cocoa Agreement, Introductory Note," 50 *Amer. Soc. Int'l L.* 669 (2011).

King, B.G., & Soule, S.A., "Social Movements as Extra-Institutional Entrepreneurs: The Effect of Protests on Stock Price Returns," 52 *Admin. Sci. Q.* 413 (2007).

Kinley, D., & Chambers, R., "The UN Human Rights Norms for Corporations: the Private Implications of Public International Law," 6 *Hum. Rts. L. Rev.* 447 (Part I) (2006).

Koh, H., "Separating Myth from Reality about Corporate Responsibility Litigation," 7 *J. Int'l Econ. L.* 293 (2004).

Koven Levit, Janet, "Bottom-Up International Lawmaking: Reflections on the New Haven School of International Law," 32 *Yale J. Int'l L.* 393 (2007).

Laplante, Lisa J., & Spears, Suzanne A., "Out of the Conflict Zone: The Case for Community Consent Processes in the Extractive Sector," 11 *Yale Hum. Rts. & Dev. L.J.* 69–116.

Lashgari, M.K., & Gant, D.R., "Social Investing: The Sullivan Principles," *Rev. Soc. Econ.* 47, 74–83 (Spring 1989).

LeBaron, Genevieve, Lister, Jane, & Dauvergne, Peter, "Governing Global Supply Chain Sustainability through the Ethical Audit Regime," 14 *Globalizations* 6, 958–975 (2017).

Lee, Jegoo & Maxfield, Sylvia, "Doing Well by Doing Good? Reporting Corporate Responsibility and Corporate Performance," 120 *Bus. & Soc'y Rev.* 577 (2005).

Lee, Jyh-An & Liu, Ching-Yi, "Forbidden City Enclosed by the Great Firewall: the Law and Power of Internet Filtering in China," 13 *Minn. J.L. Sci. & Tech.* 125 (Winter 2012).
Leissle, Kristy, "Invisible West Africa: The Politics of Single Origin Chocolate," 13 *Gastronomica: J. of Food & Culture* 22 (2013).
Lynn, D., "The Dodd-Frank Act's Specialized Corporate Disclosure: Using the Securities Laws to Address Public Policy Issues," 6 *J. Bus. & Tech. L.* 327 (2011) (Murphy).
Manner, G., "The Object-Theory of the Individual in International Law," 46 *Am. J. Int'l L.* 428 (1952).
Manzo, Kate, "Modern Slavery, Global Capitalism, Deproletarianisation in West Africa," 32 *R. of Afr. Pol. Econ.* 521.
Margolis, Joshua D., & Walsh, James P., "Misery Loves Companies: Rethinking Social Initiatives by Business," 48 *Admin. Sci. Q.* 268, 277–78 (2003).
Martin, Jena, "Hiding in the Light: The Misuse of Disclosure to Advance the Business and Human Rights Agenda, *Colum. J. Transnat'l L.* 56, 530 (2017).
McBeth, Adam, "Crushed by an Anvil: A Case Study on Responsibility for Human Rights in the Extractive Sector," 11 *Yale Hum. Rts. & Dev. L.J.* 127 (2008).
McLean, Janet, "The Transnational Corporation in History: Lessons for Today?," *Ind. L.J.* 79 (2004).
Mena, S., & Palazzo, G., "Input and Output Legitimacy of Multi-Stakeholder Initiatives," 22 *Bus. Ethics Q.* 527–556 (2012).
Metcalf, C., "Corporate Responsibility as Global Public Law: Third Party Rankings as Regulation by Information," 28 *Pace Envtl. L. Rev.* 145 (2010).
Meyerstein, A., "Transnational Private Financial Regulation and Sustainable Development: An Empirical Assessment of the Implementation of the Equator Principles," 45 *N.Y.U. J. Int'l L. & Pol.* 487.
Michalski, Roger M., "Rights Come with Responsibilities: Personal Jurisdiction in the Age of Corporate Personhood," 50 *San Diego L. Rev.* 125, 131–132 (2013).
Millon, David, "Theories of the Corporation," *Duke L.J.* 201 (1990).
Muchlinski, Peter T., "Human Rights and Multinationals: Is There a Problem?," 77 *Int'l Aff.* 31, 35–36, 38–39 (2001).
Mull, L. Diane, & Kirkhorn, Steven R., "Child Labor in Ghana Cocoa Production: Focus upon Agricultural Tasks, Ergonomic Exposures, and Associated Injuries and Illness," 120 *Public Health Reports* 649 (2005).
Mushkat, Roda, "Corporate Social Responsibility, International Law, and Business Economics: Convergences and Divergences," 12 *Or. Rev. Int'l L.* 55, 66–73 (2010).
Narula, S., "The Right to Food," *Colum. Transnat'l L.J.* (2007).
Nikolaeva, R., & Bicho, M., "The Role of Institutional and Reputational Factors in the Voluntary Adoption of Corporate Social Responsibility Reporting Standards," 39 *J. Acad. Marketing Sci.* 136–157 (2011).
Öberseder, M., Schlegelmilch, B.B., & Gruber, V., "'Why Don't Consumers Care About CSR?': A Qualitative Study Exploring the Role of CSR in Consumption Decisions," 104 *J. Bus. Ethics* 449–460 (2011).
Olsen, Tricia, "Law, Business and Human Rights: Bridging the Gap," 25 *Bus. Ethics Q.* 590–593 (2015).
Ontiveros, Maria L., "Lessons from the Fields: Female Farmworkers and the Law," 55 *Me. L. Rev.* 157, 183–184 (2003).
Orlitzky, Marc et al., "Corporate Social and Financial Performance: A Meta-Analysis," 24 *Org. Stud.* 403 (2003).

O'Rourke, D., "Multi-stakeholder Regulation: Privatizing or Socializing Global Labor Standards?," 34 *World Dev.* 899–918 (2006).

Paust, J., "Human Rights Responsibilities of Private Corporations," 35 *Vand. J. Transnat'l L.* 801 (2002).

Peloza, J., & Shang, J., "How Can Corporate Social Responsibility Activities Create Value for Stakeholders? A Systematic Review," 39 *J. Acad. Marketing Sci.* 117–135 (2011).

Penney, Jonathon W., "Internet Access Rights: A Brief History and Intellectual Origins," 38 *Wm. Mitchell L. Rev.* 10 (2011).

Perrini, F. et al., "Deconstructing the Relationship Between Corporate Social and Financial Performance," 102 *J. Bus. Ethics* 59–76 (2011).

Peters, R., & Mullen, M.R., "Some Evidence of the Cumulative Effects of Corporate Social Responsibility on Financial Performance," 3 *J. Global Bus. Issues* 1 (2009).

Phillips, Joe, & Lim, Suk-Jun, "Their Brothers' Keeper: Global Buyers and the Legal Duty to Protect Suppliers' Employees," 61 *Rutgers L. Rev.* 333 (2009).

Piety, Tamara R., "The First Amendment and the Corporate Civil Rights Movement," 11 *J. Bus. & Tech. L.* 1, 2 (2016).

Porter, Michael E., & Kramer, Mark R., "Creating Shared Value: How to Reinvent Capitalism—And Unleash a Wave of Innovation and Growth," *Harv. Bus. Rev.* (Jan.–Feb. 2011)+Pirella, Kish.

Porter, Michael E., & Kramer, Mark R., "Strategy & Society: The Link Between Competitive Advantage and Corporate Social Responsibility," *Harv. Bus. Rev.* (Dec. 2006).

Pronto, Arnold N., "Understanding the Hard/Soft Distinction in International Law," 48 *Vand. J. Transnat'l L.* 941 (2015).

Raj, Shannon, "Blood Electronics: Congo's Conflict Minerals and the Legislation That Could Cleanse the Trade," 84 *S. Cal. L. Rev.* 981–1033.

Ramasatry, A., "Corporate Complicity From Nuremberg to Rangoon: An Examination of Forced Labor Cases and Their Impact on the Liability of Multinational Corporations," 20 *Berkeley J. Int'l* 91 (2002).

Ramasatry, Anita, "Corporate Social Responsibility Versus Business and Human Rights: Bridging the Gap Between Responsibility and Accountability," 14 *J. Hum. Rts.* 2, 237–259 (2015).

Ratner, Steven R., "Corporations and Human Rights: A Theory of Legal Responsibility," 111 *Yale L.J.* 443 (2001).

Revak, Haley, "Corporate Codes of Conduct: Binding or Ideal Publicity?," 63 *Hastings L.J.* 1645 (2012).

Richemond-Barak, Daphne, "Can Self-Regulation Work? Lessons from the Private Security and Military Industry," 35 *Mich. J. Int'l L.* 773 (2014).

Robbins, Allie, "Toxic Sweatshops: Regulating the Import of Hazardous Electronics," 18 *CUNY L. Rev.* 267, 284–285 (2015).

Robins, Nick, "Loot: In Search of the East India Company, the World's First Transnational Corporation," 14 *Env't & Urban.* 79 (2002).

Ruggie, J., "Business and Human Rights: The Evolving International Agenda," 101 *Am. J. Int'l L.* 819 (2007).

Rupp, D.E., Williams, C.A., & Aguilera, R.V., "Increasing Corporate Social Responsibility Through Stakeholder Value Internalization (And the Catalyzing Effect of New Governance): An Application of Organizational Justice, Self-Determination, and Social Influence Theories," *Managerial Ethics: Managing the Psychology of Morality* 69–88 (2011).

Rutherford, P., "How Have International Business Discourses on the Environment Changed over the Last Decade?," 6 *Global Soc. Pol'y* 79 (2006).
Sarfaty, Galit A., "Shining Light on Global Supply Chains," 56 *Harv. Int'l L.J.* 419, 425 (2015).
Scheltema, M., "Assessing Effectiveness of International Private Regulation in the CSR Arena," 13 *Rich. J. Global L. & Bus.* 263.
Schwartz, M., "A Code of Ethics for Corporate Code of Ethics," 41 *J. Bus. Ethics* 27–43 (2002).
Schwartz, M., "Universal Moral Values for Corporate Codes of Ethics," 59 *J. Bus. Ethics* 27–44 (2005).
Sethi, S.P., "Dimensions of Corporate Social Performance: An Analytic Framework," 17 *Cal. Mgmt. Rev.* 58–64 (1975).
Sethi, S.P., "Values for Corporate Conduct in the International Arena: Challenges and Opportunities for Multinational Corporations," 107 *Bus. & Soc'y Rev.* 20–40 (2002).
Sethi, S. Prakash, "The Effectiveness of Industry-Based Codes in Serving Public Interest: The Case of the International Council on Mining and Metals," 14 *Transnat'l Corp.* 55–99 (2005).
Sethi, S. Prakash, & Emelianova, Olga, "A Failed Strategy of Using Voluntary Codes of Conduct by the Global Mining Industry," 6 *Corp. Gov.* 226–238 (2006).
Skibola, Nicola, "Navigating the Voluntary Sustainability Reporting Maze," *Bus. Insider* (Feb. 23, 2011).
Skinner, Gwynne L., "Beyond Kiobel: Providing Access to Judicial Remedies for Violations of International Human Right Norms by Transnational Corporations in New (Post Kiobel) World," 46 *Colum. HR L. Rev.* 158 (2014).
Slack, Keith, "Mission Impossible?: Adopting a CSR-Based Business Model for Extractive Industries in Developing Countries," 37 *Res. Pol'y* 179 (2012).
Slawotsky, J., "The Global Corporation As International Law Actor," 52 *Va. J. Int'l L.* 79 (2012).
Soleimani, A., Schneper, W.D., & Newburry, W., "The Impact of Stakeholder Power on Corporate Reputation: A Cross-Country Corporate Governance Perspective," 25 *Org. Sci.* 991–1008 (2014).
Spence, David, "Corporate Social Responsibility in the Oil and Gas Industry: The Importance of Reputational Risk," 86 *Chi.-Kent L. Rev.* 59 (2011).
Stephens, Beth, "The Amorality of Profit, Transnational Corporations and Human Rights," 20 *Berkeley J. of Int'l L.* 45 (2002).
Stevelman, Faith, "Global Finance, Multinationals and Human Rights: With Commentary on Backer's Critique of the 2008 Report by John Ruggie," 9 *Santa Clara J. Int'l L.* 101, 116 (2011).
Taub, Jennifer, "Is Hobby Lobby a Tool for Limiting Corporate Constitutional Rights?," 30 *Const. Comment.* 403–429. (2015).
Timberg, Sigmund, "Corporate Fictions: Logical, Social and International Implications," *Color. L. Rev.* 46 (1946).
Timberg, Sigmund, "The Corporation as a Technique of International Administration," *U. Chi. L. Rev.* 19 (1951).
Timberg, Sigmund, "International Combines and National Sovereigns," *U. Pa. L. Rev.* 95 (1947).
Tonello, Matteo (ed.), "The Business Case for Corporate Social Responsibility," *Harv. L. Sch. F. on Corp. Governance & Fin. Reg.* (June 26, 2011, 11:46 AM), http://blogs.

law.harvard.edu/corpgov/2011/06/26/the-business-case-for-corporate-social-responsibility/.

Tsuk Mitchell, D., "Shareholders as Proxies: The Contours of Shareholder Democracy," 63 *Wash. & Lee L. Rev.* 1503 (2006).

Vaghts, Detlev, "The Multinational Enterprise: A New Challenge for Transnational Law," 83 *Harv. L. Rev.* 739 (1970).

Vazquez, C., "Direct vs. Indirect Obligations of Corporations Under International Law," 43 *Colum. J. Transnat'l L.* 927 (2004–2005).

Vlachos, P.A. et al., "Corporate Social Responsibility: Attributions, Loyalty, and the Mediating Role of Trust," 37 *J. Acad. Marketing Sci.* 170–180 (2009).

Vogel, D., "The Private Regulation of Global Corporate Conduct: Achievements and Limitations," 49 *Bus. & Soc'y* 68–87 (2010).

Waddell, S., & Khagram, S., "Multi-stakeholder global networks: emerging systems for the global common good," *Partnerships, governance and sustainable development: Reflections on theory and practice*, 261 (2007).

Waddock, S., "Building a New Institutional Infrastructure for Corporate Responsibility," 22 *Acad. Mgmt. Persp.* 87–108 (2008).

Weissbrodt, David, "Keynote Address: International Standard-Setting on the Human Rights Responsibilities of Business," 26 *Berkeley J. Int'l L.* 373–391.

Weissbrodt, David & Kruger, Muria, "Norms on the Responsibilities of Transnational Corporations and Other Business Enterprises with Regard to Human Rights," 97 *Am. J. Int'l L.* 901–922 (2003).

Weitzner, D., & Deutsch, Y., "Understanding Motivation and Social Influence in Stakeholder Prioritization," *Org. Stud.* 0170840615585340 (2015).

Wells, C.A. Harwell, "The Cycles of Corporate Social Responsibility: An Historical Retrospective for the Twenty-First Century," 51 *U. Kan. L. Rev.* 77 (2002).

Wettstein, Florian, "CSR and the Debate on Business and Human Rights: Bridging the Great Divide," 22 *Bus. Ethics Q.* 739–770 (2012).

Wettstein, Florian & Waddock, Sandra, "Voluntary or Mandatory: That Is (Not) the Question: Linking Corporate Citizenship to Human Rights Obligations for Business," 6 zfwu 304 (2005).

White, R., & Kare, D., "The Impact of Consumer Boycotts on the Stock Prices of Target Firms," 6 *J. Applied Bus. Res.* 63–72 (1990). (Murphy)

Williams, Cynthia, "Civil Society Initiatives and 'Soft Law' in the Oil and Gas Industry," 36 *N.Y.U. J. Int'l L. & Pol.* 457 (2004).

Williams, Cynthia A., "The Securities and Exchange Commission and Corporate Social Transparency," 112 *Harv. L. Rev.* 1197 (1999).

Williams, O., "The UN Global Compact: The Challenge and the Promise," 14 *Bus. Ethics Q.* 755–774 (2004).

Wotruba, T.R., "Industry Self-Regulation: A Review and Extension to a Global Setting," 16 J. *Pub. Pol'y & Marketing* 38–54 (1997).

Xie, C., Bagozzi, R.P., & Grønhaug, K.,"The Role of Moral Emotions and Individual Differences in Consumer Responses to Corporate Green and Non-Green Actions," 43 *J. Acad. Marketing Sci.* 333–356 (2015).

Zyglidopoulos, S.C. et al., "Does Media Attention Drive Corporate Social Responsibility?," 65 *J. Bus. Res.* 1622–1627 (2012).

## Treaties

African Charter on Human and Peoples Rights, 1981.
African Union Convention on Preventing and Combating Corruption, 2003.
Agreement on Trade Related Aspects of Intellectual Property Law, 1994.
Declaration on the Right to Development, 1986.
Draft Norms on the Responsibilities on the Responsibilities of Transnational Corporations and Other Business Enterprises with Respect to Human Rights, 2003.
Inter-American Convention against Corruption, 1996.
International Covenant on Civil and Political Rights, 1966.
International Covenant on Economic Social and Cultural Rights, 1976.
OECD Convention on Combating Bribery of Foreign Public Officials in International Business Transactions, 1997.
Rio Declaration, Agenda 21 United Nations Conference on Environment and Declaration, 1992.
Rome Statute of the ICC, 1998.
Universal Declaration of Human Rights, 1948.
United Nations Charter, 1945.
United Nations Convention against Corruption, 2003.
United Nations, *Guiding Principles on Business and Human Rights: Implementing the United Nations "Protect, Respect and Remedy" Framework*, New York: United Nations Publications, 2011.
Vienna Convention on the Law of Treaties, 1969.
Vienna Declaration and Programme of Action, 1993.

## Cases and Statutes

United States
28 U.S.C. Section1350. The Alien Tort Statute (ATS).
Abdullah v. Pfizer, Inc. 562 F.3d 163 (2d Cir. 2009).
Aldana v. Del Monte Fresh Produce, N.A., Inc. 416 F. 3d 1242 (11th Cir. 2005).
Baloco ex rel. Tapia v. Drummond Co., Inc., 640 F.3d 1338 (11th Cir. 2011).
Beanal v. Freeport-McMoran, Inc., 197 F.3d 161 (5th Cir. 1999)
Bowoto v. Chevron Corp. 2010 WL 3516437 (9th Cir. Sept. 10, 2010).
Burwell v. Hobby Lobby Stores, 573 U.S. 682 (2014).
Citizens United v. Fed. Election Comm'n, 558 U.S. 310 (2010).
Dodge v. Ford, 170 NW 668 (Mich. 1919).
Doe v. Exxon Mobil Corp., 473 F.3d 345 (D.C. Cir. 2007).
Doe v. Exxon Mobil Corp., 654 F.3d 11 (D.C. Cir. 2011).
Doe I v. Nestle USA, Inc., 738 F.3d 1048 (9th Cir. 2013).
Doe v. Nestle, S.A., 929 F.3d 623 (9th Cir. 2019).
Doe v. Wal-Mart Stores, Inc., 572 F.3d 677 (9th Cir. 2009).
*Filartiga v. Pena-Irala*, 630 F.2d 876, 878 (2d Cir. 1980).
Flomo v. Firestone Nat. Rubber Co., LLC, 643 F.3d 1013 (7th Cir. 2011).
*In re* Chiquita Brands Int'l, Inc., 792 F. Supp. 2d 1301 (S.D. Fla. 2011).

Jesner v. Arab Bank, 138 S.Ct. 1386 (2018).
Khulumani v. Barclay Nat. Bank Ltd., 504 F.3d 254 (2nd Cir. 2007).
Kiobel v. Royal Dutch Petroleum Co., 621 F.3d 111 (2d Cir. 2010).
Kiobel v. Royal Dutch Petroleum, 133 S. Ct. 1659 (2013).
La. Mun. Police Employees' Retirement System v. Hershey Co., 2013 WL 1776668 (Del. Ch. 2013).
Nike Inc. v. Kasky 539 U.S 654 (2003).
Presbyterian Church of Sudan v. Talisman Energy, 582 F.3d 244 (2009).
Rio Tinto PLC v. Sarei, 133 S. Ct. 1995 (2013).
Santa Clara Cty. v. S. Pac. R. Co., 118 U.S. 394, 6 S. Ct. 1132, 30 L. Ed. 118 (1886).
Sarei v. Rio Tinto, PLC, 671 F.3d 736, 748 (9th Cir. 2011).
Sinaltrainal v. Coca-Cola Co., 256 F. Supp. 2d 1345 (S.D. Fla. 2003).
Sosa v. Alvarez-Machain 124 S. Ct 2709 (2004)
*Doe v. Unocal Corp.*, 963 F. Supp. 880 (C.D. Cal. 1997).
Vietnam Ass'n for Victims of Agent Orange v. Dow Chem. Co., 517 F.3d 104 (2d Cir. 2008).
Villeda Aldana v. Del Monte Fresh Produce N.A., Inc., 578 F.3d 1283 (11th Cir. 2009).
Wang Xiaoning v. Yahoo! Inc., 2007 WL 9812491 (2007).
Wiwa v. Royal Dutch Petroleum Co., 226 F. 3d 88: 29 (2002).
United Kingdom
Abacha v. The Secretary of State for the Home Department [2001] EWHC Admin 787.
Vedanta Resources PLC v. Lungowe [2019] UKSC 20.

## Reports

Amnesty International, Undermining Freedom of Expression in China: The Role of Yahoo!, Microsoft and Google, Amnesty International, London, UK, 2006.
Brookings Institution, Transparency, Conflict Minerals and Natural Resources: Debating Sections 1502 and 1504 of the Dodd-Frank Act (2011).
Bus. & Human Rights Res. Ctr., EU Requirements on Companies' Non-Financial Reporting (2014).
Bus. & Human Rights Res. Ctr, Shared Space Under Pressure: Business Support for Civic Freedoms and Human Rights Defenders: Guidance for Companies (Sept. 2018).
BSR, Conducting an Effective Human Rights Impact Assessment: Guidelines, Steps, and Examples (Mar. 2013).
BSR, Going Beyond the Supply Chain in the Democratic Republic of Congo: Responsible Multistakeholder Action on Development and Capacity-Building in Eastern DRC (2012).
BSR, The Nice Consumer: Toward a Framework for Sustainable Fashion Consumption in the EU (2012).
BSR, Applying the UN Guiding Principles on Business and Human Rights to the ICT Industry (2011).
BSR, Environmental, Social and Governance: Moving to Mainstream Investing? (June 25, 2008).
Castan Centre for Human Rights Law-Monash University, Human Rights Translated: A Business Reference Guide (2008).

Center for Business and Human Rights-NYU Stern, Harmful Conent: The Role of Internet Platform Companies in Fighting Terrorist Incitement and Politically Motivated Disinformation (2017).
Global Witness, Oil and Mining in Violent Places: Why Voluntary Codes for Companies Don't Guarantee Human Rights (2007).
GRI, Carrots and Sticks—Promoting Transparency and Sustainability: An Update on Trends in Voluntary and Mandatory Approaches to Sustainability Reporting 4 (2016).
GRI, A Resource Guide to Corporate Human Rights Reporting 1, 10 (2009).
Human Rights Watch, On the Margins of Profit: Rights at Risk in the Global Economy (2008) Volume 20, No. 3(G).
Human Rights Watch, A New Accountability Agenda: Human Rights and the Extractive Industries Transparency Initiative (2013).
Human Rights Watch, Race to the Bottom: Corporate Complicity in Chinese Internet Censorship (2006).
Human Rights Watch, Whoever Raises their Head Suffers the Most: Worker Rights in Bangladesh Garment Factories (2015).
Human Rights Watch, The Dark Side of Green Growth: Human Rights Impacts of Weak Governance in Indonesia's Forestry Sector (2013).
IPIECA, Human Rights and Ethics in the Oil and Gas Industry (2008).
Institute for Human Rights and Business, Calvert Investments, and the Interfaith Center on Corporate Responsibility, Investing the Rights Way: A Guide for Investors on Business and Human Rights (2013).
Shift, Dissecting Human Rights Disclosure: A Tool for Investors (2020).
Shift, Human Rights Reporting: Are Companies Telling Investors What They Need to Know? (May 2017).
Shift, Human Rights Reporting and Assurance Frameworks Initiative-RAFI (May 2015).
Shift, Evidence of Corporate Disclosure relevant to the UN Guiding Principles on Business and Human Rights, New York, (2014).

# Index

*For the benefit of digital users, indexed terms that span two pages (e.g., 52–53) may, on occasion, appear on only one of those pages.*

Tables, figures and boxes are indicated by *t*, *f* and *b* following the page number